FREE COLLARS KINGDOM
フリーカラーズキングダム

KINGDOM

2

TAKUYA FUJIMA

TRANSLATED AND ADAPTED BY
William Flanagan

LETTERED BY
North Market Street Graphics

BALLANTINE BOOKS • NEW YORK

Free Collars Kingdom volume 2 is a work of fiction. Names, characters, places, and incidents are the products of the author's imagination or are used fictitiously. Any resemblance to actual events, locales, or persons, living or dead, is entirely coincidental.

A Del Rey Trade Paperback Original

Published in the United States by Del Rey Books,
an imprint of The Random House Publishing Group,
a division of Random House, Inc., New York.

Publication rights arranged through Kodansha Ltd.

First published in Japan in 2003 by Kodansha Ltd., Tokyo.

ISBN 978-0-345-49266-1

Printed in the United States of America

www.delreymanga.com

9 8 7 6 5 4 3 2 1

Translator/adapter: William Flanagan
Lettering: North Market Street Graphics

Contents

AUTHOR'S NOTE

Maybe it's because I never let my Scotty (♂) go out-
side that he's a real coward. When I arranged to breed
him, he got very scared just because of the change of
scenery. He wouldn't move, and so the session ended
without him getting anywhere near the female cat. I
guess he's just led a too-sheltered life. But really . . .
I wanted to raise Scotty's kittens.

 Here's volume 2. This one starts up with our cat-
eared people having adventures in Ikebukuro! Please
watch over them as if you were their owner.

Takuya Fujima

HONORIFICS EXPLAINED

Throughout the Del Rey Manga books, you will find Japanese honorifics left intact in the translations. For those not familiar with how the Japanese use honorifics and, more important, how they differ from American honorifics, we present this brief overview.

Politeness has always been a critical facet of Japanese culture. Ever since the feudal era, when Japan was a highly stratified society, use of honorifics—which can be defined as polite speech that indicates relationship or status—has played an essential role in the Japanese language. When addressing someone in Japanese, an honorific usually takes the form of a suffix attached to one's name (example: "Asuna-san"), is used as a title at the end of one's name, or appears in place of the name itself (example: "Negi-sensei," or simply "Sensei!").

Honorifics can be expressions of respect or endearment. In the context of manga and anime, honorifics give insight into the nature of the relationship between characters. Many English translations leave out these important honorifics and therefore distort the feel of the original Japanese. Because Japanese honorifics contain nuances that English honorifics lack, it is our policy at Del Rey not to translate them. Here, instead, is a guide to some of the honorifics you may encounter in Del Rey Manga.

-san: This is the most common honorific and is equivalent to Mr., Miss, Ms., or Mrs. It is the all-purpose honorific and can be used in any situation where politeness is required.

-sama: This is one level higher than "-san" and is used to confer great respect.

-dono: This comes from the word "tono," which means "lord." It is an even higher level than "-sama" and confers utmost respect.

-kun: This suffix is used at the end of boys' names to expr[e]ss [fa]miliarity or endearment. It is also sometimes used by men a[mong] friends, or when addressing someone younger or of a lower s[ta]tion.

-chan: This is used to express endearment, mostly toward girls. It is also used for little boys, pets, and even among lovers. It gives a sense of childish cuteness.

Bozu: This is an informal way to refer to a boy, similar to the English terms "kid" and "squirt."

**Sempai/
Senpai:** This title suggests that the addressee is one's senior in a group or organization. It is most often used in a school setting, where underclassmen refer to their upperclassmen as "sempai." It can also be used in the workplace, such as when a newer employee addresses an employee who has seniority in the company.

Kohai: This is the opposite of "sempai" and is used toward underclassmen in school or newcomers in the workplace. It connotes that the addressee is of a lower station.

Sensei: Literally meaning "one who has come before," this title is used for teachers, doctors, or masters of any profession or art.

[blank]: This is usually forgotten in these lists, but it is perhaps the most significant difference between Japanese and English. The lack of honorific means that the speaker has permission to address the person in a very intimate way. Usually, only family, spouses, or very close friends have this kind of permission. Known as *yobisute,* it can be gratifying when someone who has earned the intimacy starts to call one by one's name without an honorific. But when that intimacy hasn't been earned, it can be very insulting.

CULTURAL NOTES

Nyan:
The same way cats say *meow* in English-speaking countries, they say *nyan* in Japan. Through the course of this book, the reader may see quite a few references to *nyan* made in the form of puns or other cat allusions.

Nyan-Man:
The place where our feline heroes live is called Nyan-Nyan's Mansion. It is a high-rise apartment building, and its name is shortened, in typical Japanese style, to Nyan-Man.

Ikebukuro:
Tokyo has quite a few city centers, the most popular of which are the Ginza for those with expensive tastes, Shibuya for young people, and Shinjuku for more average folks. Ikebukuro has all of the same attractions as the other city centers, such as stores, restaurants, theaters, cinemas, and other forms of entertainment, but recently it has become a haven for female *otaku*. It also has a partially deserved reputation as a destination for gangs of street punks.

フリーカラーズキングダム

FREE COLLARS KINGDOM

2

Takuya Fujima

CONTENTS

Cat Tale 6 Cat-Ear Report

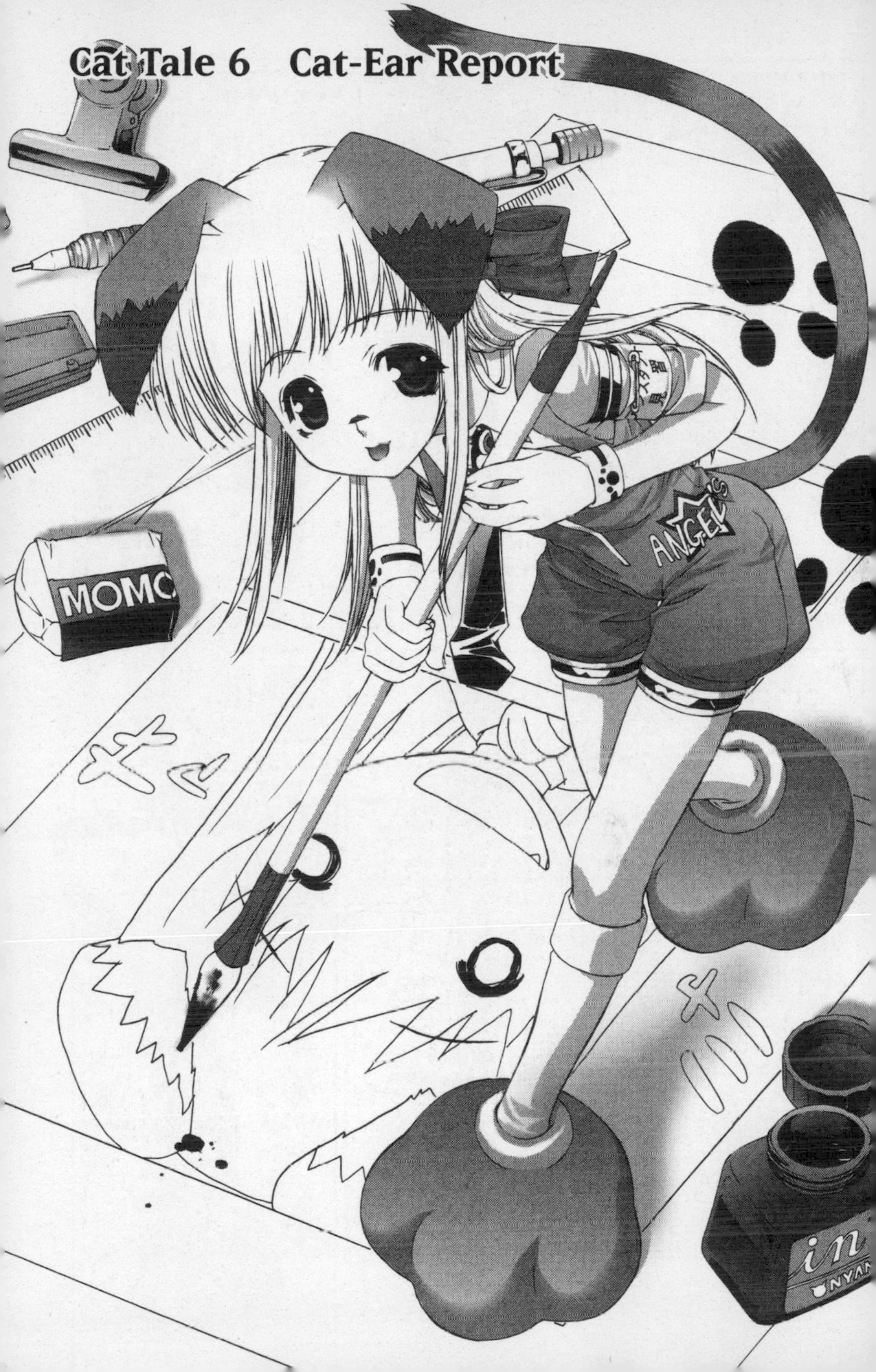

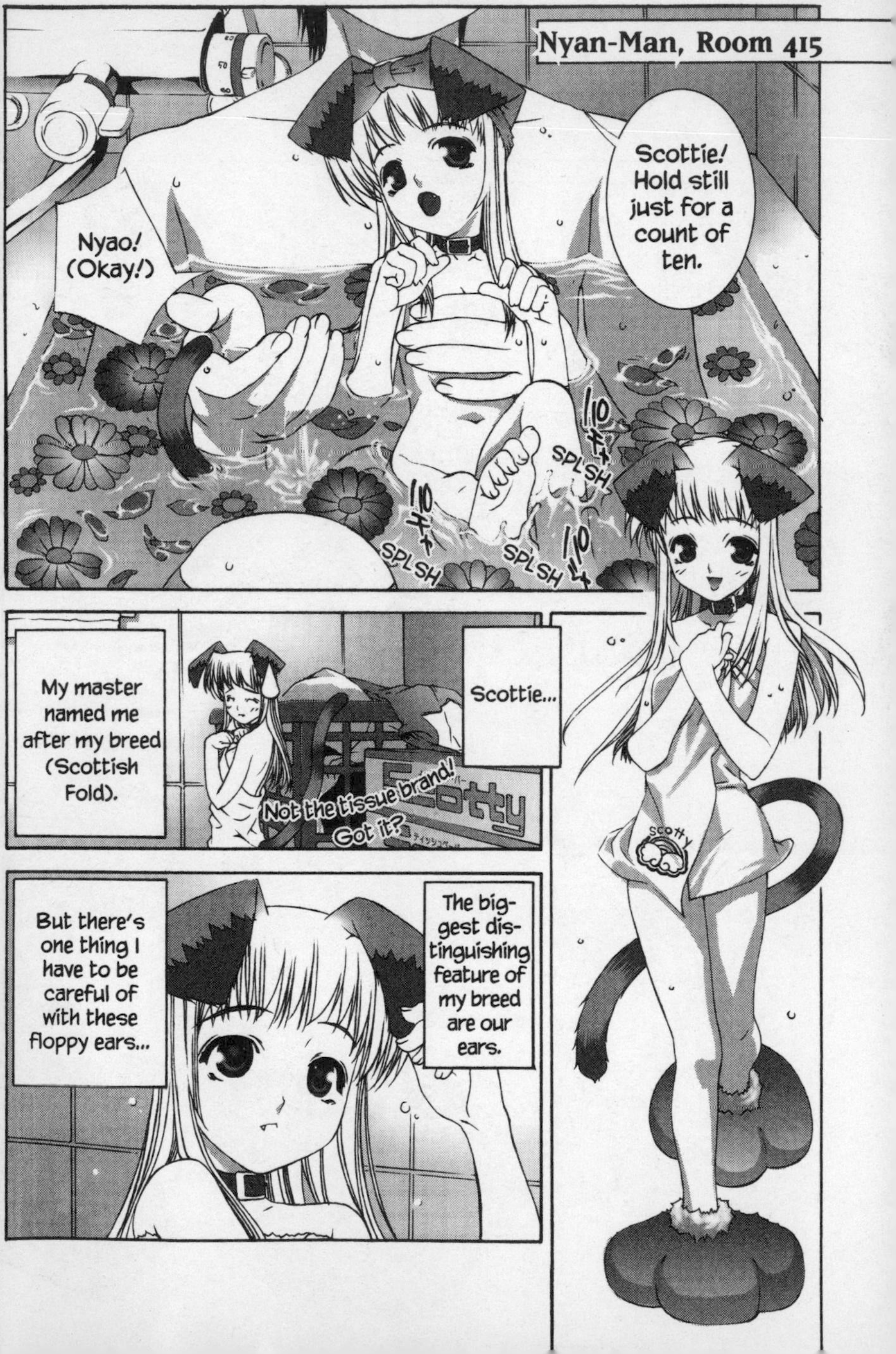
Nyan-Man, Room 415
Scottie! Hold still just for a count of ten.
Nyao! (Okay!)
SPLSH
SPLSH
SPLSH
Scottie...
My master named me after my breed (Scottish Fold).
Not the tissue brand! Got it?
Scotty
scotty
The big-gest dis-tinguishing feature of my breed are our ears.
But there's one thing I have to be careful of with these floppy ears...

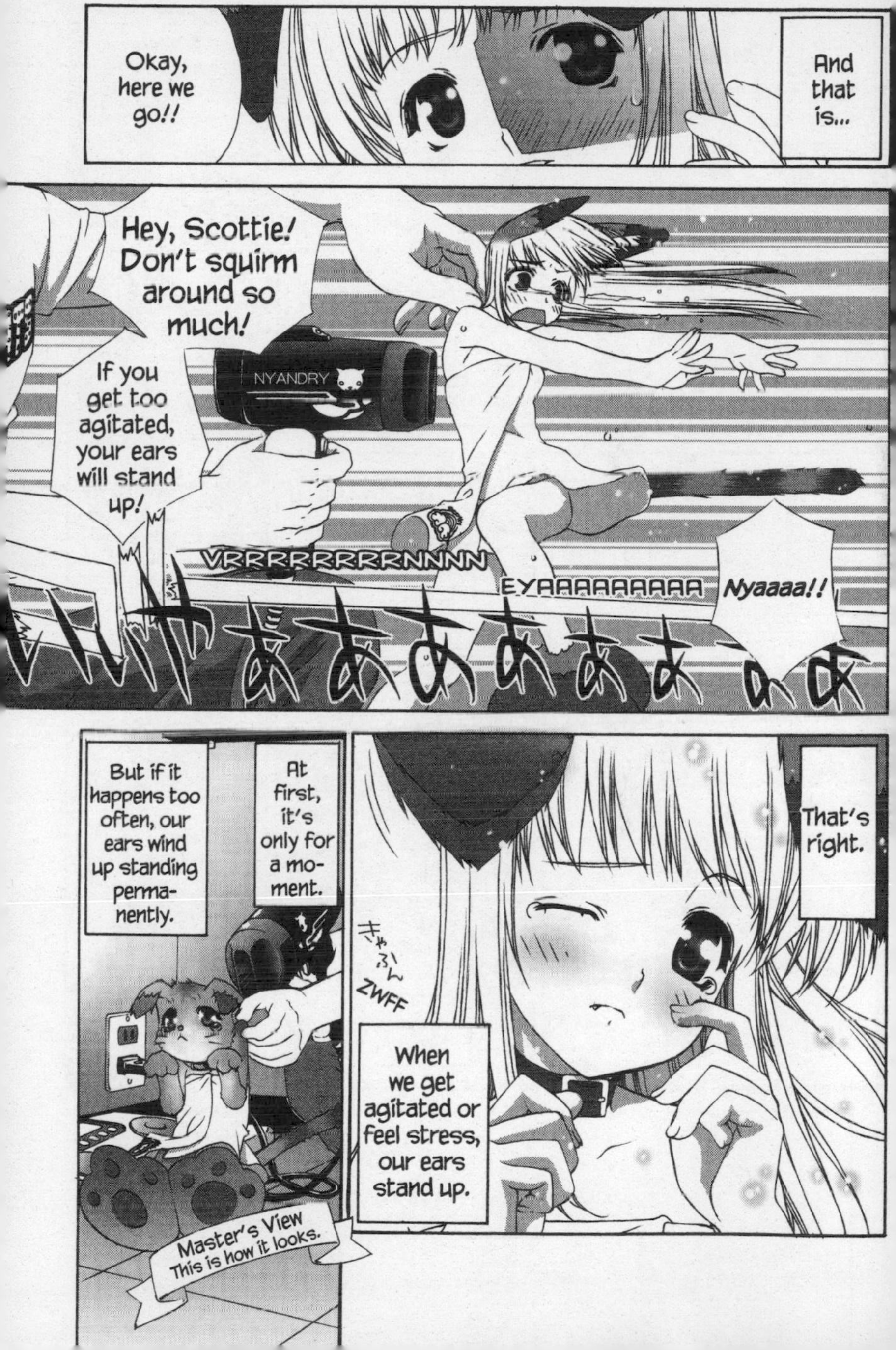
And that is...
Okay, here we go!!
Nyaaaa!!
EYAAAAAAAAAA
Hey, Scottie! Don't squirm around so much!
If you get too agitated, your ears will stand up!
VRRRRRRRRRNNNNN
That's right.
When we get agitated or feel stress, our ears stand up.
きゃふん
ZWFF
At first, it's only for a moment.
But if it happens too often, our ears wind up standing permanently.
Master's View
This is how it looks.

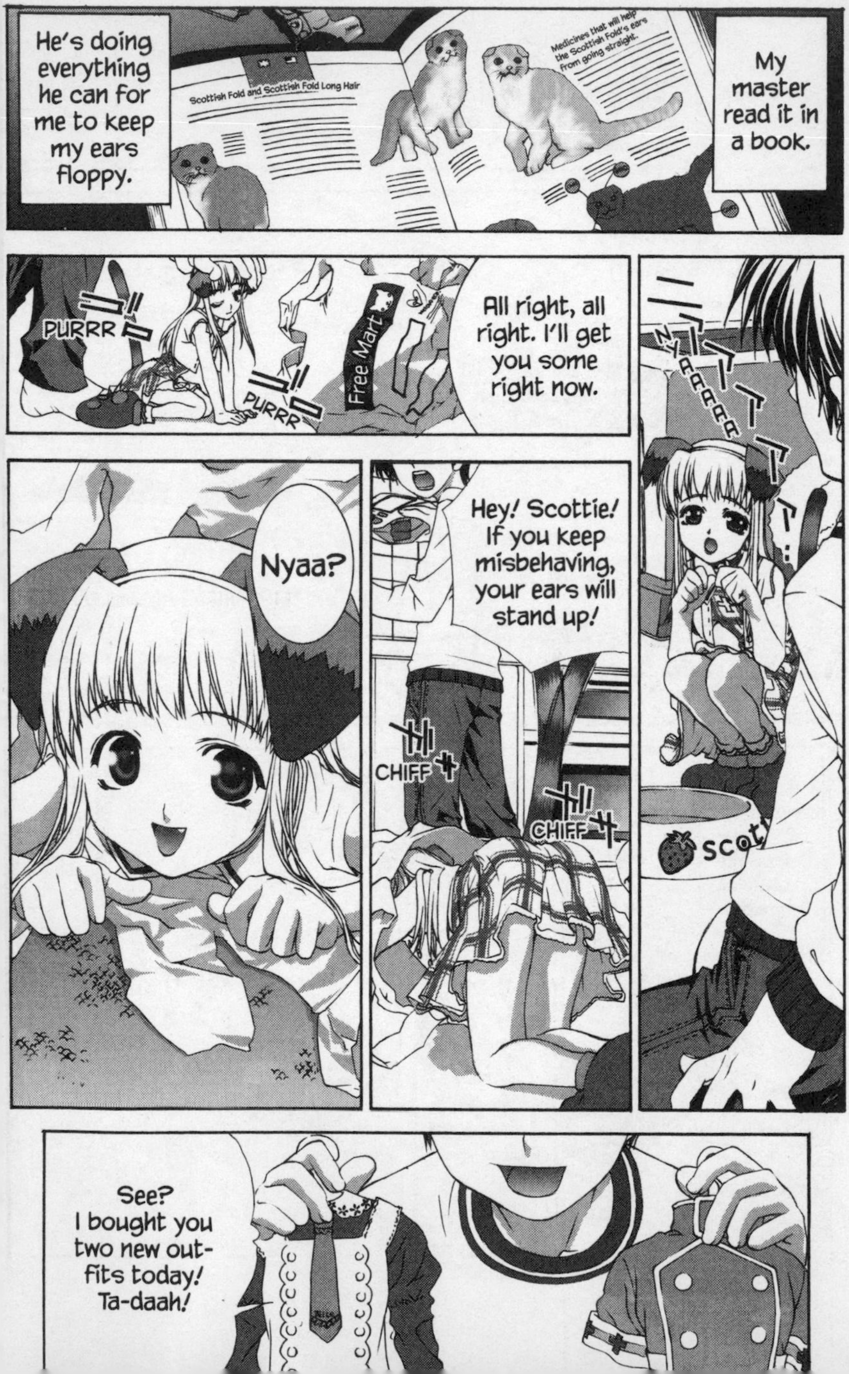
My master read it in a book.
Medicines that will help the Scottish Fold's ears from going straight.
Scottish Fold and Scottish Fold Long Hair
He's doing everything he can for me to keep my ears floppy.
NYAAAAAA
scot
All right, all right. I'll get you some right now.
Free Mart
PURRR
PURRR
Hey! Scottie! If you keep misbehaving, your ears will stand up!
CHIFF
CHIFF
Nyaa?
See? I bought you two new outfits today! Ta-daah!

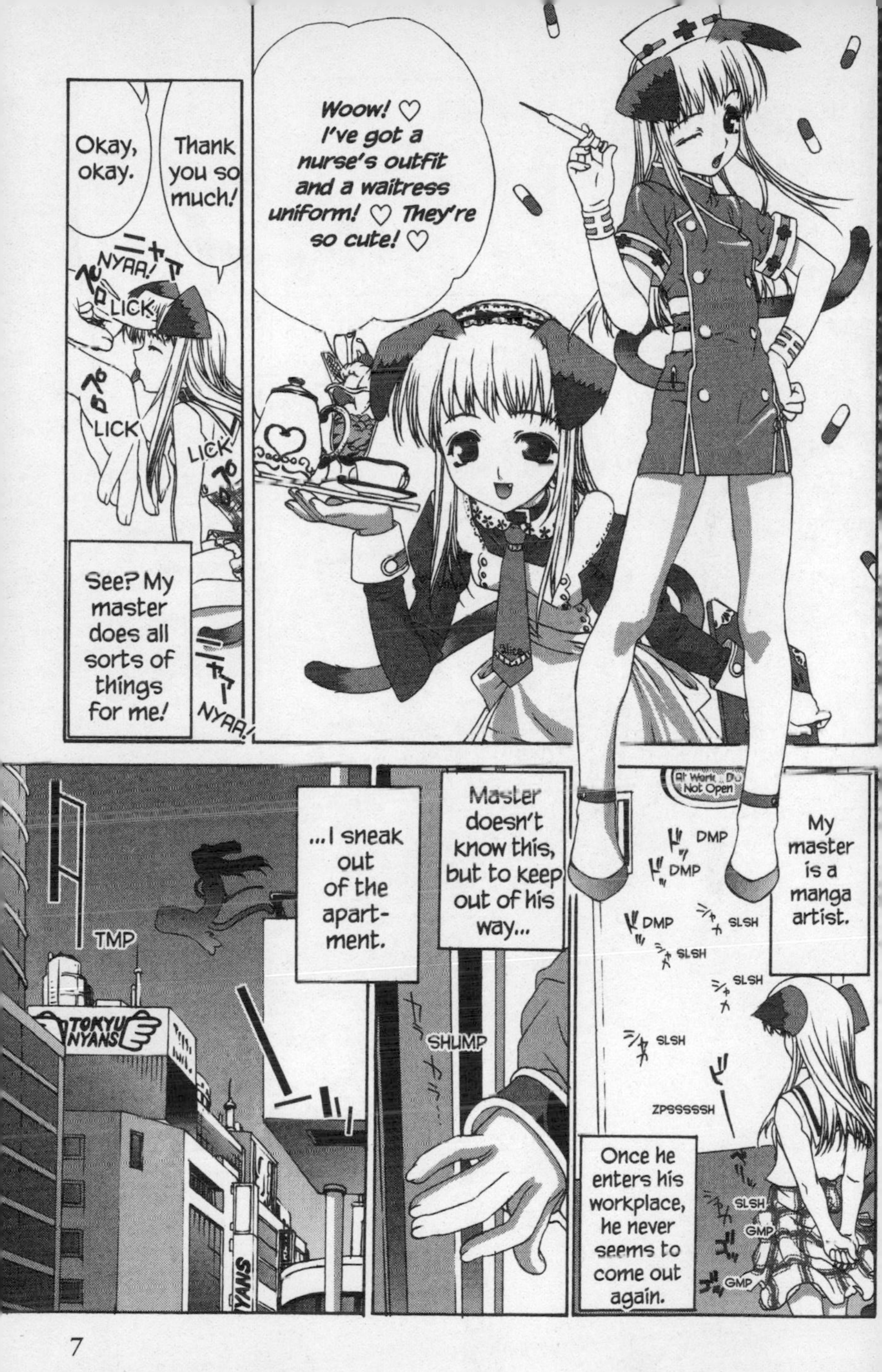
Woow! ♡ I've got a nurse's outfit and a waitress uniform! ♡ They're so cute! ♡
Thank you so much!
Okay, okay.
NYAA!
LICK
LICK
LICK
See? My master does all sorts of things for me!
NYAA!
My master is a manga artist.
At Work... Do Not Open
DMP
DMP
DMP
SLSH
SLSH
SLSH
SLSH
ZPSSSSSH
SLSH
GMP
GMP
Once he enters his workplace, he never seems to come out again.
Master doesn't know this, but to keep out of his way...
SHUMP
...I sneak out of the apartment.
TMP
TOKYU NYANS
NYANS

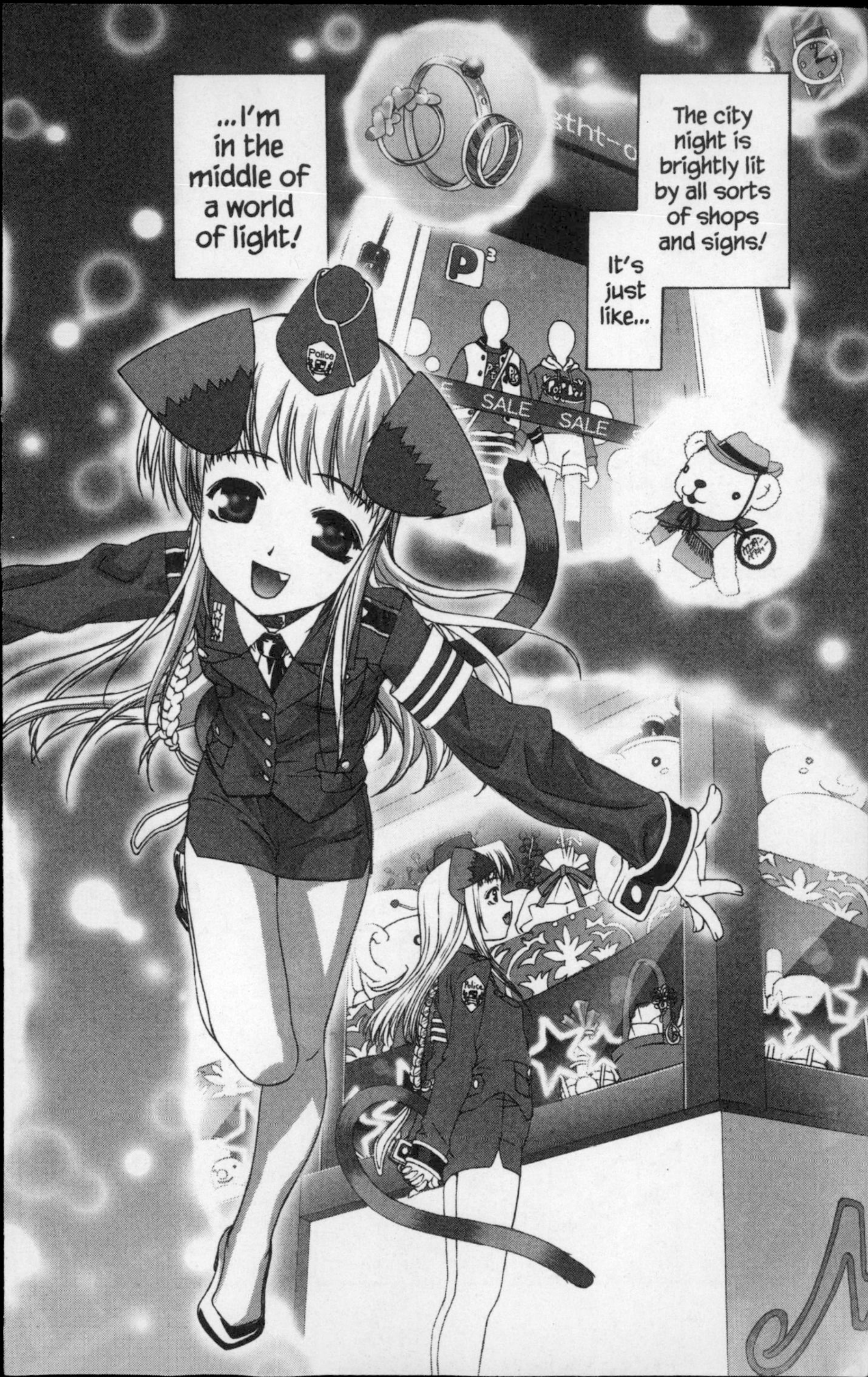
The city night is brightly lit by all sorts of shops and signs!
It's just like...
...I'm in the middle of a world of light!
SALE
SALE
Police
Police

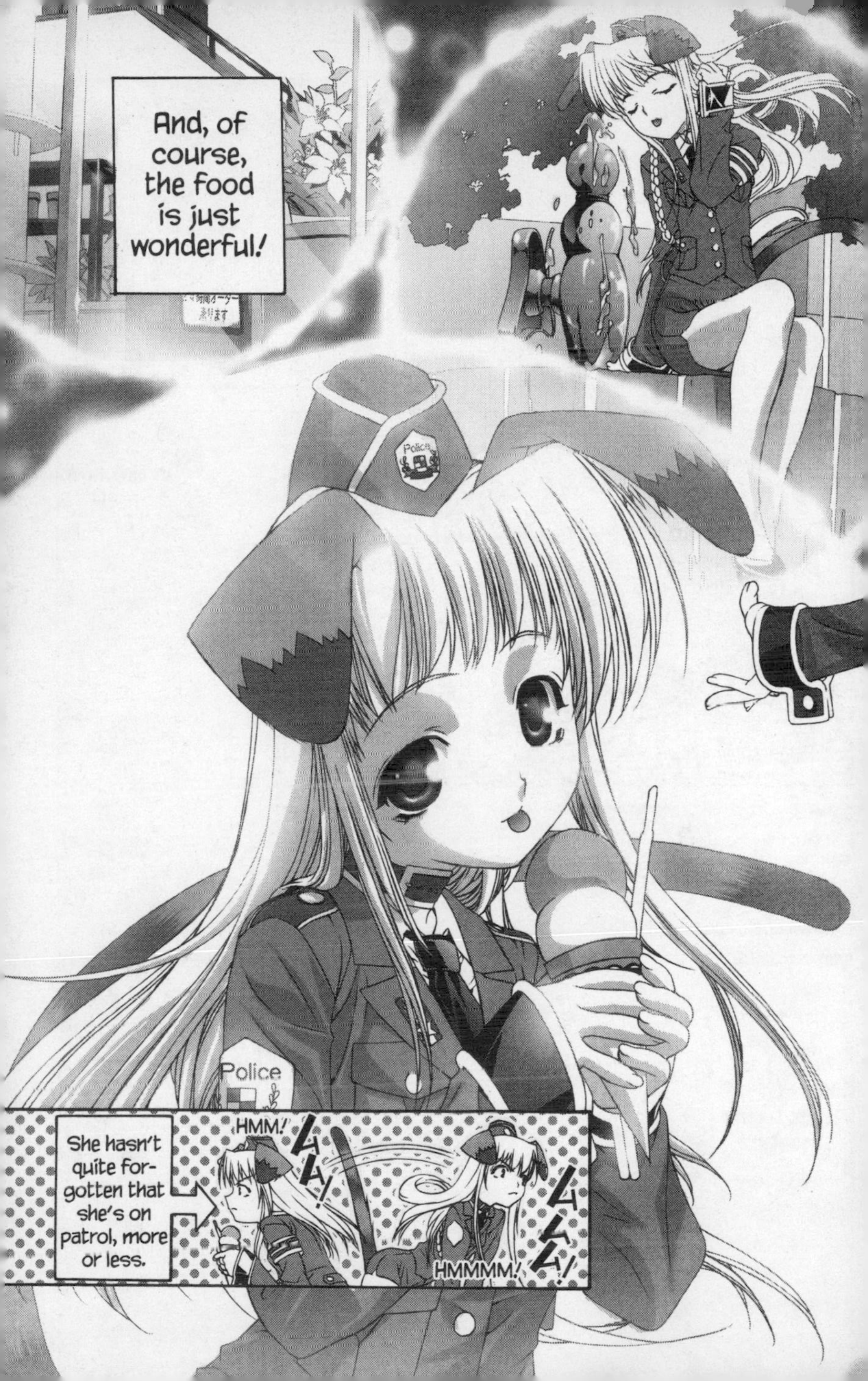
And, of course, the food is just wonderful!
HMM!
ムム!
ムムム!
HMMMM!
She hasn't quite for-gotten that she's on patrol, more or less.

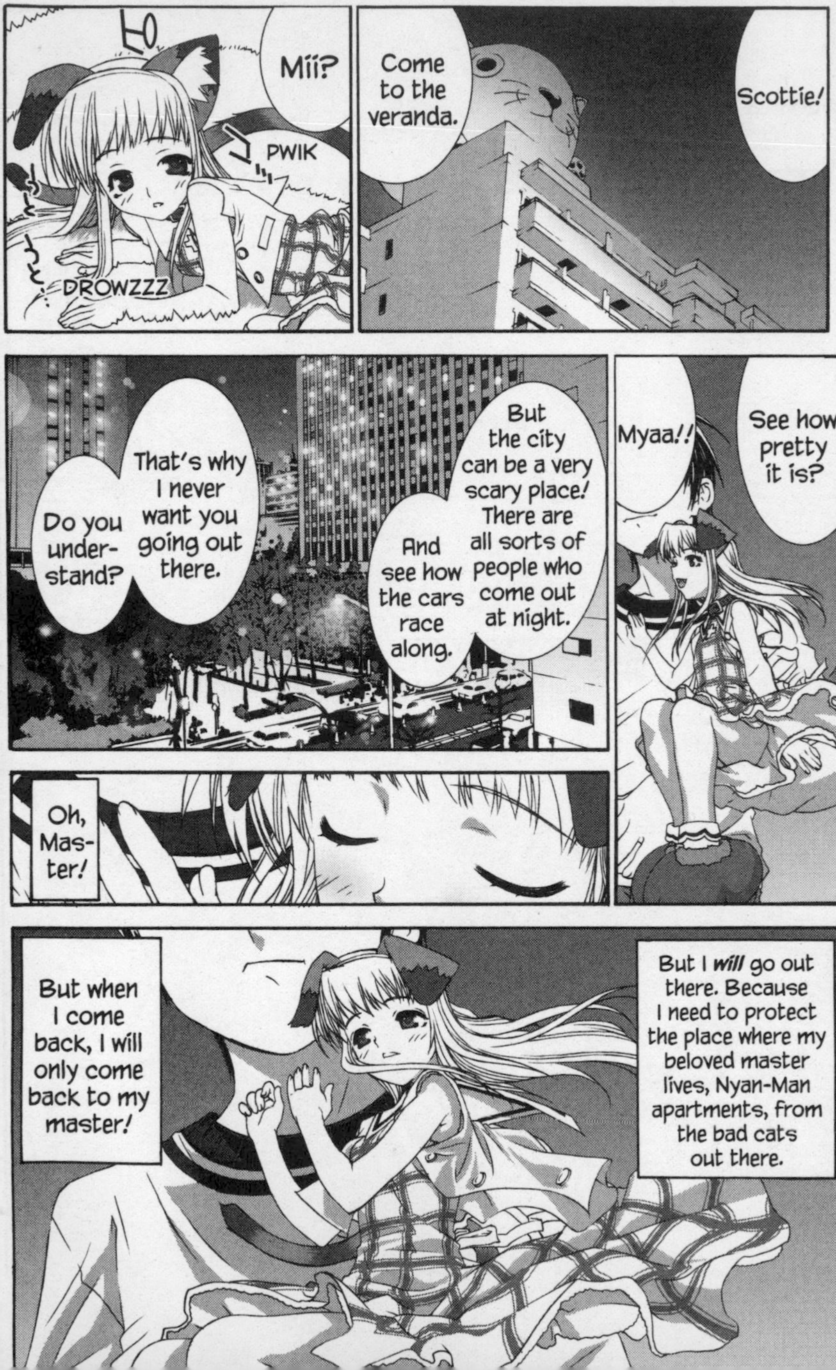
Scottie!
Come to the veranda.
Mii?
PWIK
DROWZZZ
See how pretty it is?
Myaa!!
And see how the cars race along.
But the city can be a very scary place! There are all sorts of people who come out at night.
That's why I never want you going out there.
Do you under-stand?
Oh, Mas-ter!
But I *will* go out there. Because I need to protect the place where my beloved master lives, Nyan-Man apartments, from the bad cats out there.
But when I come back, I will only come back to my master!

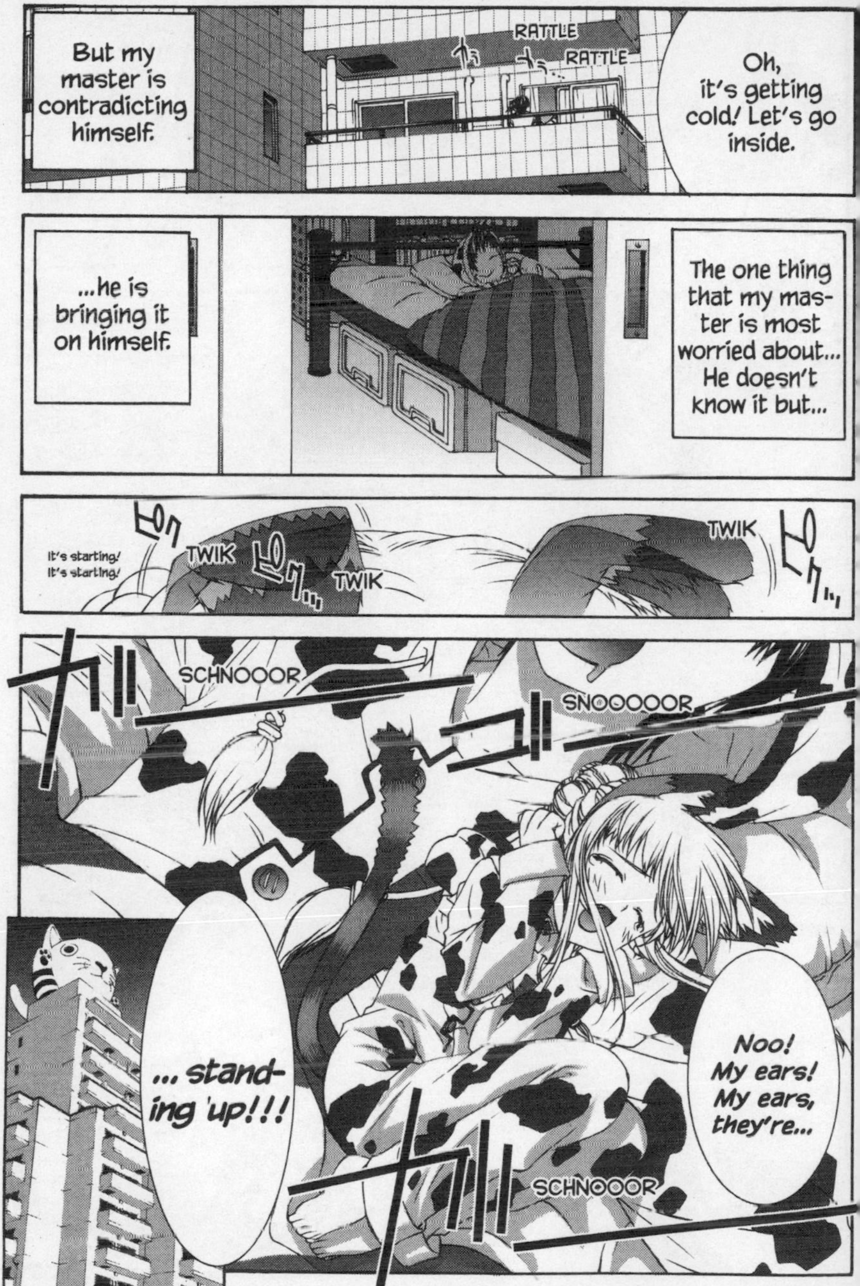
Oh, it's getting cold! Let's go inside.
RATTLE
RATTLE
But my master is contradicting himself.
The one thing that my master is most worried about... He doesn't know it but...
...he is bringing it on himself.
TWIK
TWIK
TWIK
It's starting! It's starting!
SNOOOOOR
SCHNOOOR
Noo! My ears! My ears, they're...
... standing 'up!!!
SCHNOOOR

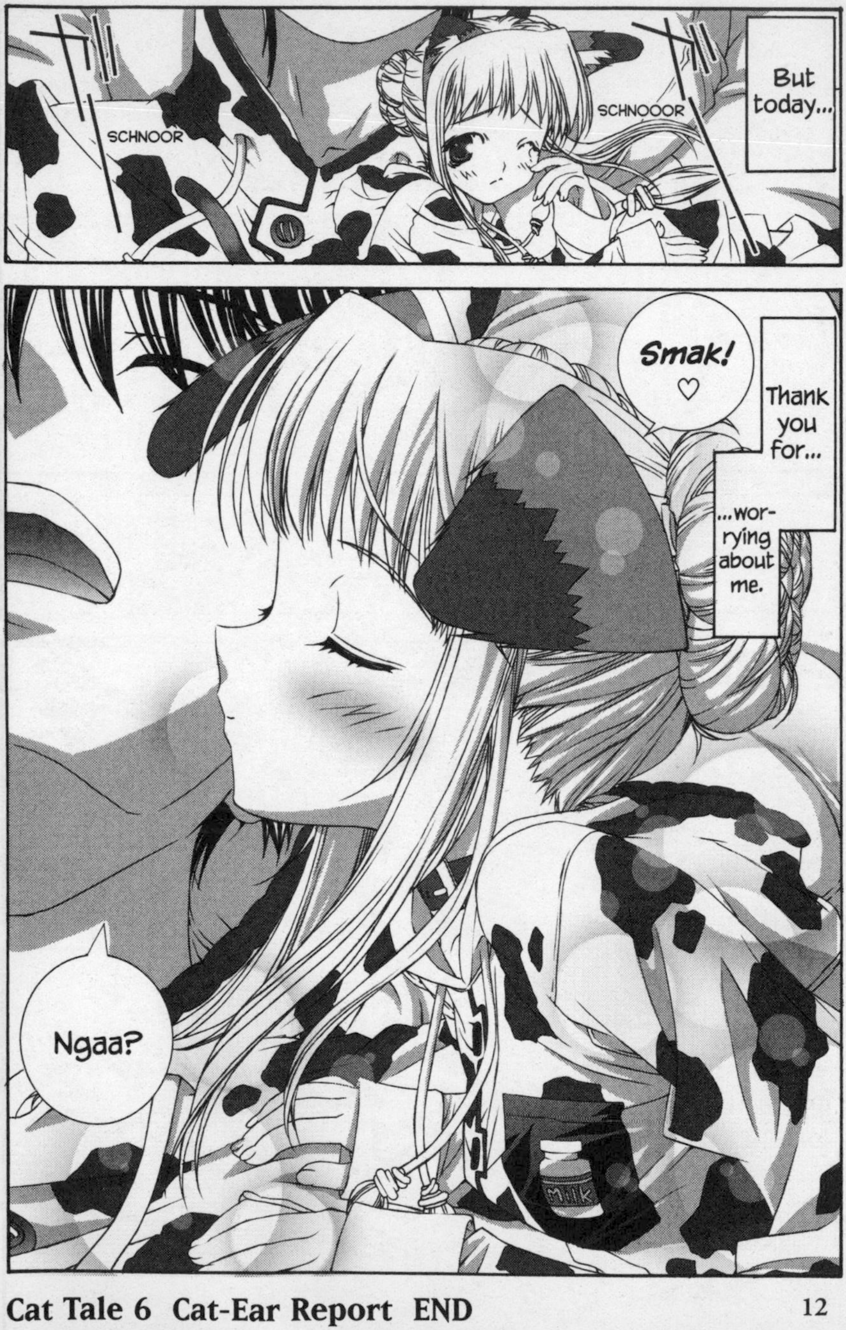
But today...
SCHNOOOR
SCHNOOR
Thank you for...
...wor-rying about me.
Smak! ♡
Ngaa?

Cat Tale 6 Cat-Ear Report END

Free Collars Side Story 1
Cat-Ear Jobs

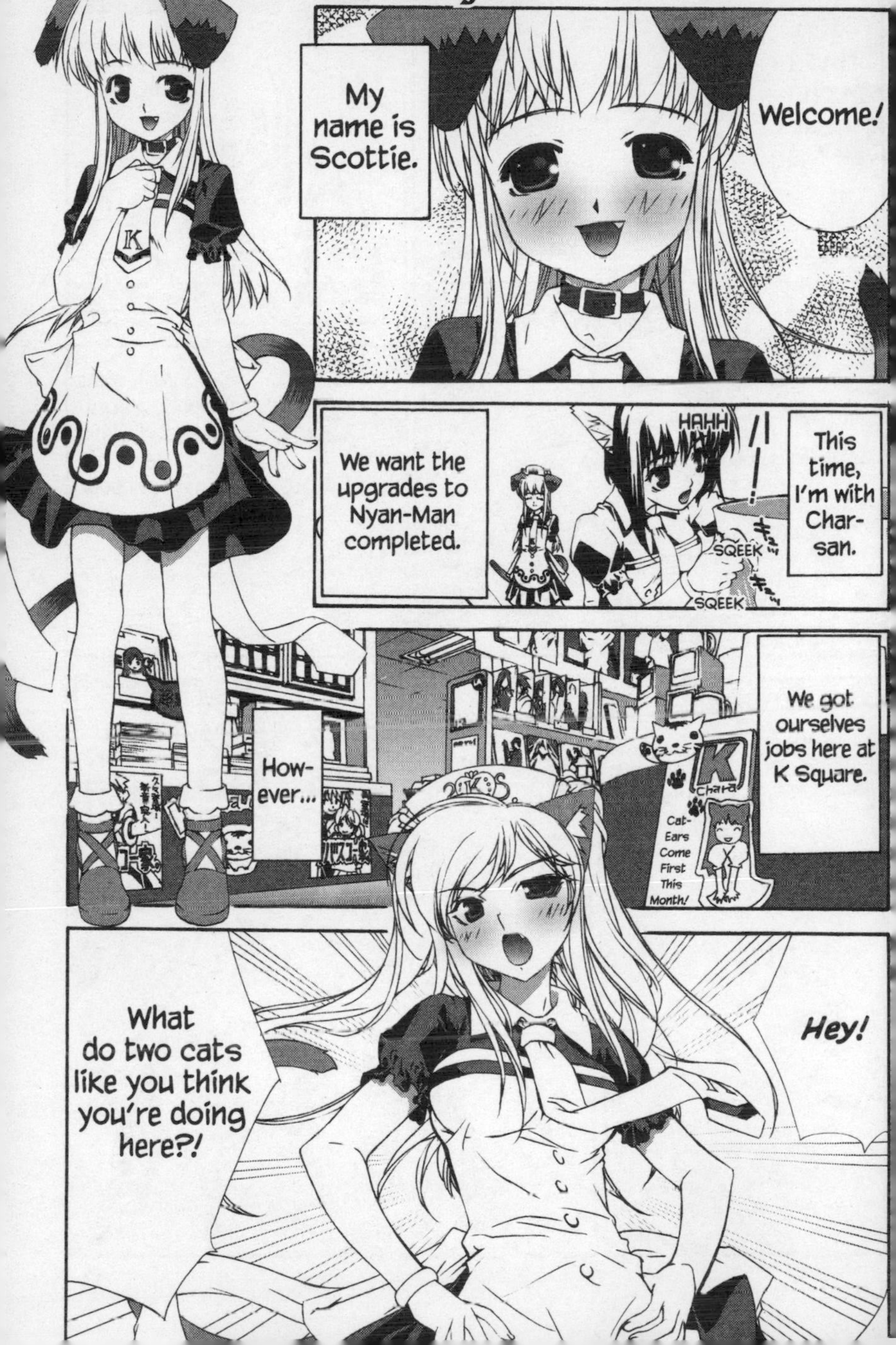
Welcome!
My name is Scottie.
This time, I'm with Char-san.
HAHH
SQEEK
SQEEK
We want the upgrades to Nyan-Man completed.
We got ourselves jobs here at K Square.
K Chara
Cat-Ears Come First This Month!
How-ever...
Hey!
What do two cats like you think you're doing here?!

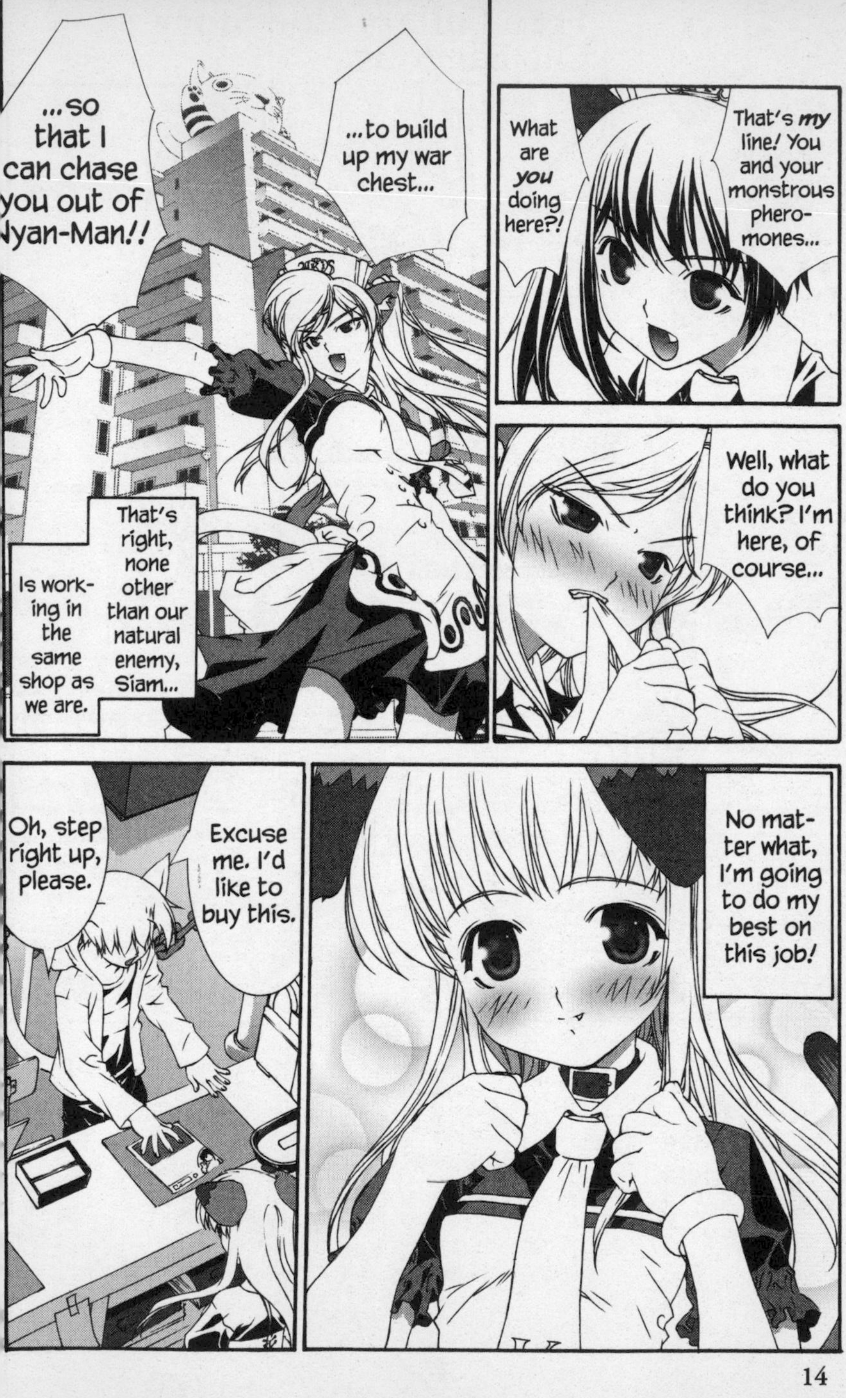
What are *you* doing here?!
That's *my* line! You and your monstrous phero-mones...
Well, what do you think? I'm here, of course...
...to build up my war chest...
...so that I can chase you out of Nyan-Man!!
That's right, none other than our natural enemy, Siam...
Is work-ing in the same shop as we are.
No mat-ter what, I'm going to do my best on this job!
Excuse me. I'd like to buy this.
Oh, step right up, please.

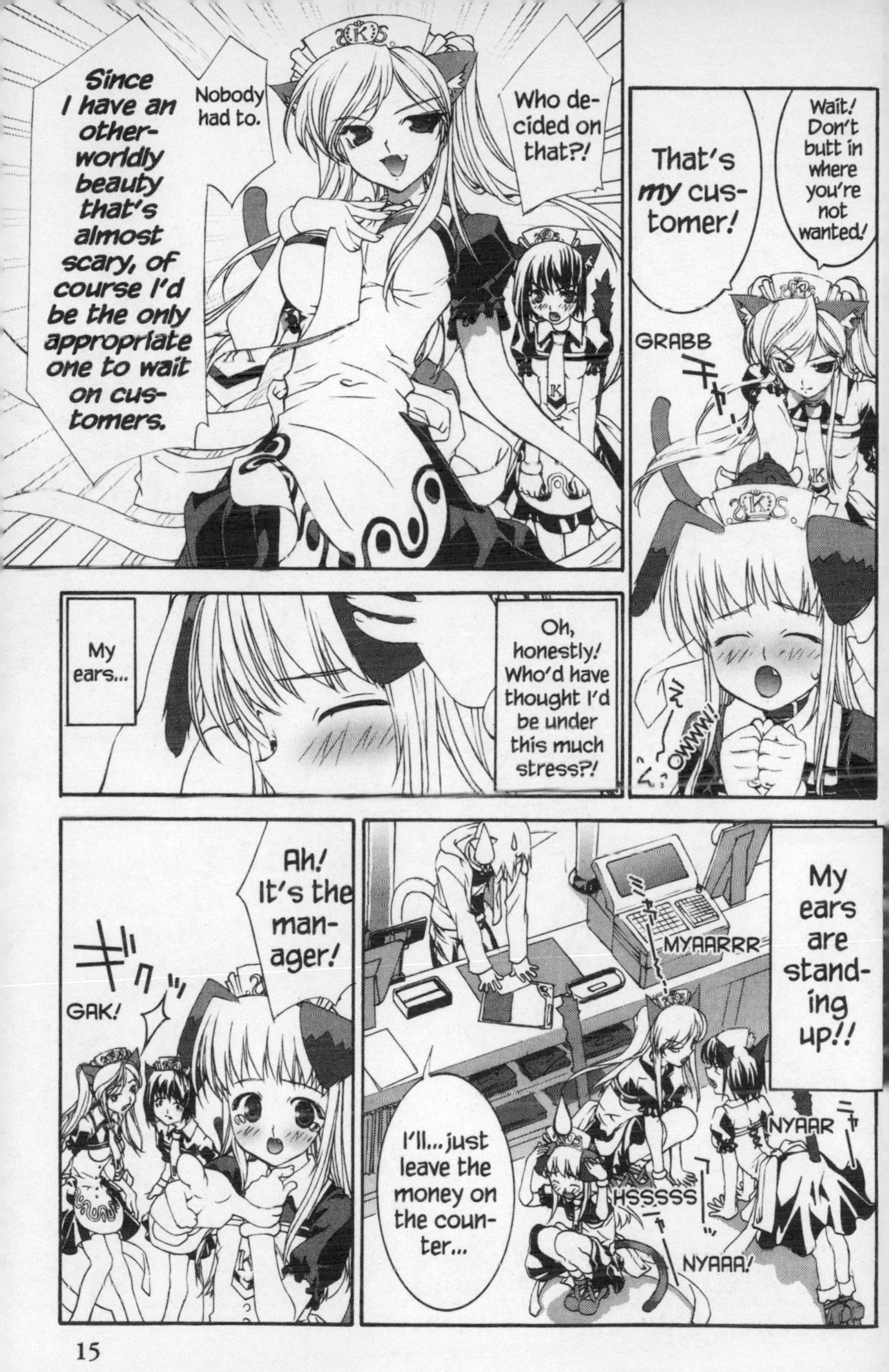
Wait! Don't butt in where you're not wanted!
That's my customer!
GRABB
OWWW!
Who de-cided on that?!
Nobody had to.
Since I have an other-worldly beauty that's almost scary, of course I'd be the only appropriate one to wait on cus-tomers.
Oh, honestly! Who'd have thought I'd be under this much stress?!
My ears...
My ears are stand-ing up!!
MYAARRR
NYAAR
I'll...just leave the money on the coun-ter...
HSSSSS
NYAAA!
Ah! It's the man-ager!
GAK!

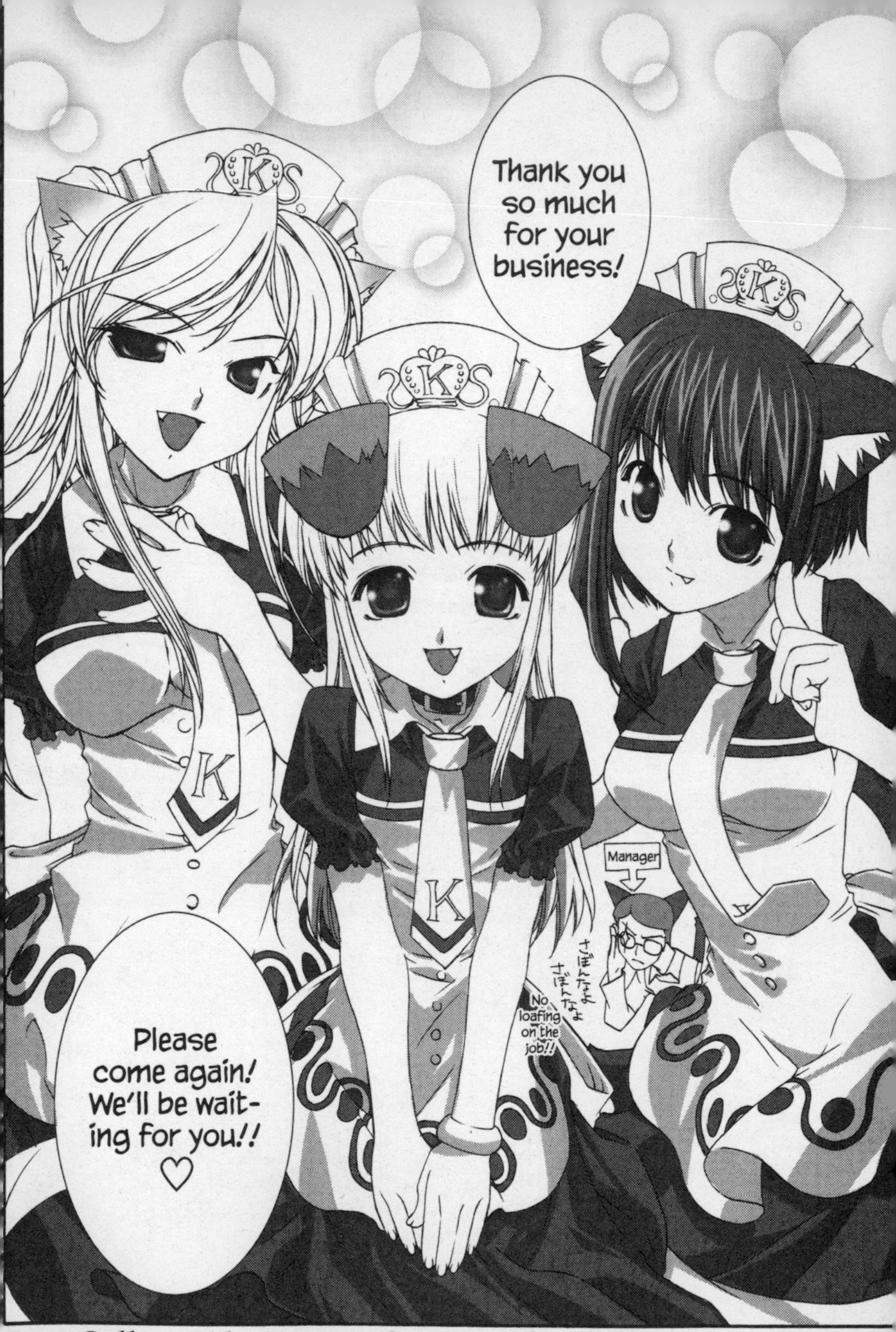
Thank you so much for your business!
Manager
さぼんなよ さぼんなよ
No loafing on the job!!
Please come again! We'll be wait-ing for you!! ♡

Free Collars Side Story 1 Cat-Ear Jobs END

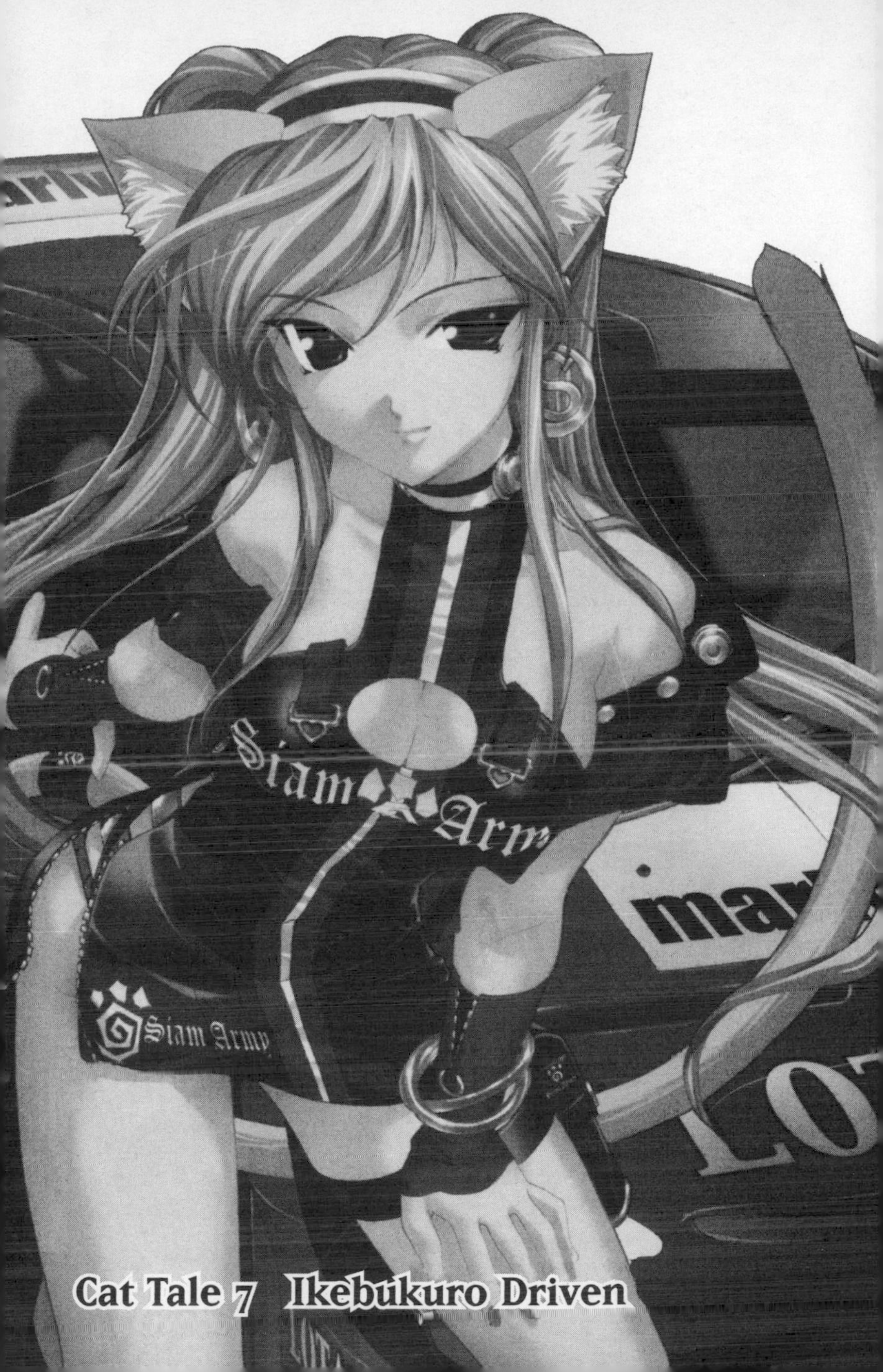
Siam Army
Siam Army

Cat Tale 7 Ikebukuro Driven

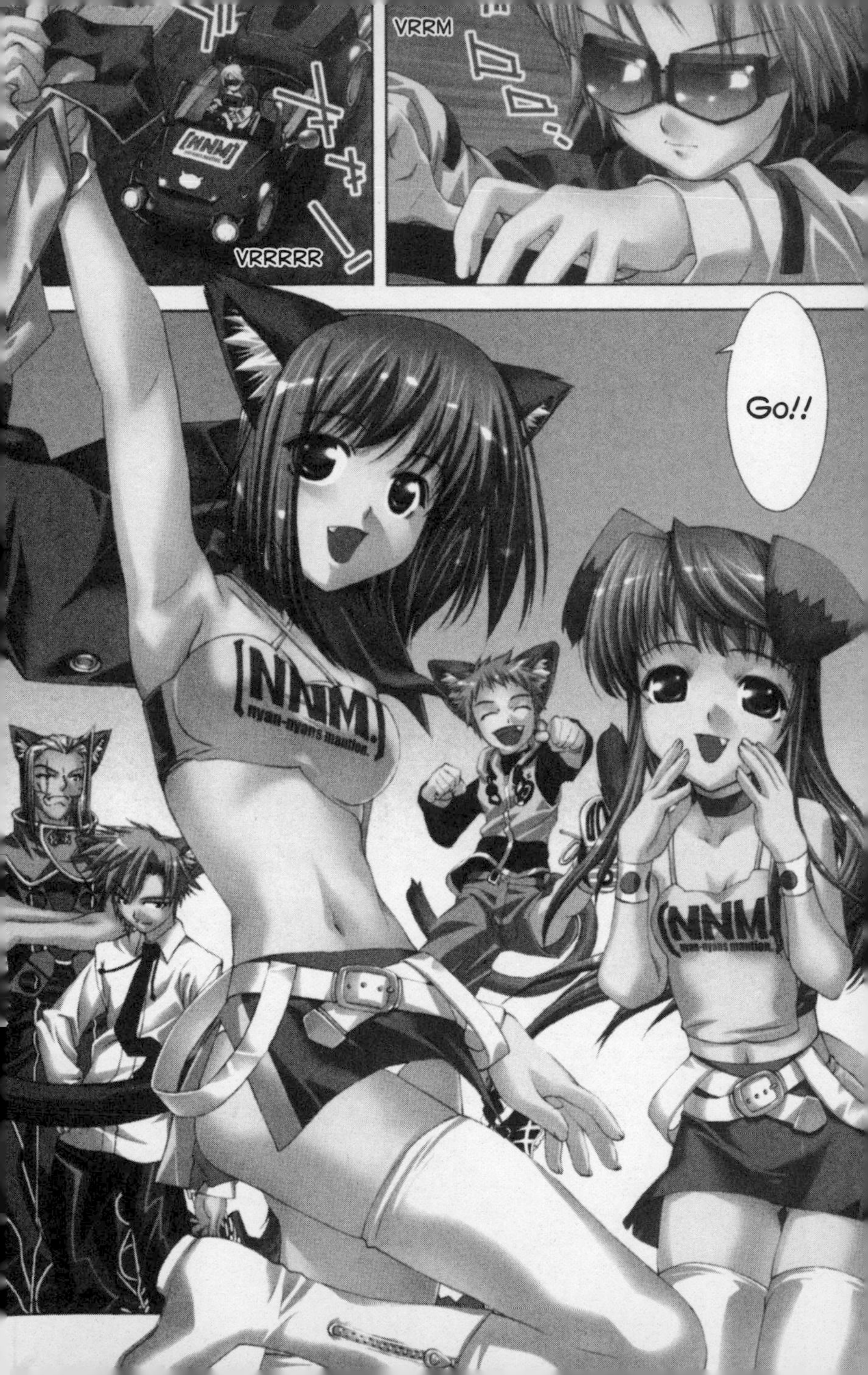
VRRM
VRRRRR
Go!!

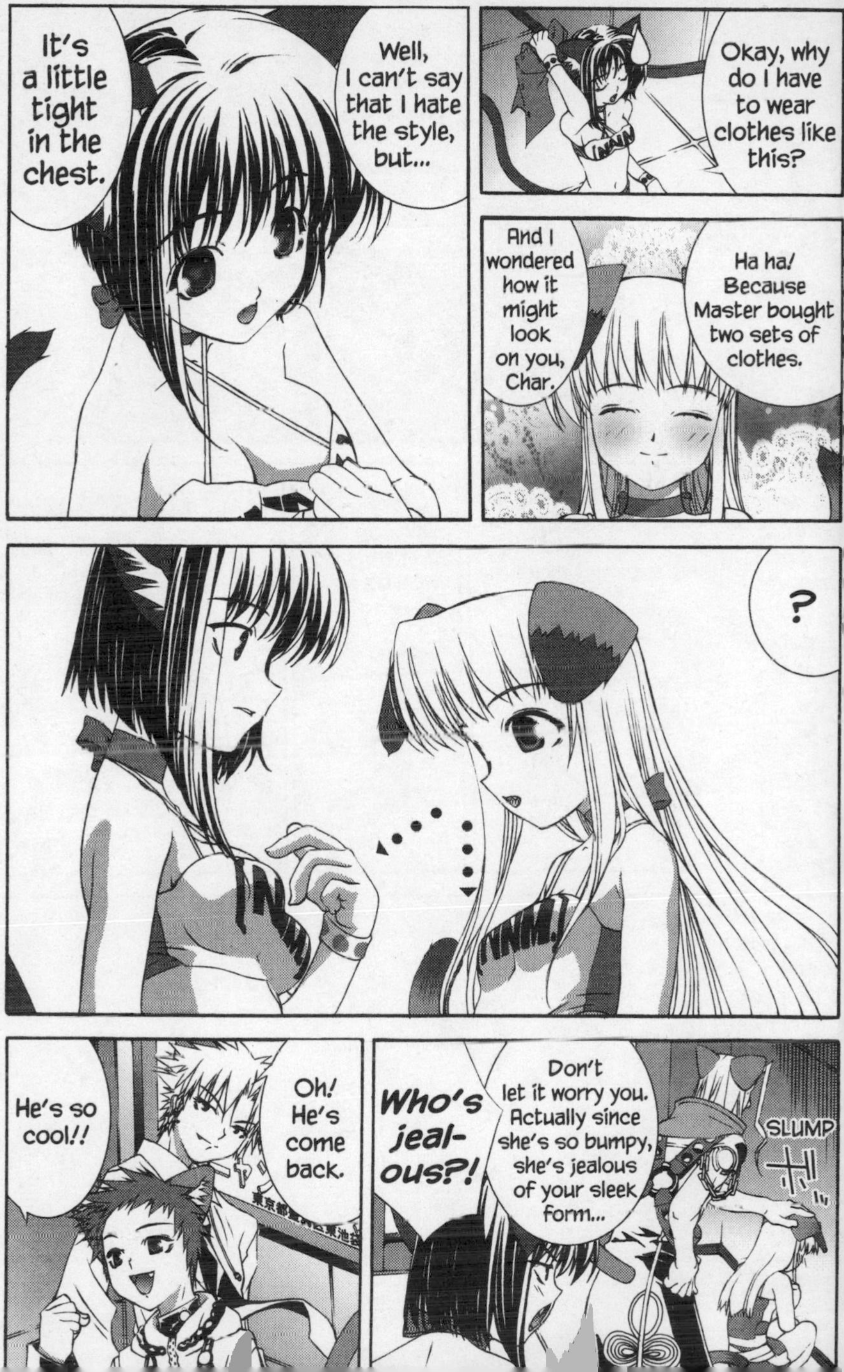

Okay, why do I have to wear clothes like this?
Ha ha! Because Master bought two sets of clothes.
And I wondered how it might look on you, Char.
Well, I can't say that I hate the style, but...
It's a little tight in the chest.
?
Don't let it worry you. Actually since she's so bumpy, she's jealous of your sleek form...
SLUMP
Who's jeal-ous?!
Oh! He's come back.
He's so cool!!

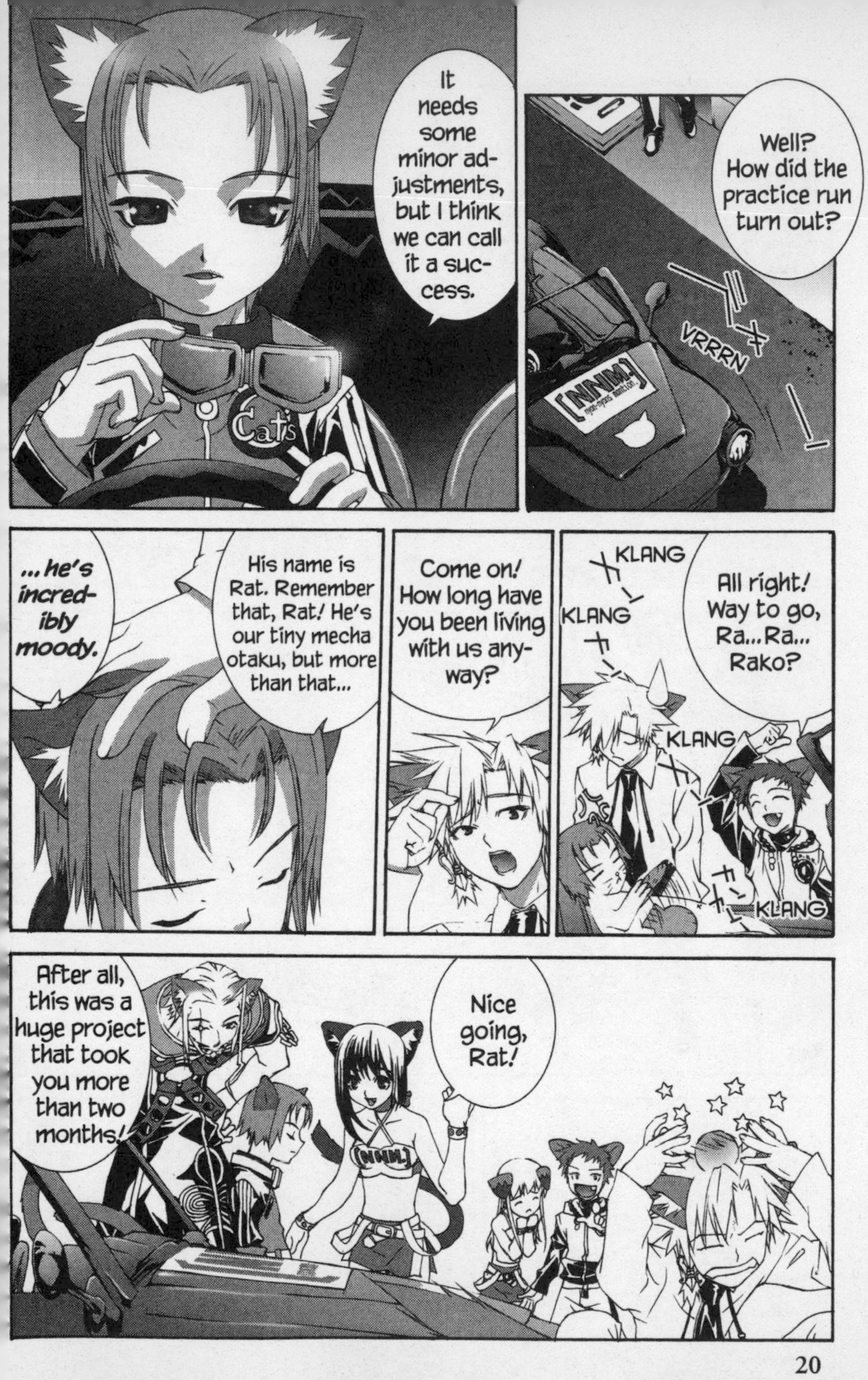
Well? How did the practice run turn out?
VRRRN
It needs some minor adjustments, but I think we can call it a success.
KLANG
KLANG
All right! Way to go, Ra...Ra... Rako?
KLANG
KLANG
Come on! How long have you been living with us anyway?
His name is Rat. Remember that, Rat! He's our tiny mecha otaku, but more than that...
...he's incredibly moody.
Nice going, Rat!
After all, this was a huge project that took you more than two months!

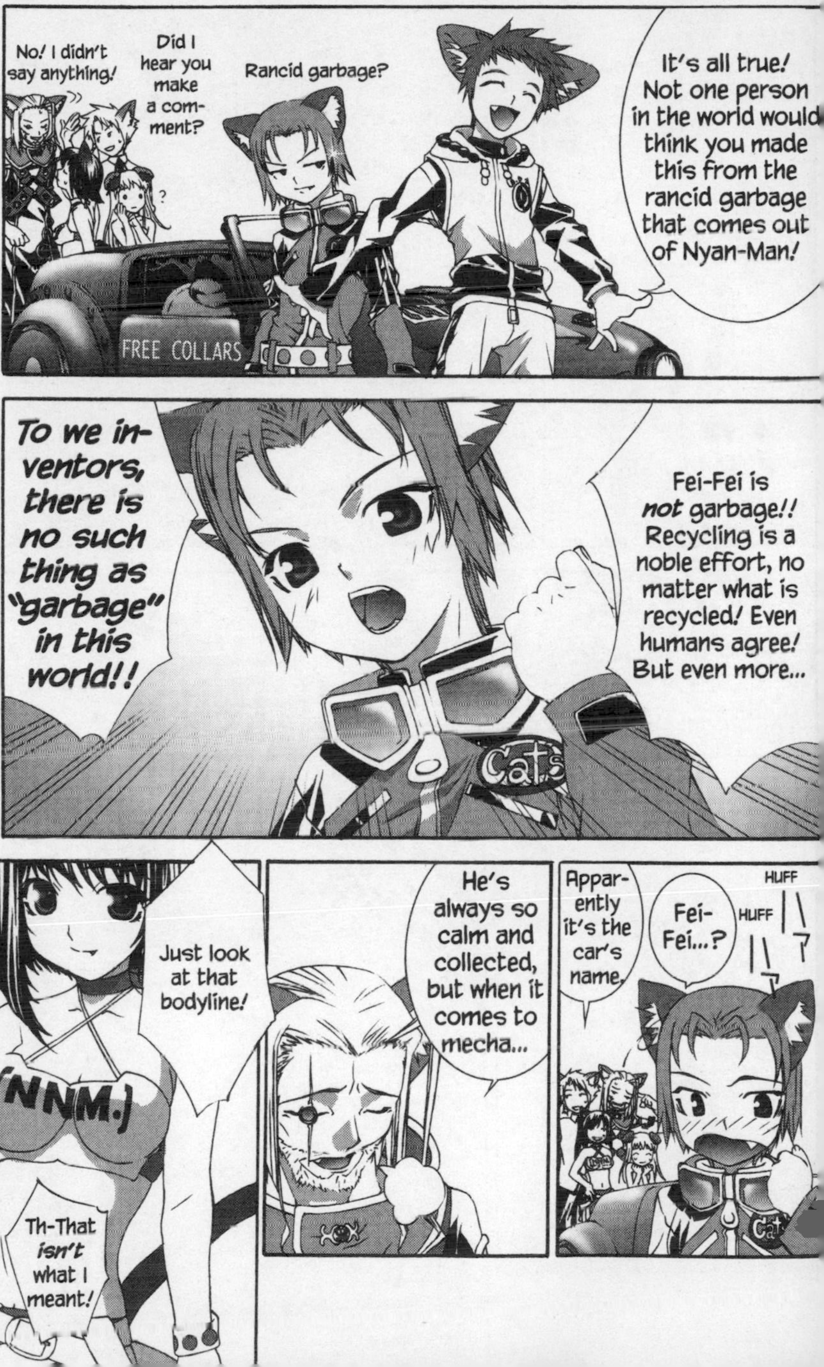
It's all true! Not one person in the world would think you made this from the rancid garbage that comes out of Nyan-Man!
Rancid garbage?
Did I hear you make a com-ment?
No! I didn't say anything!
?
FREE COLLARS
Fei-Fei is *not* garbage!! Recycling is a noble effort, no matter what is recycled! Even humans agree! But even more...
To we in-ventors, there is no such thing as "garbage" in this world!!
Cats
HUFF
HUFF
Fei-Fei...?
Appar-ently it's the car's name.
He's always so calm and collected, but when it comes to mecha...
Just look at that bodyline!
?
(NNM.)
Th-That *isn't* what I meant!

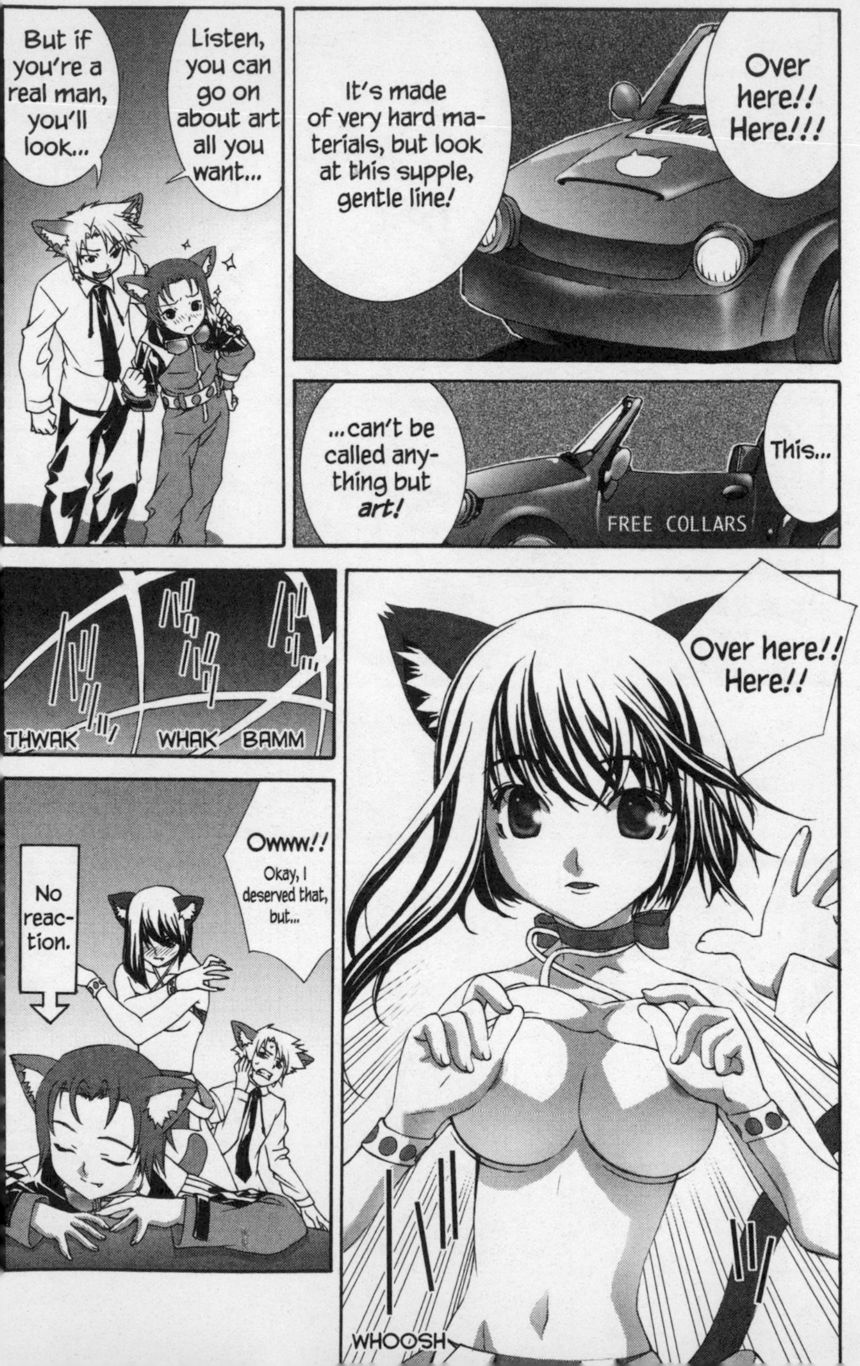
Over here!! Here!!!
It's made of very hard materials, but look at this supple, gentle line!
This...
...can't be called anything but *art*!
FREE COLLARS
Listen, you can go on about art all you want...
But if you're a real man, you'll look...
Over here!! Here!!
WHOOSH
BAMM
WHAK
THWAK
Owww!!
Okay, I deserved that, but...
No reaction.

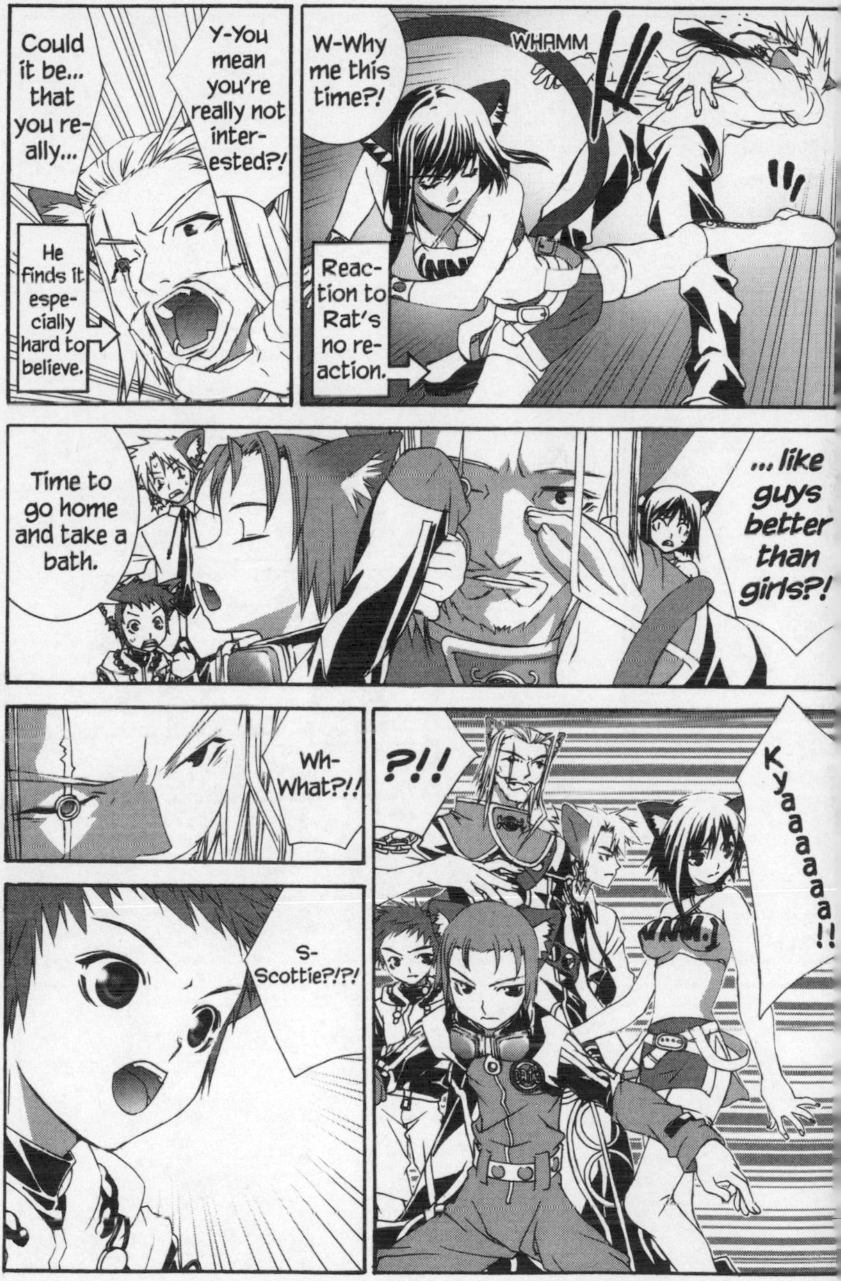

WHAMM
W-Why me this time?!
Reaction to Rat's no reaction.
Y-You mean you're really not interested?!
Could it be... that you really...
He finds it especially hard to believe.
...like guys better than girls?!
Time to go home and take a bath.
Kyaaaaaa!!
?!!
Wh-What?!!
S-Scottie?!?!

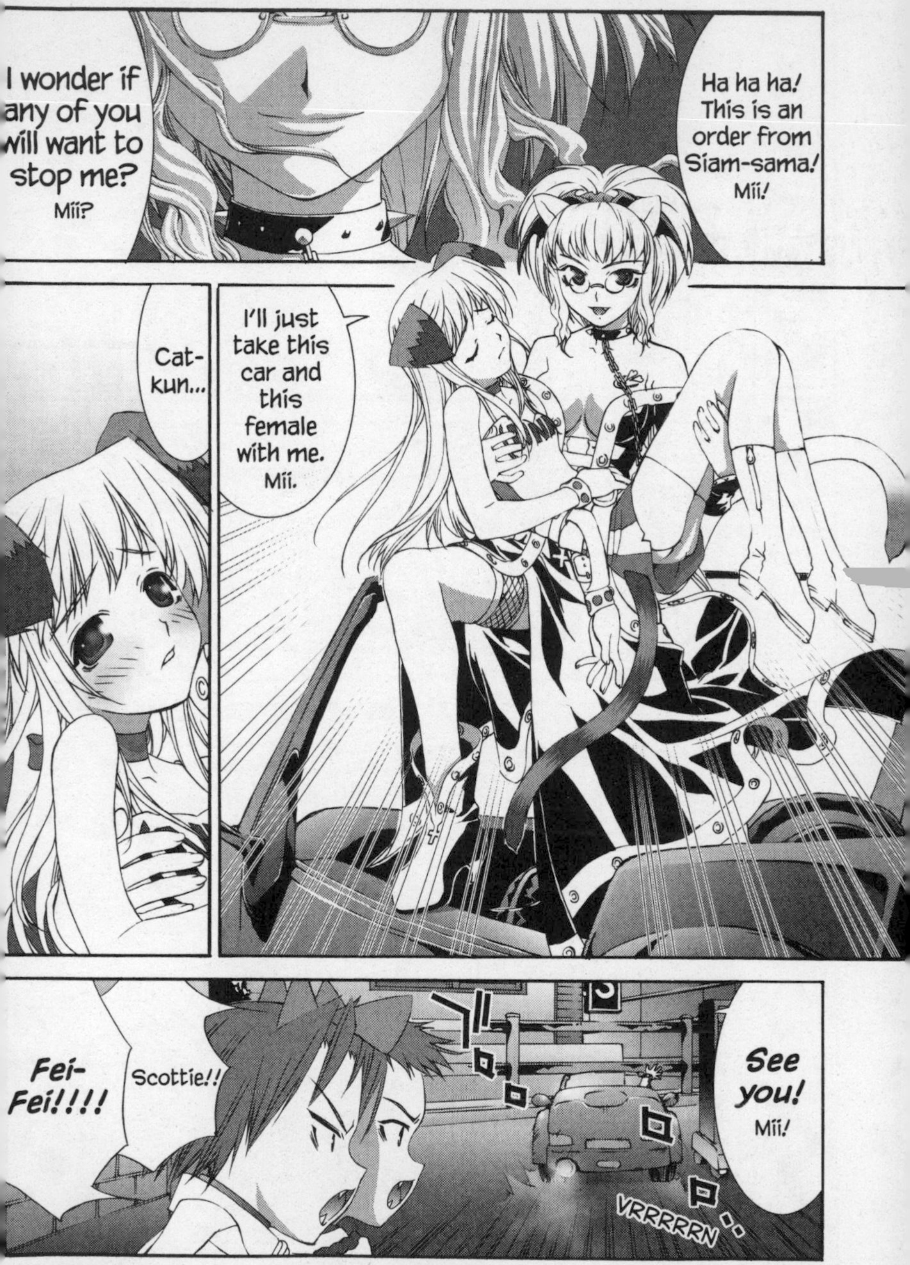
Ha ha ha! This is an order from Siam-sama! Mii!
I wonder if any of you will want to stop me? Mii?
I'll just take this car and this female with me. Mii.
Cat-kun...
See you! Mii!
VRRRRRN
Scottie!!
Fei-Fei!!!!

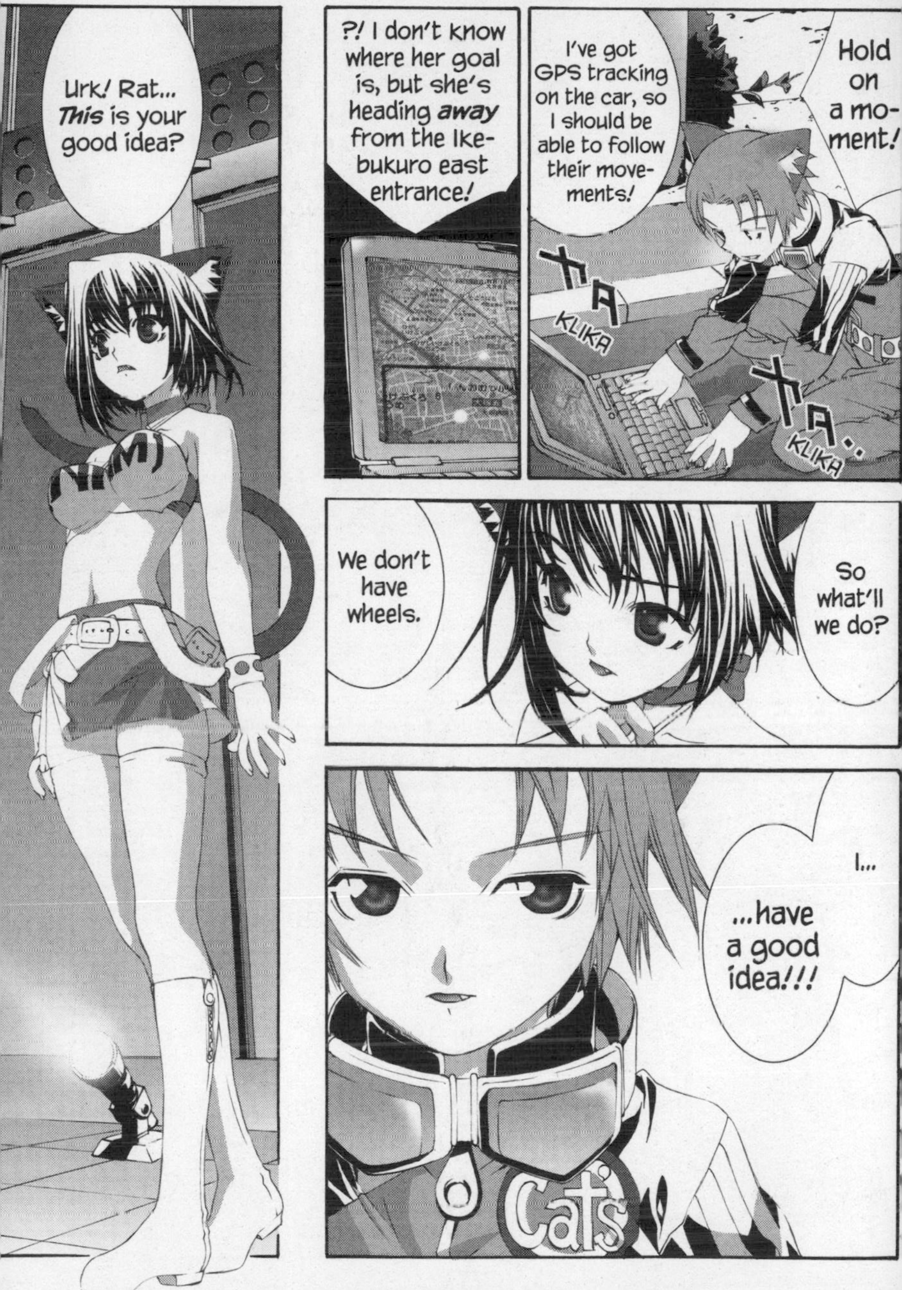

Hold on a moment!
I've got GPS tracking on the car, so I should be able to follow their movements!
KLIKA
KLIKA
?! I don't know where her goal is, but she's heading *away* from the Ikebukuro east entrance!
So what'll we do?
We don't have wheels.
I...
...have a good idea!!!
Cats
Urk! Rat... *This* is your good idea?

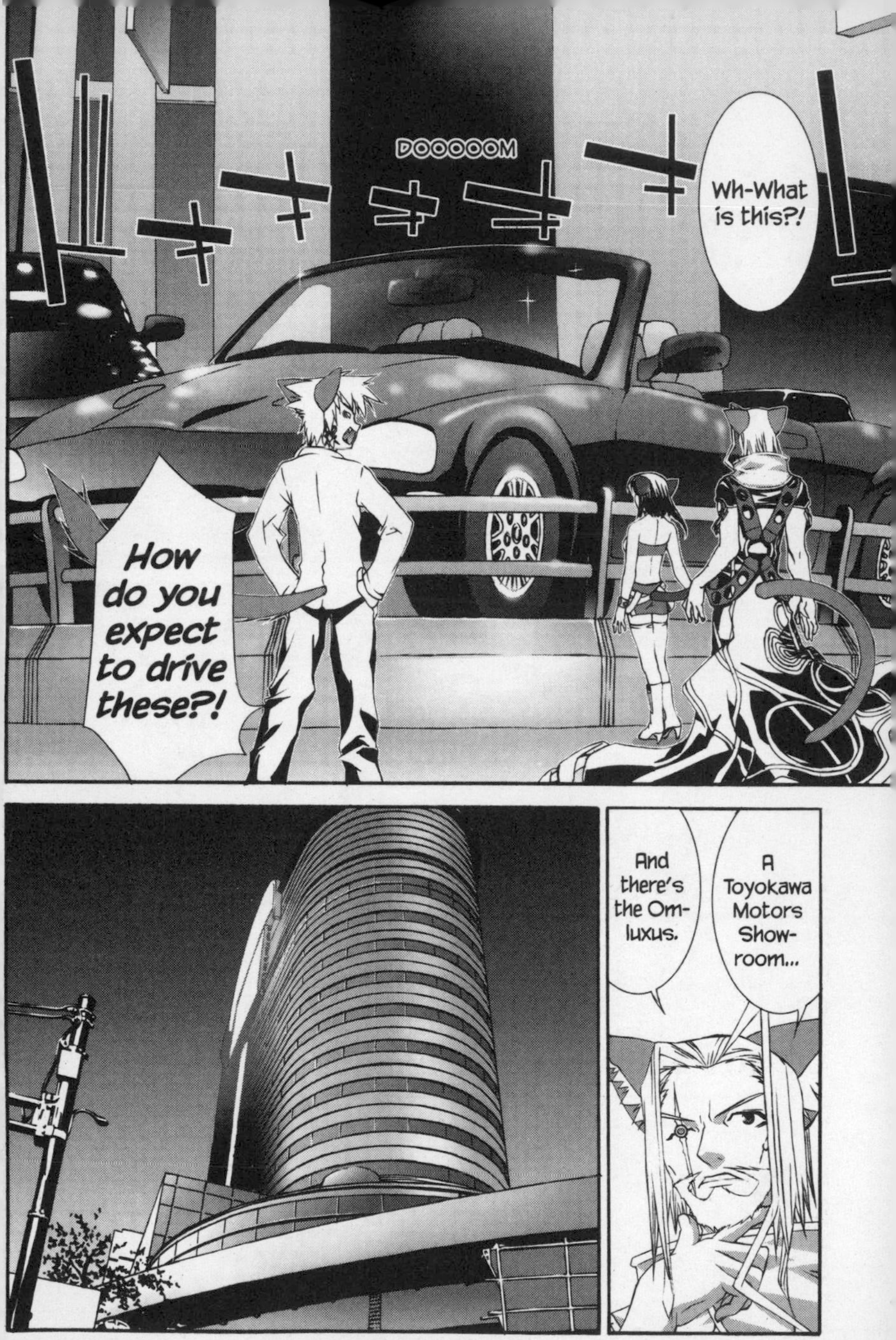
Wh-What is this?!
DOOOOOM
How do you expect to drive these?!
A Toyokawa Motors Show-room...
And there's the Om-luxus.

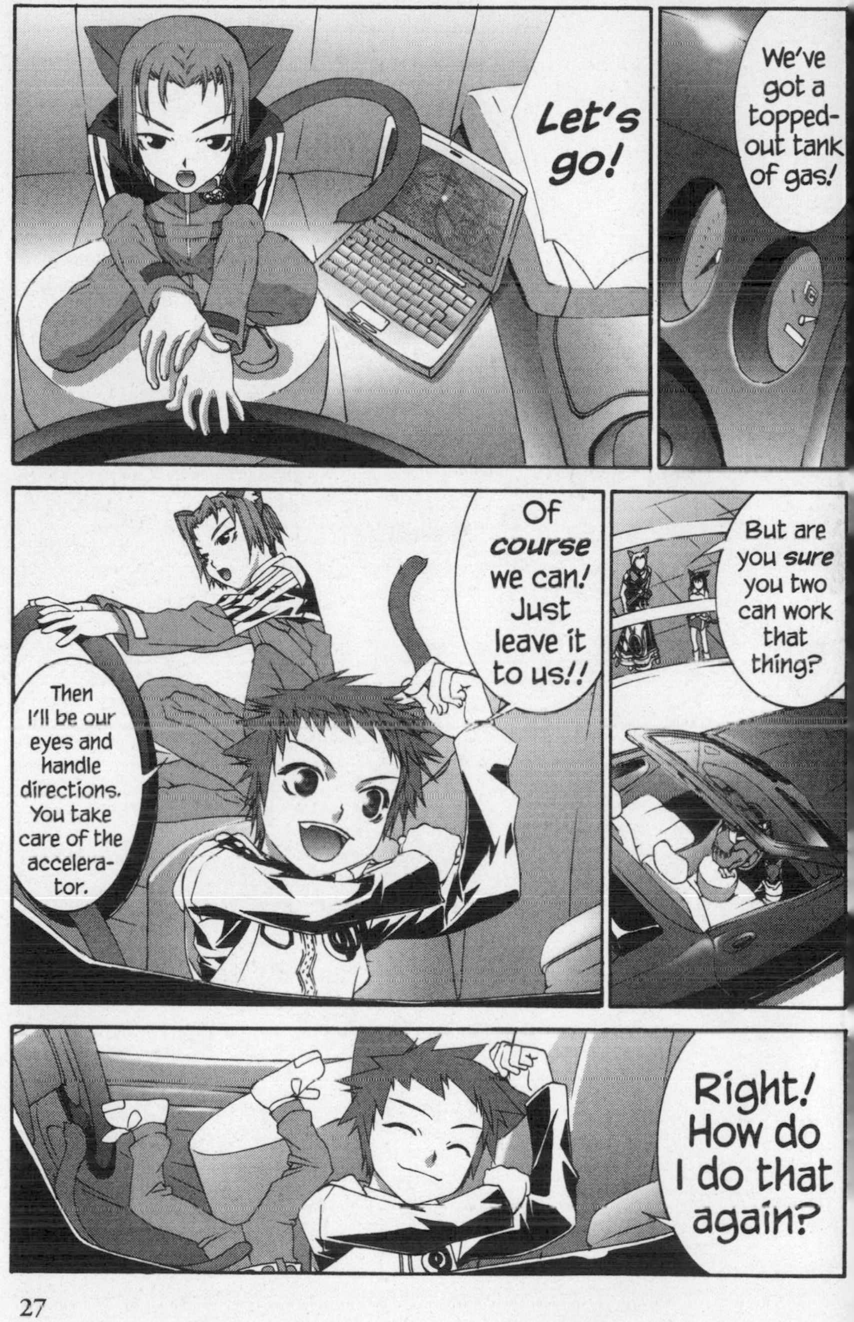
We've got a topped-out tank of gas!
Let's go!
But are you *sure* you two can work that thing?
Of *course* we can! Just leave it to us!!
Then I'll be our eyes and handle directions. You take care of the accelerator.
Right! How do I do that again?

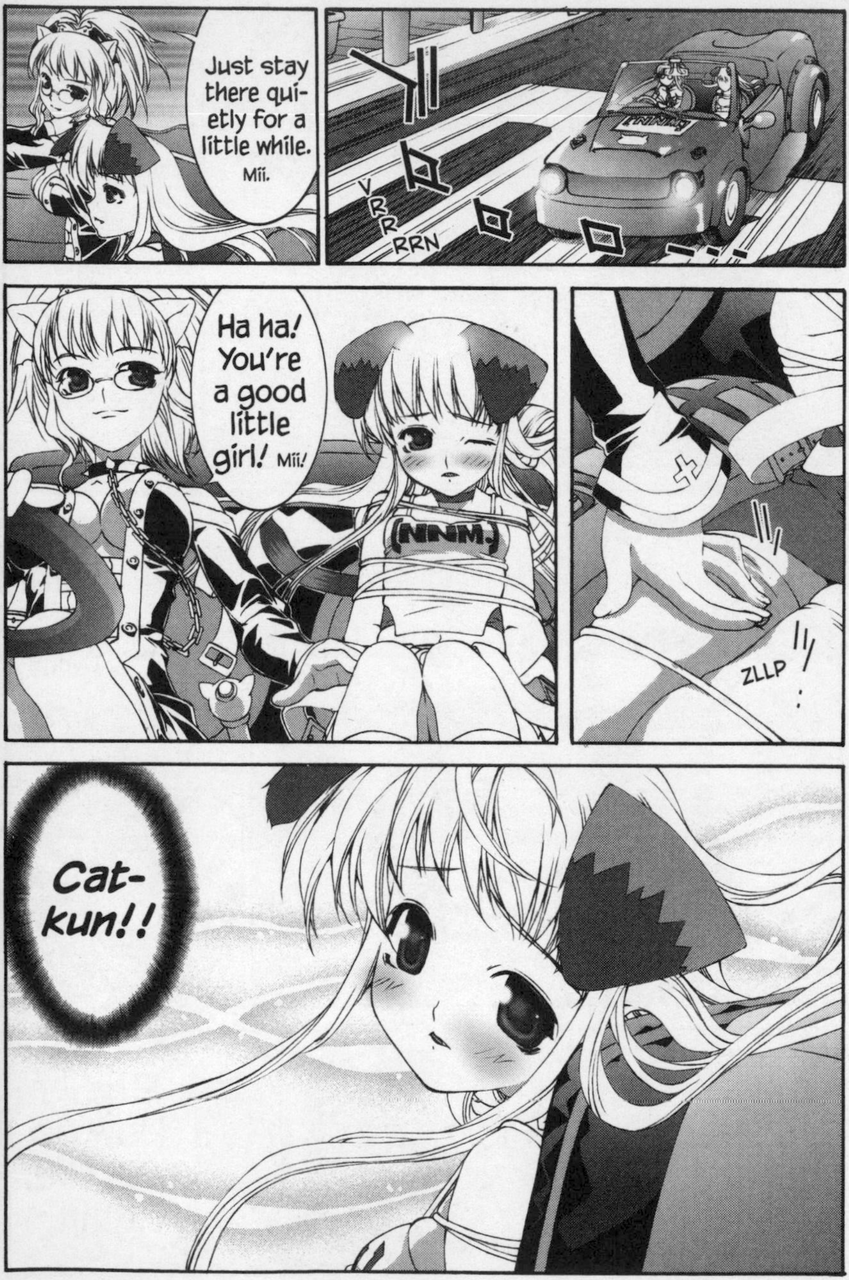
VRRRRN
Just stay there qui-etly for a little while.
Mii.
ZLLP
Ha ha! You're a good little girl!
Mii!
Cat-kun!!

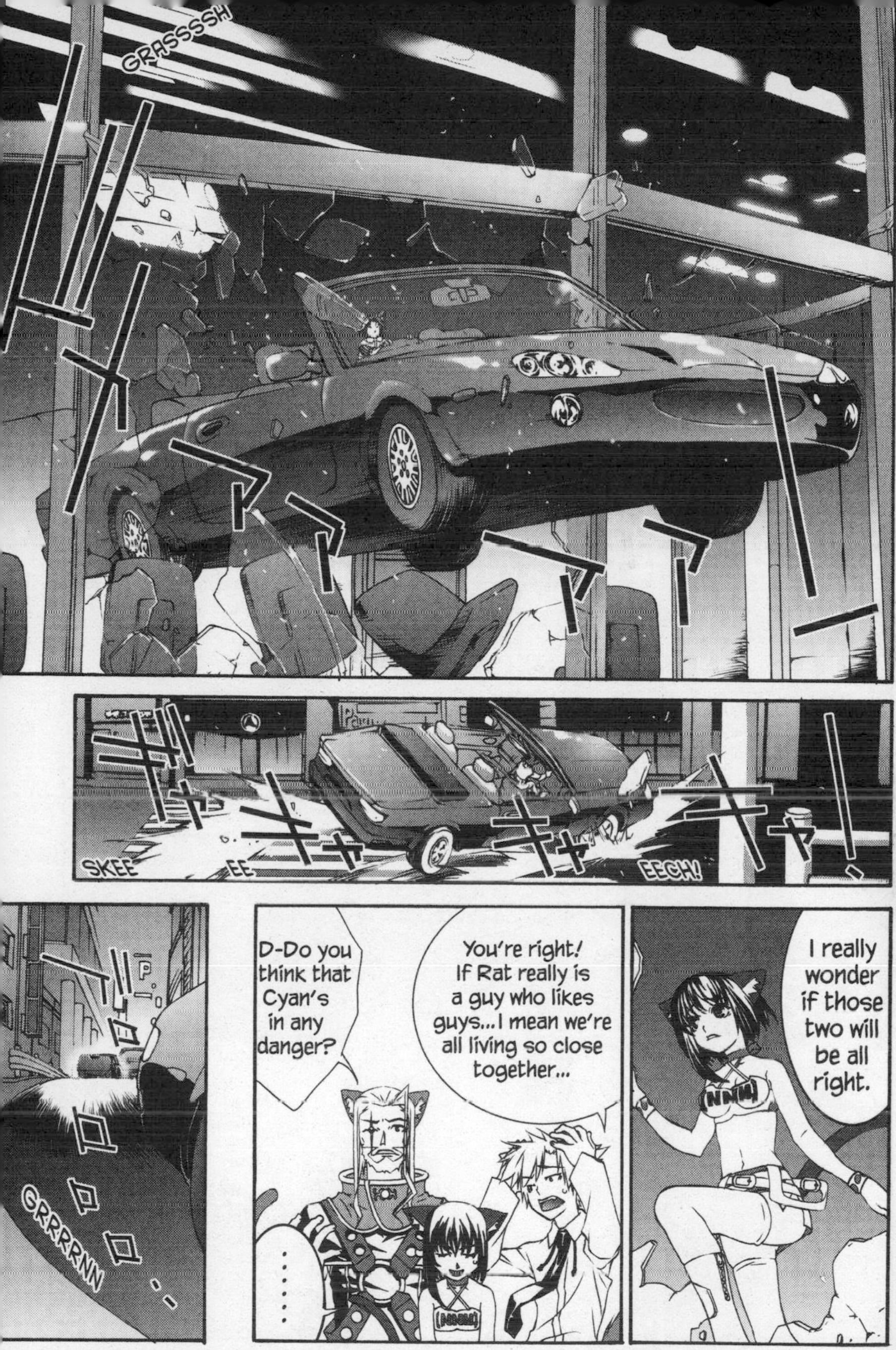
GRASSSSH
SKEE
EE
EECH!
I really wonder if those two will be all right.
You're right! If Rat really is a guy who likes guys...I mean we're all living so close together...
D-Do you think that Cyan's in any danger?
......
GRRRRNN

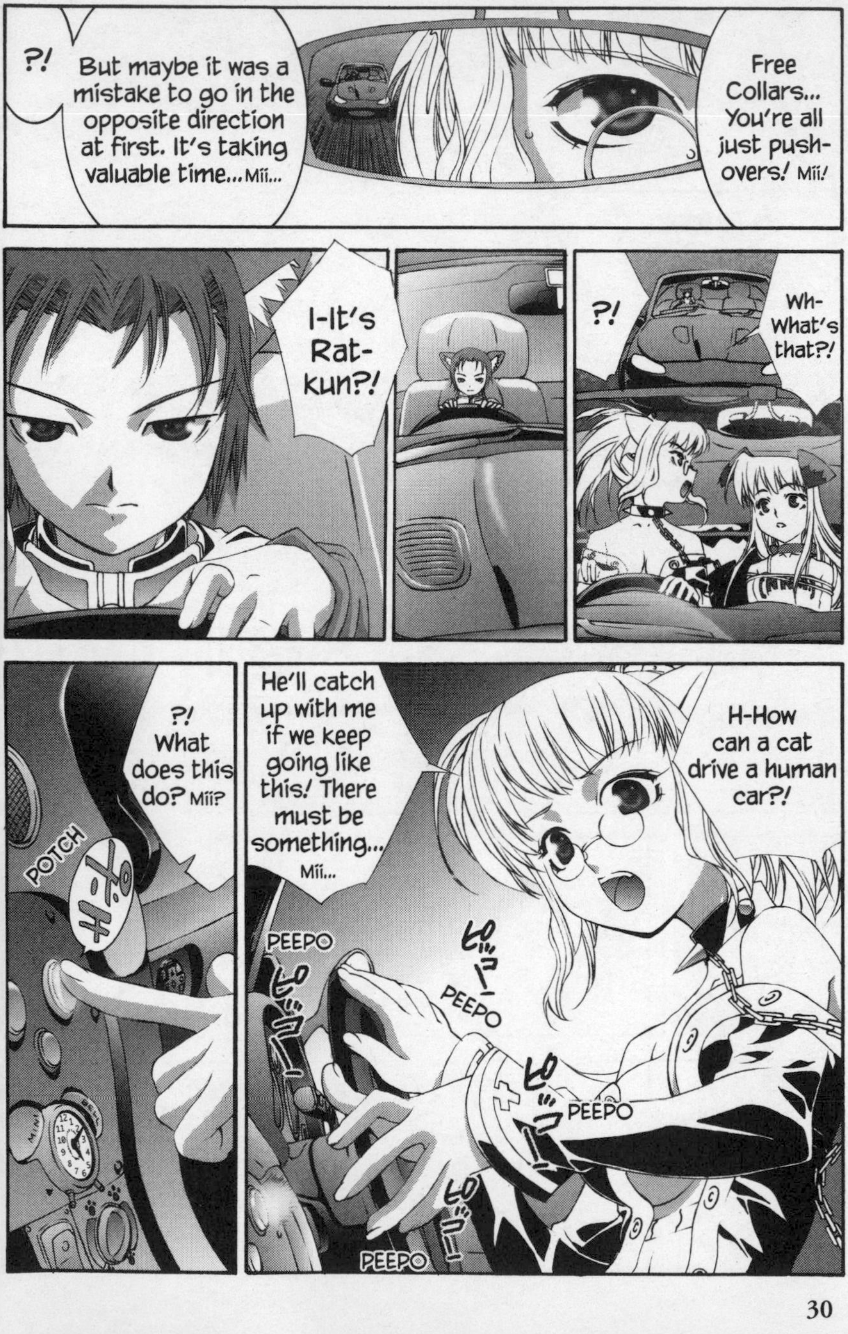

Free Collars... You're all just push-overs! Mii!
?!
But maybe it was a mistake to go in the opposite direction at first. It's taking valuable time... Mii...
Wh- What's that?!
?!
I-It's Rat-kun?!
H-How can a cat drive a human car?!
He'll catch up with me if we keep going like this! There must be something... Mii...
PEEPO
PEEPO
PEEPO
PEEPO
?! What does this do? Mii?
POTCH

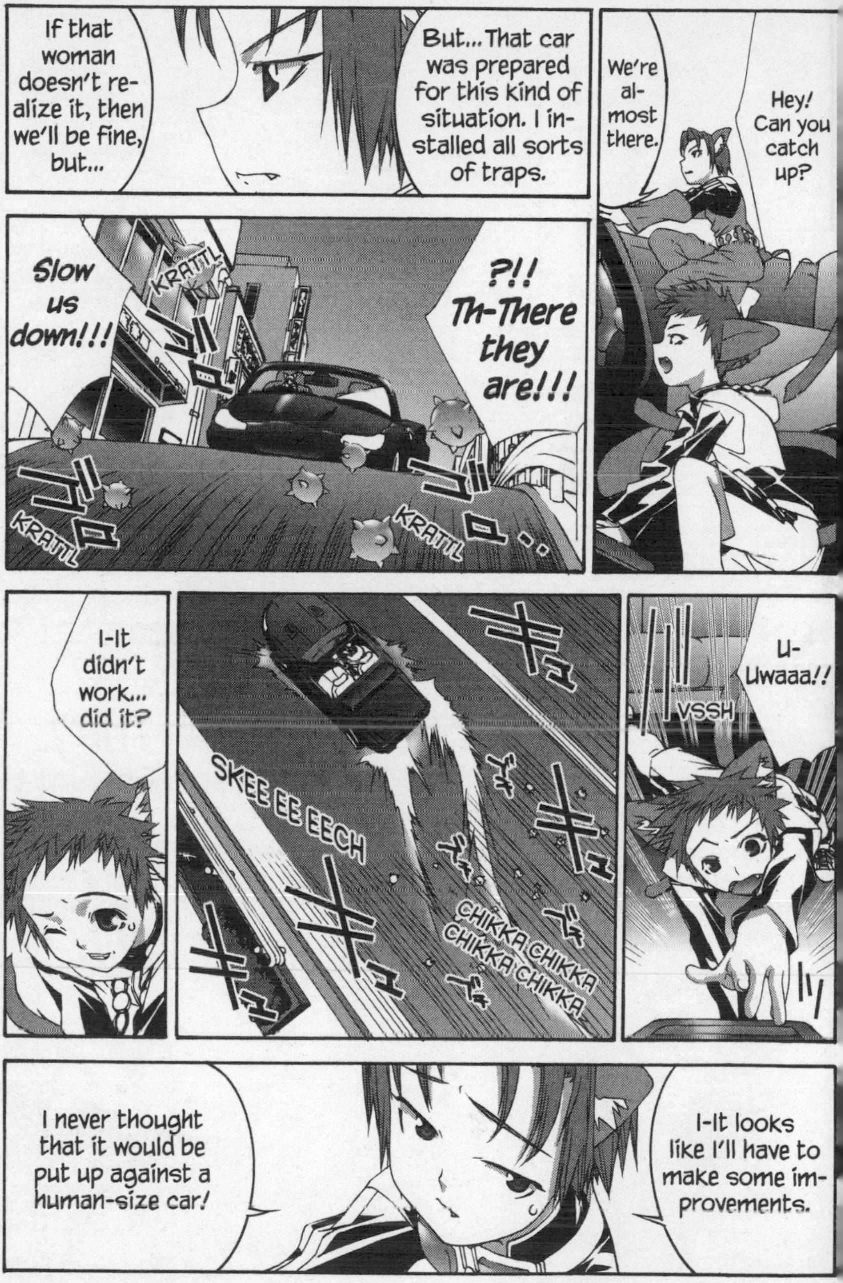
Hey! Can you catch up?
We're almost there.
But...That car was prepared for this kind of situation. I installed all sorts of traps.
If that woman doesn't realize it, then we'll be fine, but...
?!! Th-There they are!!!
KRATTL
KRATTL
KRATTL
Slow us down!!!
U-Uwaaa!!
VSSH
SKEE EE EECH
CHIKKA CHIKKA CHIKKA CHIKKA
I-It didn't work... did it?
I-It looks like I'll have to make some improvements.
I never thought that it would be put up against a human-size car!

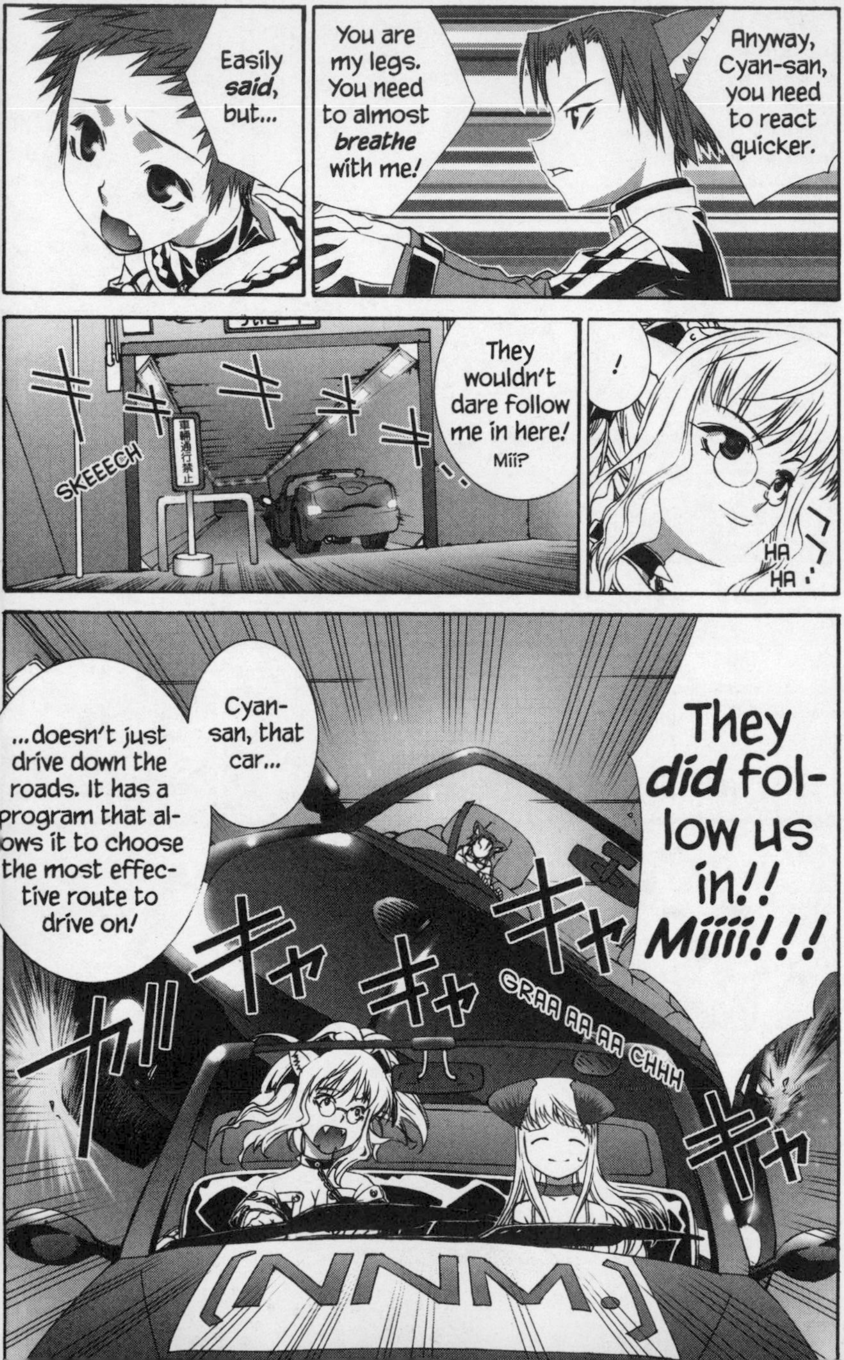
Anyway, Cyan-san, you need to react quicker.
You are my legs. You need to almost *breathe* with me!
Easily *said*, but...
!
HA HA
They wouldn't dare follow me in here!
Mii?
車輛通行禁止
SKEEECH
They *did* fol-low us in!! Miiii!!!
Cyan-san, that car...
...doesn't just drive down the roads. It has a program that al-lows it to choose the most effec-tive route to drive on!
GRAA AA AA CHHH
(NNM.)

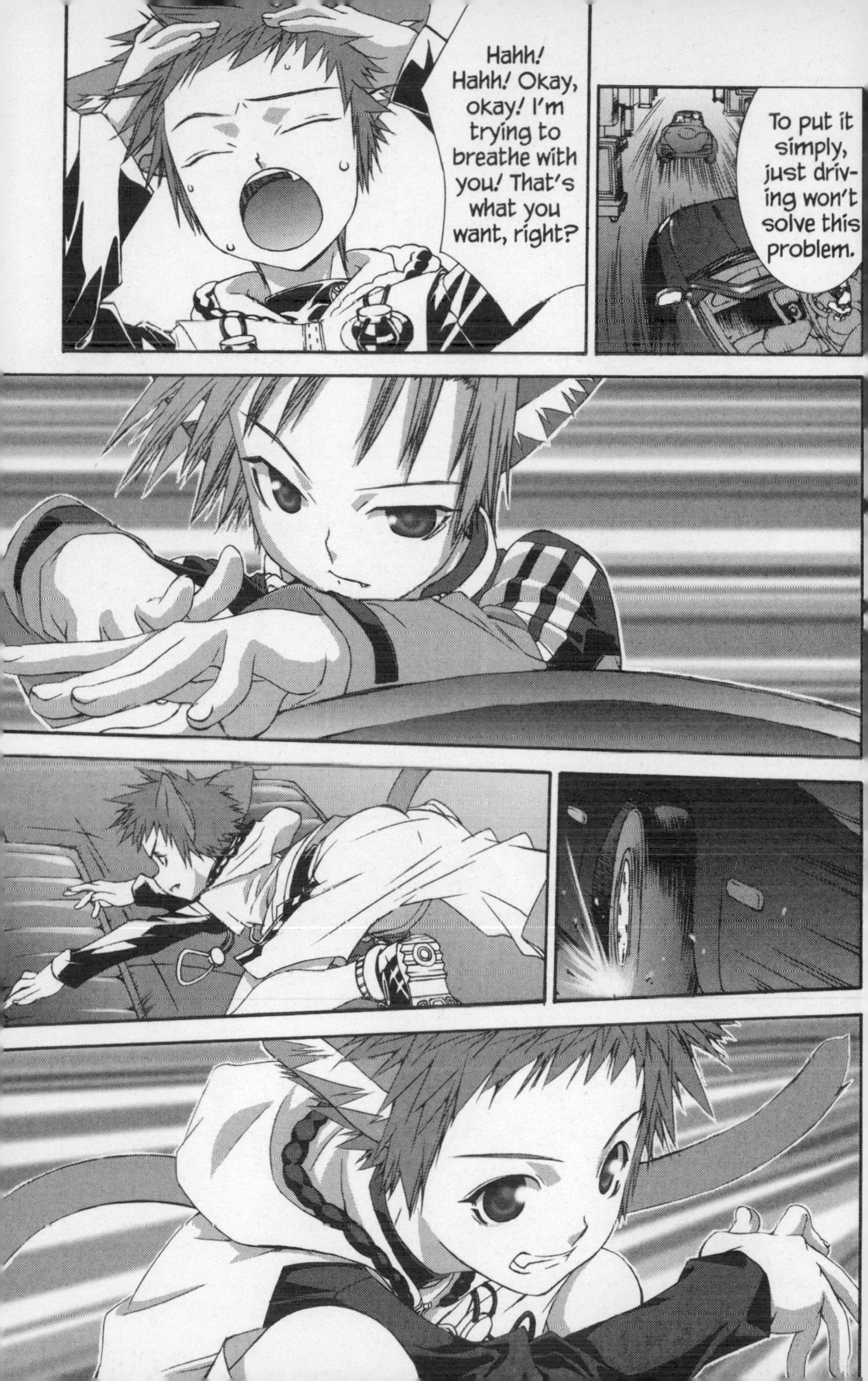
To put it simply, just driv-ing won't solve this problem.
Hahh! Hahh! Okay, okay! I'm trying to breathe with you! That's what you want, right?

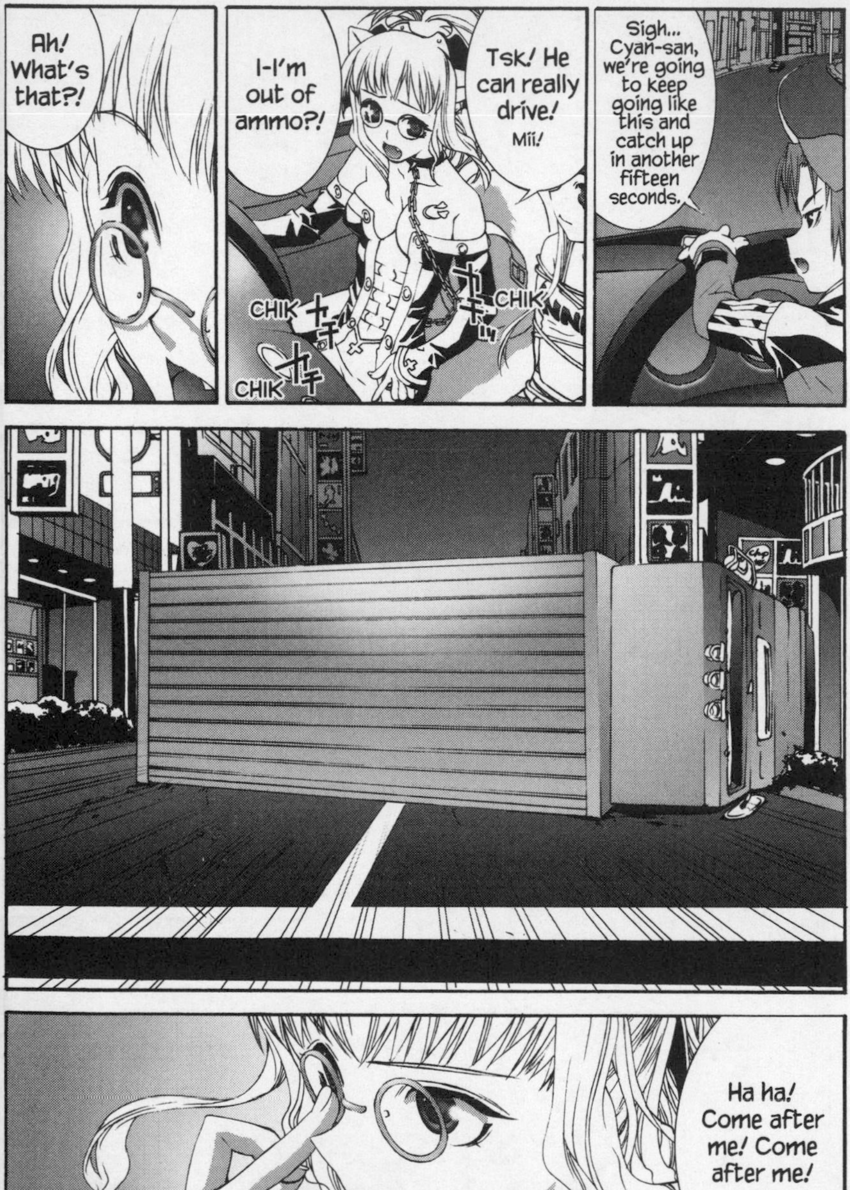
Sigh... Cyan-san, we're going to keep going like this and catch up in another fifteen seconds.
Tsk! He can really drive! Mii!
I-I'm out of ammo?!
CHIK
CHIK
CHIK
Ah! What's that?!
Ha ha! Come after me! Come after me! Mii!

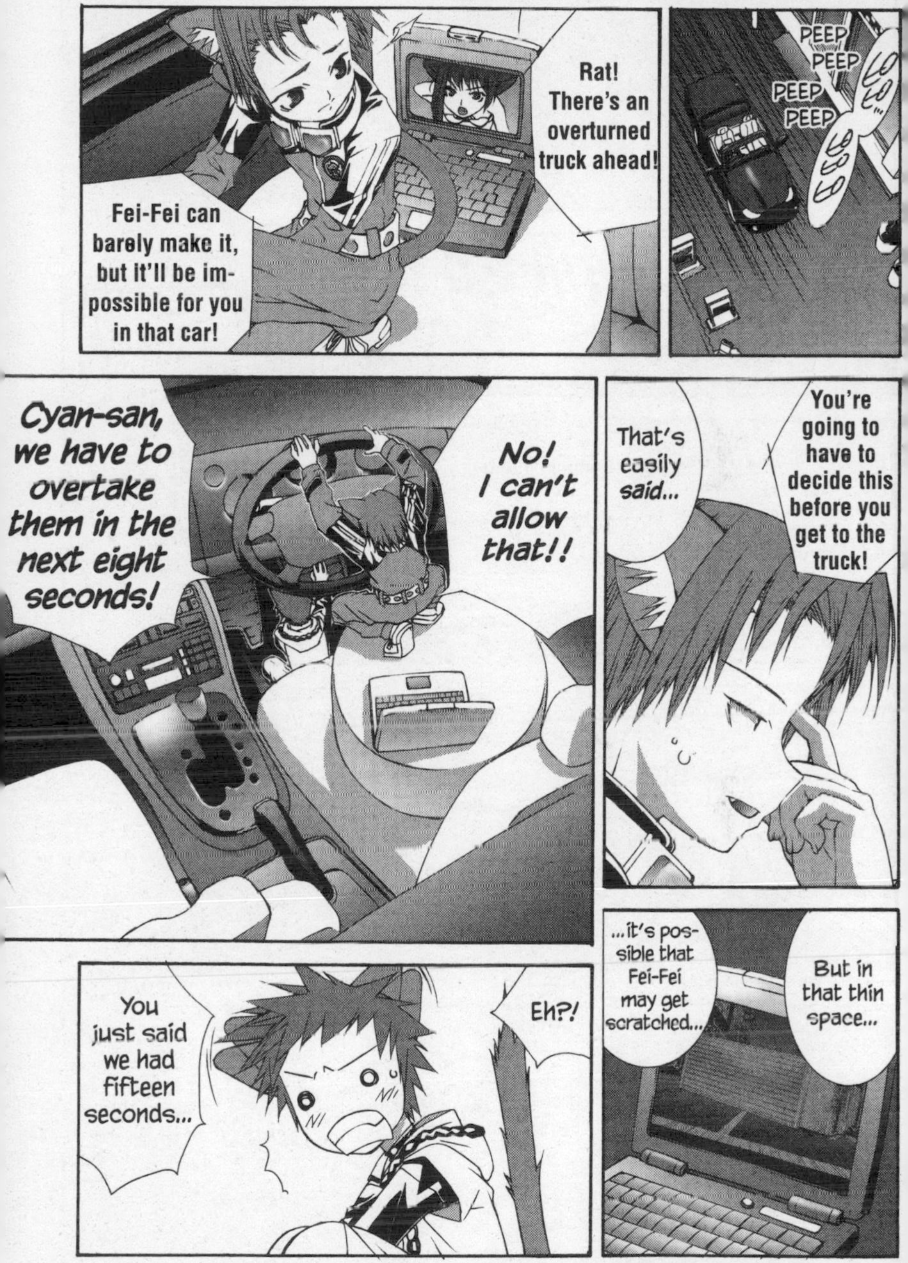
PEEP PEEP PEEP PEEP
Rat! There's an overturned truck ahead!
Fei-Fei can barely make it, but it'll be impossible for you in that car!
You're going to have to decide this before you get to the truck!
That's easily said...
No! I can't allow that!!
Cyan-san, we have to overtake them in the next eight seconds!
But in that thin space...
...it's possible that Fei-Fei may get scratched...
Eh?!
You just said we had fifteen seconds...

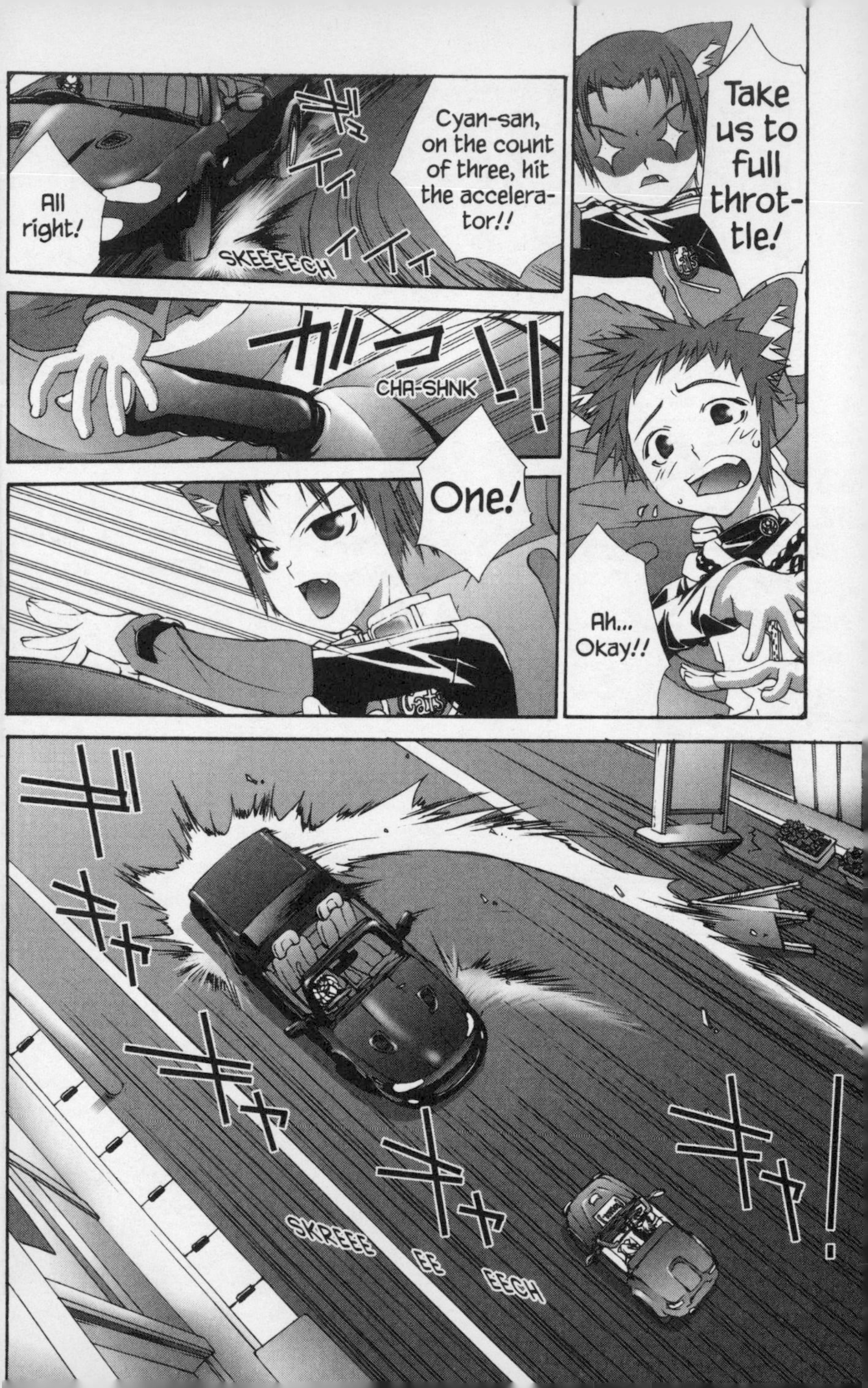

Take us to full throttle!
Ah... Okay!!
Cyan-san, on the count of three, hit the accelerator!!
All right!
SKEEEECH
ガコッ!!
CHA-SHNK
One!
SKREEE EE EECH

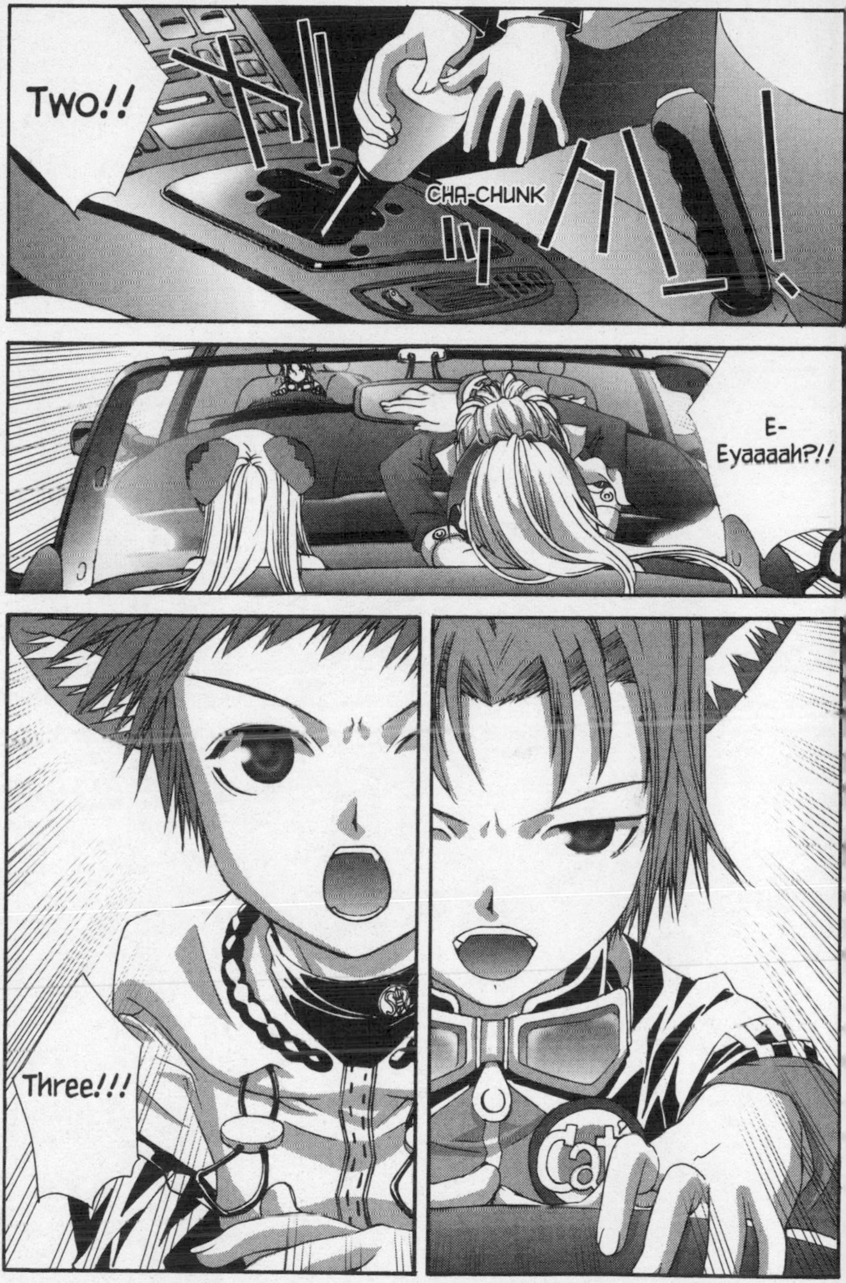
Two!!
CHA-CHUNK
E-
Eyaaaah?!!
Three!!!

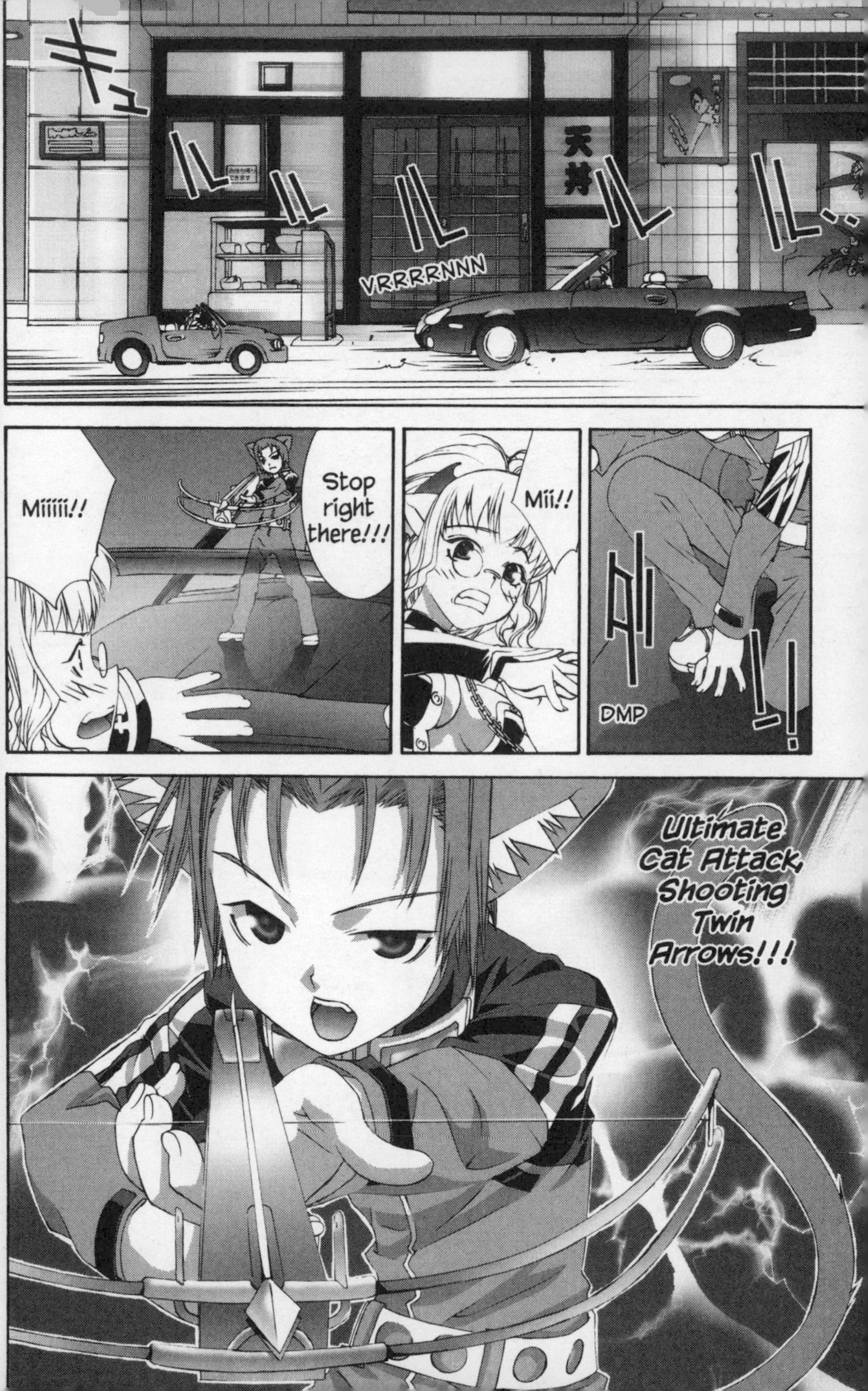
キュルルルルル..
天丼
VRRRRNNN
DMP
Mii!!
Stop right there!!!
Miiiii!!
Ultimate Cat Attack, Shooting Twin Arrows!!!

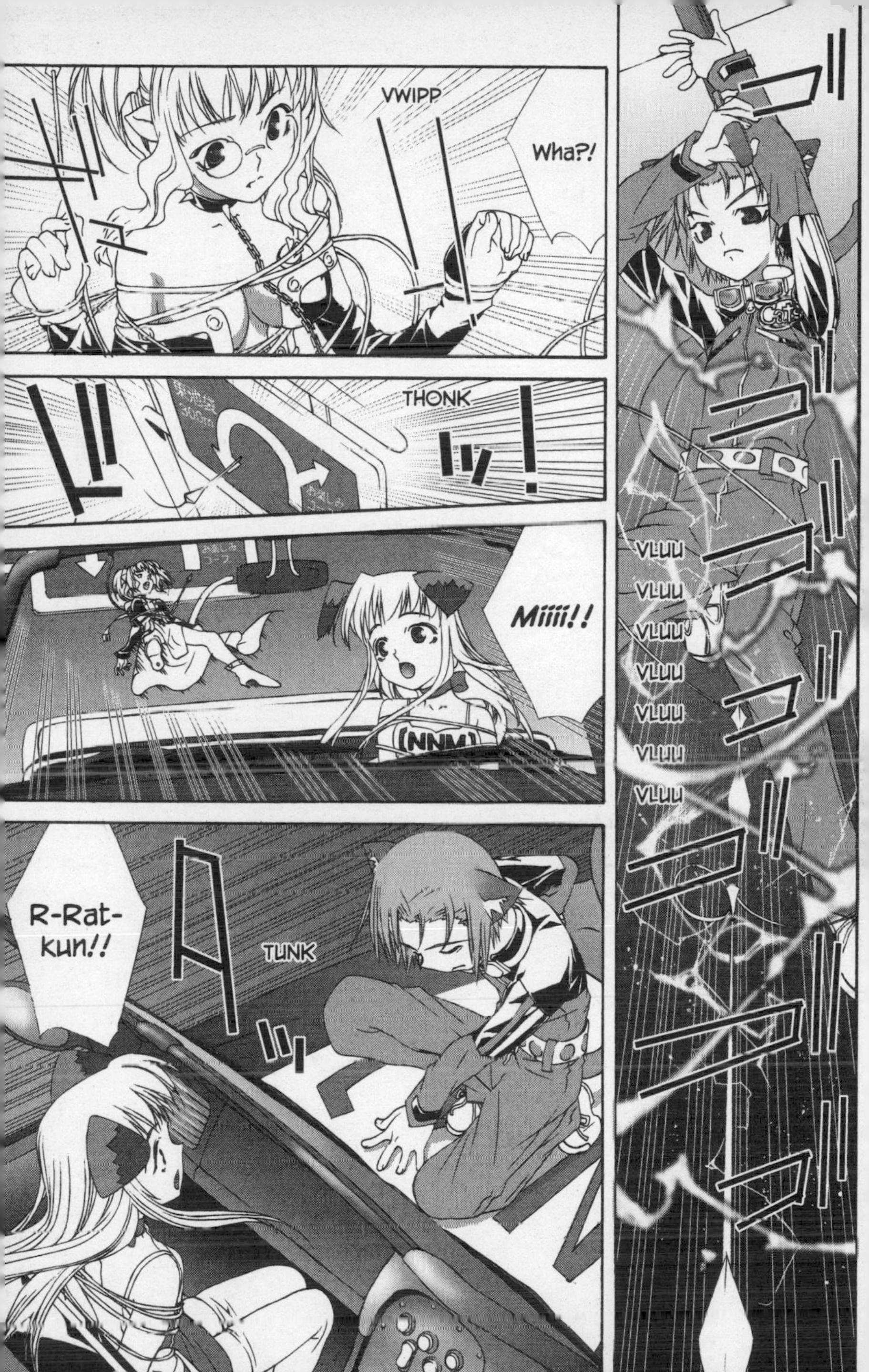
VLUU
VLUU
VLUU
VLUU
VLUU
VLUU
VLUU
VWIPP
Wha?!
THONK
Miiii!!
R-Rat-kun!!
TUNK

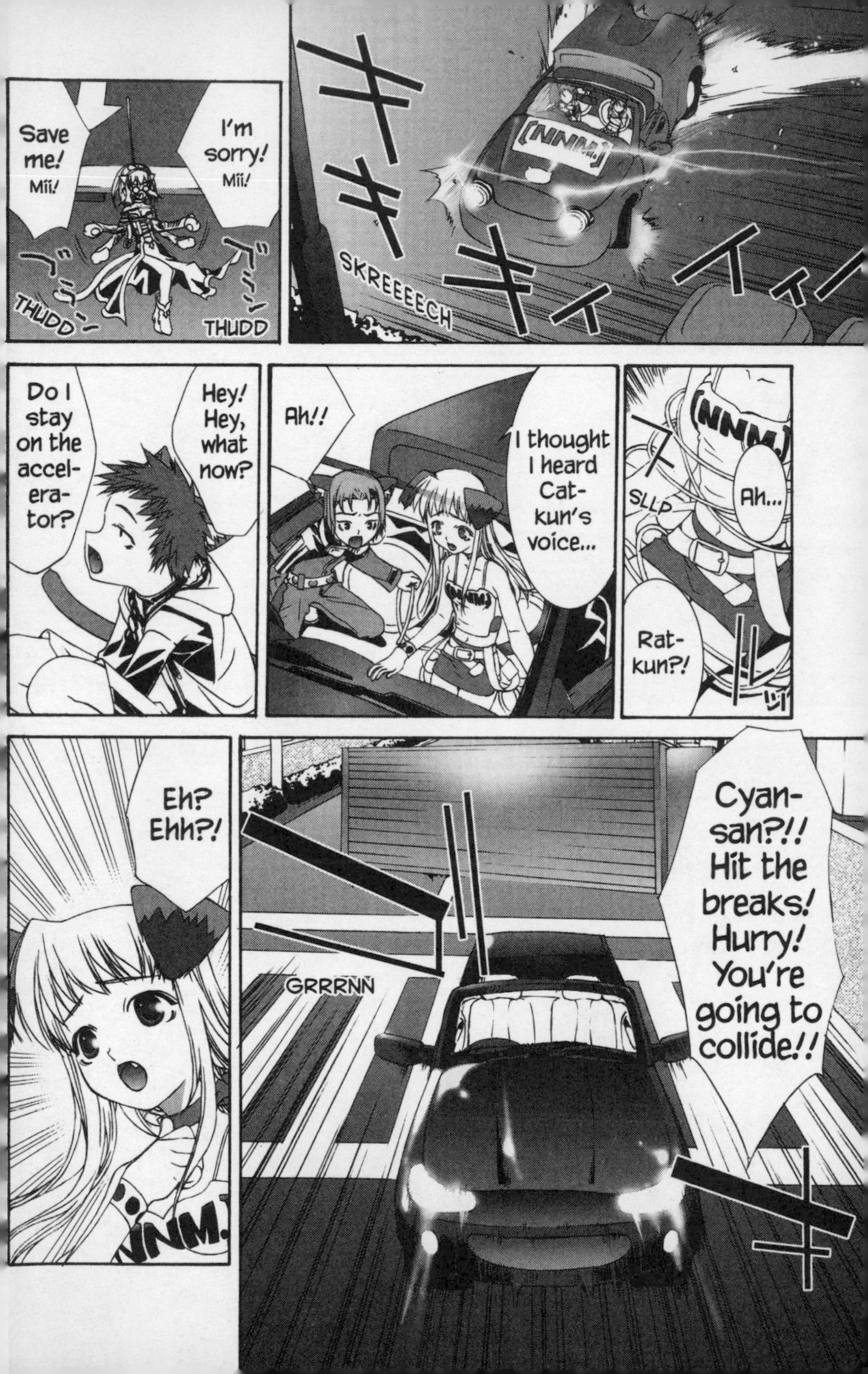
SKREEEEECH
I'm sorry! Mii!
Save me! Mii!
THUDD
THUDD
Ah...
SLLP
Rat-kun?!
I thought I heard Cat-kun's voice...
Ah!!
Hey! Hey, what now?
Do I stay on the accel-erator?
Cyan-san?!! Hit the breaks! Hurry! You're going to collide!!
GRRRNN
Eh? Ehh?!

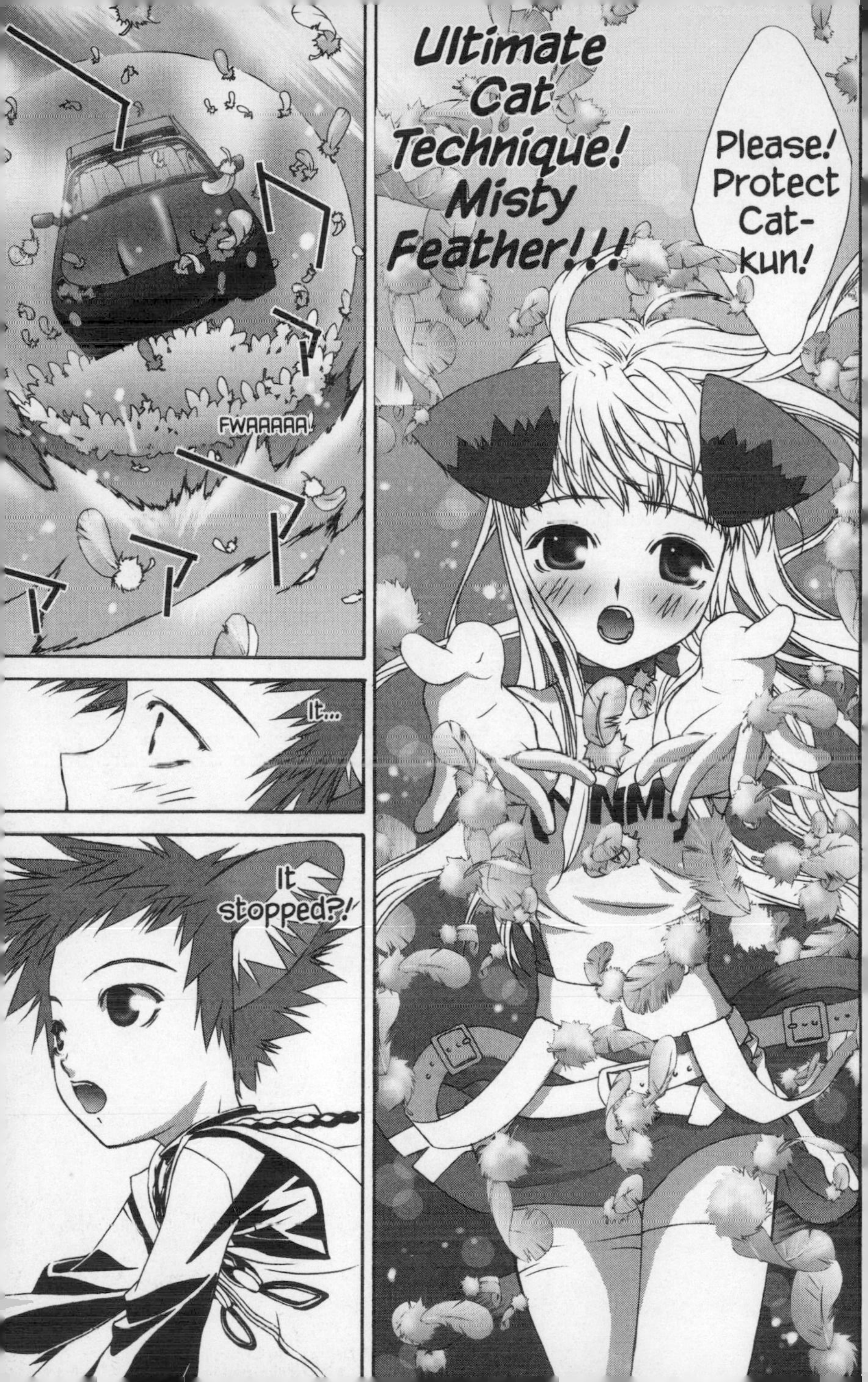
Please! Protect Cat-kun!
Ultimate Cat Technique! Misty Feather!!!
NM
FWAAAAA!
It...
It stopped?!

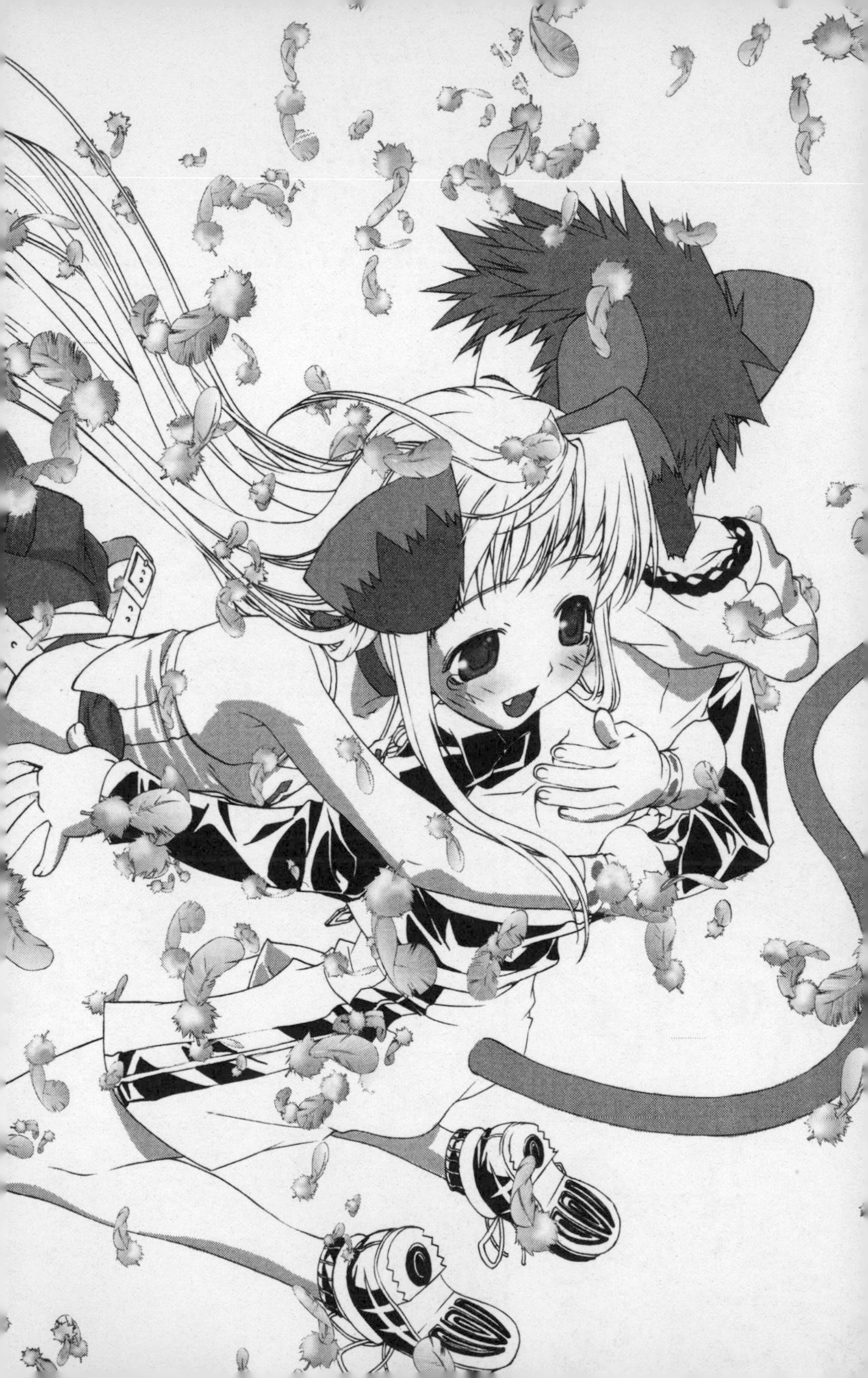

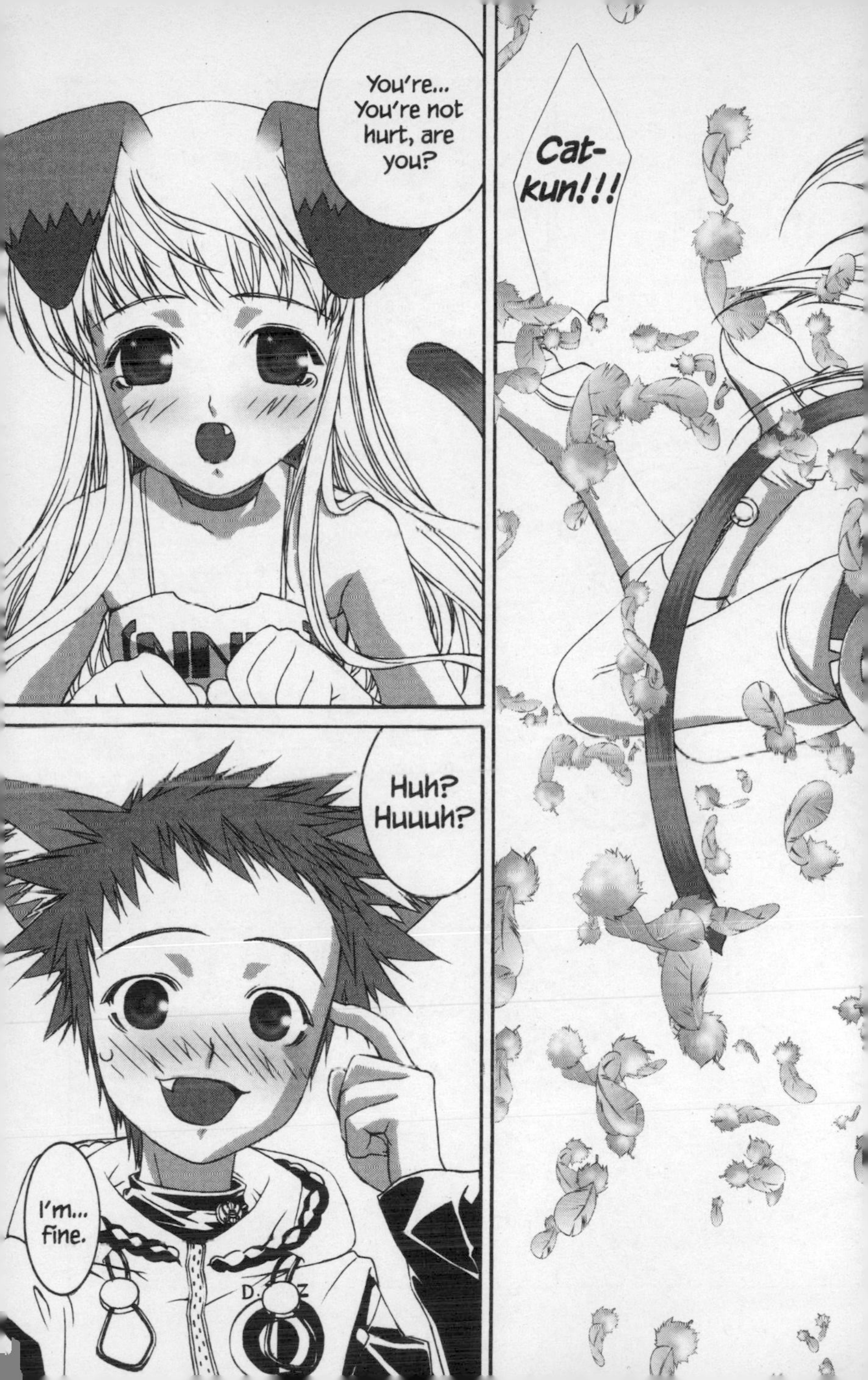
Cat-kun!!!
You're... You're not hurt, are you?
Huh? Huuuh?
I'm... fine.

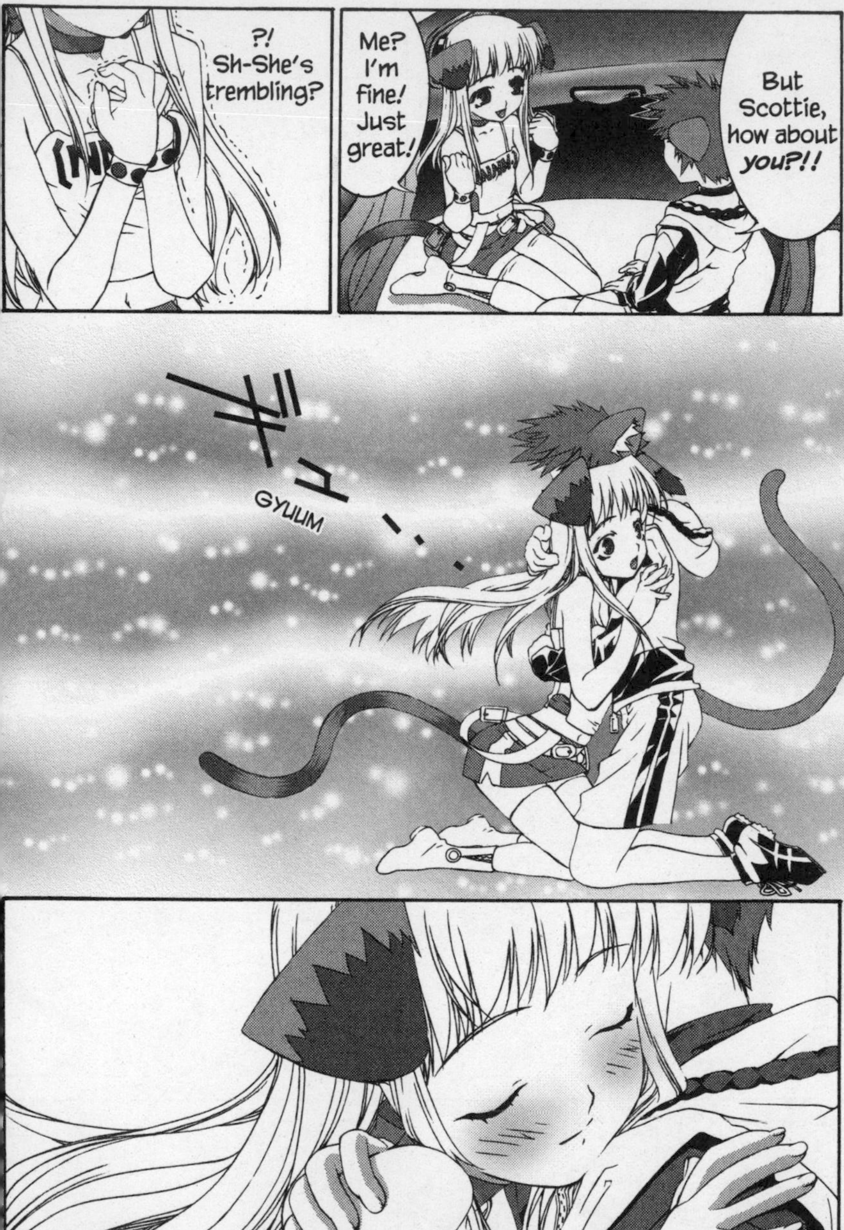
But Scottie, how about you?!!
Me? I'm fine! Just great!
?! Sh-She's trembling?
ギュ…
GYUUM

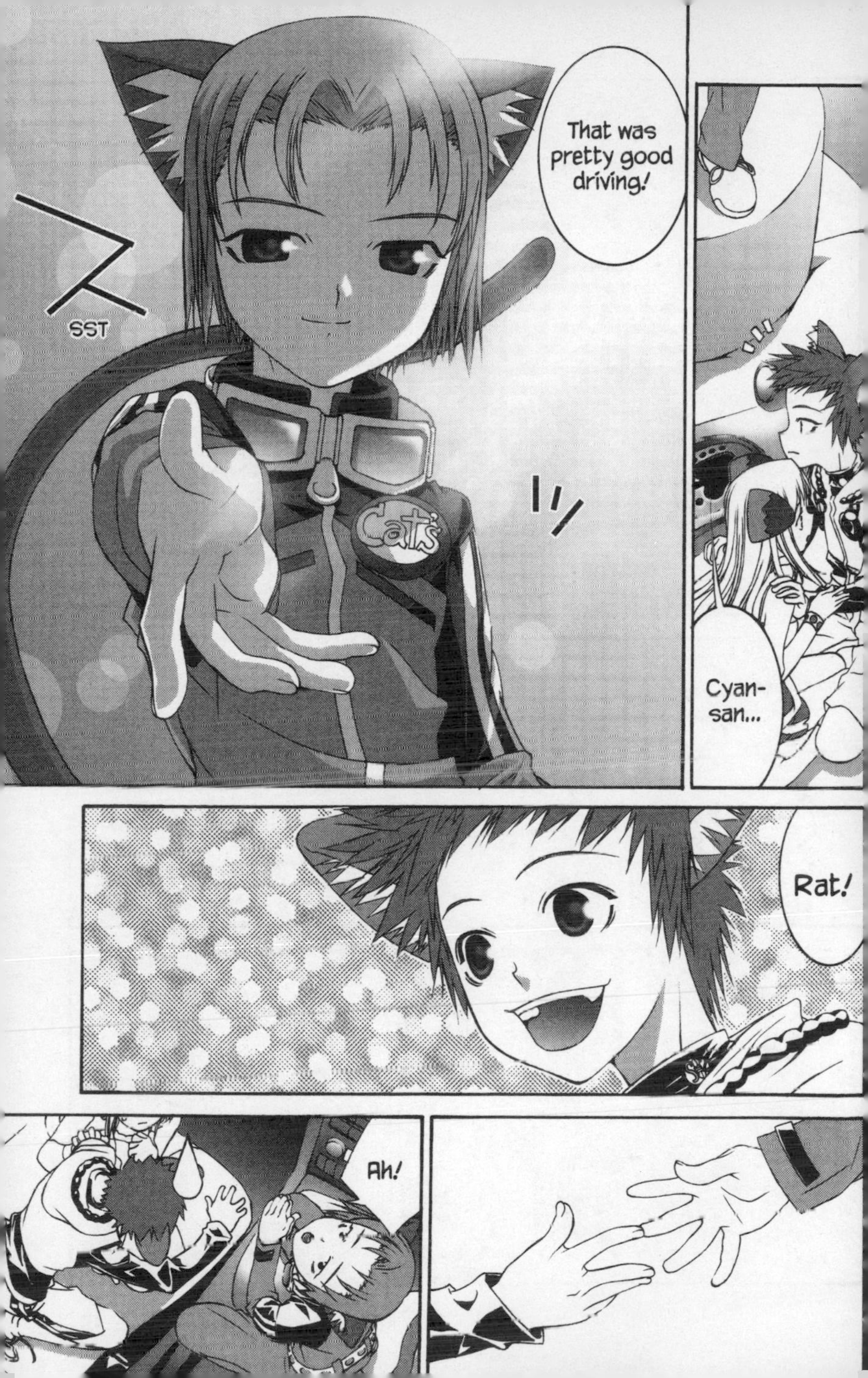
Cyan-
san...
That was pretty good driving!
SST
Rat!
Ah!

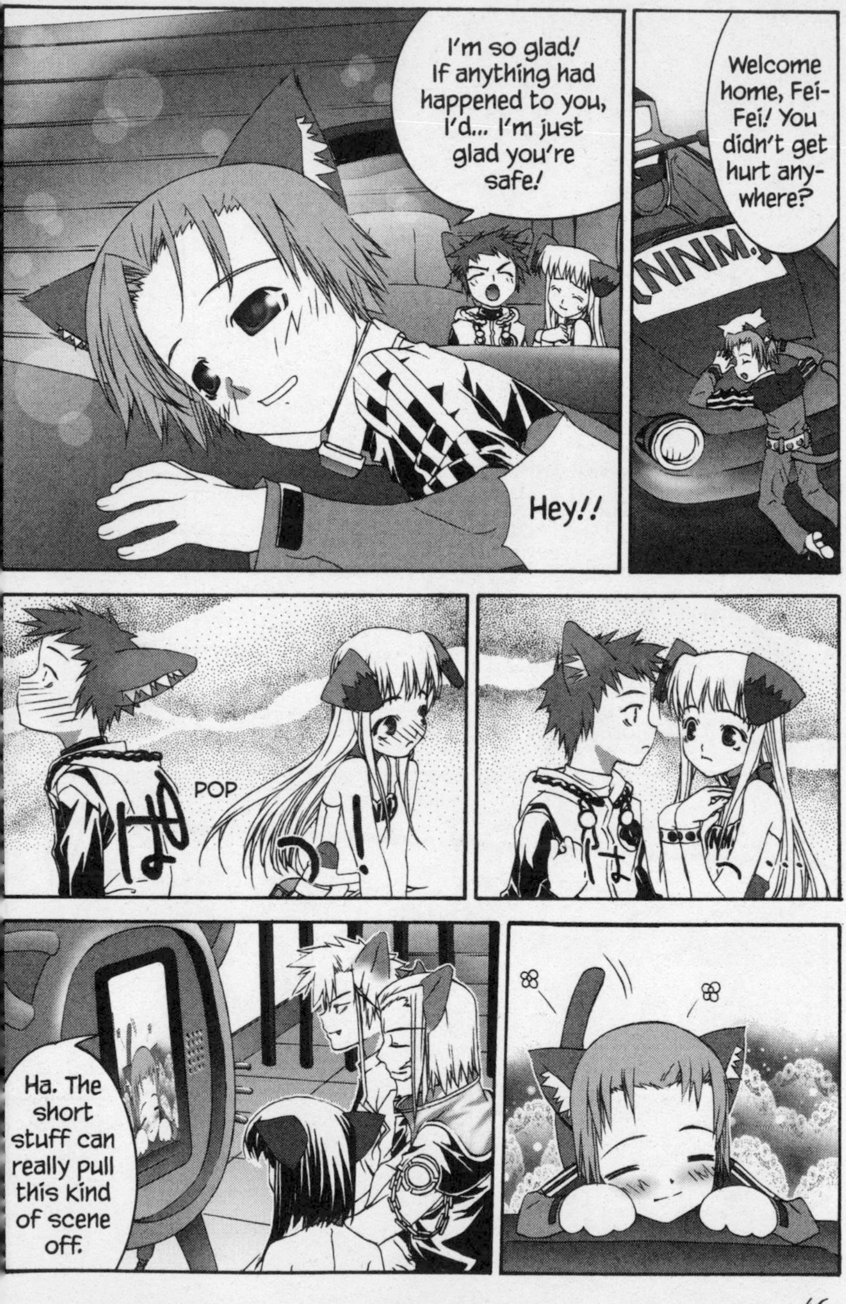
Welcome home, Fei-Fei! You didn't get hurt anywhere?
I'm so glad! If anything had happened to you, I'd... I'm just glad you're safe!
Hey!!
はっ…
POP
ぱっ!
Ha. The short stuff can really pull this kind of scene off.

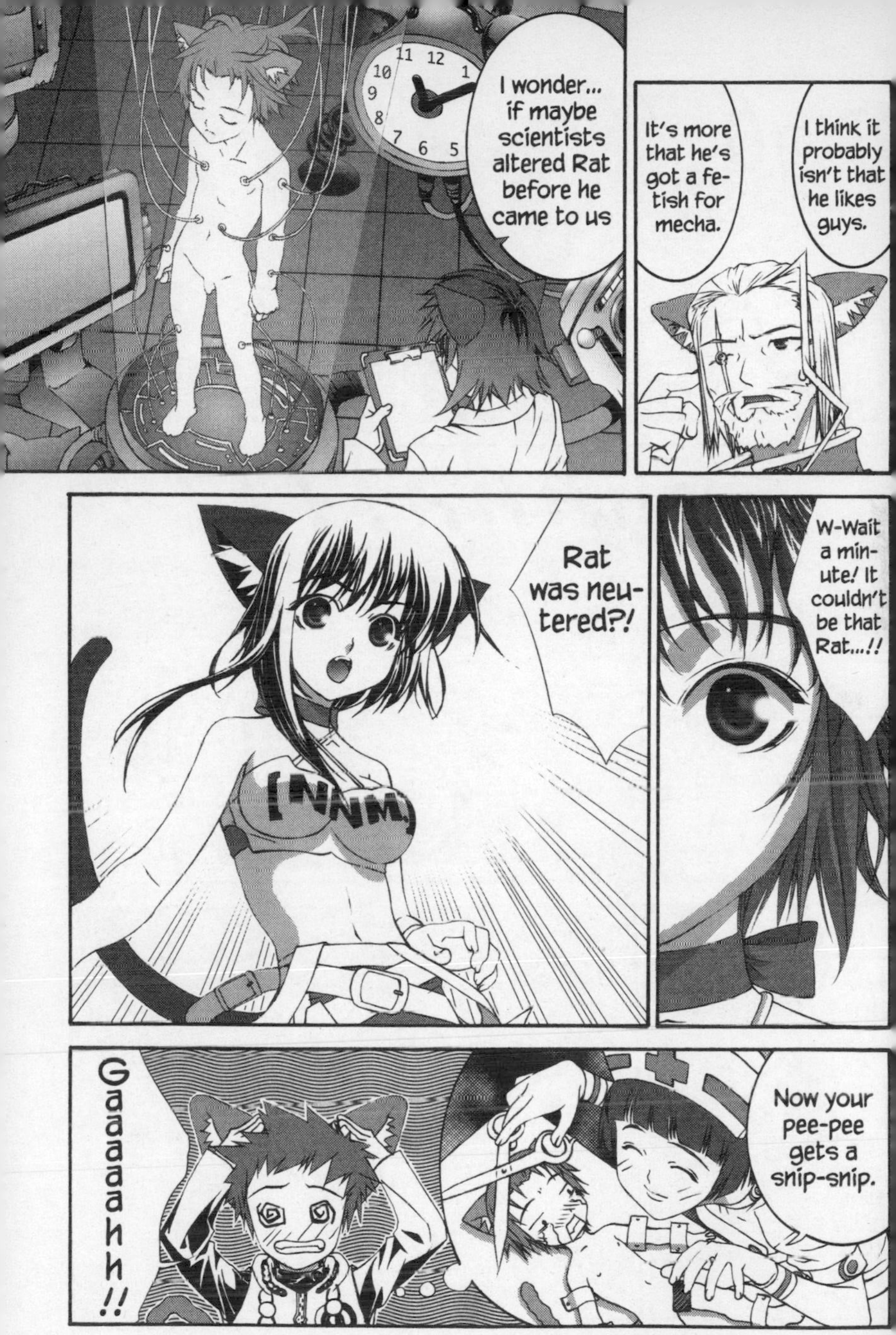
I think it probably isn't that he likes guys.
It's more that he's got a fetish for mecha.
I wonder... if maybe scientists altered Rat before he came to us
W-Wait a minute! It couldn't be that Rat...!!
Rat was neutered?!
(NNM)
Now your pee-pee gets a snip-snip.
Gaaaaahh!!

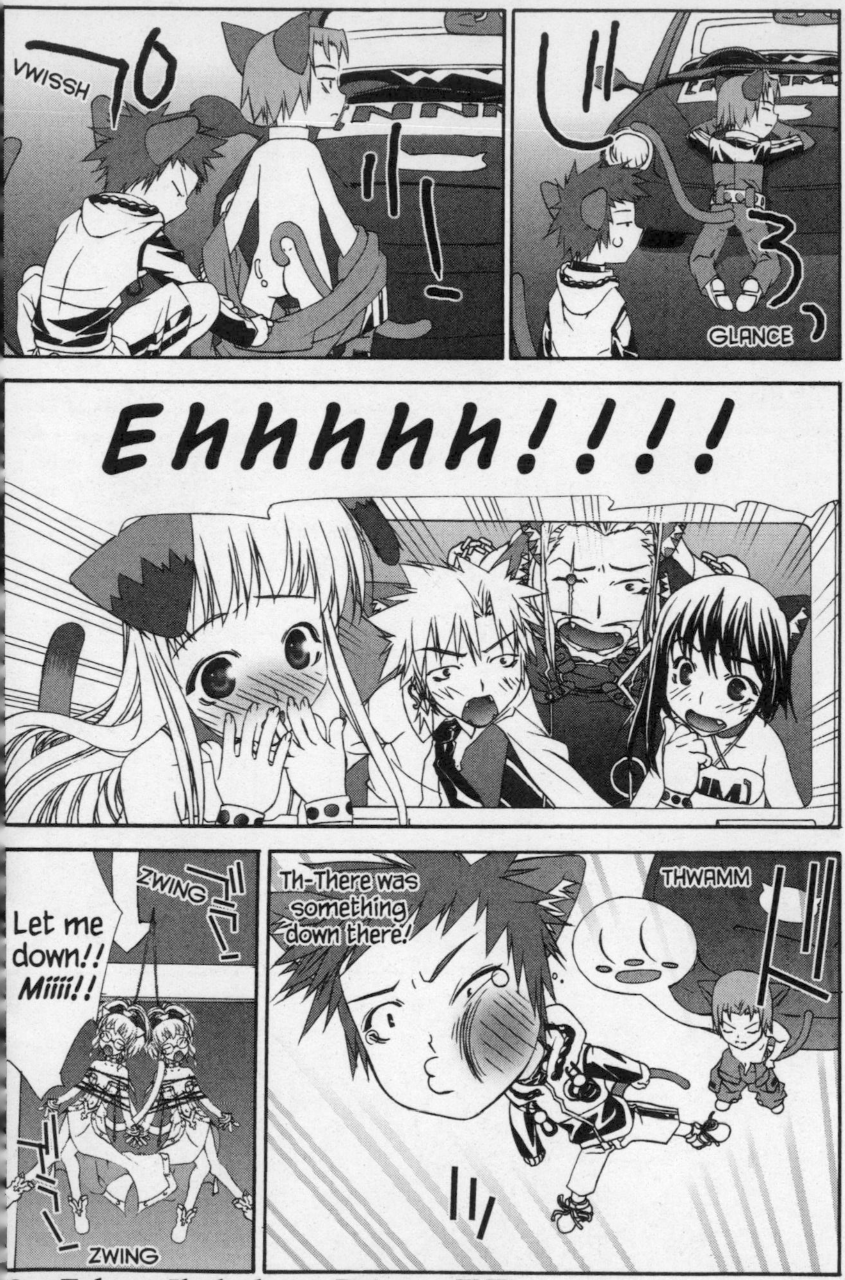
GLANCE
VWISSH
Ehhhhh!!!!
THWAMM
Th-There was something down there!
ZWING
Let me down!! Miiii!!
ZWING

Cat Tale 7 Ikebukuro Driven END

Cat Tale 8 Siamese Cat Boogie

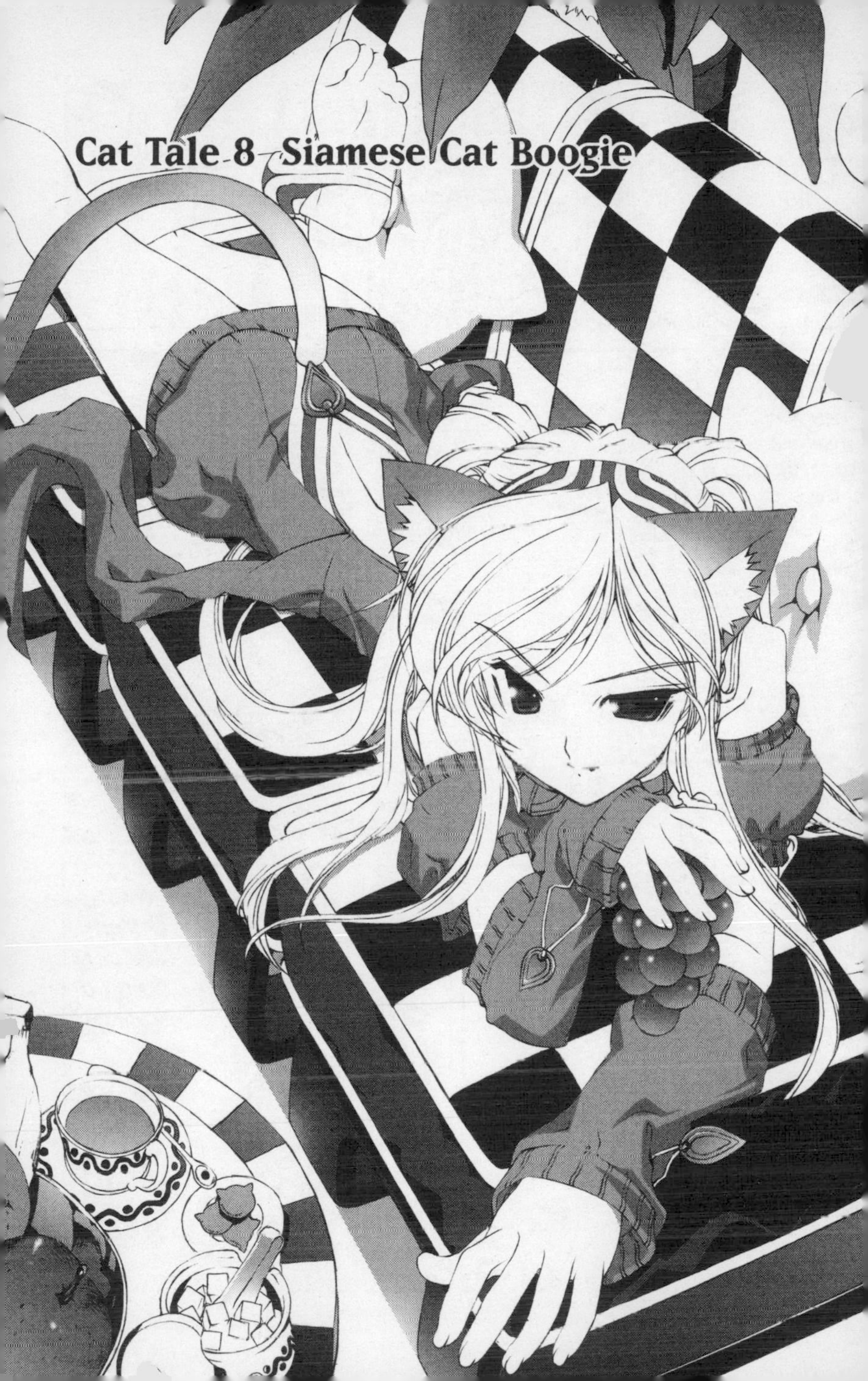

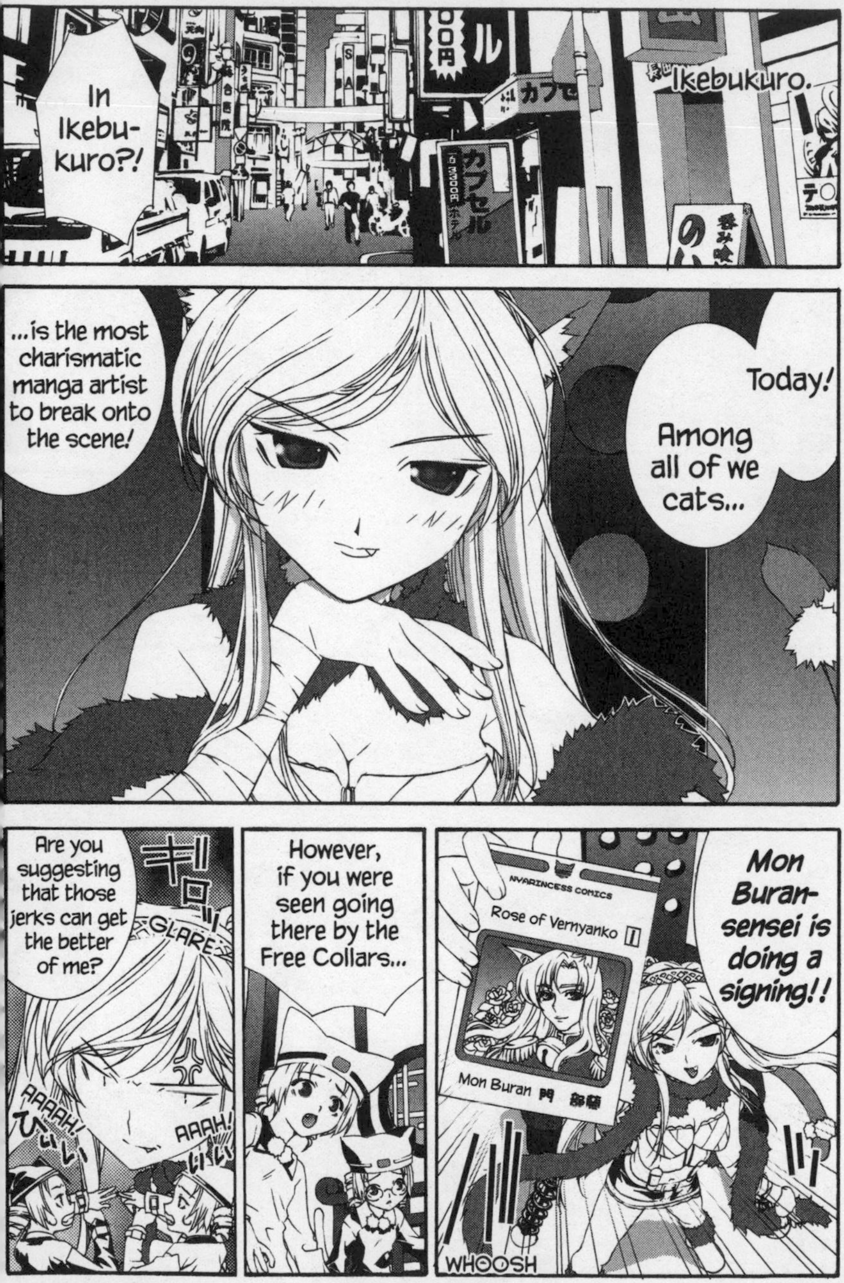
Ikebukuro.
In Ikebukuro?!
Today!
Among all of we cats...
...is the most charismatic manga artist to break onto the scene!
Mon Buran-sensei is doing a signing!!
NYARINCESS COMICS
Rose of Vernyanko 1
Mon Buran
WHOOSH
However, if you were seen going there by the Free Collars...
Are you suggesting that those jerks can get the better of me?
GLARE
AAAAH!
AAAH!

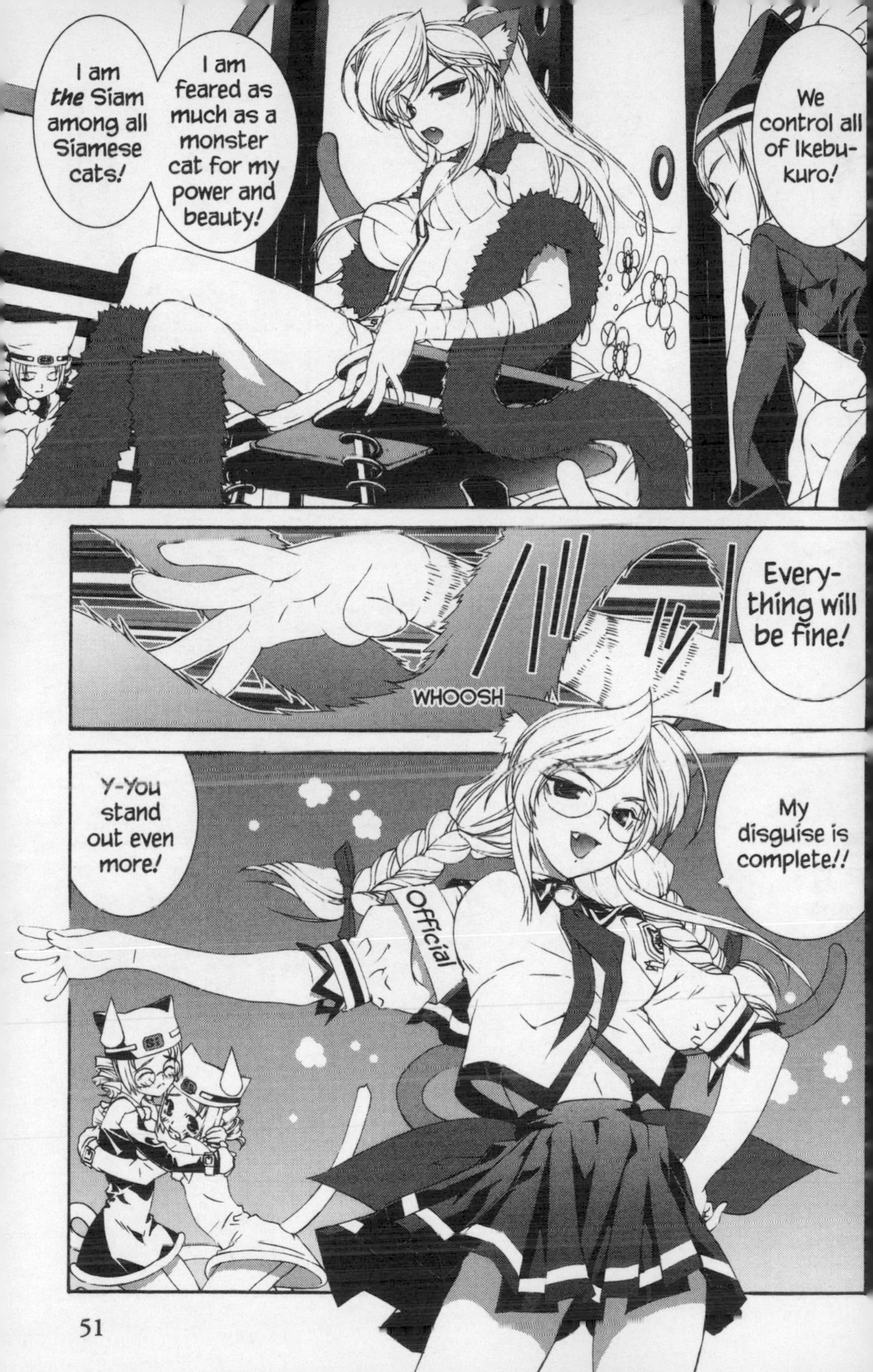
We control all of Ikebukuro!
I am feared as much as a monster cat for my power and beauty!
I am the Siam among all Siamese cats!
Everything will be fine!
WHOOSH
My disguise is complete!!
Y-You stand out even more!
Official

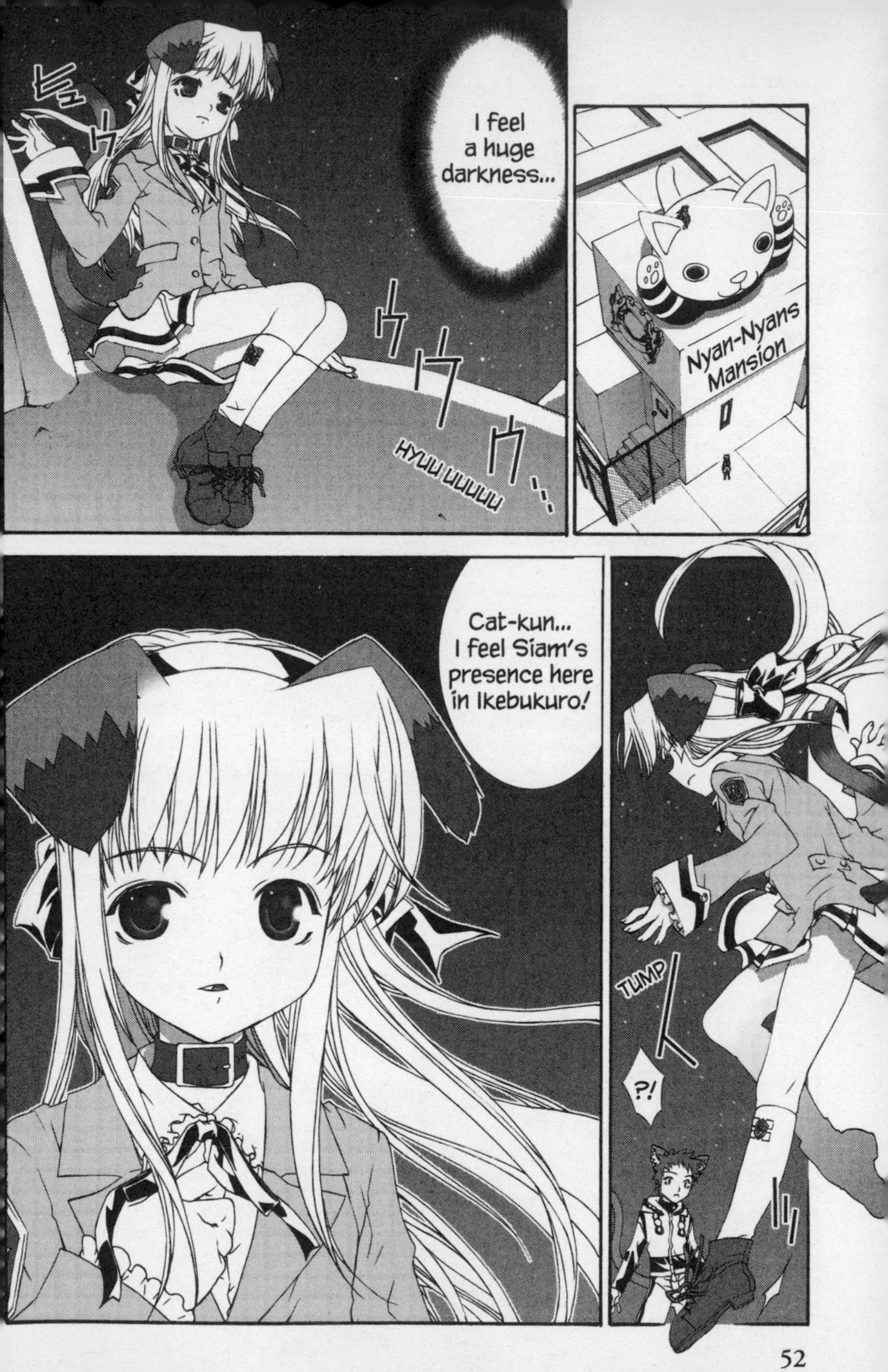
Nyan-Nyans Mansion
I feel a huge darkness...
HYUU UUUUU
TUMP
?!
Cat-kun... I feel Siam's presence here in Ikebukuro!

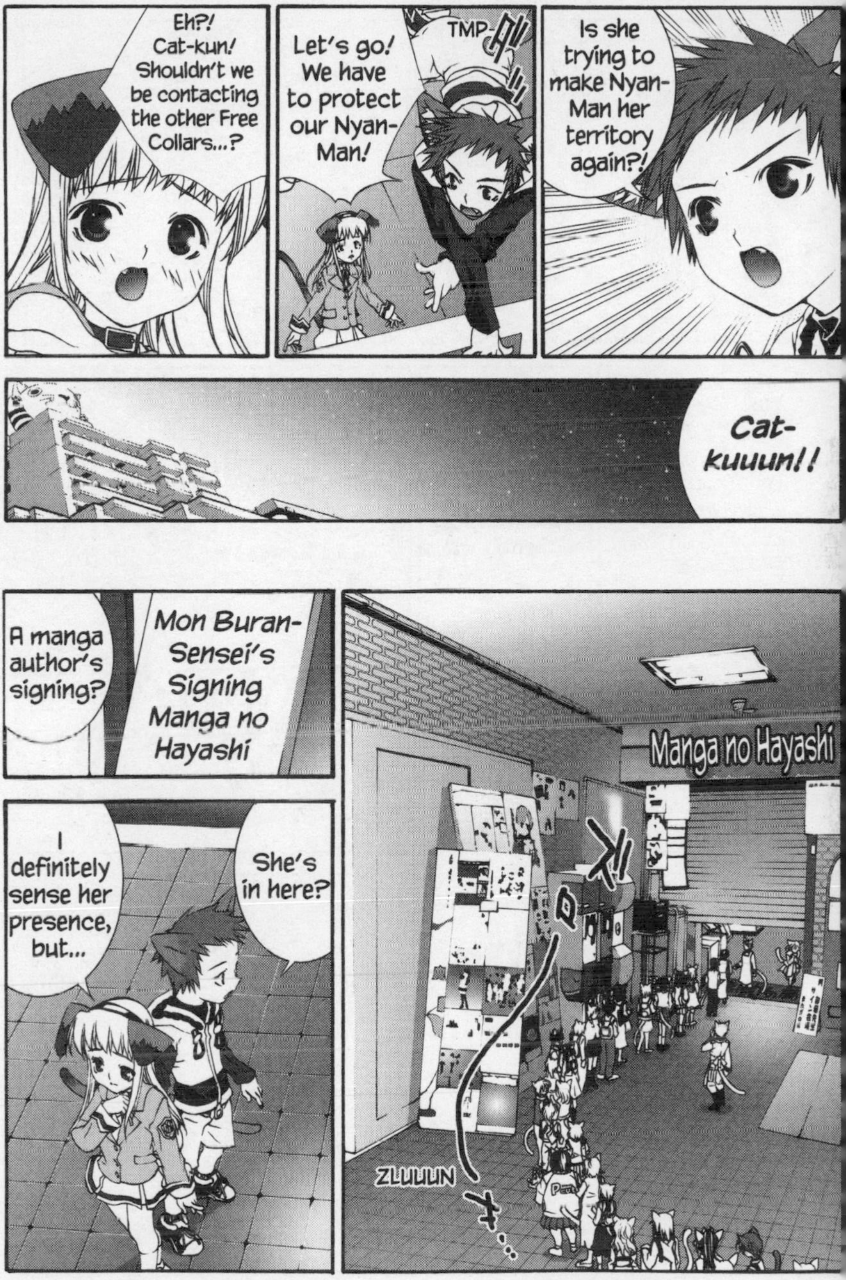

Is she trying to make Nyan-Man her territory again?!
TMP-
Let's go! We have to protect our Nyan-Man!
Eh?! Cat-kun! Shouldn't we be contacting the other Free Collars...?
Cat-kuuun!!
Manga no Hayashi
ZLUUUN
Mon Buran-Sensei's Signing Manga no Hayashi
A manga author's signing?
She's in here?
I definitely sense her presence, but...

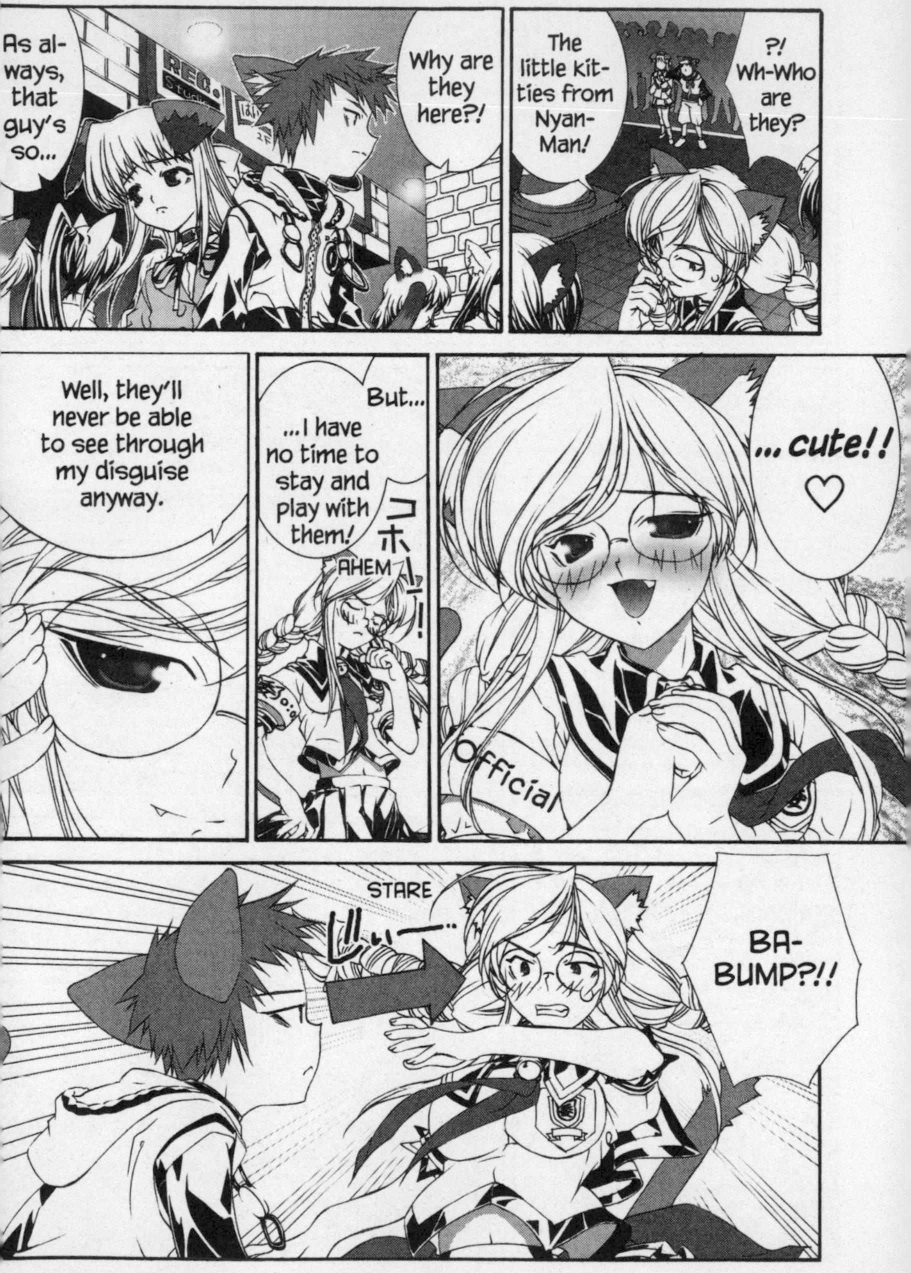
?! Wh-Who are they?
The little kitties from Nyan-Man!
Why are they here?!
As always, that guy's so...
...cute!! ♡
Official
But...
...I have no time to stay and play with them!
コホー!
AHEM
Well, they'll never be able to see through my disguise anyway.
BA-BUMP?!!
STARE
じぃー…

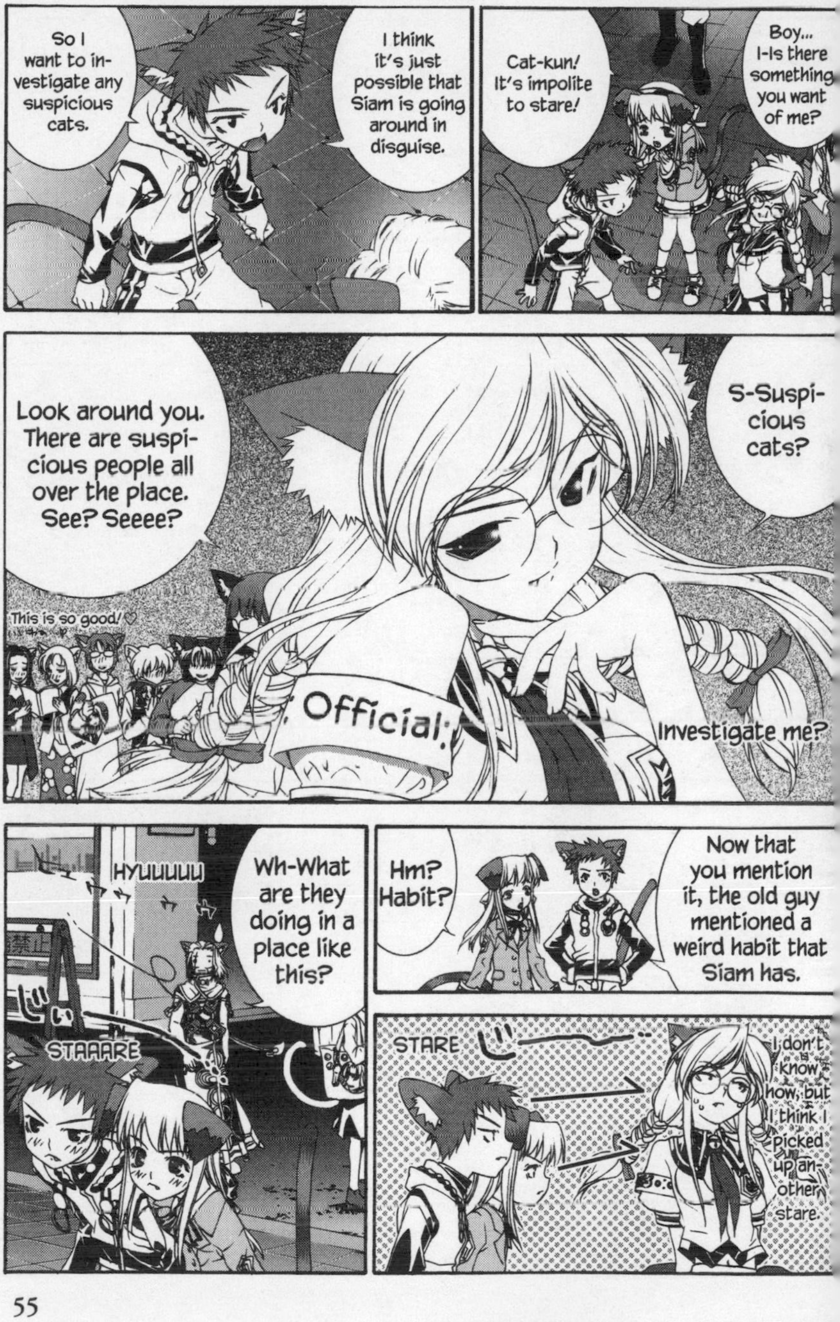
Boy... I-Is there something you want of me?
Cat-kun! It's impolite to stare!
I think it's just possible that Siam is going around in disguise.
So I want to investigate any suspicious cats.
S-Suspicious cats?
Investigate me?
Look around you. There are suspicious people all over the place. See? Seeee?
Official
This is so good!♡
Now that you mention it, the old guy mentioned a weird habit that Siam has.
Hm? Habit?
STARE
I don't know how, but I think I picked up another stare.
Wh-What are they doing in a place like this?
HYUUUUU
STAAARE

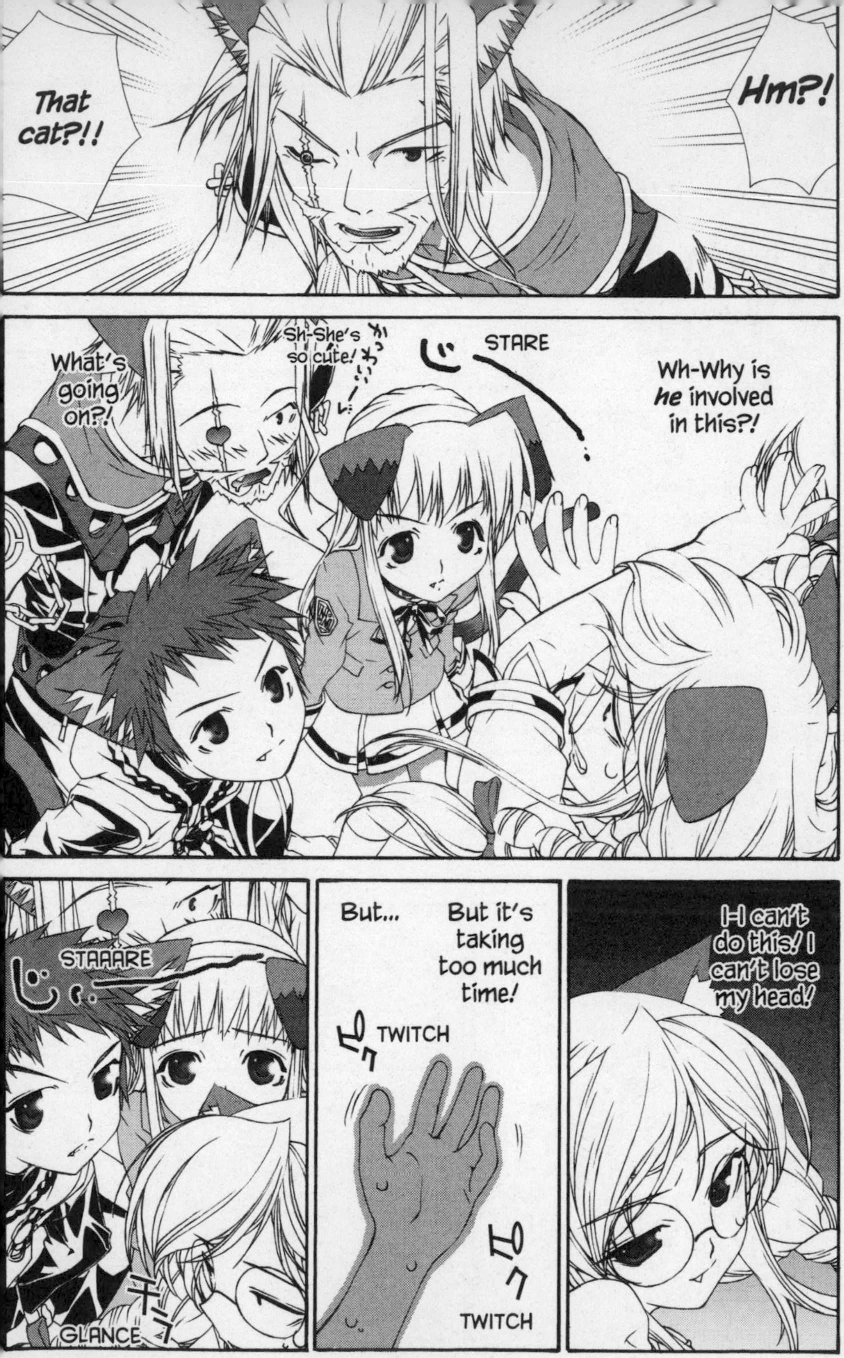
Hm?!
That cat?!!
Wh-Why is *he* involved in this?!
STARE
Sh-She's so cute!
What's going on?!
I-I can't do this! I can't lose my head!
But it's taking too much time!
But...
TWITCH
TWITCH
STAAARE
GLANCE

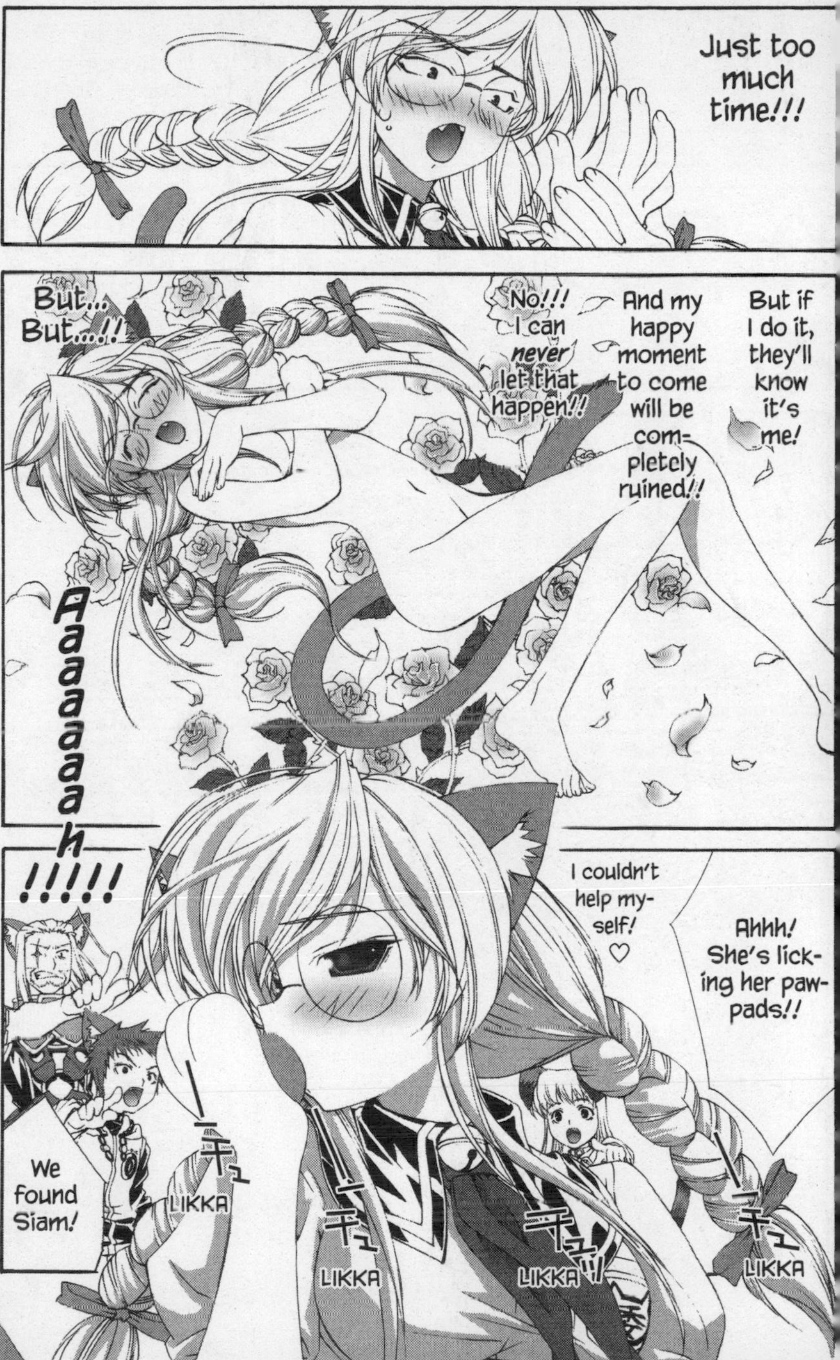

Just too much time!!!
But if I do it, they'll know it's me!
And my happy moment to come will be com-pletcly ruined!!
No!!! I can *never* let that happen!!
But... But...!!
Aaaaaaaaah!!!!!!
Ahhh! She's lick-ing her paw-pads!!
I couldn't help my-self! ♡
LIKKA
LIKKA
LIKKA
LIKKA
We found Siam!

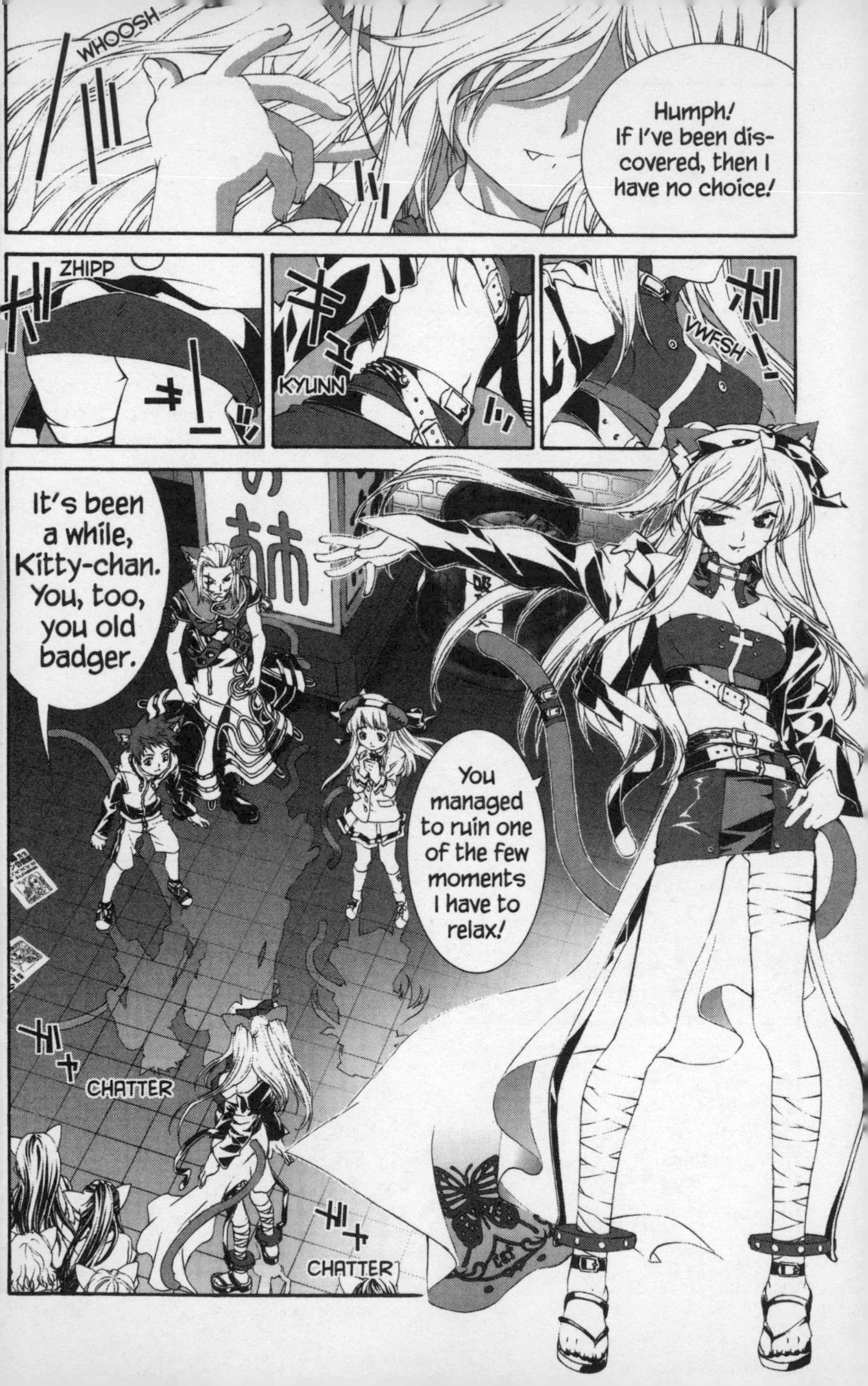
Humph! If I've been dis- covered, then I have no choice!
WHOOSH
VWFSH
KYUNN
ZHIPP
It's been a while, Kitty-chan. You, too, you old badger.
You managed to ruin one of the few moments I have to relax!
CHATTER
CHATTER

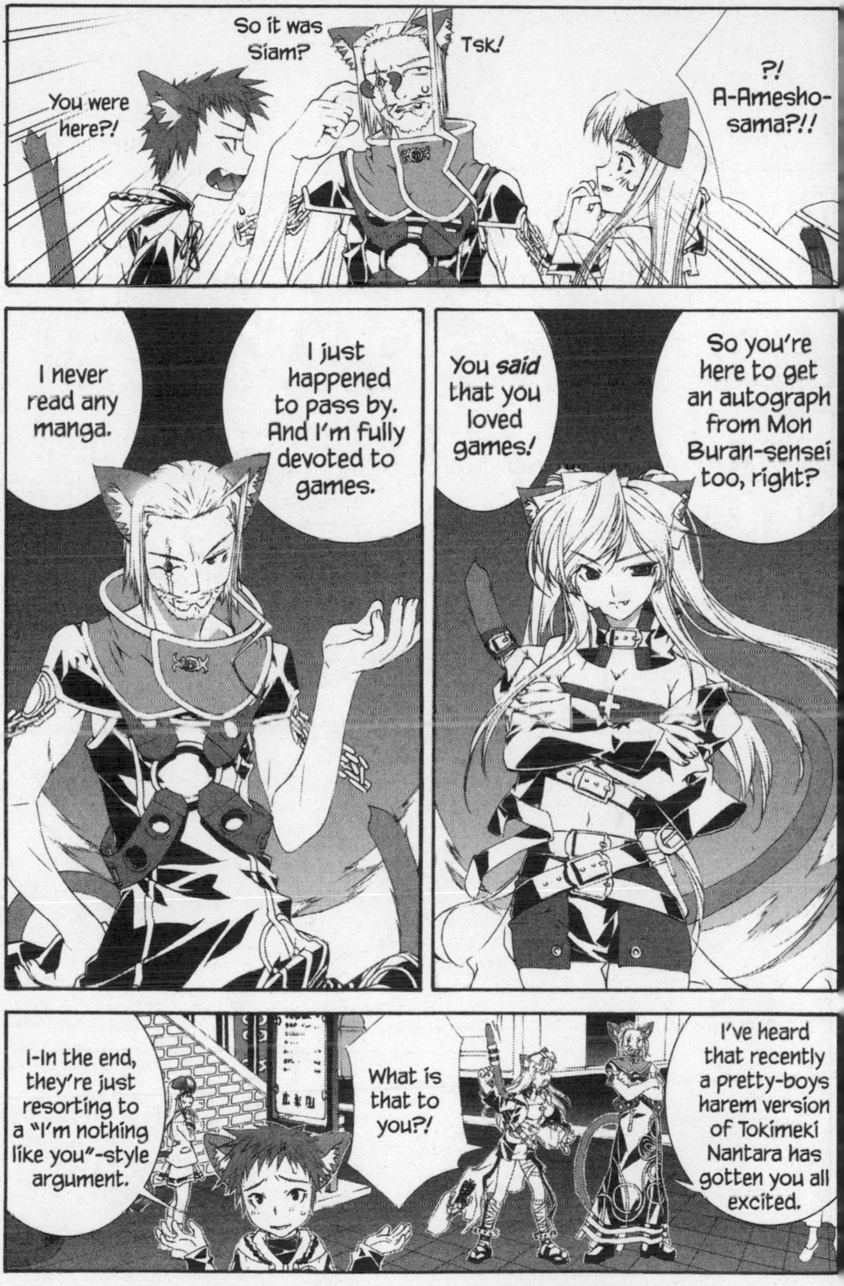
?! A-Ameshosama?!!
Tsk!
So it was Siam?
You were here?!
So you're here to get an autograph from Mon Buran-sensei too, right?
You *said* that you loved games!
I just happened to pass by. And I'm fully devoted to games.
I never read any manga.
I've heard that recently a pretty-boys harem version of Tokimeki Nantara has gotten you all excited.
What is that to you?!
I-In the end, they're just resorting to a "I'm nothing like you"-style argument.

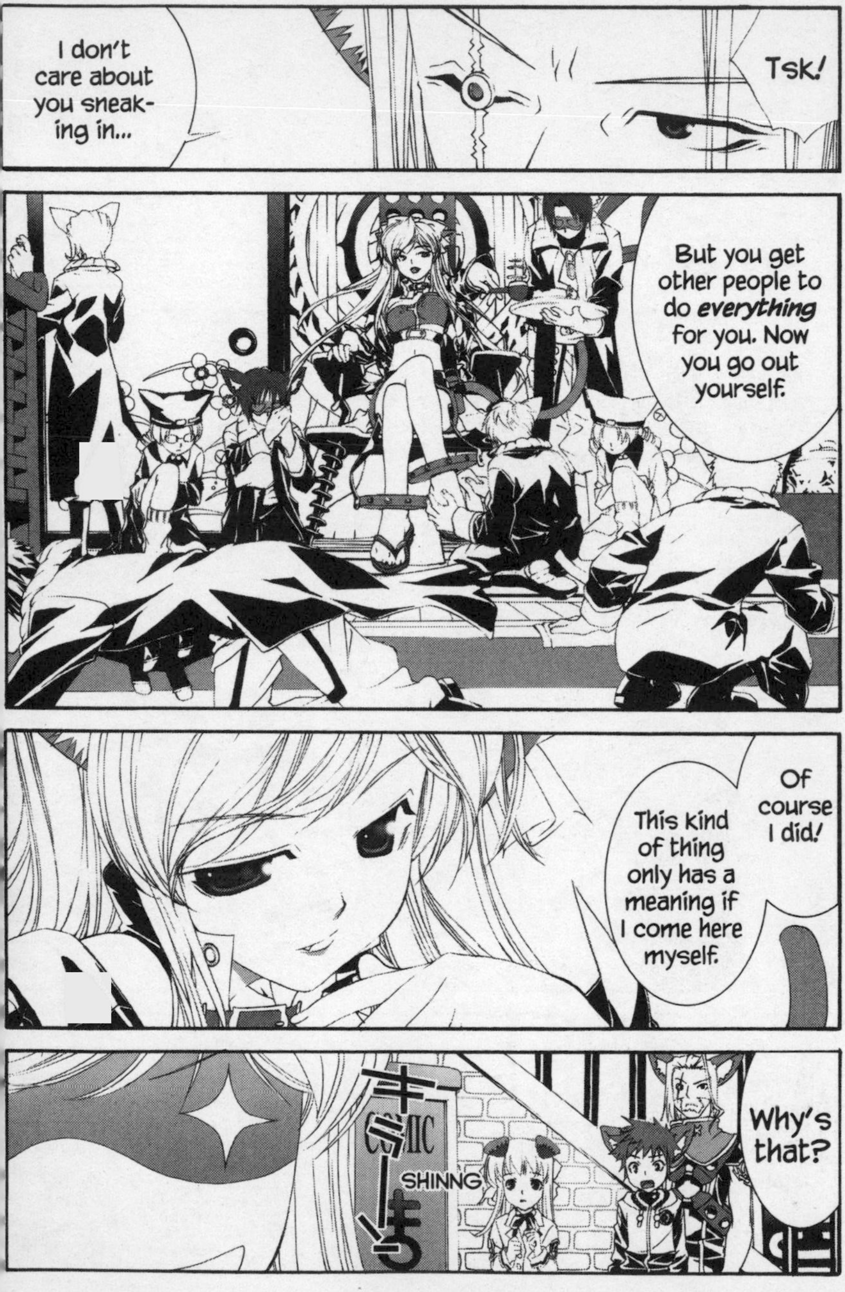
Tsk!
I don't care about you sneak-ing in...
But you get other people to do *everything* for you. Now you go out yourself.
Of course I did!
This kind of thing only has a meaning if I come here myself.
Why's that?
SHINNG

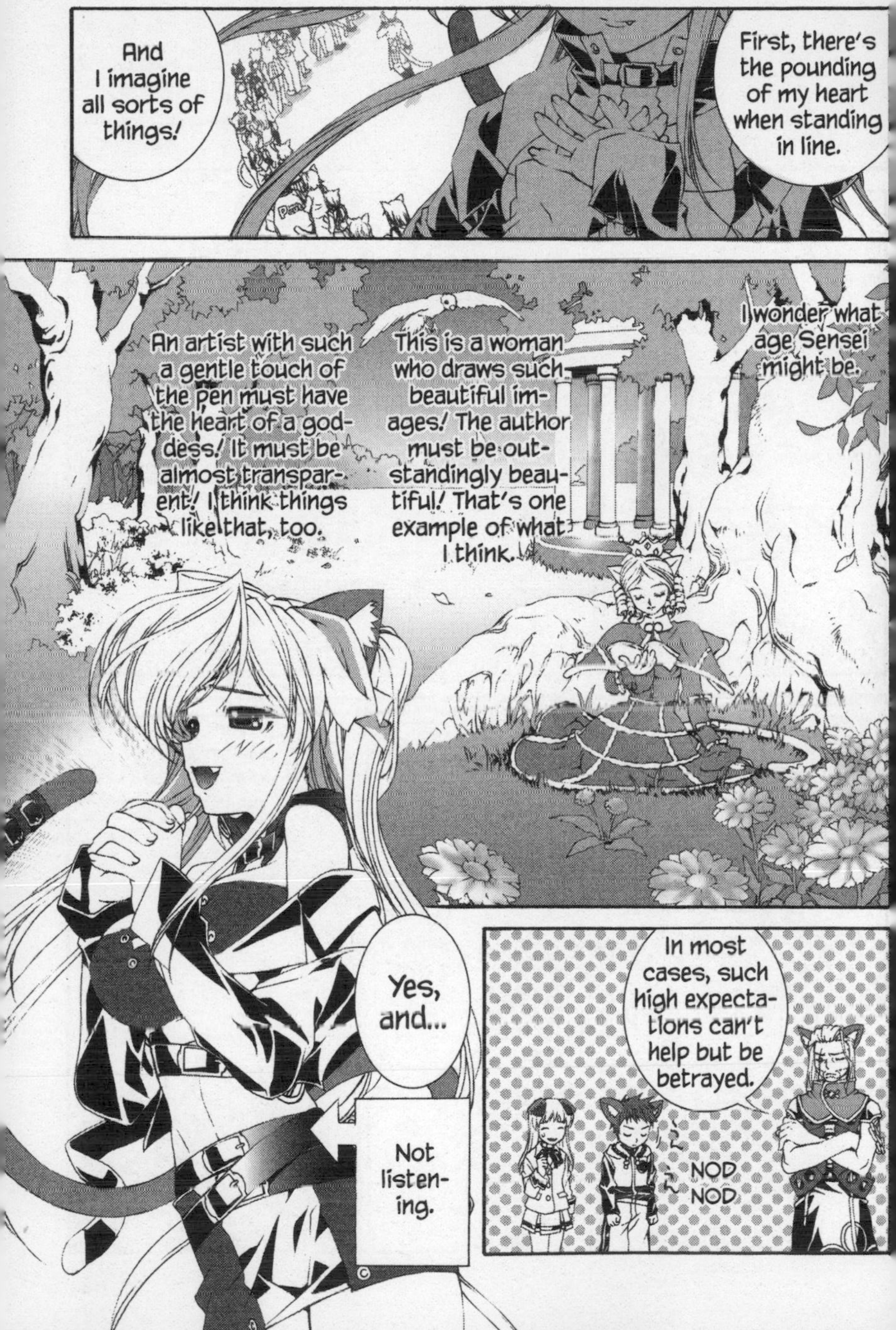
First, there's the pounding of my heart when standing in line.
And I imagine all sorts of things!
I wonder what age Sensei might be.
This is a woman who draws such beautiful images! The author must be outstandingly beautiful! That's one example of what I think.
An artist with such a gentle touch of the pen must have the heart of a goddess! It must be almost transparent! I think things like that, too.
In most cases, such high expectations can't help but be betrayed.
NOD NOD
Yes, and...
Not listening.

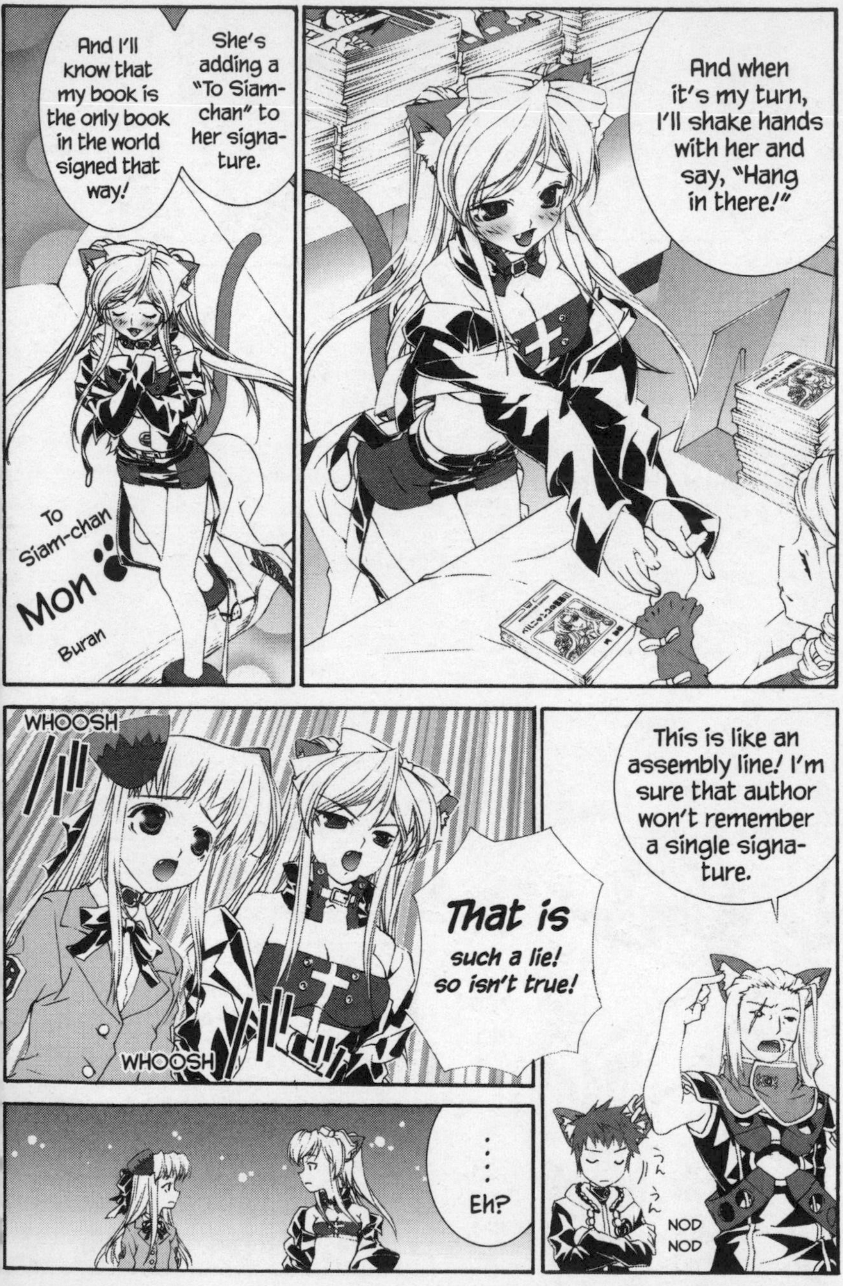
And when it's my turn, I'll shake hands with her and say, "Hang in there!"
She's adding a "To Siam-chan" to her signature.
And I'll know that my book is the only book in the world signed that way!
To Siam-chan
Mon
Buran
This is like an assembly line! I'm sure that author won't remember a single signature.
うん うん
NOD NOD
WHOOSH
That is
such a lie!
so isn't true!
WHOOSH
. . . .
Eh?

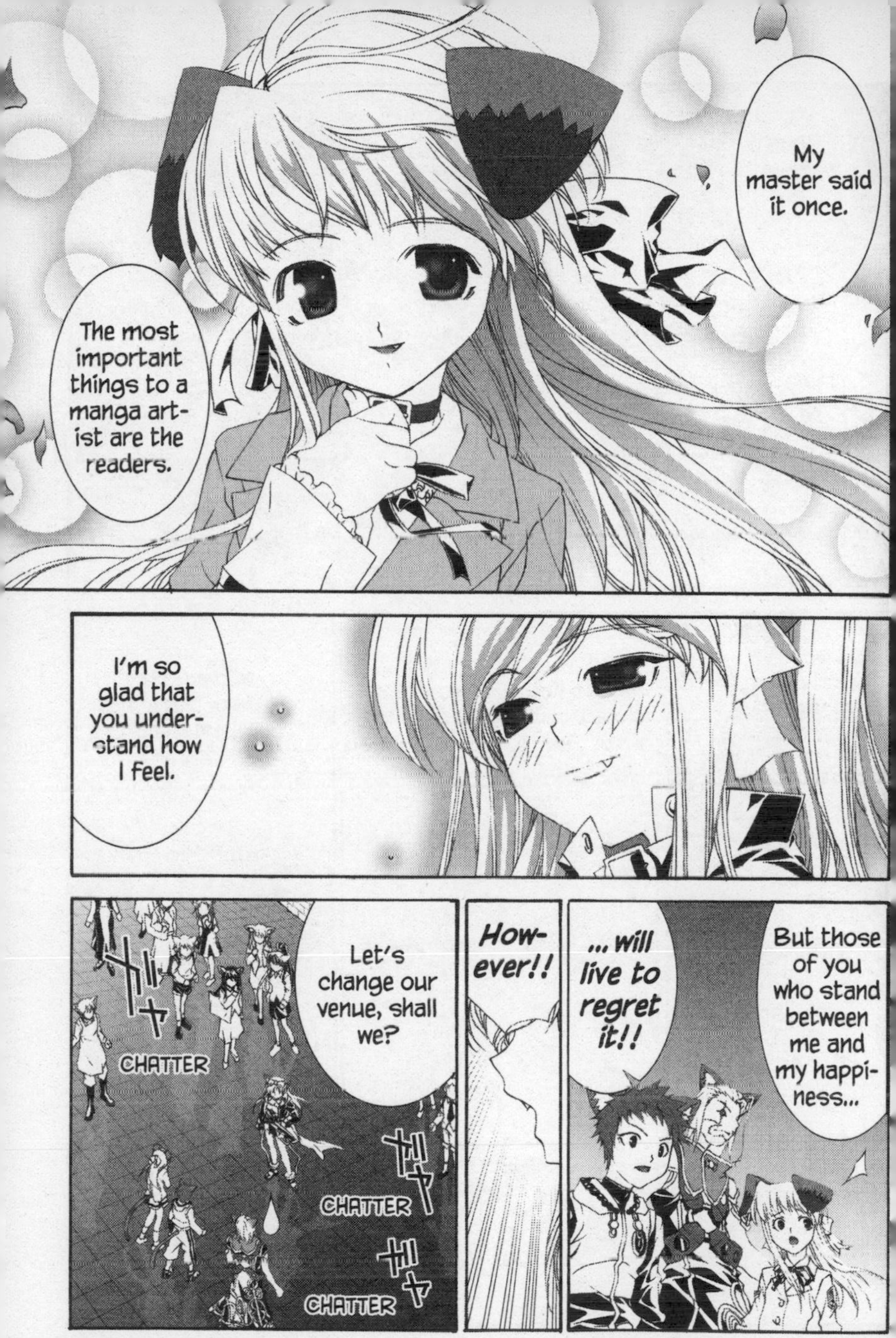
My master said it once.
The most important things to a manga art-ist are the readers.
I'm so glad that you under-stand how I feel.
But those of you who stand between me and my happi-ness...
...will live to regret it!!
How-ever!!
Let's change our venue, shall we?
CHATTER
CHATTER
CHATTER

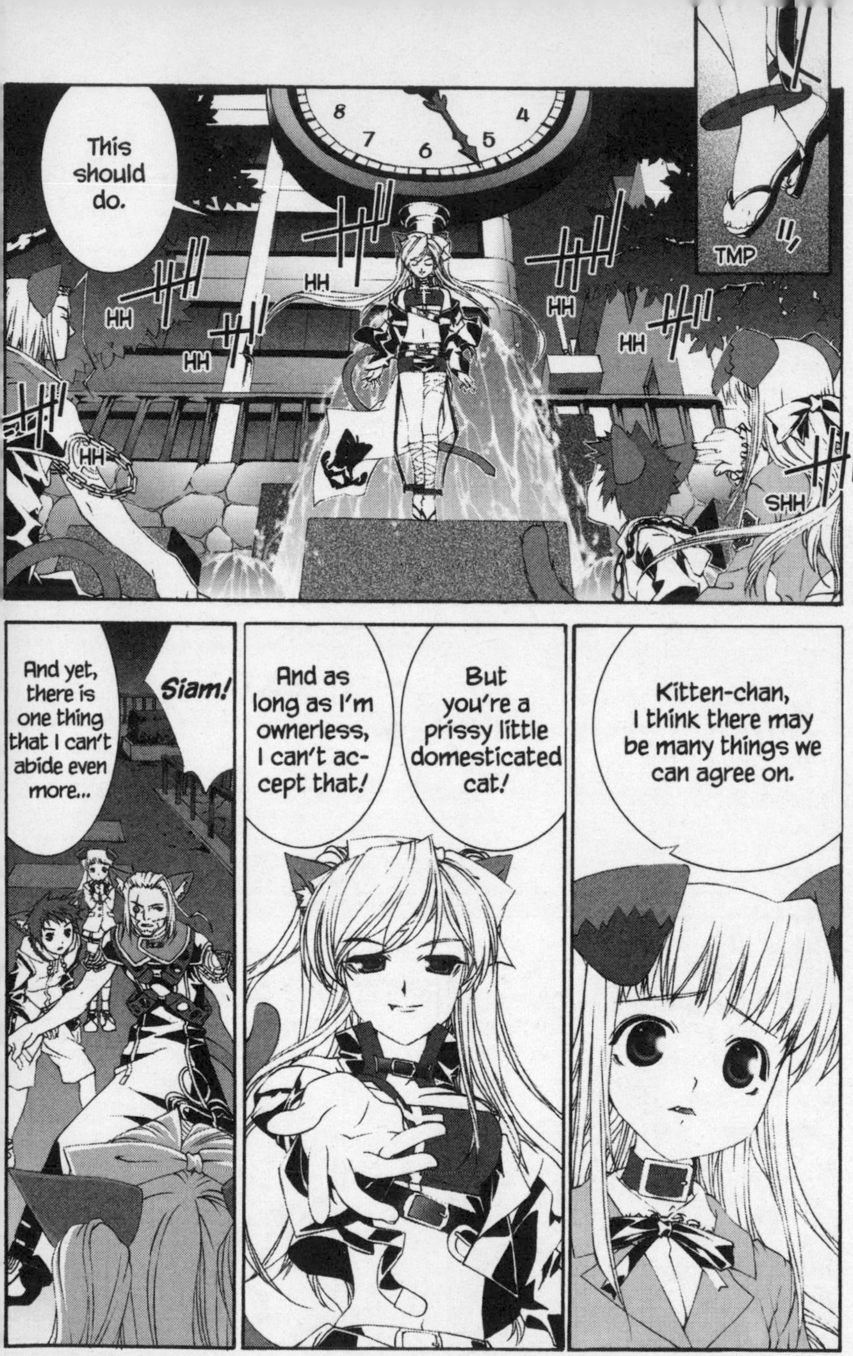
TMP
This should do.
HH
HH
HH
HH
HH
HH
SHH
Kitten-chan, I think there may be many things we can agree on.
But you're a prissy little domesticated cat!
And as long as I'm ownerless, I can't accept that!
Siam!
And yet, there is one thing that I can't abide even more...

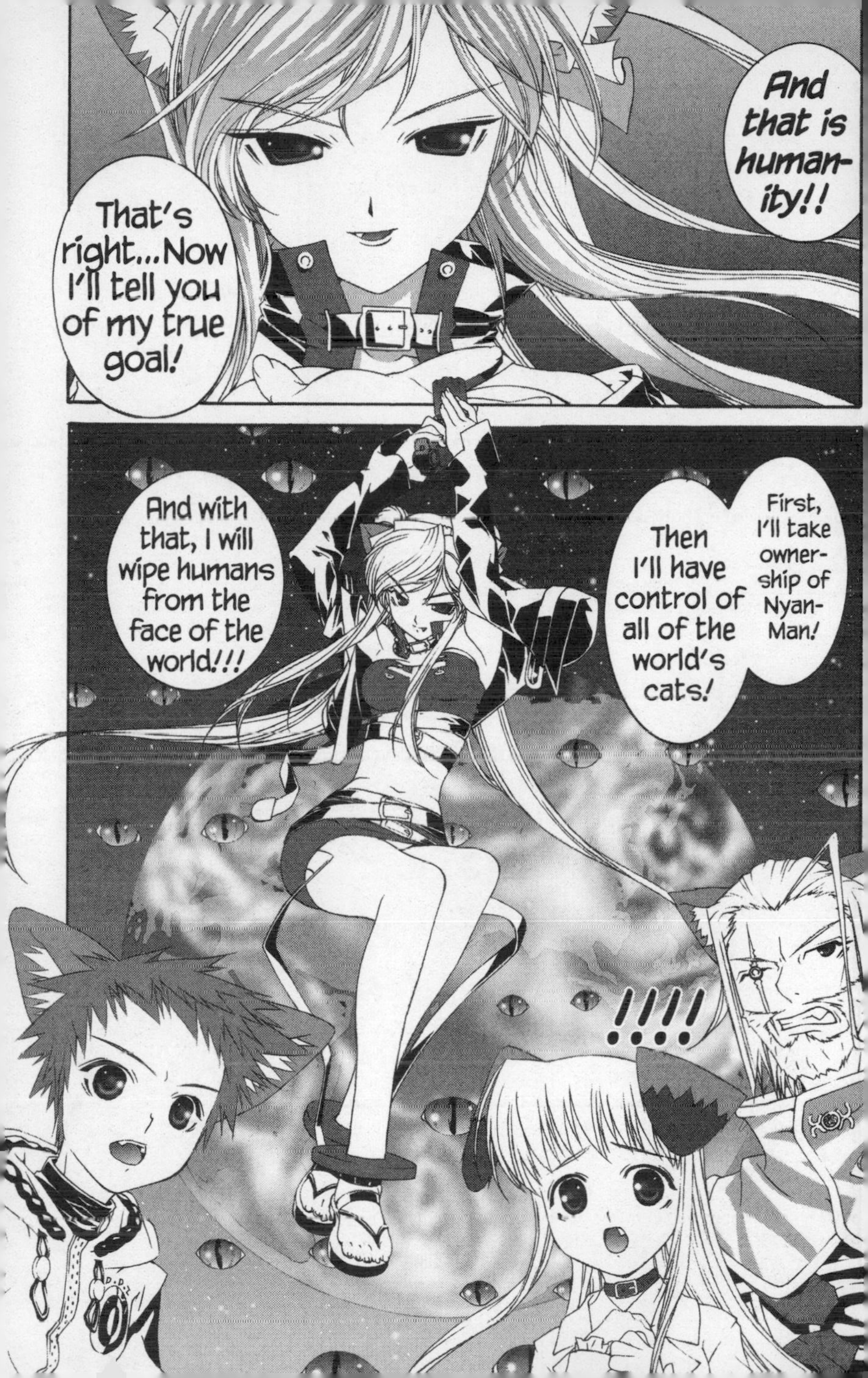
And that is humanity!!
That's right...Now I'll tell you of my true goal!
First, I'll take ownership of Nyan-Man!
Then I'll have control of all of the world's cats!
And with that, I will wipe humans from the face of the world!!!
!!!!

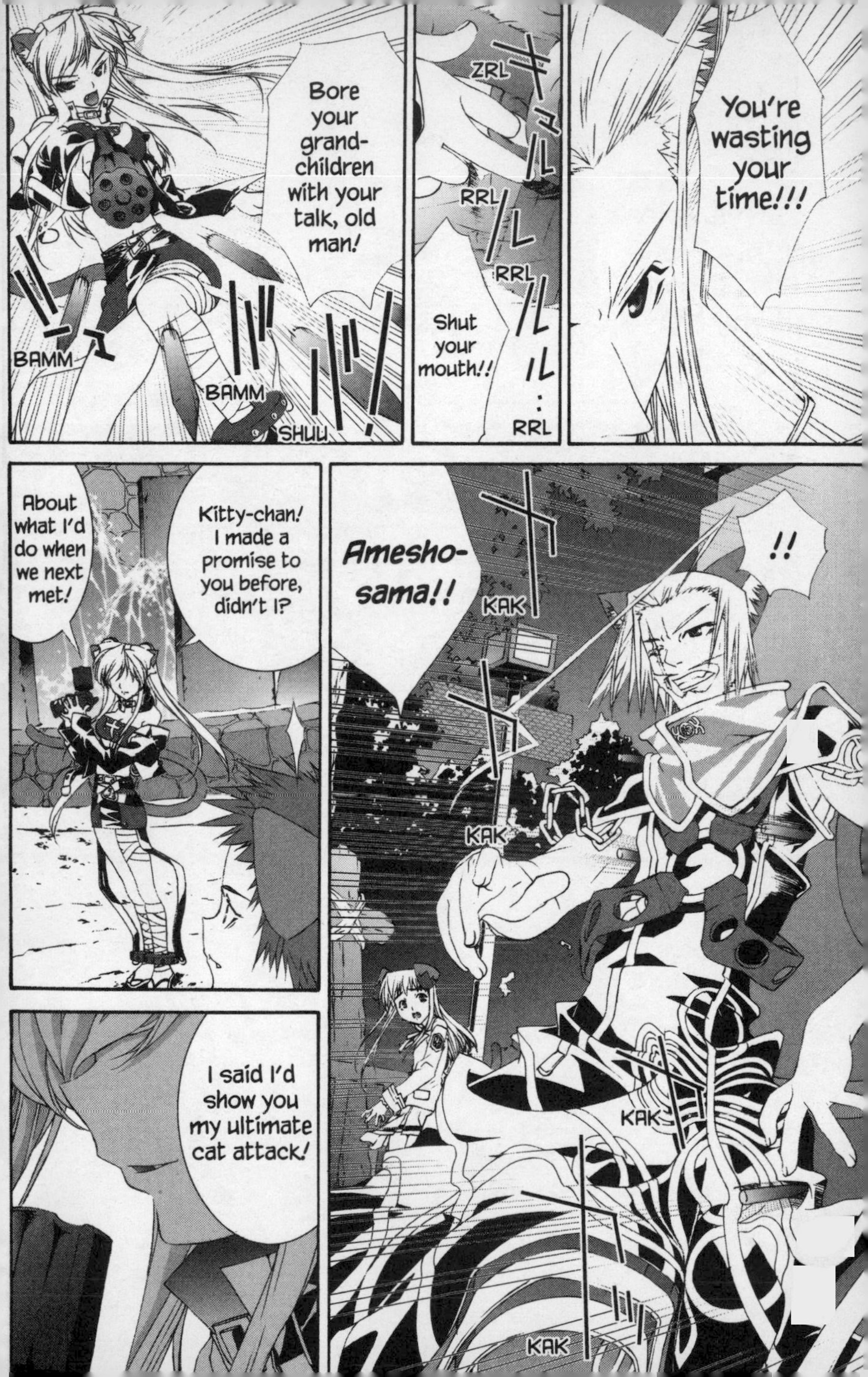

You're wasting your time!!!
ZRL
RRL
RRL
Shut your mouth!!
RRL
Bore your grand-children with your talk, old man!
BAMM
BAMM
SHUU
!!
Amesho-sama!!
KAK
KAK
KAK
KAK
Kitty-chan! I made a promise to you before, didn't I?
About what I'd do when we next met!
I said I'd show you my ultimate cat attack!

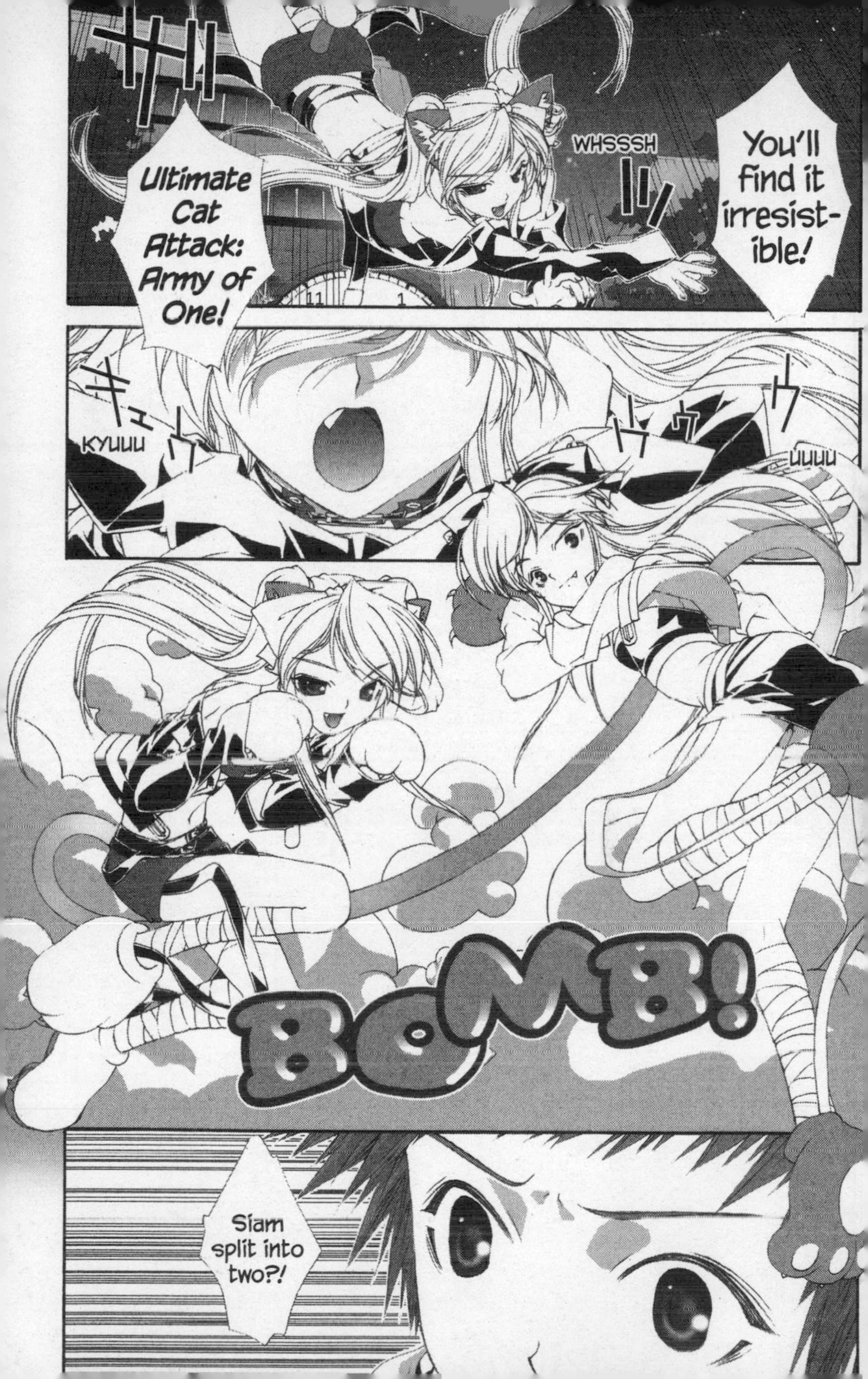
You'll find it irresistible!
WHSSSH
Ultimate Cat Attack: Army of One!
KYUUU
uuuu
BOMB!
Siam split into two?!

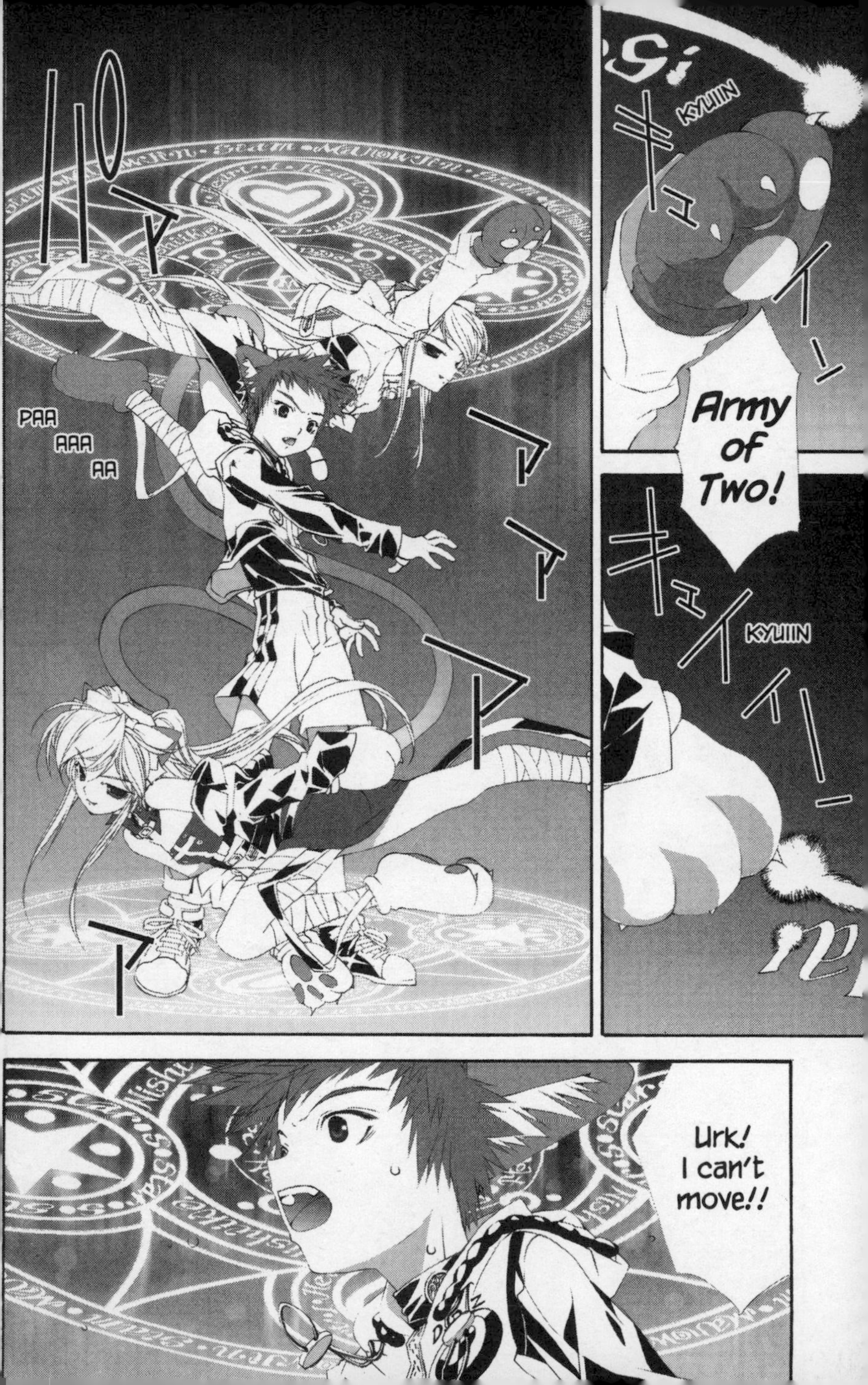
KYUIIN
Army of Two!
KYUIIN
PAA AAA AA
Urk! I can't move!!

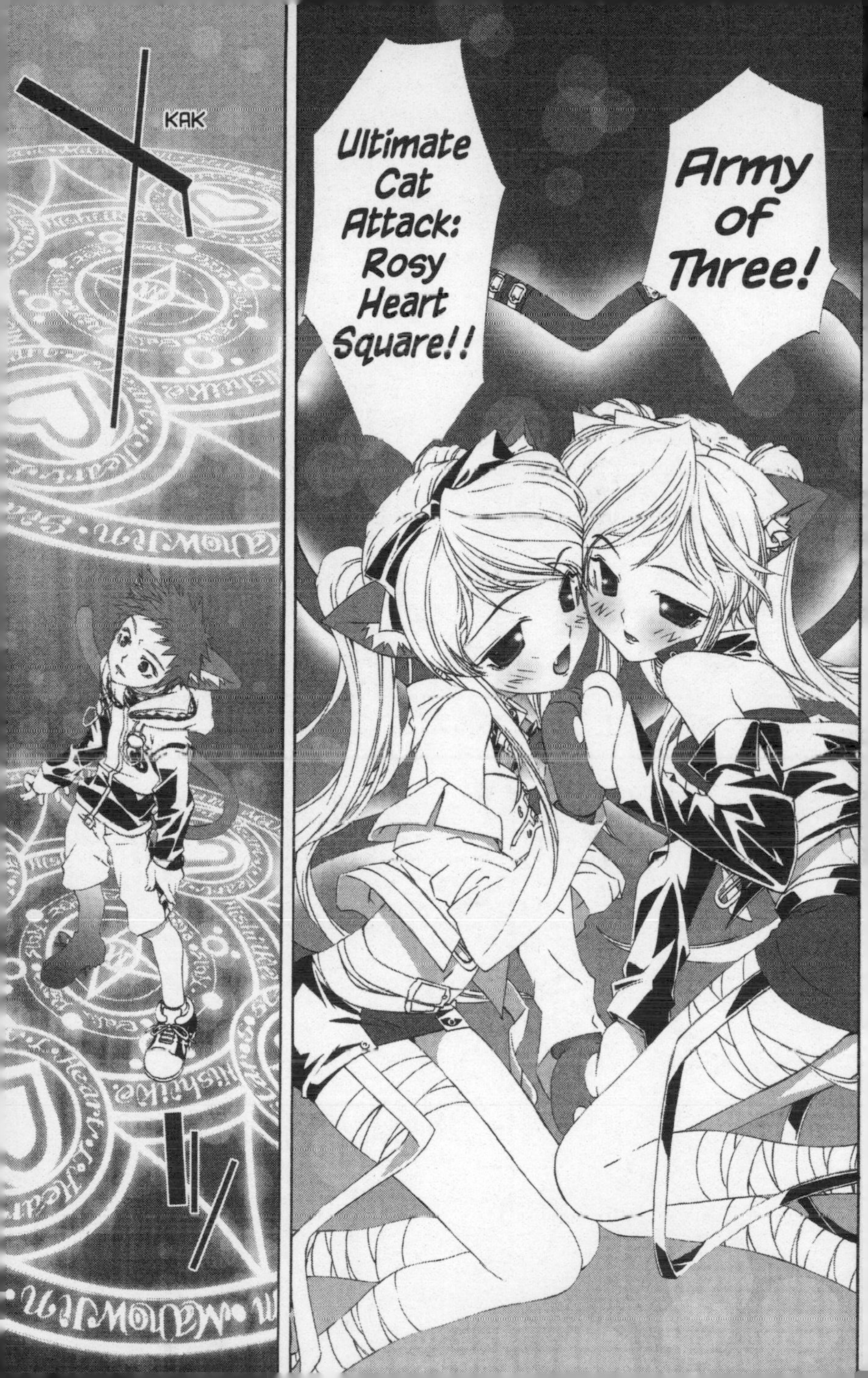
Army of Three!
Ultimate Cat Attack: Rosy Heart Square!!
KAK

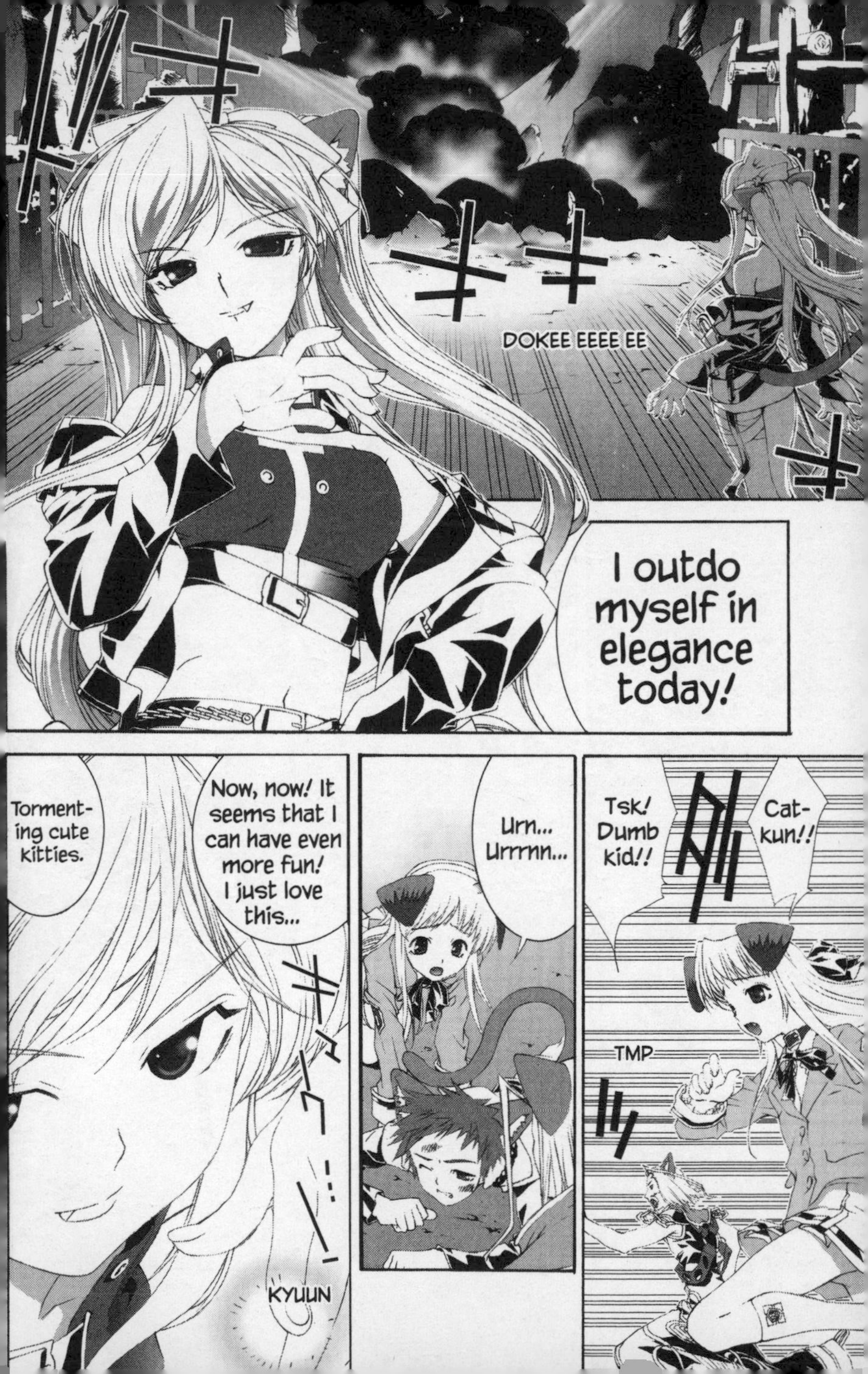
DOKEE EEEE EE
I outdo myself in elegance today!
Cat-kun!!
Tsk! Dumb kid!!
TMP
Urn... Urrrnn...
Now, now! It seems that I can have even more fun! I just love this...
Torment-ing cute kitties.
KYUUN

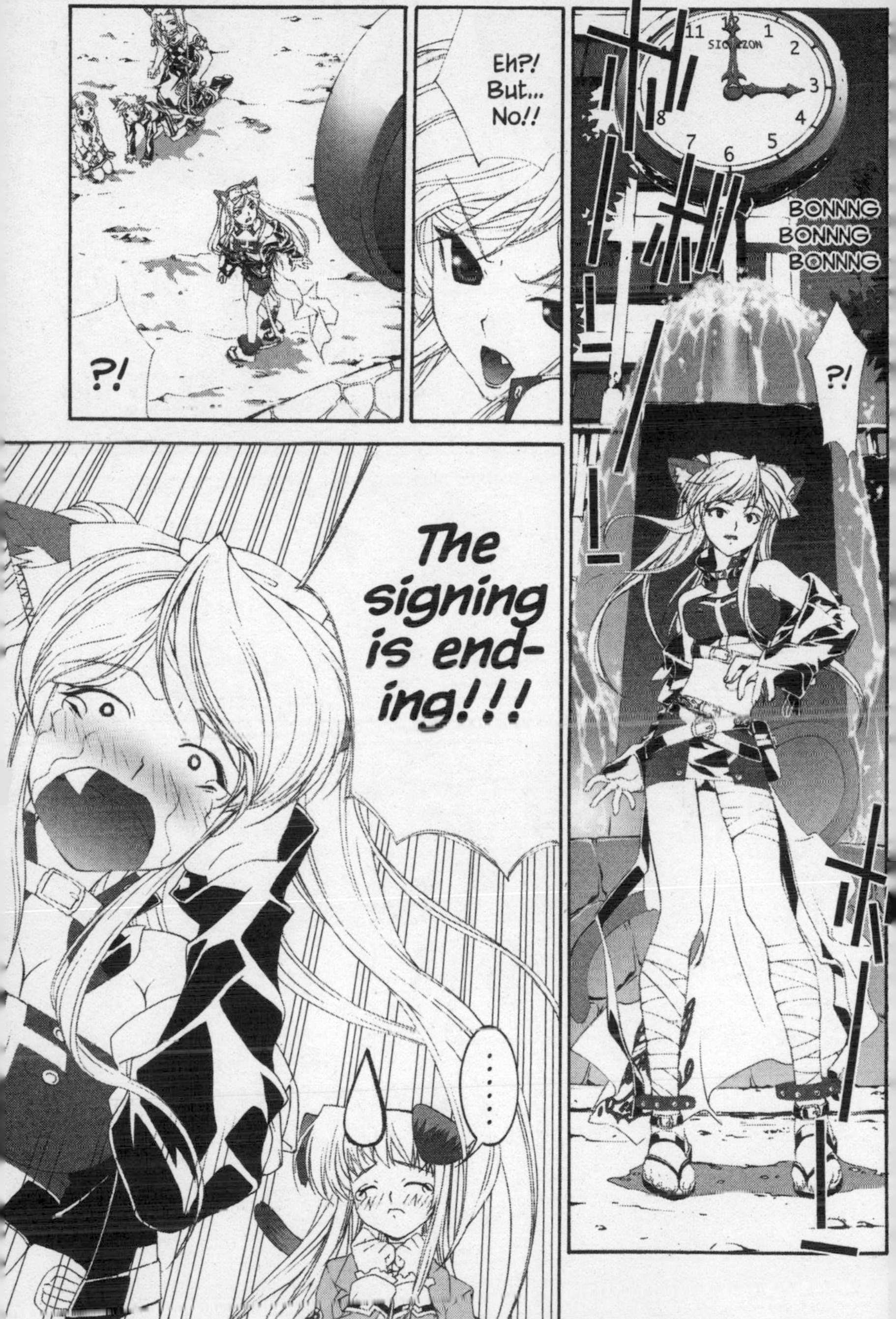
BONNNG
BONNNG
BONNNG
?!
Eh?! But... No!!
?!
The signing is end-ing!!!
......

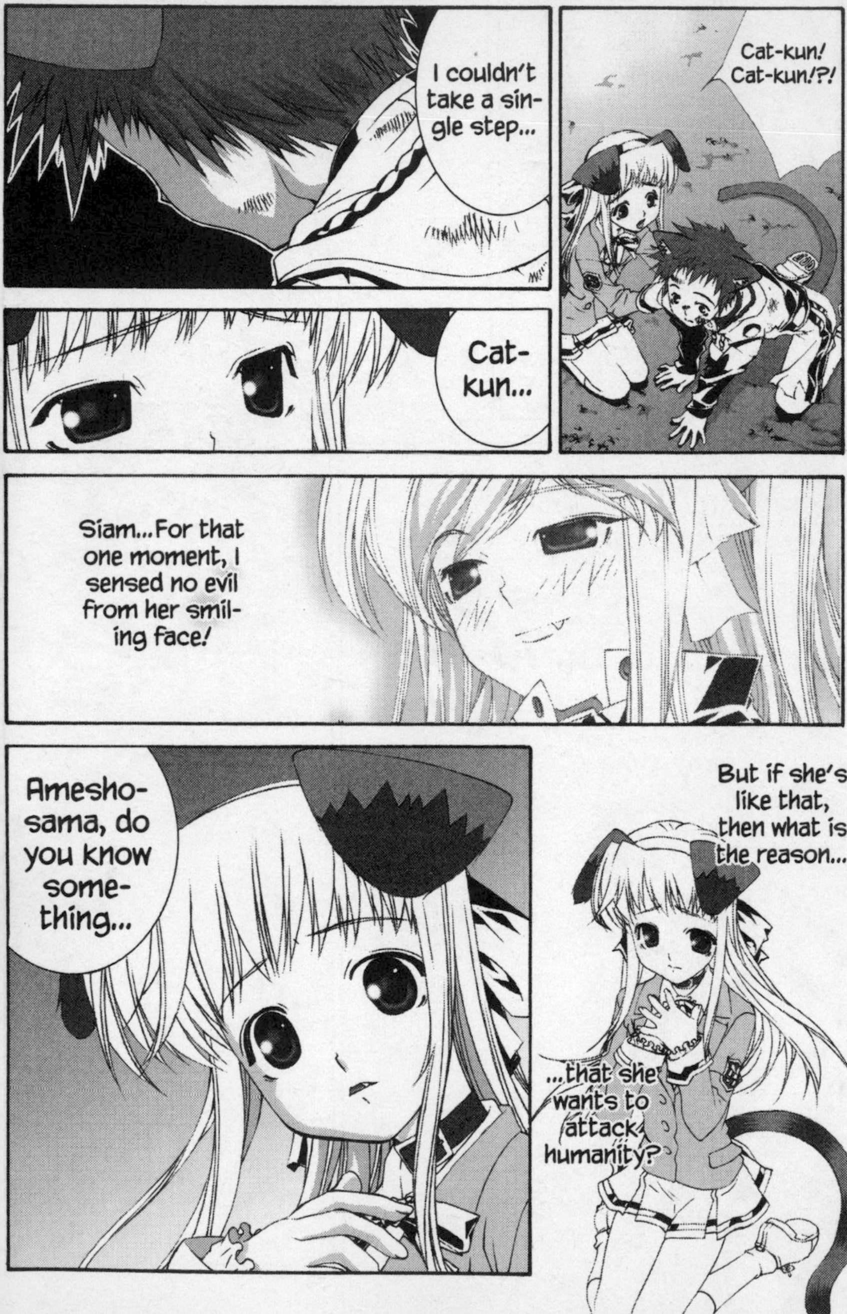
Cat-kun! Cat-kun!?!
I couldn't take a sin-gle step...
Cat-kun...
Siam...For that one moment, I sensed no evil from her smil-ing face!
But if she's like that, then what is the reason...
...that she wants to attack humanity?
Amesho-sama, do you know some-thing...

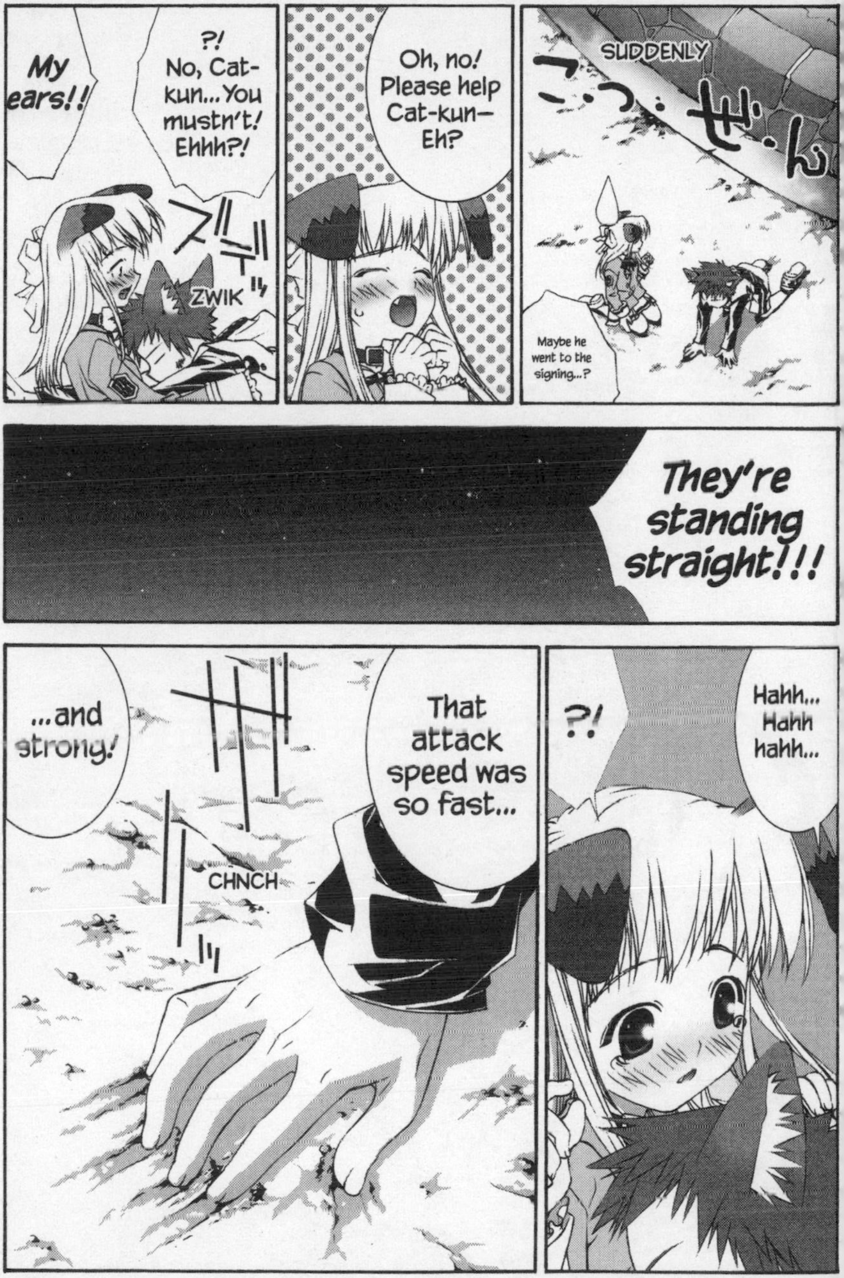
SUDDENLY
Maybe he went to the signing...?
Oh, no! Please help Cat-kun— Eh?
?! No, Cat-kun...You mustn't! Ehhh?!
My ears!!
ZWIK
They're standing straight!!!
Hahh... Hahh hahh...
?!
That attack speed was so fast...
...and strong!
CHNCH

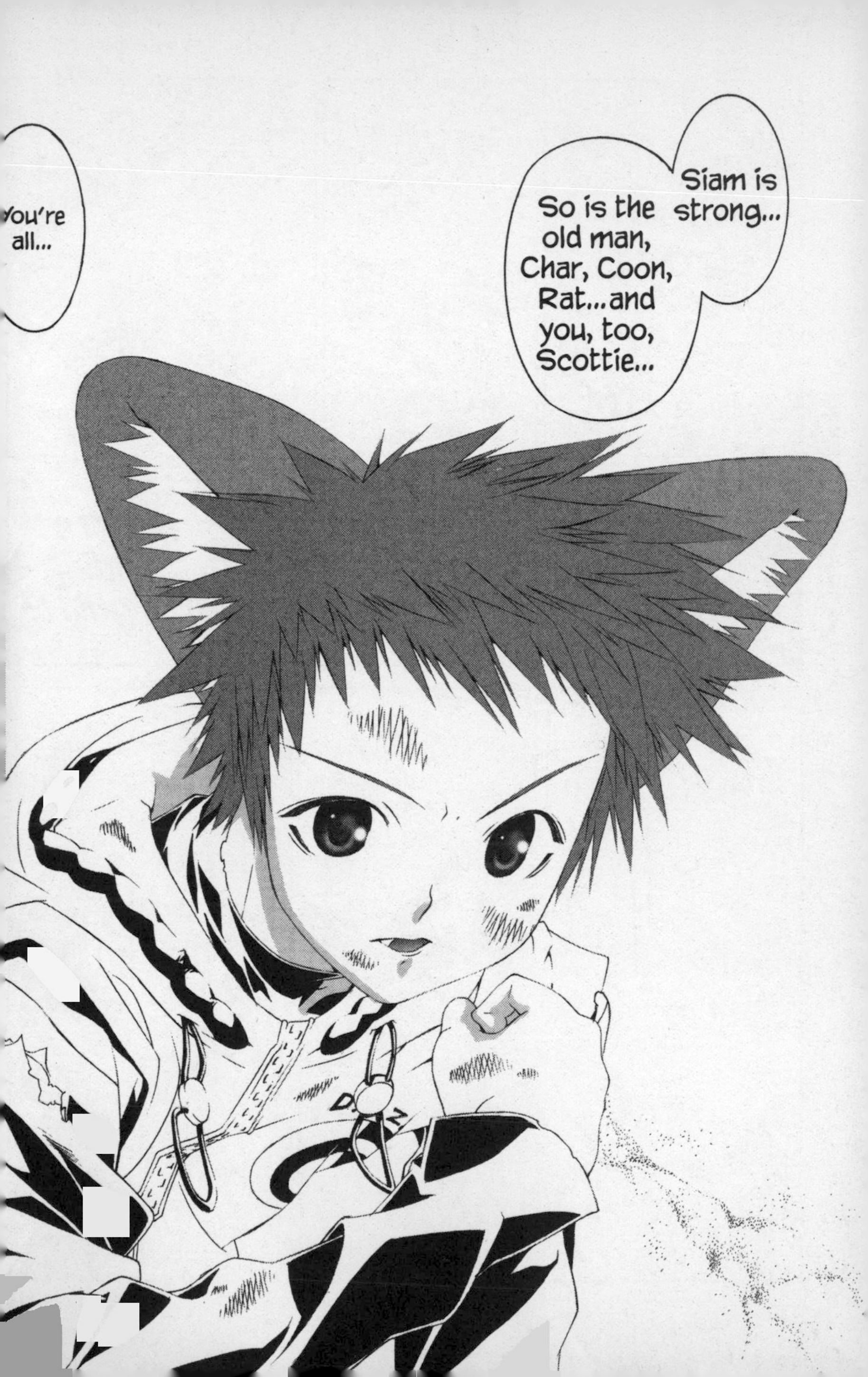
Siam is strong...
So is the old man, Char, Coon, Rat...and you, too, Scottie...
You're all...

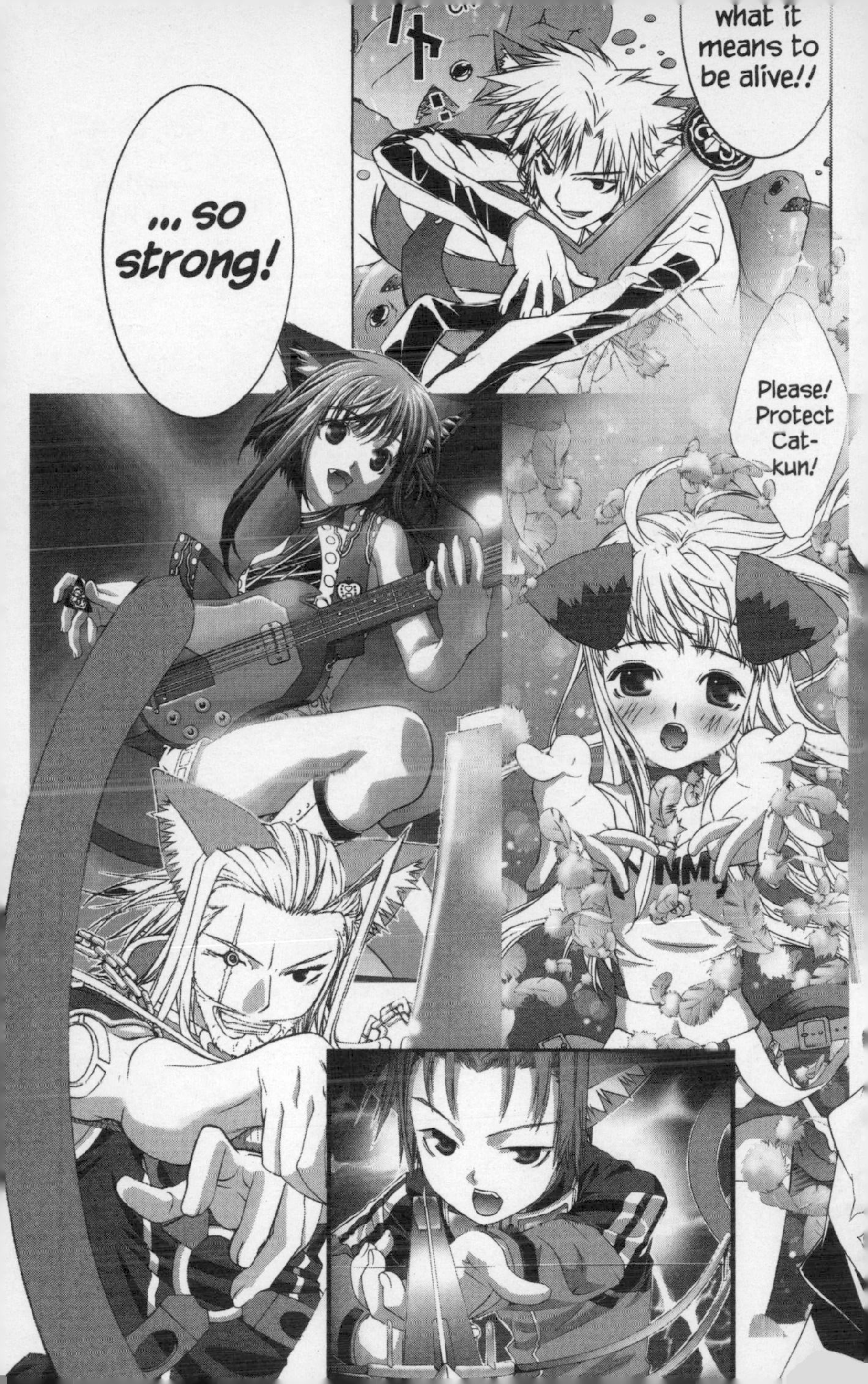
what it means to be alive!!
... so strong!
Please! Protect Cat-kun!

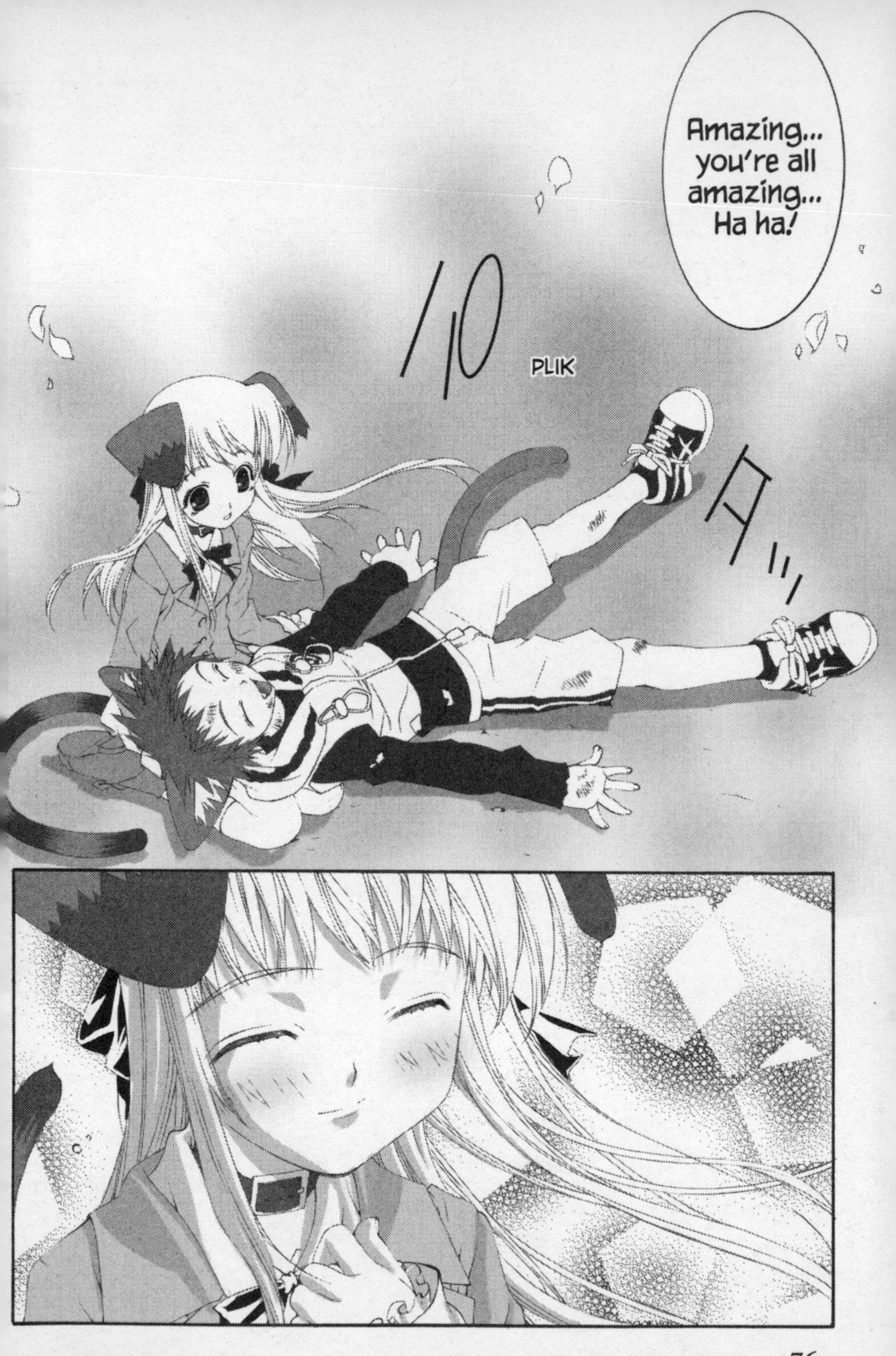
Amazing... you're all amazing... Ha ha!
PLIK

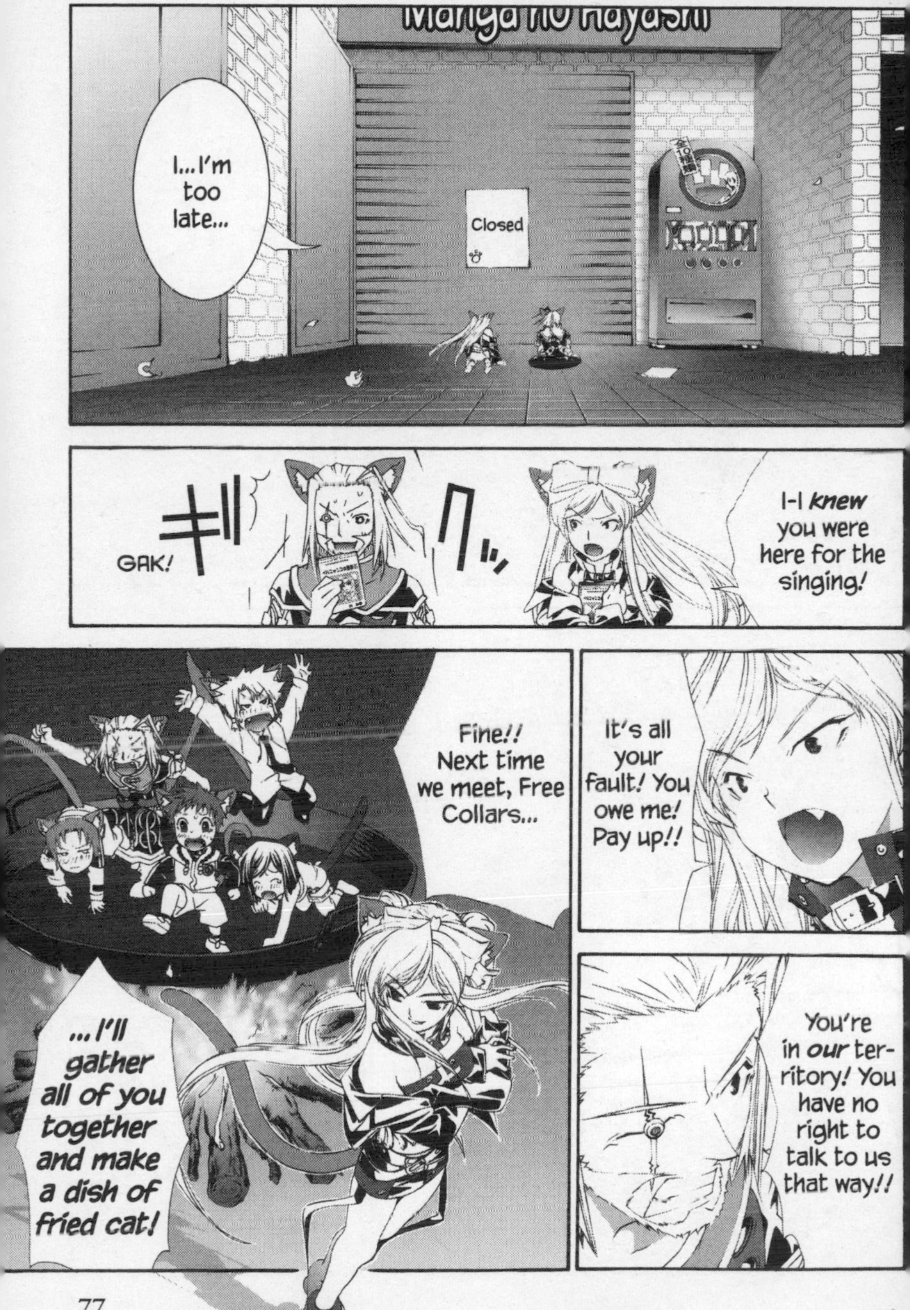
Manga no hayashi
Closed
I...I'm too late...
I-I *knew* you were here for the singing!
GAK!
It's all your fault! You owe me! Pay up!!
You're in *our* territory! You have no right to talk to us that way!!
Fine!! Next time we meet, Free Collars...
...I'll gather all of you together and make a dish of fried cat!

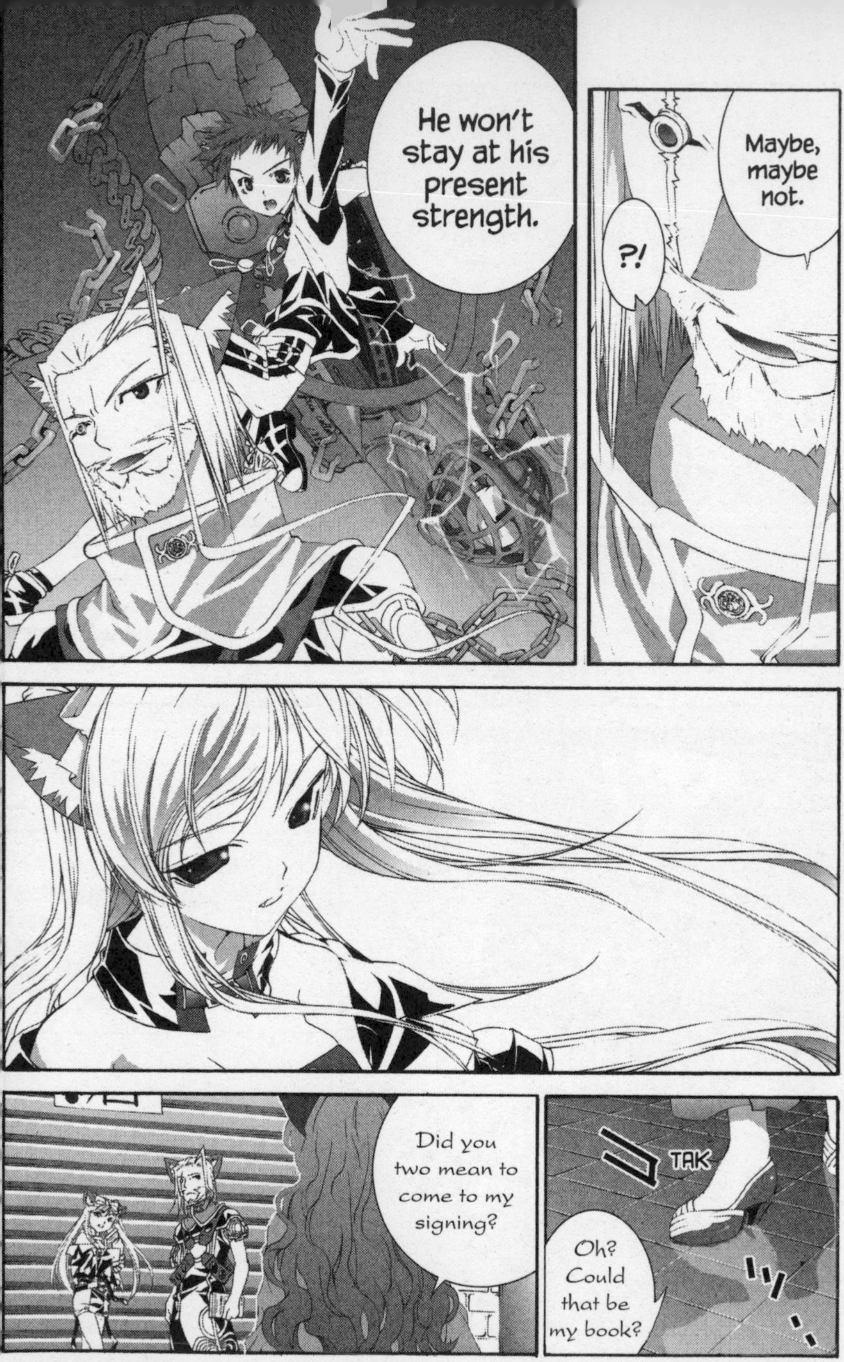
Maybe, maybe not.
?!
He won't stay at his present strength.
TAK
Oh? Could that be my book?
Did you two mean to come to my signing?

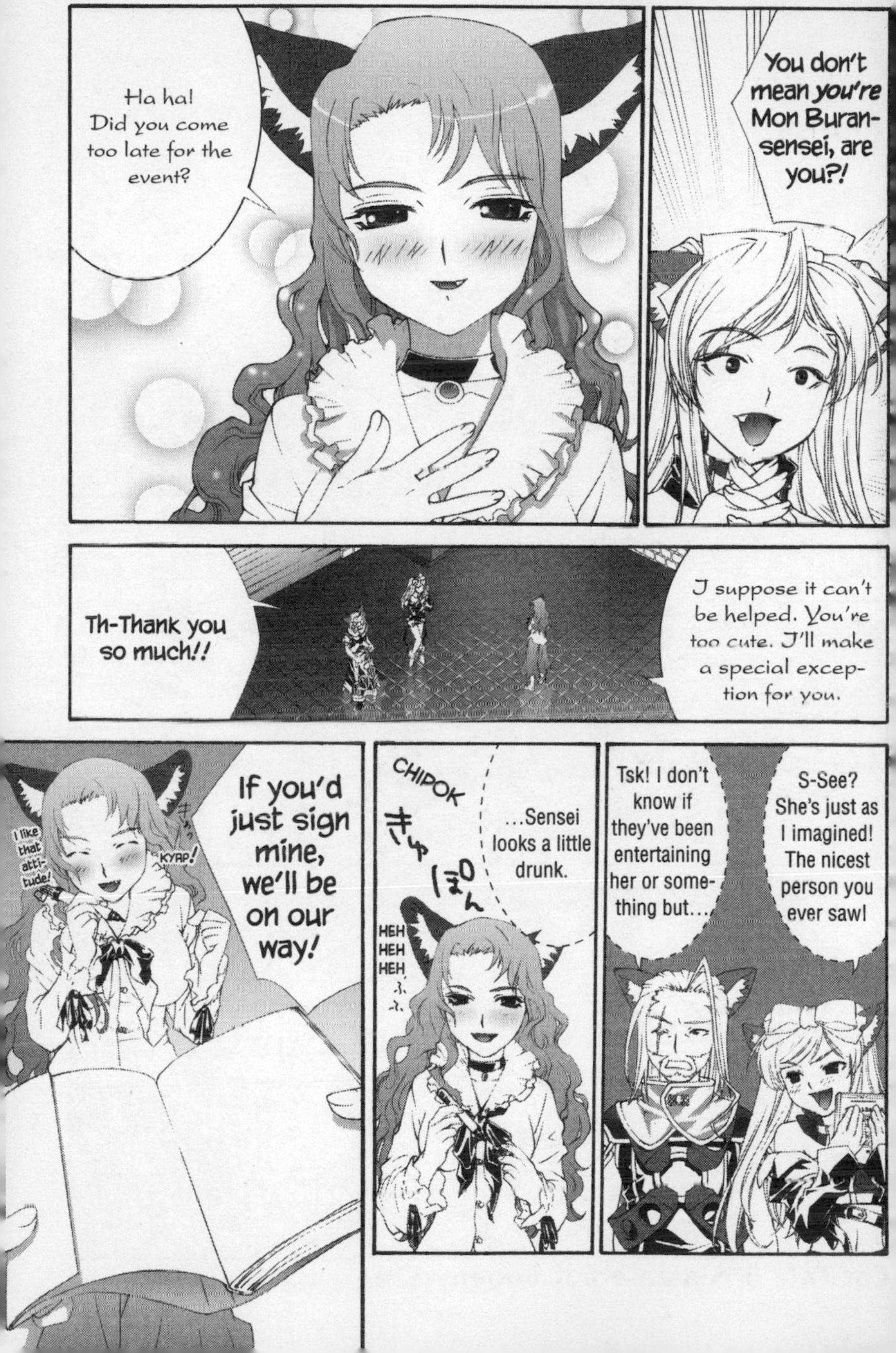
You don't mean you're Mon Buran-sensei, are you?!
Ha ha! Did you come too late for the event?
I suppose it can't be helped. You're too cute. I'll make a special exception for you.
Th-Thank you so much!!
S-See? She's just as I imagined! The nicest person you ever saw!
Tsk! I don't know if they've been entertaining her or something but…
CHIPOK
…Sensei looks a little drunk.
HEH HEH HEH
If you'd just sign mine, we'll be on our way!
KYAP!
I like that atti-tude!

Oh!! Oooooh!!

Very well, then... ♡

キュ SQEE
SQEE キュ
キュ
キュ SQEE
SQEE キュ
SQEE キュ

To Siam-chan, Mon

And for my autograph, could you put it here, please?!

EH HEH HEH HEH

Ha... ha ha!

There we go!

To Siam-chan, Mon Buran

How's *that* for you?!

Awwwww!!

To the dirty old badger, Siam-sama

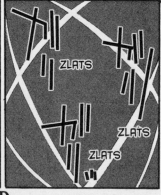

ZLATS
ZLATS
ZLATS

Cat Tale 8   Siamese Cat Boogie   END

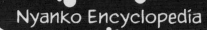

Abyssinian

Model: Cyan

■ The Abyssinian's face is the shape of a rounded V, with huge ears and almond-shaped eyes. It is said that the breed's roots include the bloodline of the ancient Egyptian house cat. It shares certain features of its appearance with the Lybica wildcat, thought to be an ancestor of the Abyssinian. Its body has a limber beauty, and there is an untamed alert quality to its movements. Normally they're quiet, and even in rut, they don't make much noise. They are very curious and show an interest in just about everything. They're perfect for living with humans.

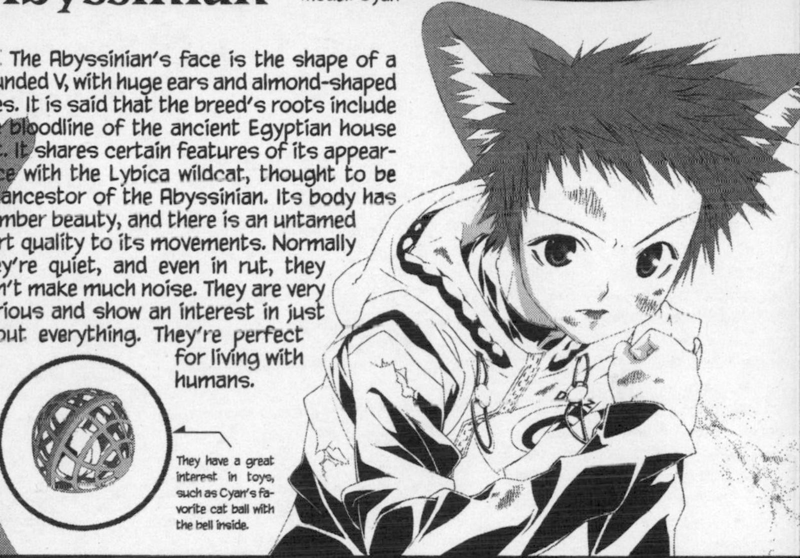

They have a great interest in toys, such as Cyan's favorite cat ball with the bell inside.

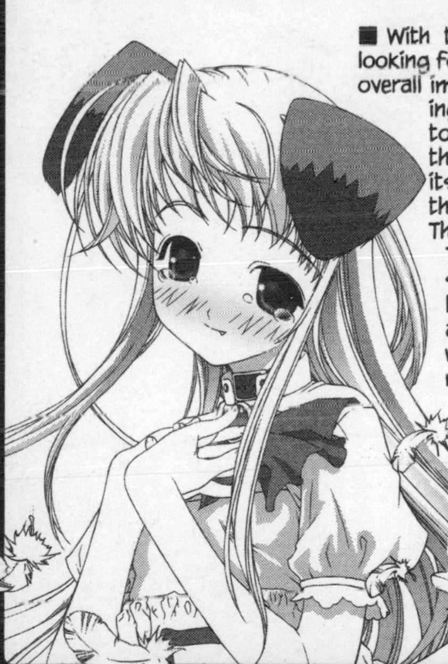

■ With their huge rounded faces, slightly forward-looking fold-over ears, and enormous round eyes, the overall impression a Scottie gives is of always wearing a loving, unself-conscious smile. Its history is not very long. On a farm in Scotland in the early 1960s, a female cat was born with its ears folded over, and that, so they say, was the origin of the entire Scottish Fold breed. Their personality is gentle, calm, and loving. They enjoy being with humans—so much so that they assume that all humans love them. They also like to play and always seem to be having fun. Filled with a lot of charm, this breed is made up of lovely ♥ cats.

Just like Scottie's, the expressions on their perfectly round faces are amazingly cute! ♥

Scottish Fold

Model: Scottie

Nyanko Encyclopedia

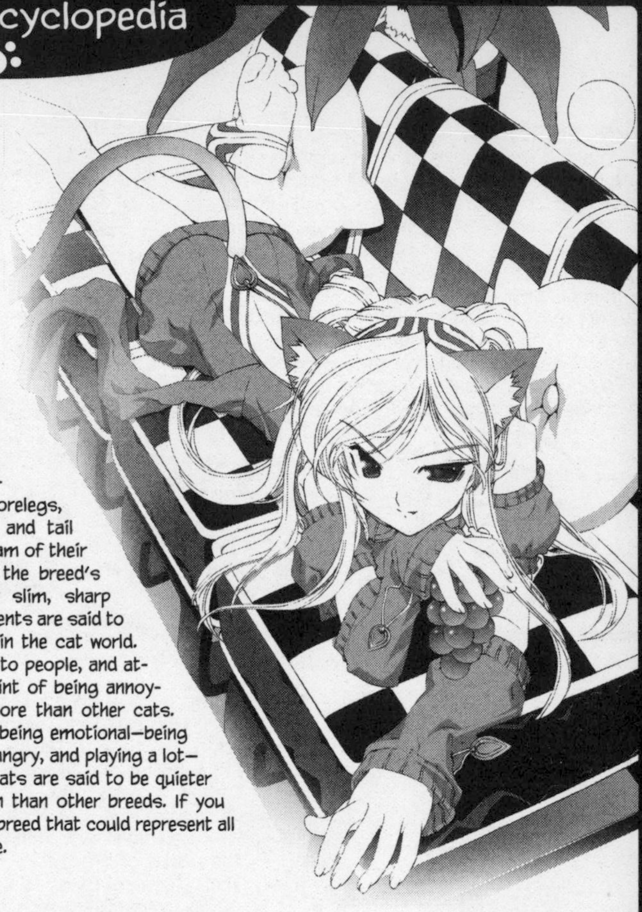

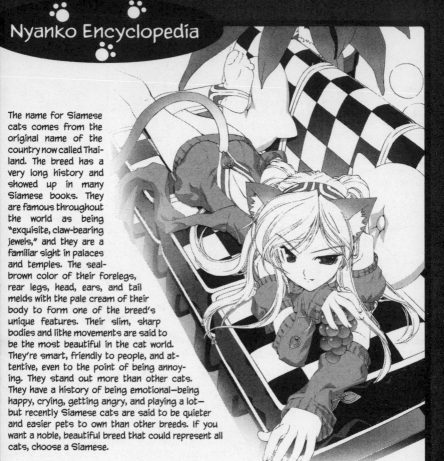

The name for Siamese cats comes from the original name of the country now called Thailand. The breed has a very long history and showed up in many Siamese books. They are famous throughout the world as being "exquisite, claw-bearing jewels," and they are a familiar sight in palaces and temples. The seal-brown color of their forelegs, rear legs, head, ears, and tail melds with the pale cream of their body to form one of the breed's unique features. Their slim, sharp bodies and lithe movements are said to be the most beautiful in the cat world. They're smart, friendly to people, and attentive, even to the point of being annoying. They stand out more than other cats. They have a history of being emotional—being happy, crying, getting angry, and playing a lot—but recently Siamese cats are said to be quieter and easier pets to own than other breeds. If you want a noble, beautiful breed that could represent all cats, choose a Siamese.

Siamese Cat

Model: Siam

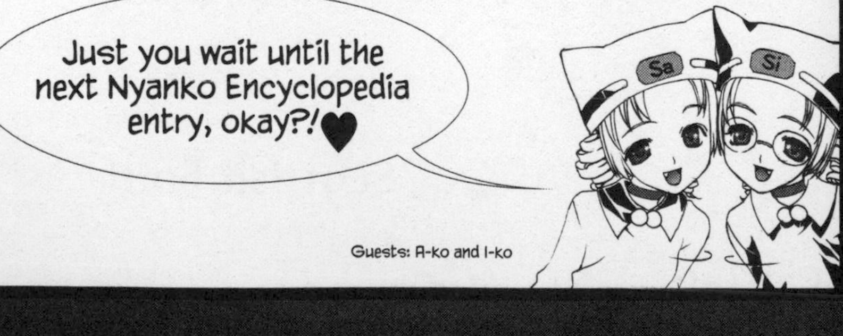
Just you wait until the next Nyanko Encyclopedia entry, okay?!♥
Sa
Si

Guests: A-ko and I-ko

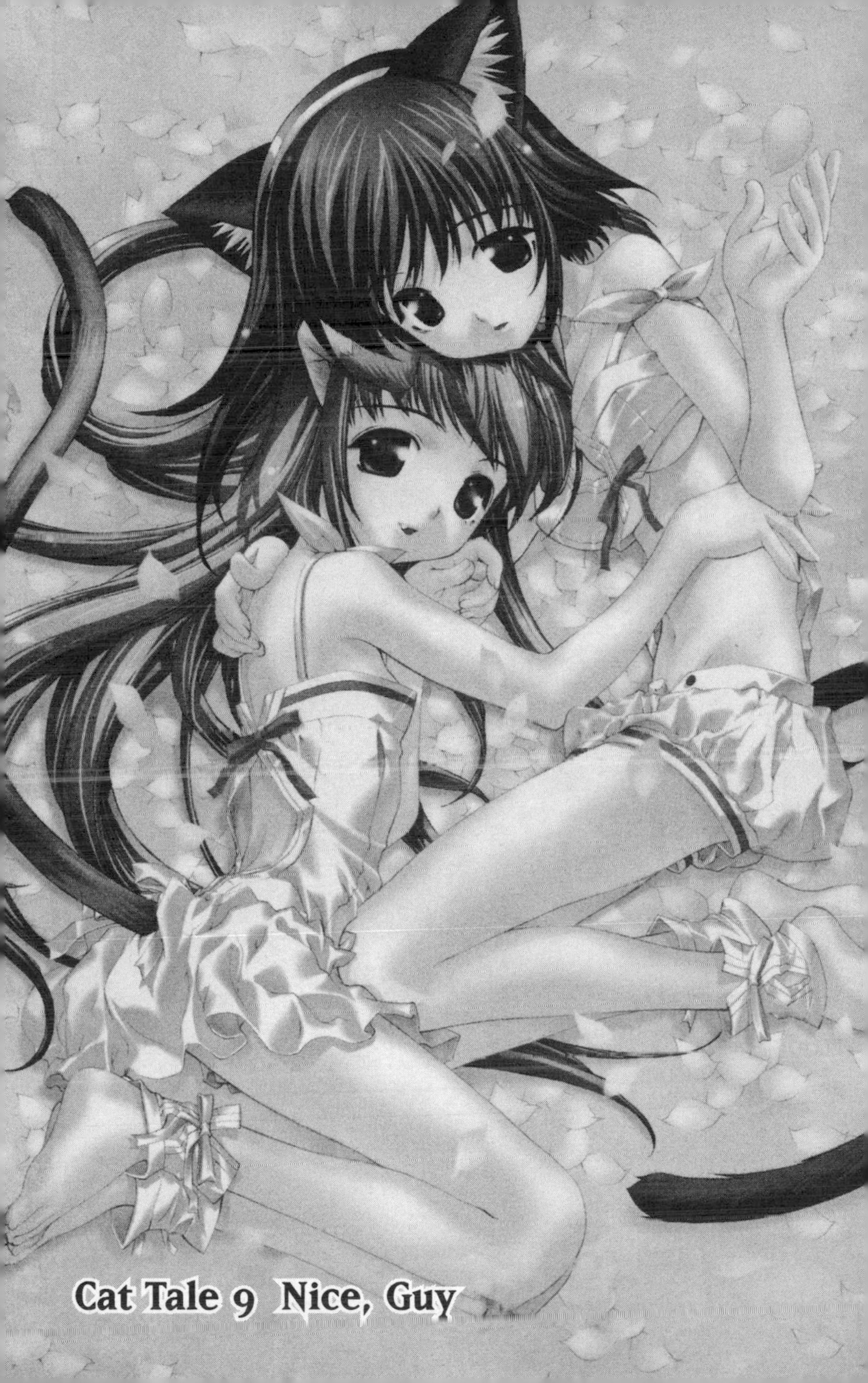

Cat Tale 9 Nice, Guy

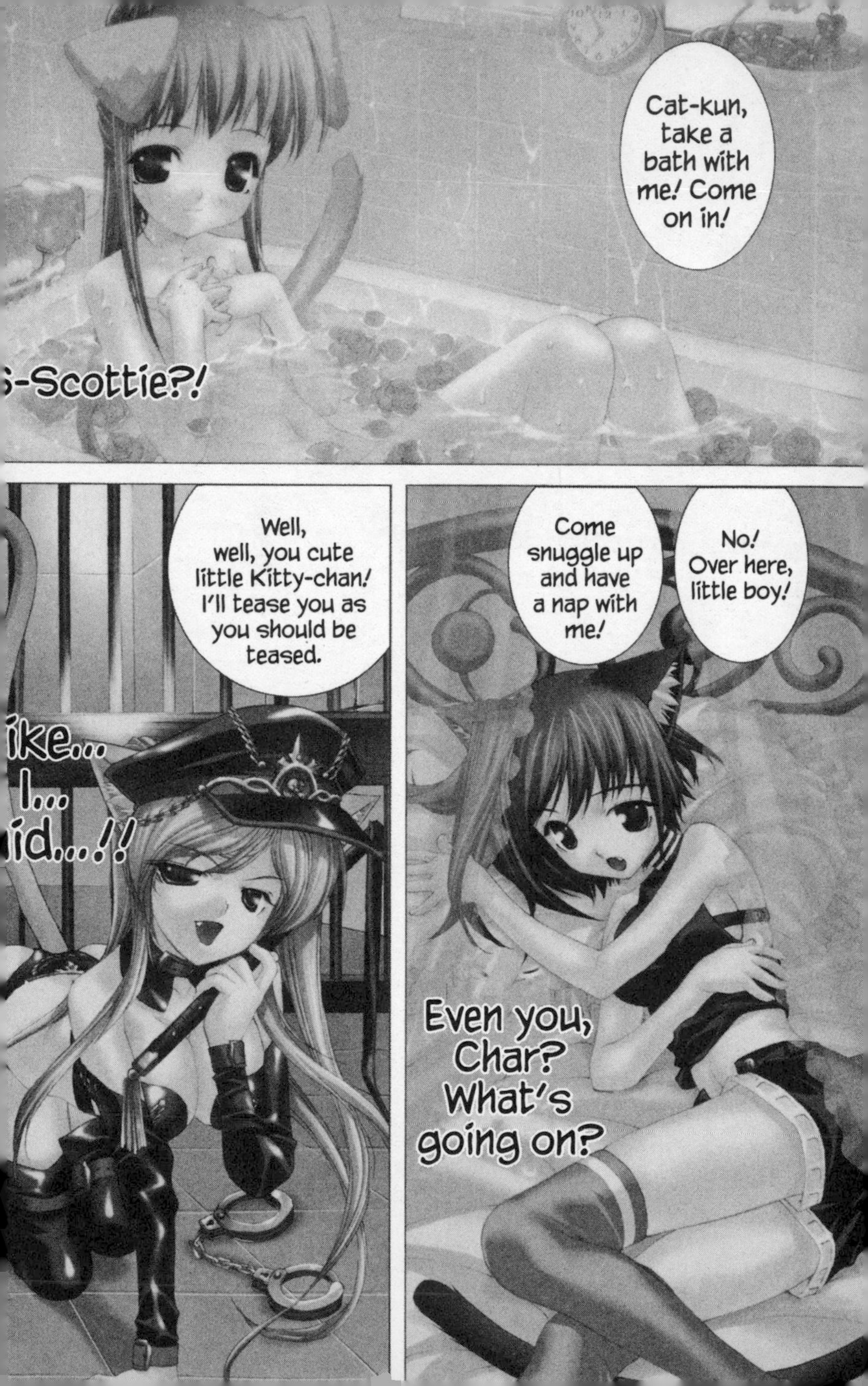
Cat-kun, take a bath with me! Come on in!
-Scottie?!
No! Over here, little boy!
Come snuggle up and have a nap with me!
Even you, Char? What's going on?
Well, well, you cute little Kitty-chan! I'll tease you as you should be teased.
ike... I... id...!!

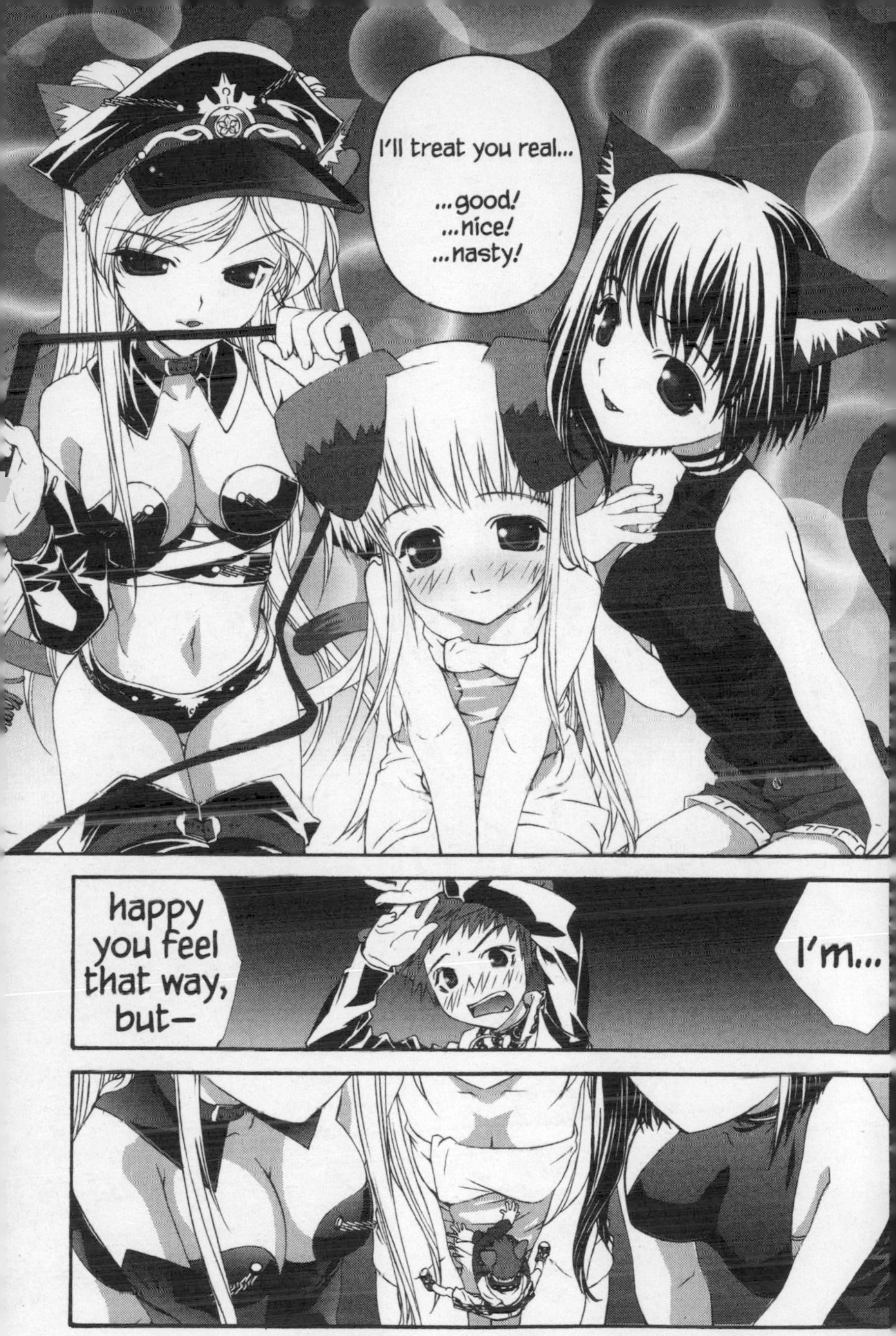
I'll treat you real...
...good! ...nice! ...nasty!
I'm...
happy you feel that way, but—

...but...!!

GAMPH

Great timing!

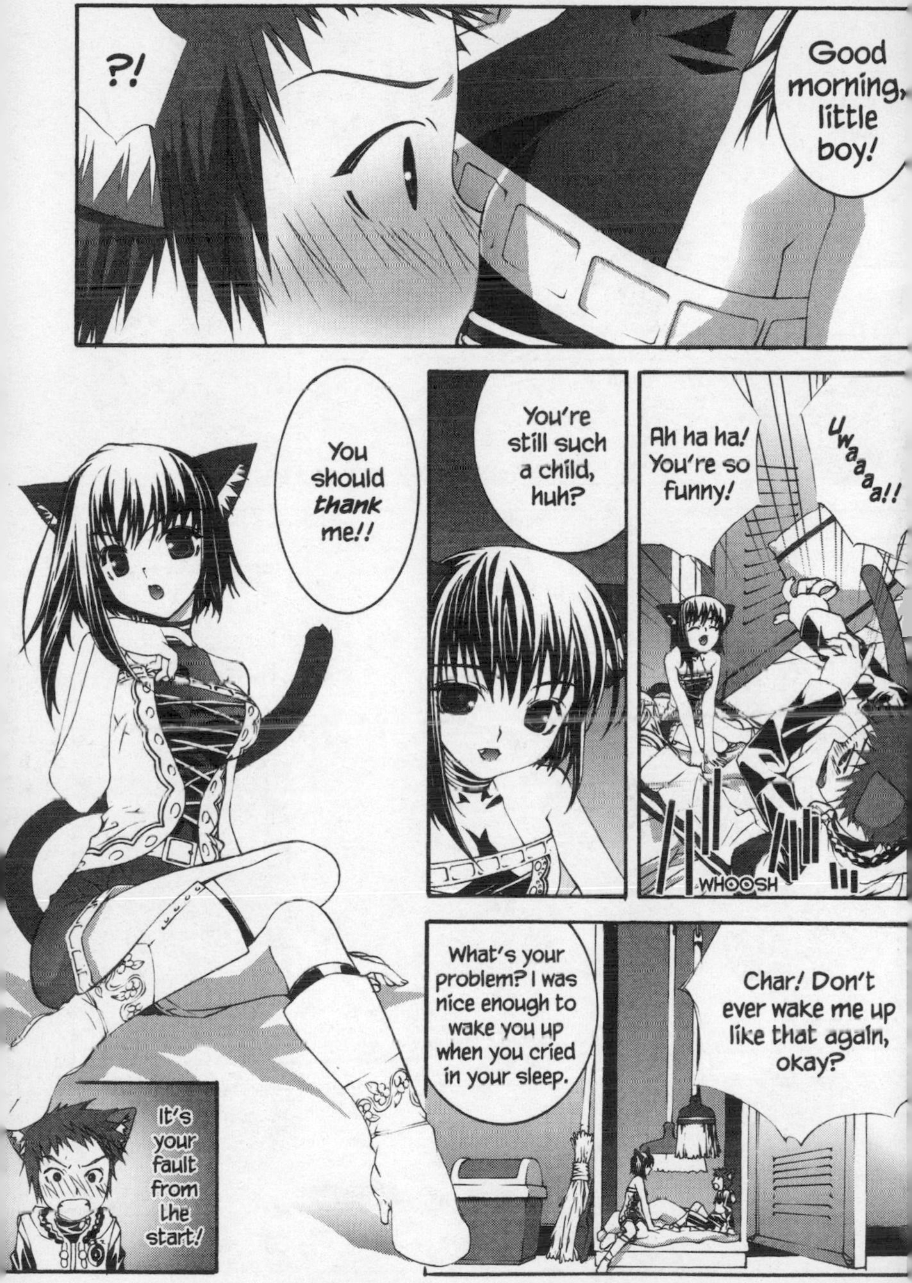
Good morning, little boy!
?!
Uwaaaaa!!
Ah ha ha! You're so funny!
WHOOSH
You're still such a child, huh?
Char! Don't ever wake me up like that again, okay?
What's your problem? I was nice enough to wake you up when you cried in your sleep.
You should *thank* me!!
It's your fault from the start!

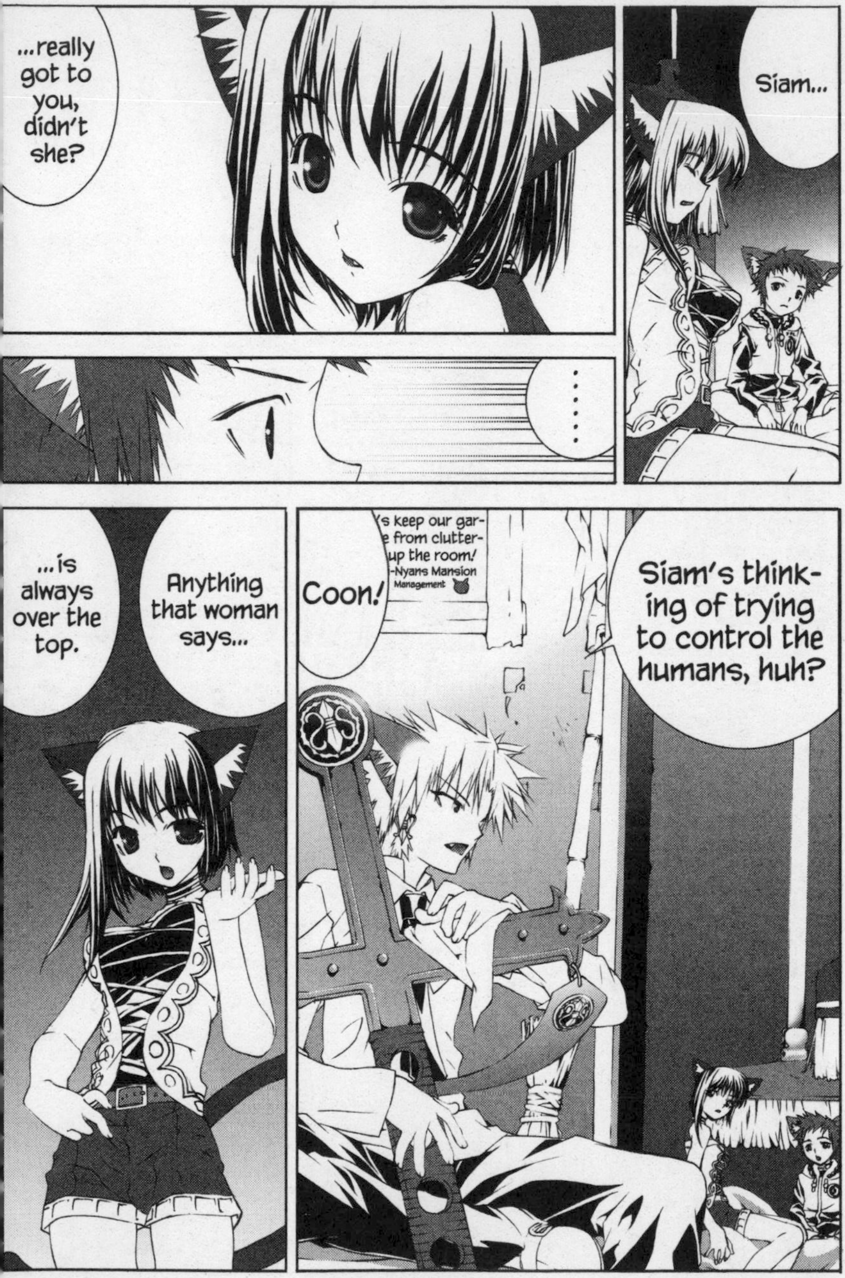
Siam...
...really got to you, didn't she?
......
Siam's thinking of trying to control the humans, huh?
Coon!
's keep our gar-
e from clutter-
up the room!
-Nyans Mansion Management
Anything that woman says...
...is always over the top.

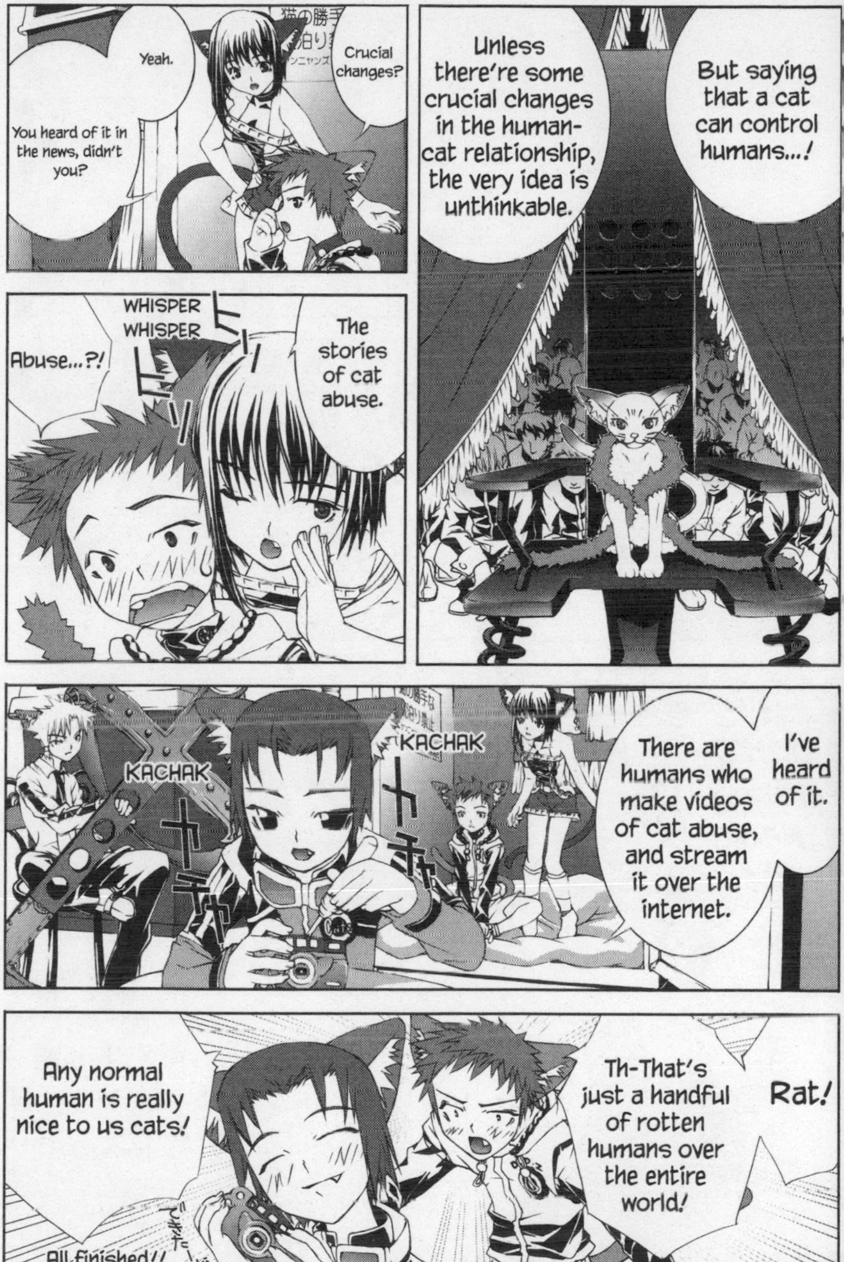

But saying that a cat can control humans...!
Unless there're some crucial changes in the human-cat relationship, the very idea is unthinkable.
Crucial changes?
Yeah.
You heard of it in the news, didn't you?
The stories of cat abuse.
WHISPER WHISPER
Abuse...?!
I've heard of it.
There are humans who make videos of cat abuse, and stream it over the internet.
KACHAK
KACHAK
Rat!
Th-That's just a handful of rotten humans over the entire world!
Any normal human is really nice to us cats!
All finished!!

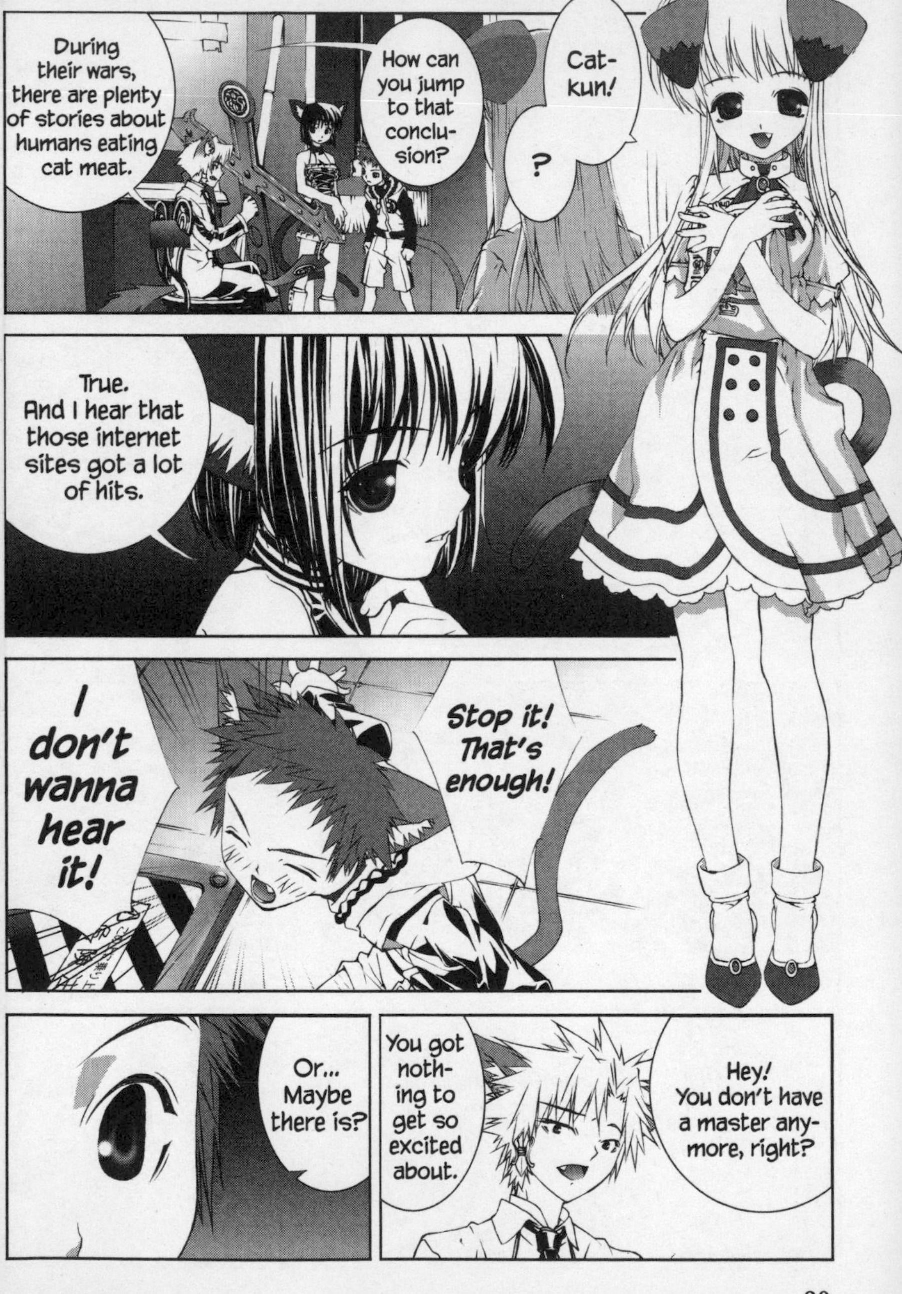

Cat-kun!
?
How can you jump to that conclusion?
During their wars, there are plenty of stories about humans eating cat meat.
True. And I hear that those internet sites got a lot of hits.
Stop it! That's enough!
I don't wanna hear it!
Hey! You don't have a master anymore, right?
You got nothing to get so excited about.
Or... Maybe there is?

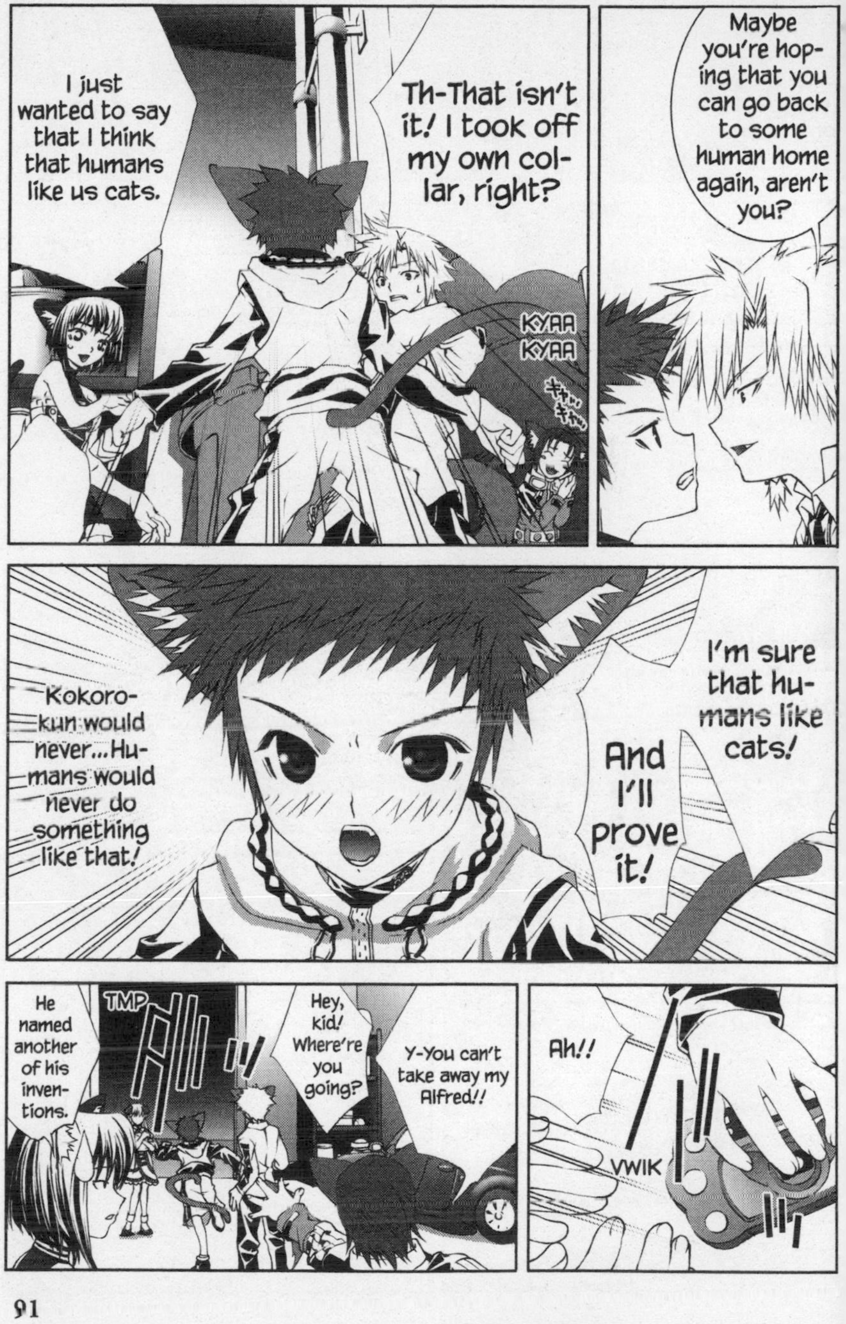
Maybe you're hoping that you can go back to some human home again, aren't you?
Th-That isn't it! I took off my own collar, right?
I just wanted to say that I think that humans like us cats.
KYAA KYAA
I'm sure that humans like cats!
And I'll prove it!
Kokoro-kun would never...Humans would never do something like that!
Ah!!
VWIK
Y-You can't take away my Alfred!!
Hey, kid! Where're you going?
TMP
He named another of his inventions.

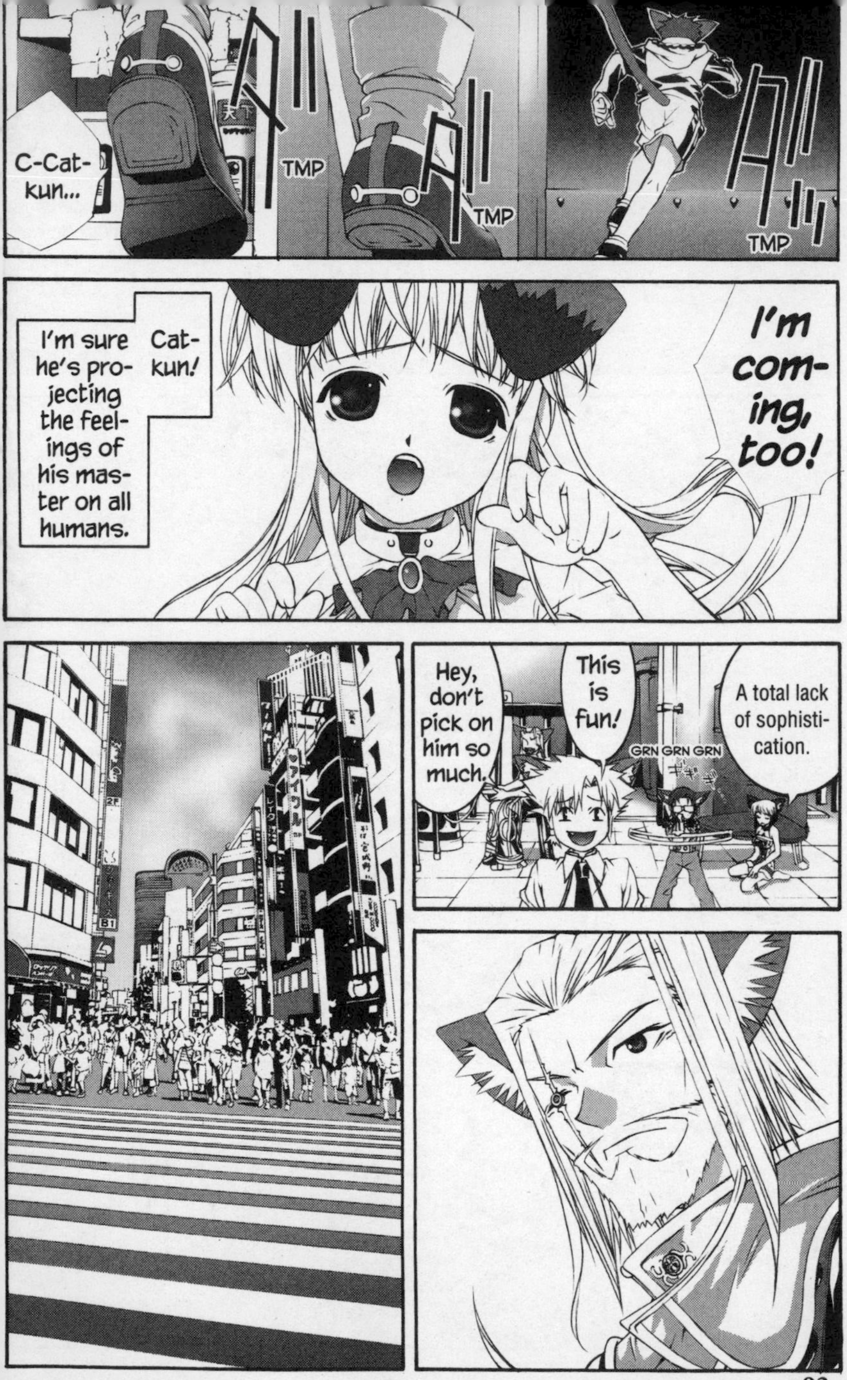
TMP
TMP
C-Cat-kun...
TMP
I'm coming, too!
Cat-kun!
I'm sure he's projecting the feelings of his master on all humans.
A total lack of sophistication.
GRN GRN GRN
This is fun!
Hey, don't pick on him so much.

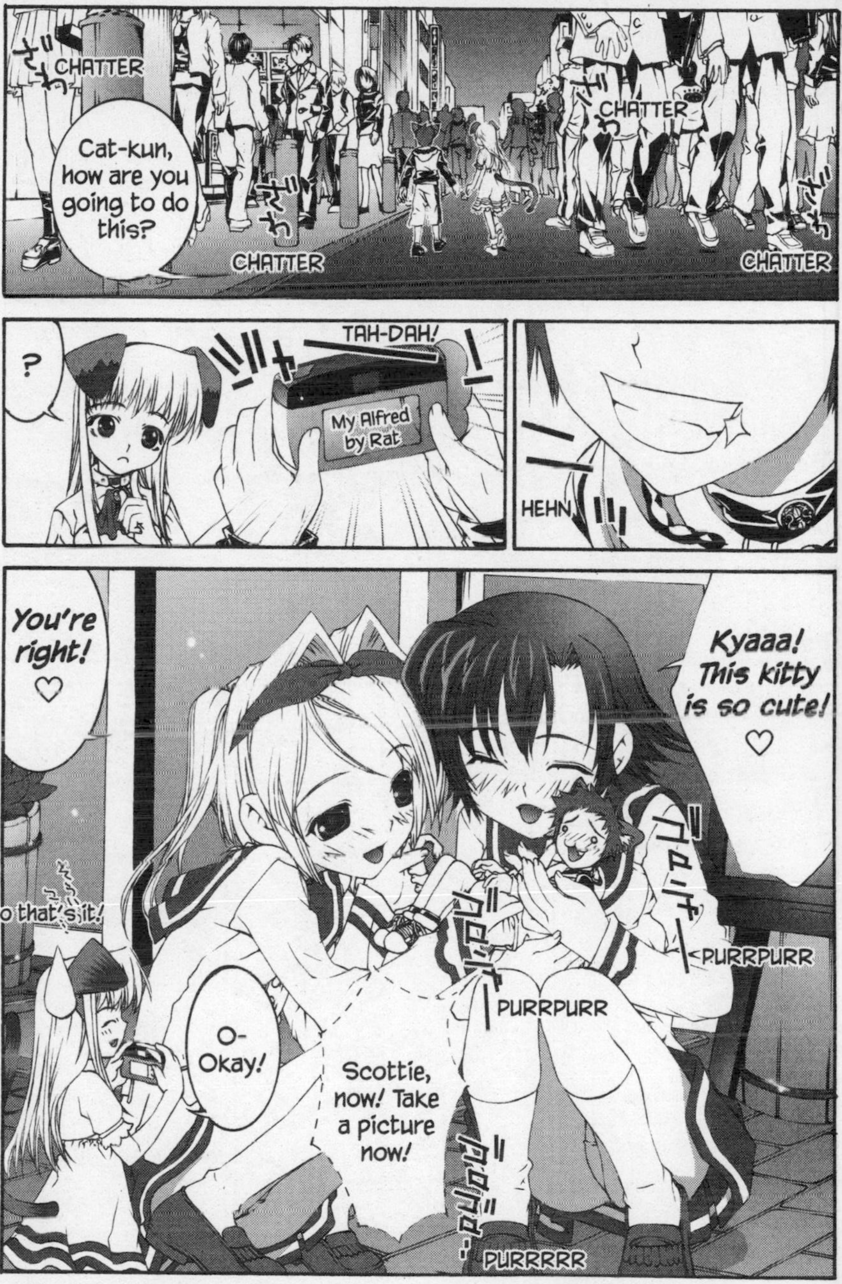
CHATTER
CHATTER
CHATTER
Cat-kun, how are you going to do this?
CHATTER
HEHN
TAH-DAH!
My Alfred by Rat
?
Kyaaa! This kitty is so cute! ♡
PURRPURR
PURRPURR
You're right! ♡
Scottie, now! Take a picture now!
PURRRRR
O-Okay!
So that's it!

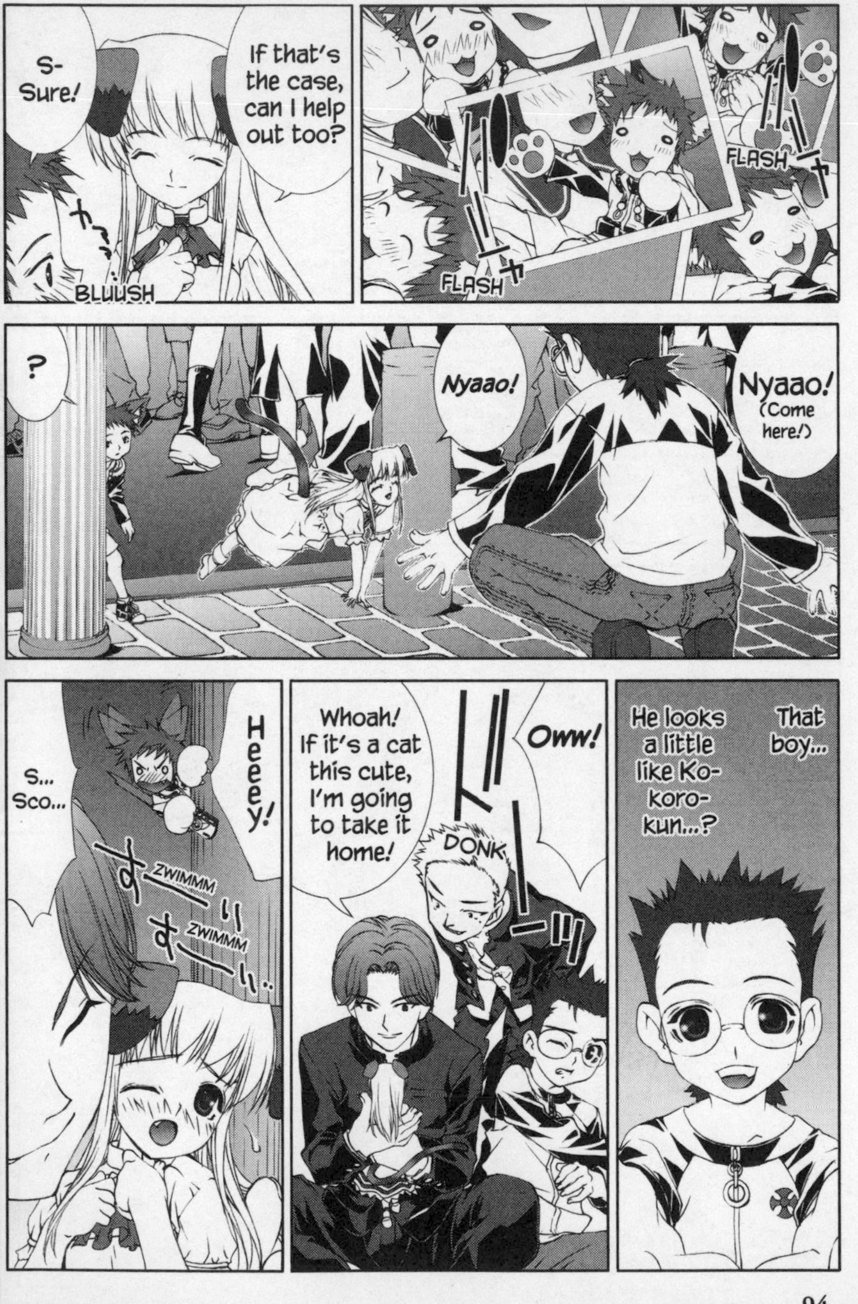
FLASH
FLASH
If that's the case, can I help out too?
S- Sure!
BLUUSH
Nyaao! (Come here!)
Nyaao!
?
That boy...
He looks a little like Ko-koro-kun...?
Oww!
DONK
Whoah! If it's a cat this cute, I'm going to take it home!
Heeeey!
S... Sco...
ZWIMMM
ZWIMMM

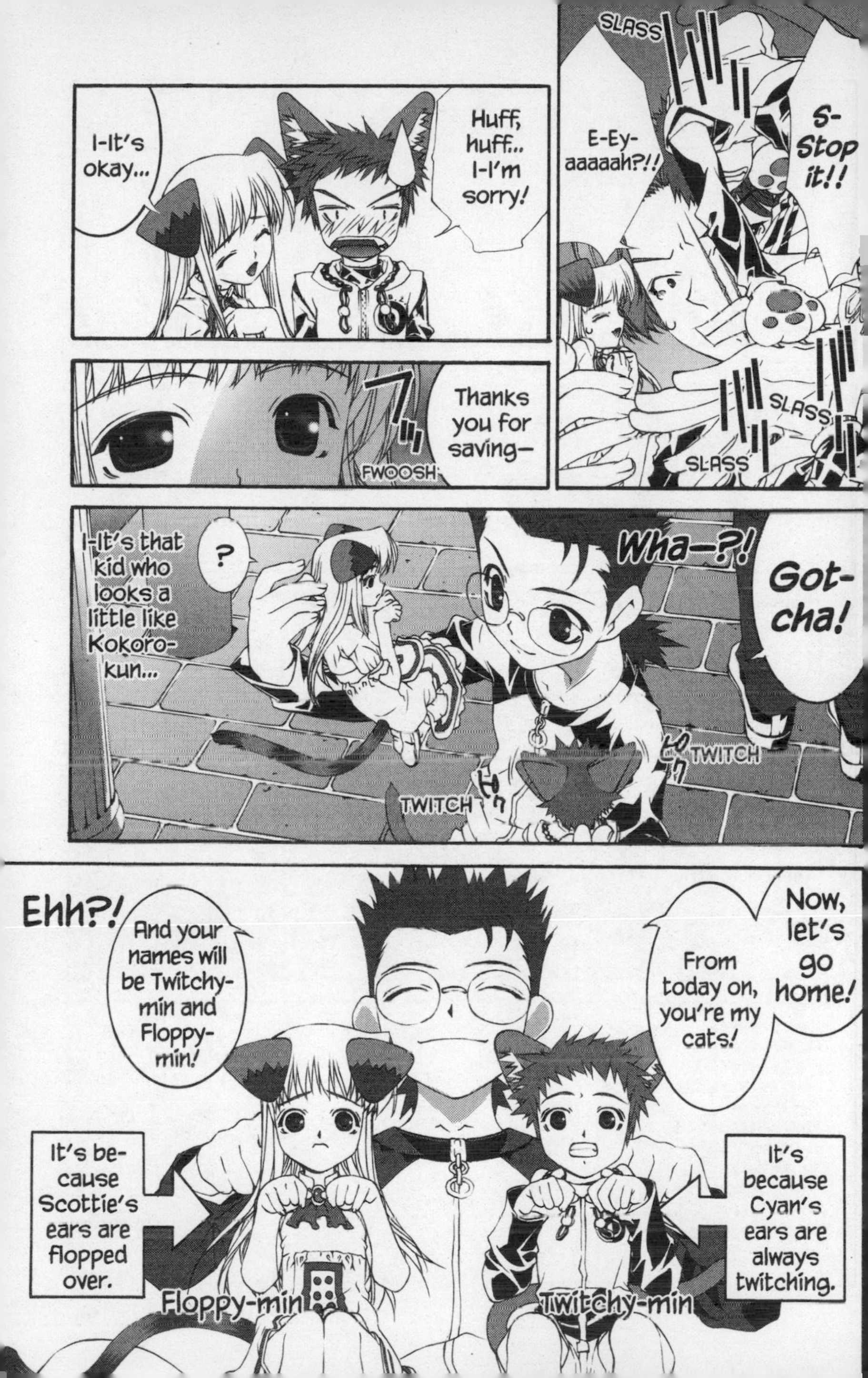
SLASS
S-Stop it!!
E-Ey-aaaaah?!!
SLASS
SLASS
Huff, huff... I-I'm sorry!
I-It's okay...
Thanks you for saving—
FWOOSH
Got-cha!
Wha—?!
?
I-It's that kid who looks a little like Kokoro-kun...
TWITCH
TWITCH
Now, let's go home!
From today on, you're my cats!
And your names will be Twitchy-min and Floppy-min!
Ehh?!
It's because Cyan's ears are always twitching.
Twitchy-min
It's because Scottie's ears are flopped over.
Floppy-min

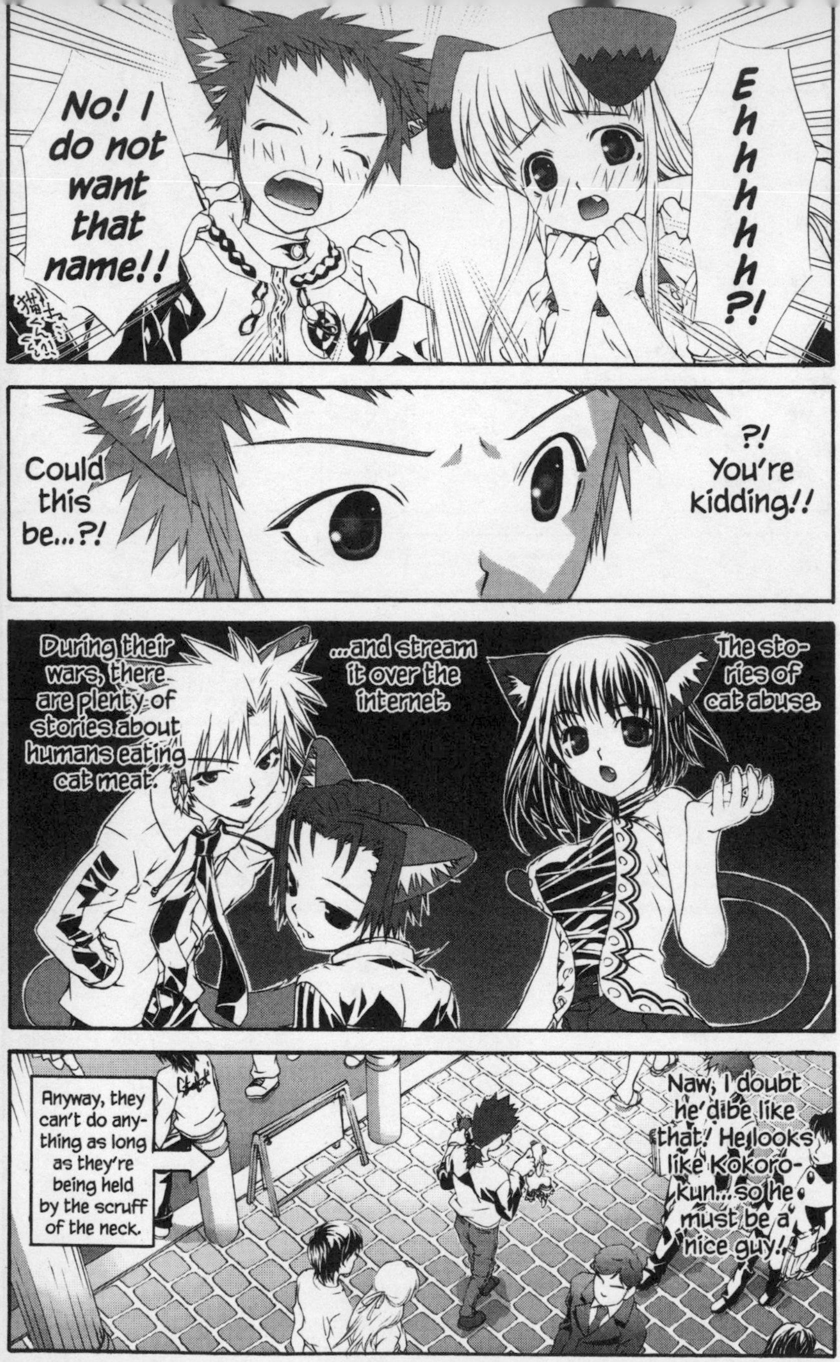
Ehhhhhh?!
No! I do not want that name!!
?! You're kidding!!
Could this be...?!
The sto-ries of cat abuse.
...and stream it over the internet.
During their wars, there are plenty of stories about humans eating cat meat.
Naw, I doubt he dibe like that! He looks like Kokoro-kun... so he must be a nice guy!
Anyway, they can't do any-thing as long as they're being held by the scruff of the neck.

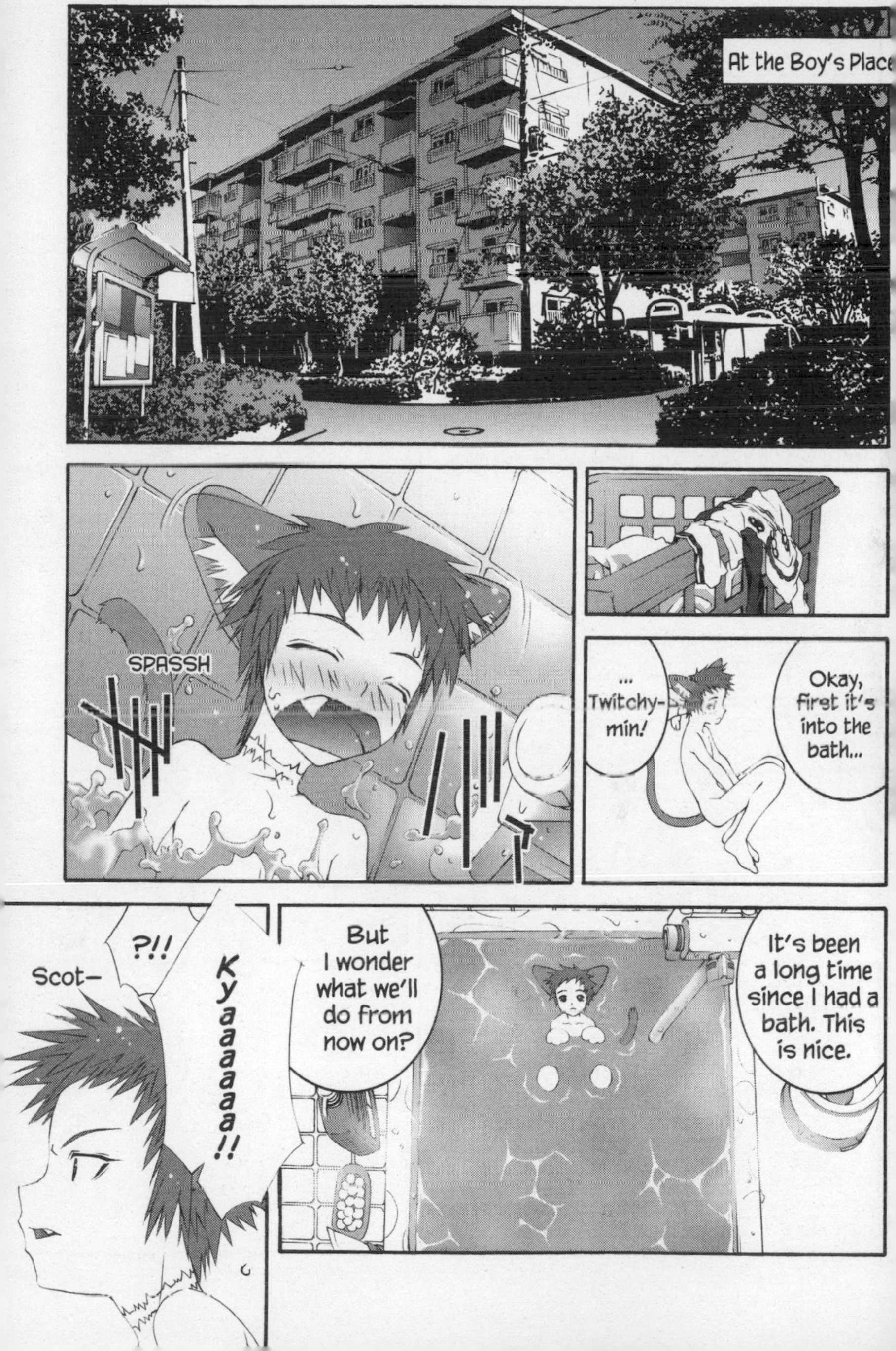

At the Boy's Place
Okay, first it's into the bath...
... Twitchy-min!
SPASSH
It's been a long time since I had a bath. This is nice.
But I wonder what we'll do from now on?
Kyaaaaaaa!!
?!!
Scot–

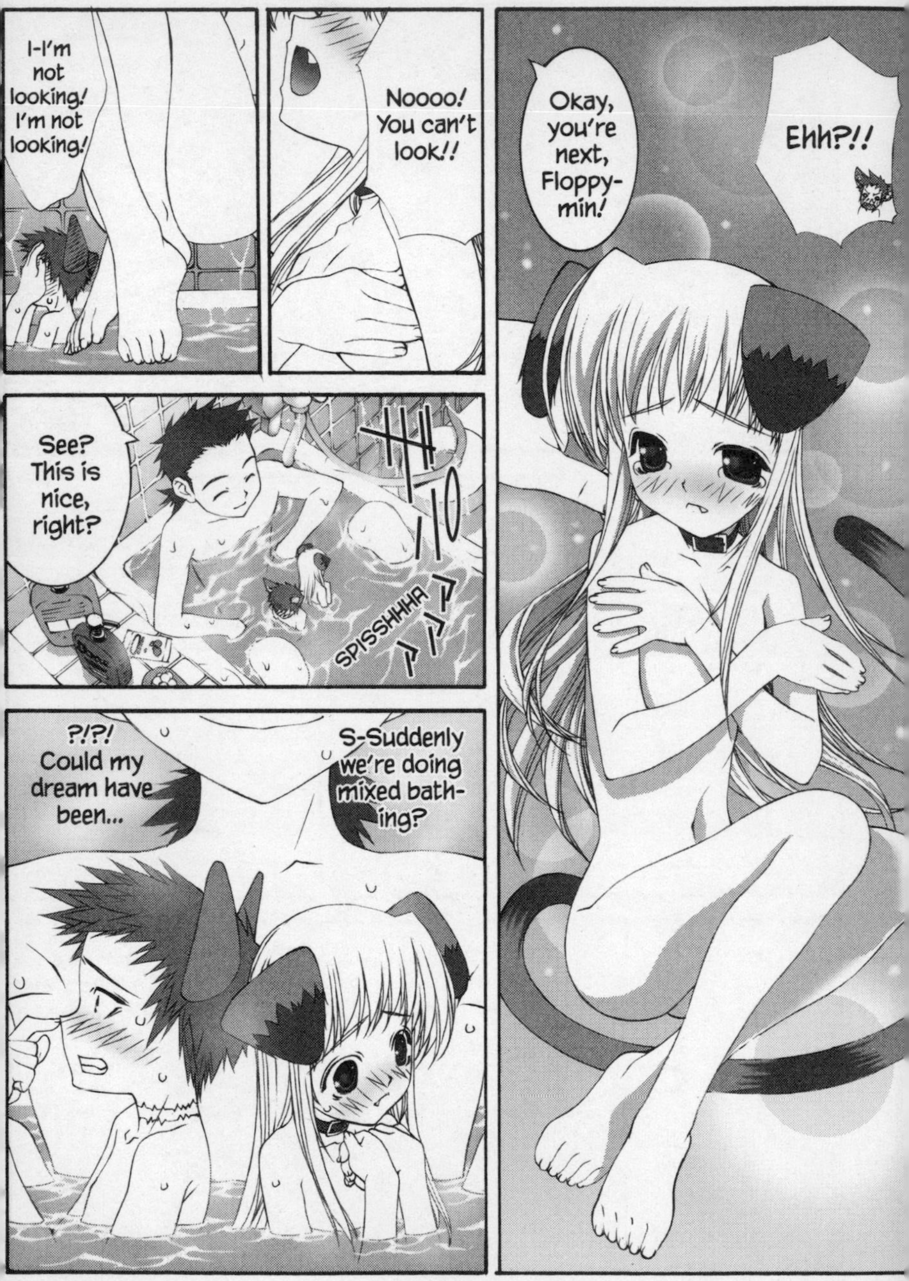
Okay, you're next, Floppy-min!
Ehh?!!
Noooo! You can't look!!
I-I'm not looking! I'm not looking!
See? This is nice, right?
SPISSHHHA
S-Suddenly we're doing mixed bath-ing?
?!?! Could my dream have been...

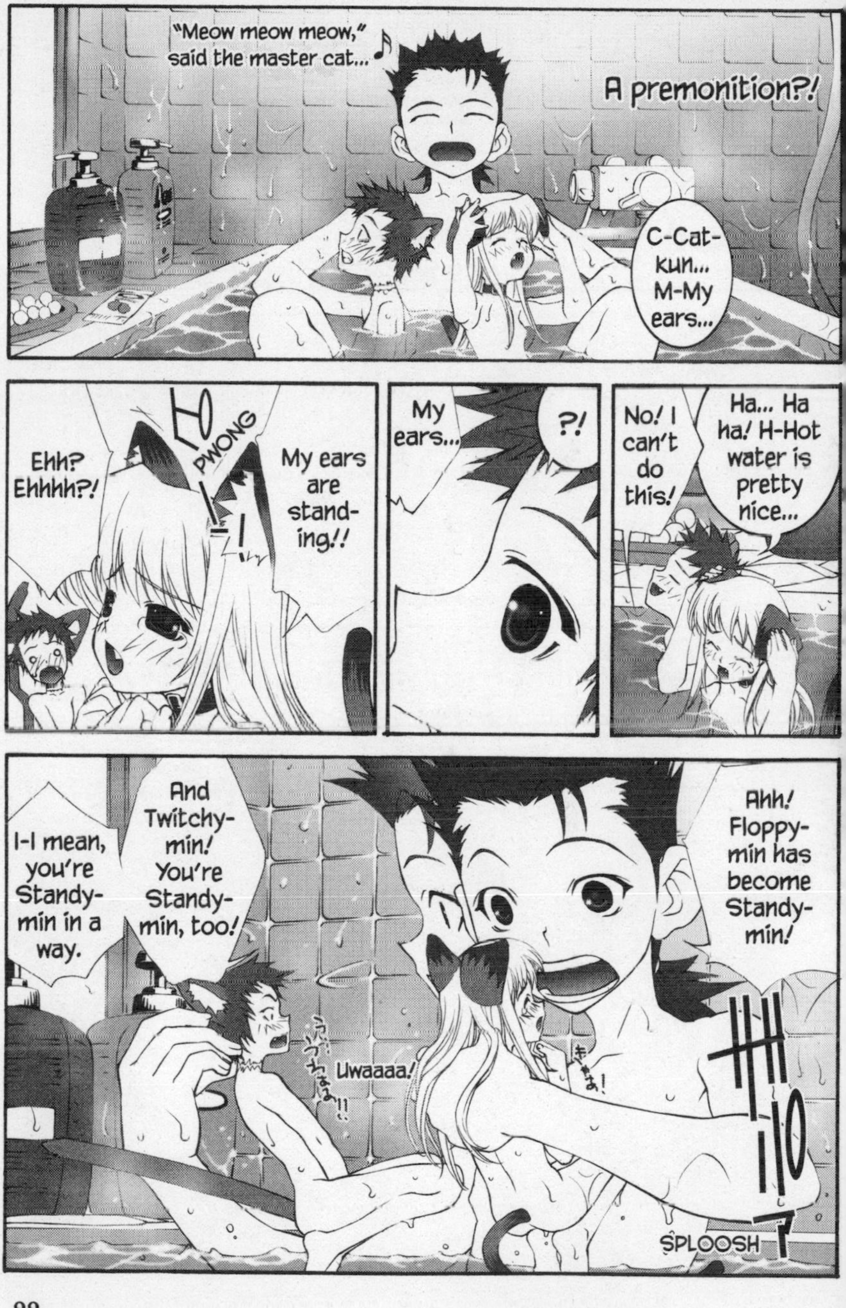
"Meow meow meow," said the master cat... ♪
A premonition?!
C-Cat-kun... M-My ears...
Ha... Ha ha! H-Hot water is pretty nice...
No! I can't do this!
?!
My ears...
My ears are standing!!
PWONG
Ehh? Ehhhh?!
Ahh! Floppy-min has become Standy-min!
SPLOOSH
Uwaaaa!
And Twitchy-min! You're Standy-min, too!
I-I mean, you're Standy-min in a way.

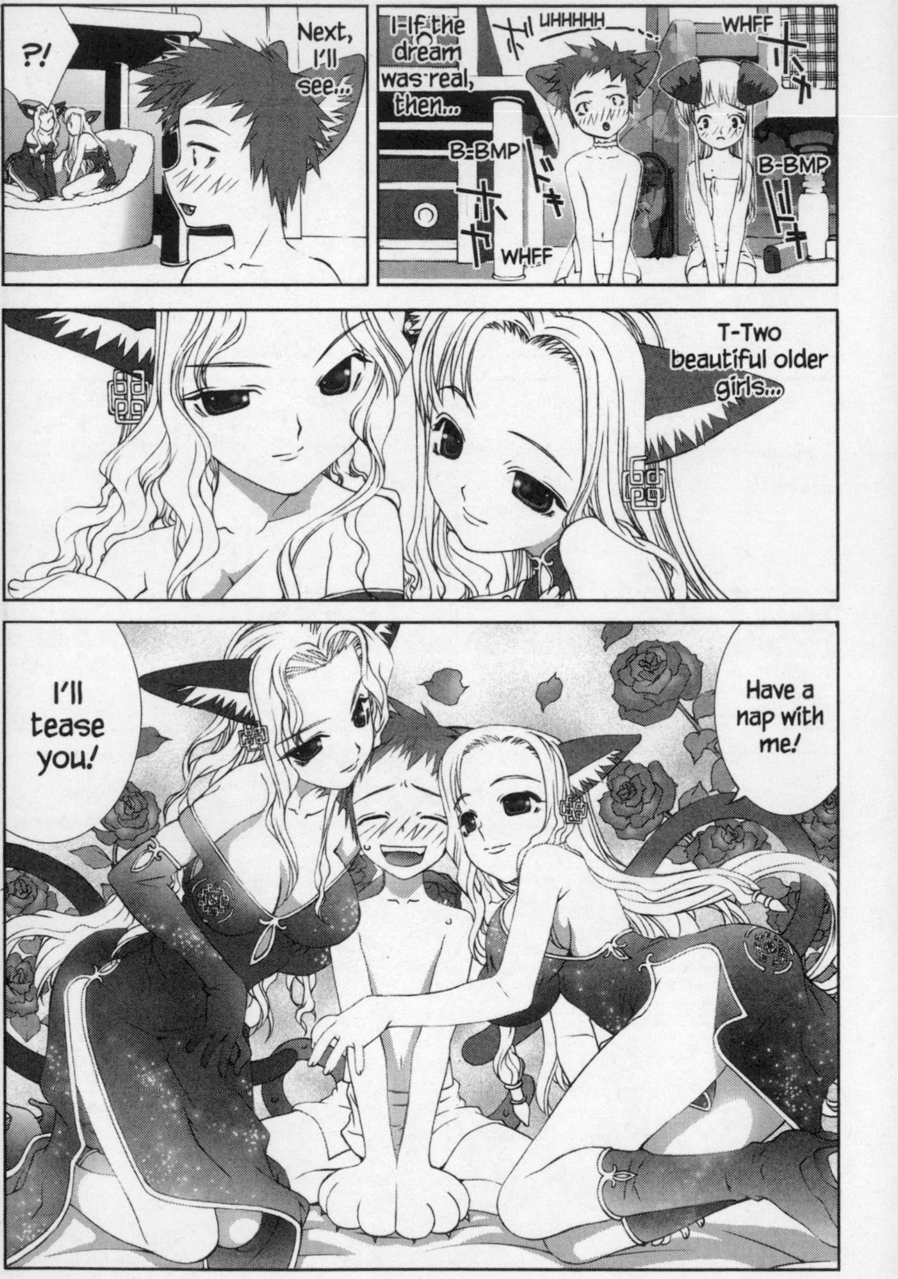
I-If the dream was real, then...
UHHHHH___...
WHFF
B-BMP
B-BMP
WHFF
Next, I'll see...
?!
T-Two beautiful older girls...
Have a nap with me!
I'll tease you!

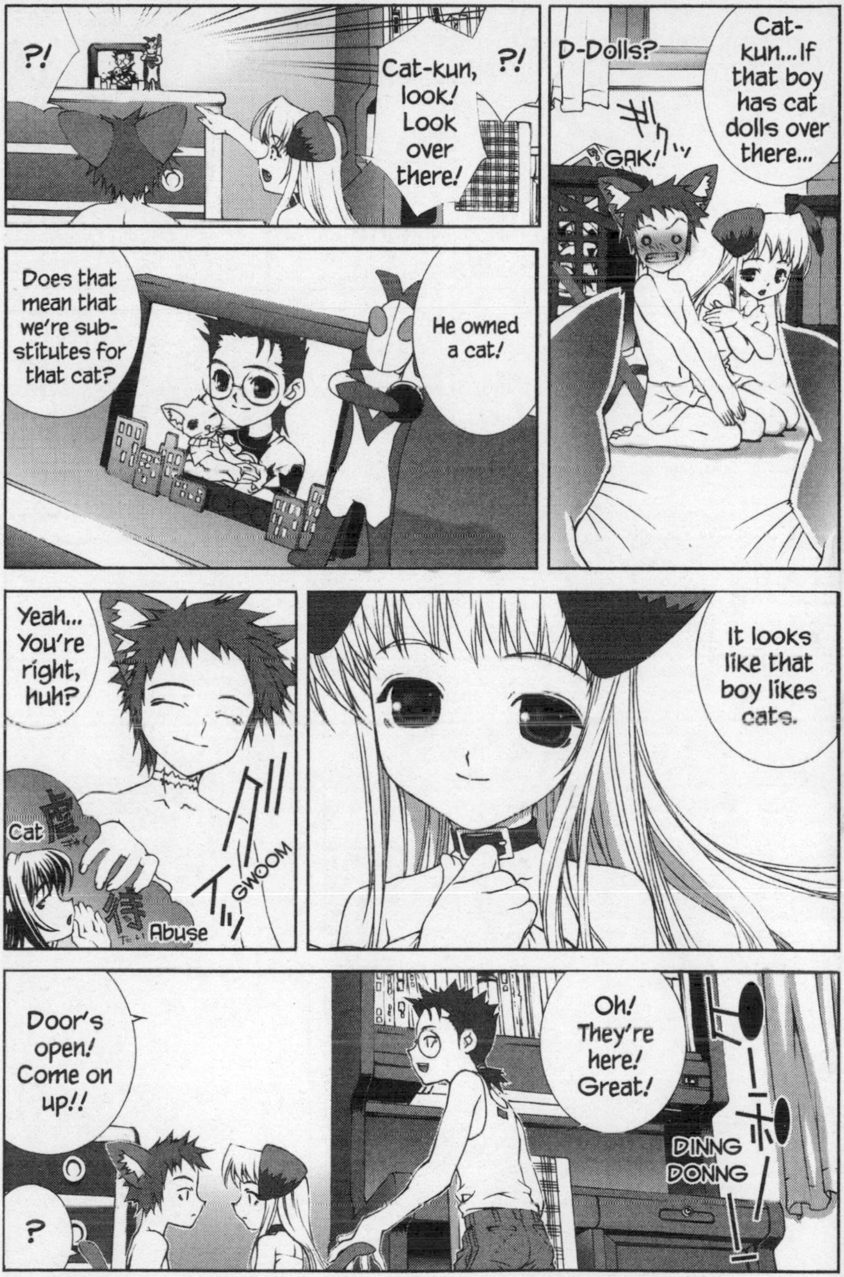
Cat-kun...If that boy has cat dolls over there...
D-Dolls?
GAK!
?!
Cat-kun, look! Look over there!
?!
He owned a cat!
Does that mean that we're substitutes for that cat?
It looks like that boy likes cats.
Yeah... You're right, huh?
GWOOM
Cat
Abuse
DINNG DONNG
Oh! They're here! Great!
Door's open! Come on up!!
?

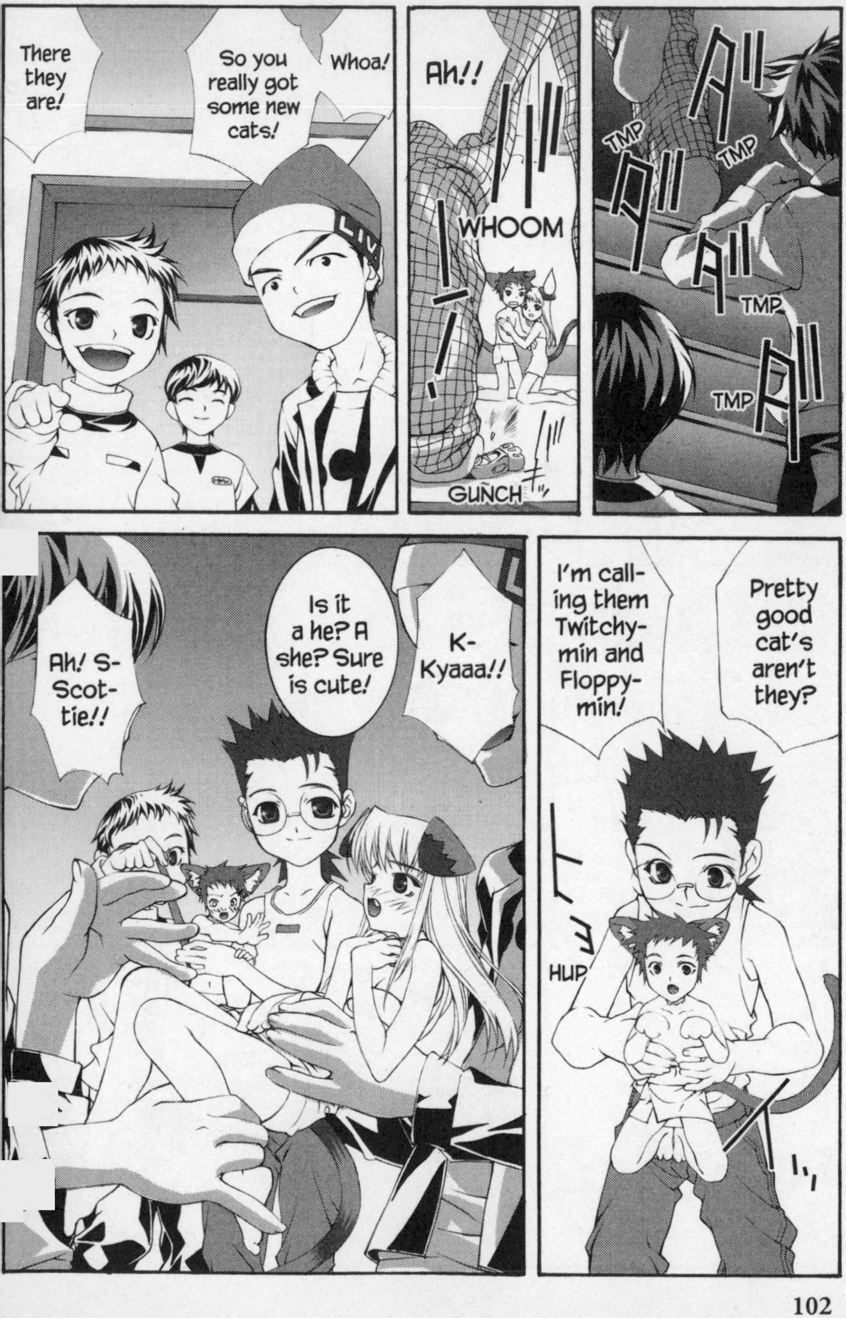
TMP
TMP
TMP
TMP
Ah!!
WHOOM
GUNCH
Whoa!
So you really got some new cats!
There they are!
Pretty good cat's aren't they?
I'm calling them Twitchy-min and Floppy-min!
HUP
K-Kyaaa!!
Is it a he? A she? Sure is cute!
Ah! S-Scottie!!

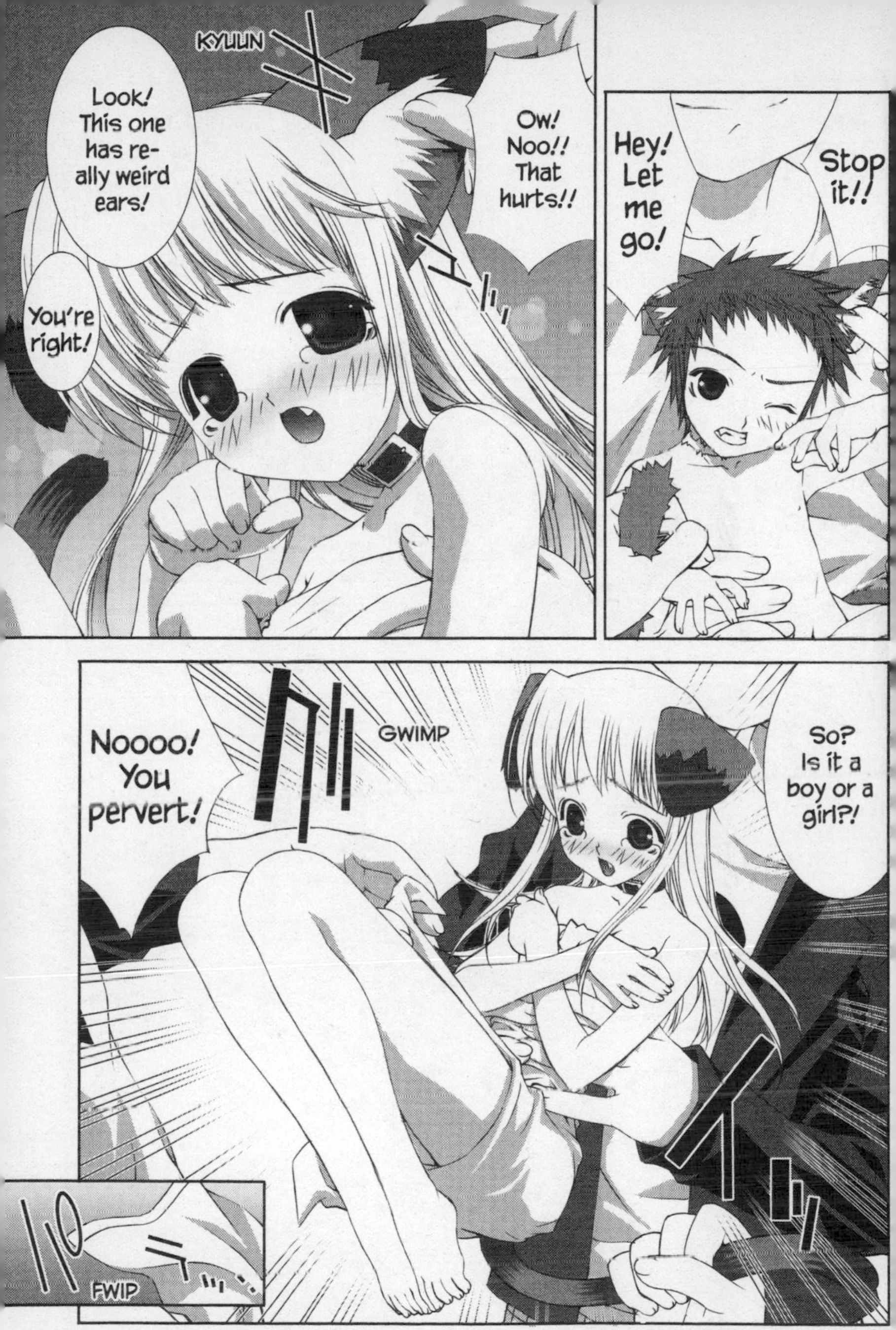
Stop it!!
Hey! Let me go!
KYUUN
Ow! Noo!! That hurts!!
Look! This one has re-ally weird ears!
You're right!
So? Is it a boy or a girl?!
GWIMP
Noooo! You pervert!
FWIP

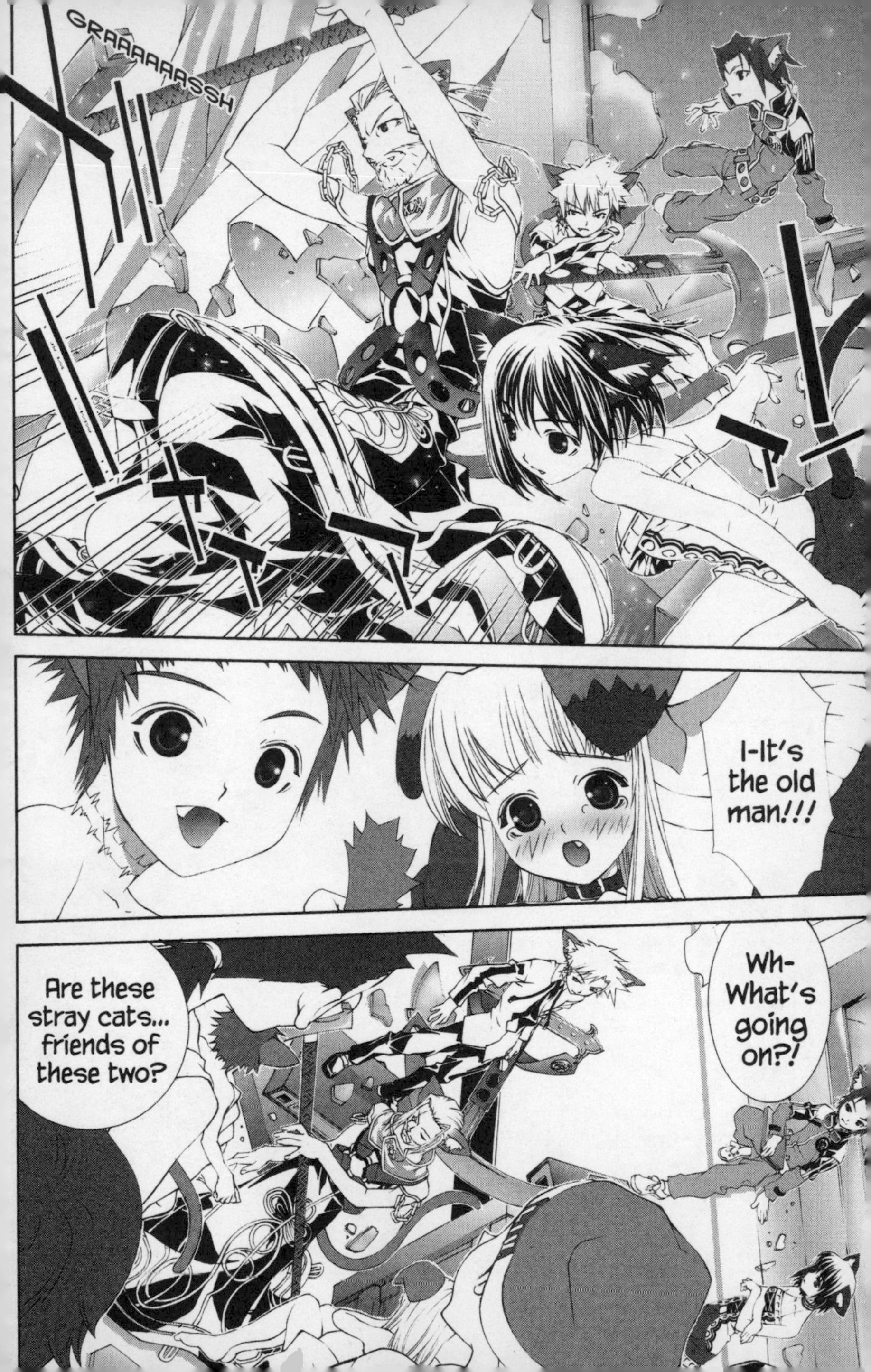
GRAAAAAAASSH
I-It's the old man!!!
Wh- What's going on?!
Are these stray cats... friends of these two?

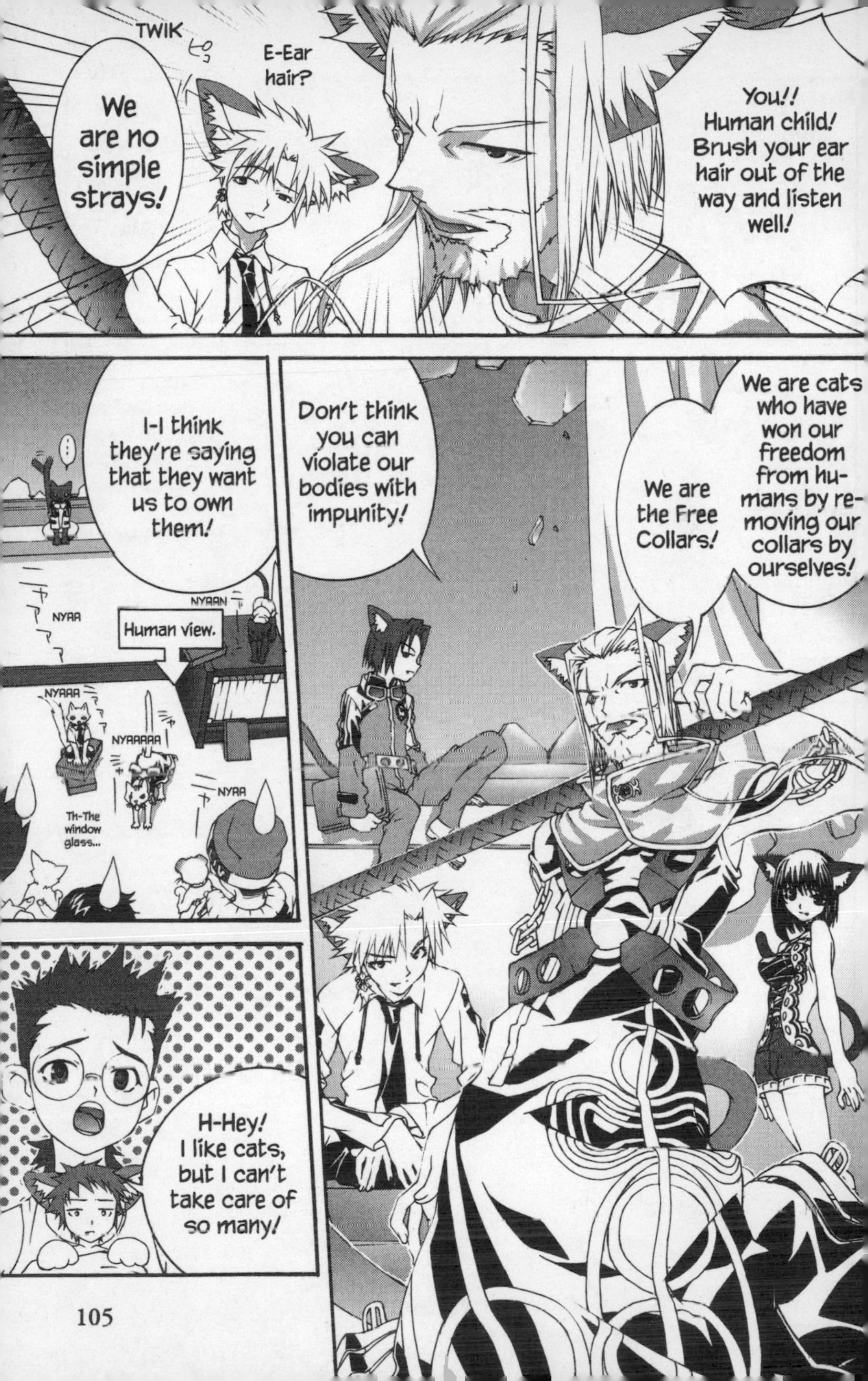
You!! Human child! Brush your ear hair out of the way and listen well!
E-Ear hair?
TWIK
We are no simple strays!
We are cats who have won our freedom from humans by removing our collars by ourselves!
We are the Free Collars!
Don't think you can violate our bodies with impunity!
I-I think they're saying that they want us to own them!
NYAAN
Human view.
NYAA
NYAAA
NYAAAAA
NYAA
Th-The window glass...
H-Hey! I like cats, but I can't take care of so many!

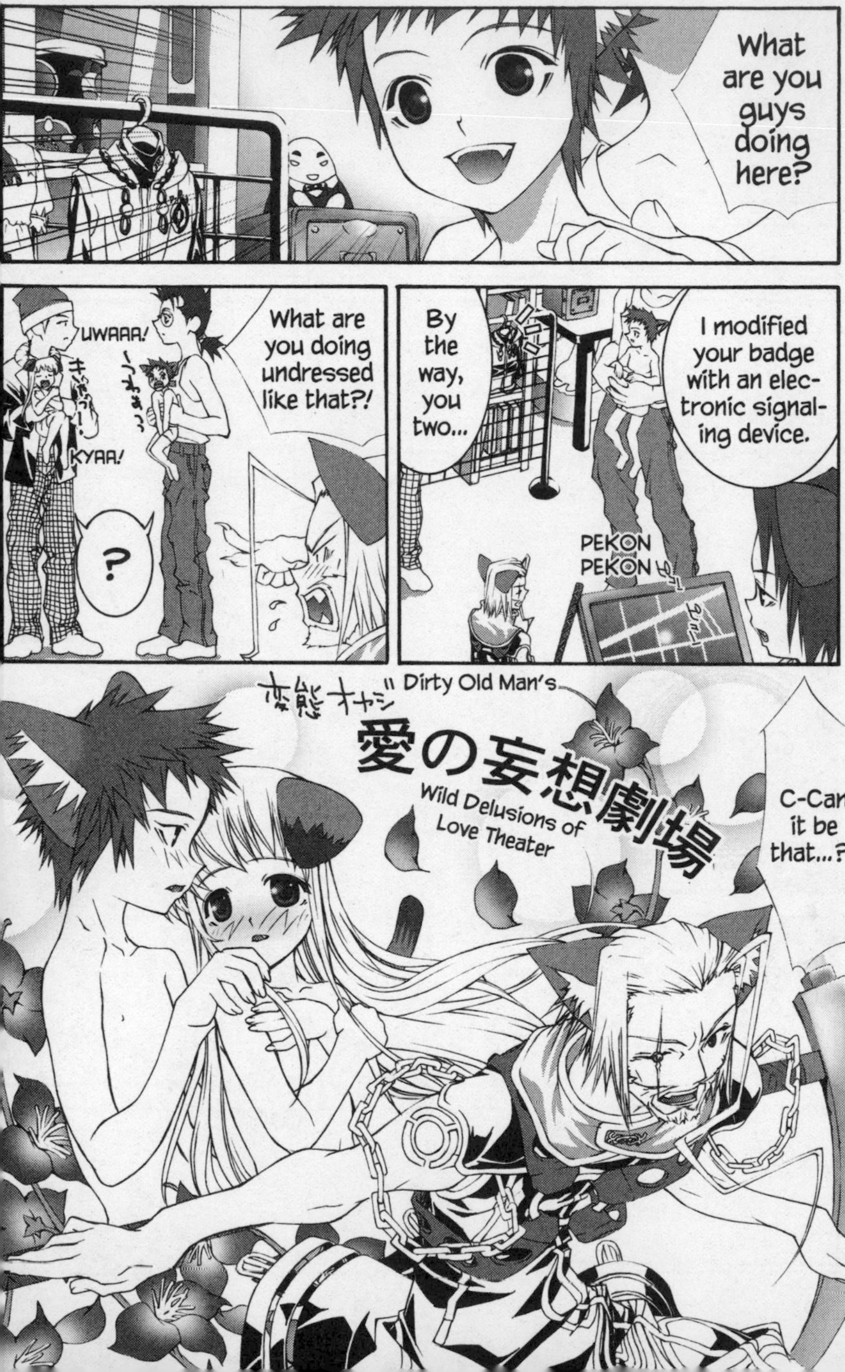

What are you guys doing here?
I modified your badge with an electronic signaling device.
By the way, you two...
PEKON PEKON
What are you doing undressed like that?!
UWAAA!
KYAA!
?
C-Can it be that...?!
変態オヤジ
Dirty Old Man's
愛の妄想劇場
Wild Delusions of Love Theater

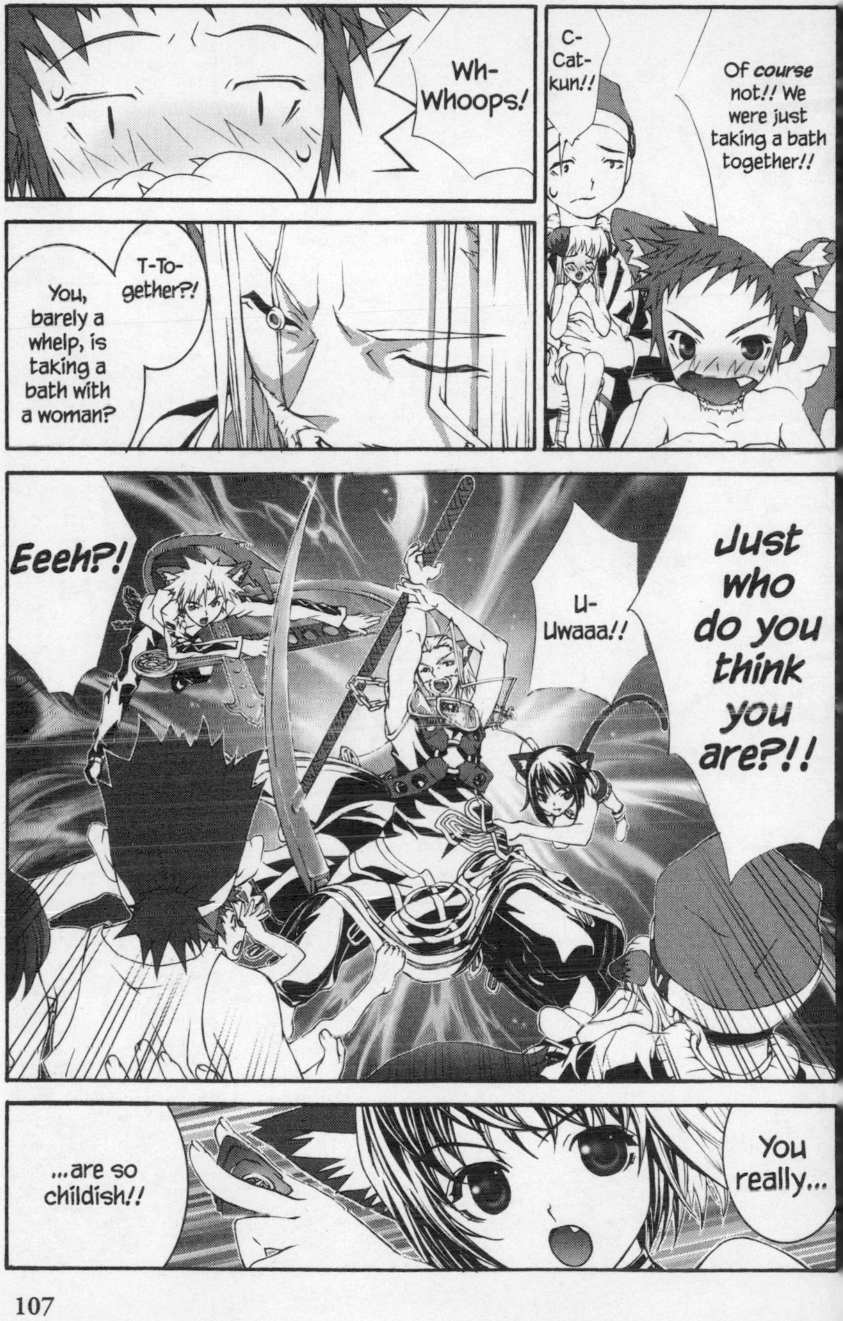
Of course not!! We were just taking a bath together!!
C-Cat-kun!!
Wh-Whoops!
T-To-gether?!
You, barely a whelp, is taking a bath with a woman?
Just who do you think you are?!!
U-Uwaaa!!
Eeeh?!
You really...
...are so childish!!

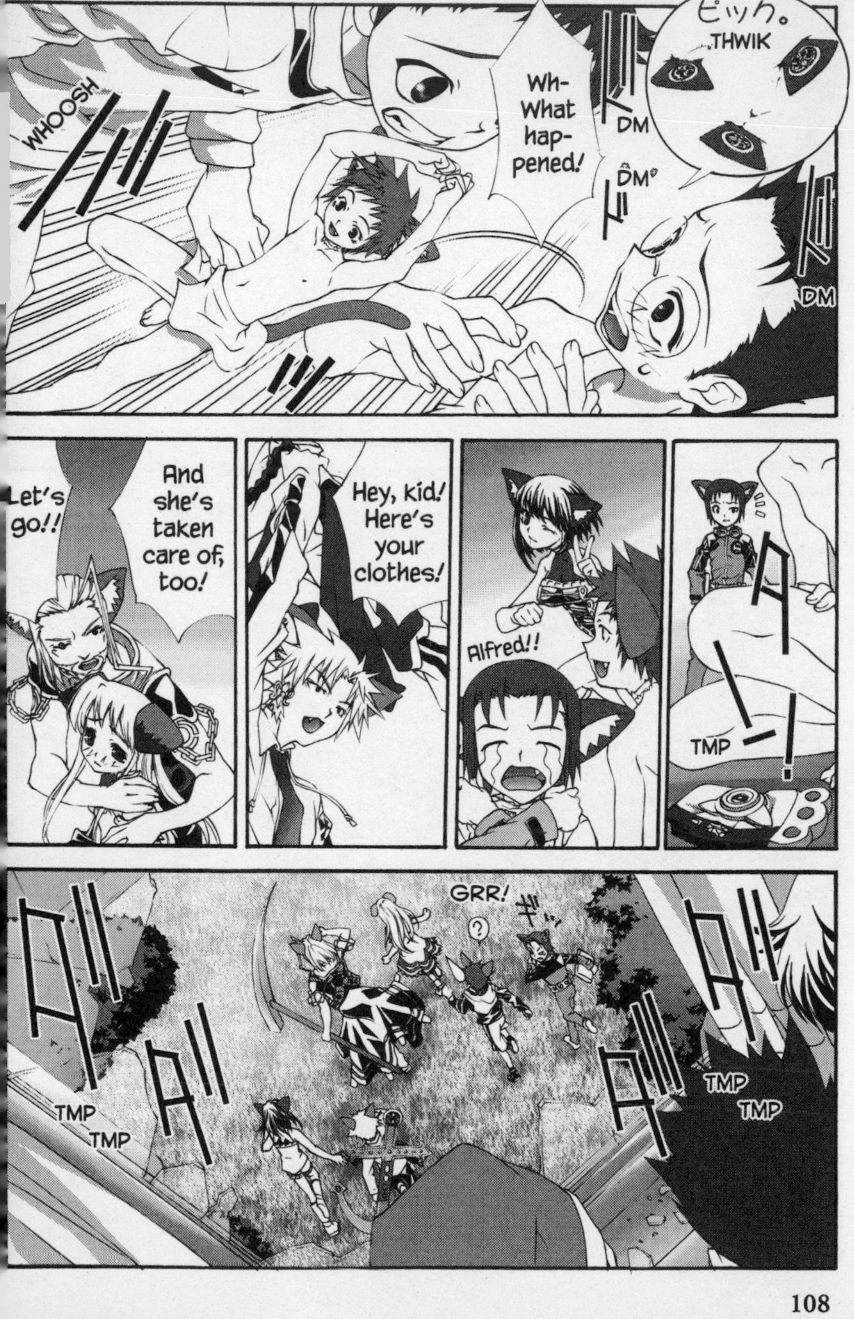

ピック。
THWIK
DM
DM
Wh- What hap- pened!
DM
WHOOSH
TMP
Alfred!!
Hey, kid! Here's your clothes!
And she's taken care of, too!
Let's go!!
GRR!
?
TMP
TMP
TMP
TMP

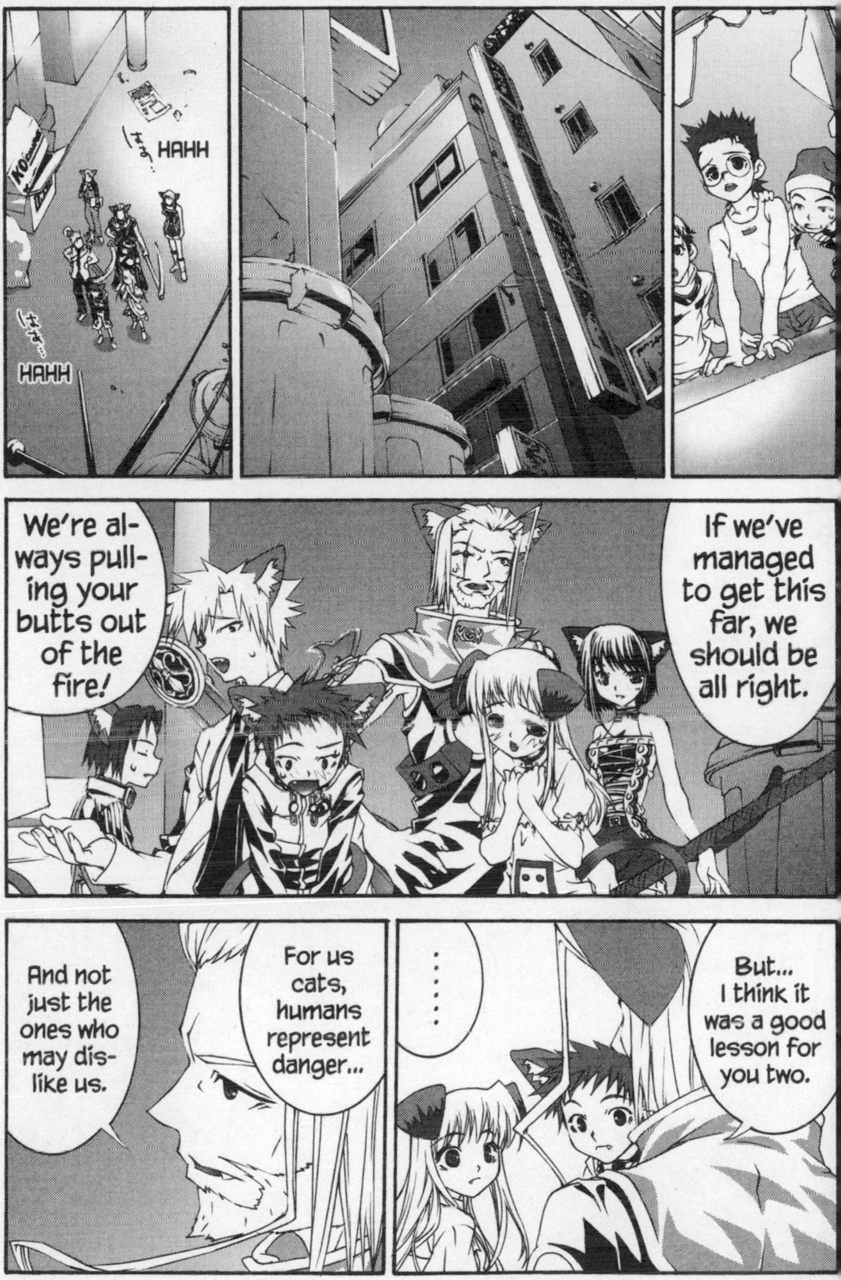
HAHH
HAHH
If we've managed to get this far, we should be all right.
We're always pulling your butts out of the fire!
But... I think it was a good lesson for you two.
......
For us cats, humans represent danger...
And not just the ones who may dislike us.

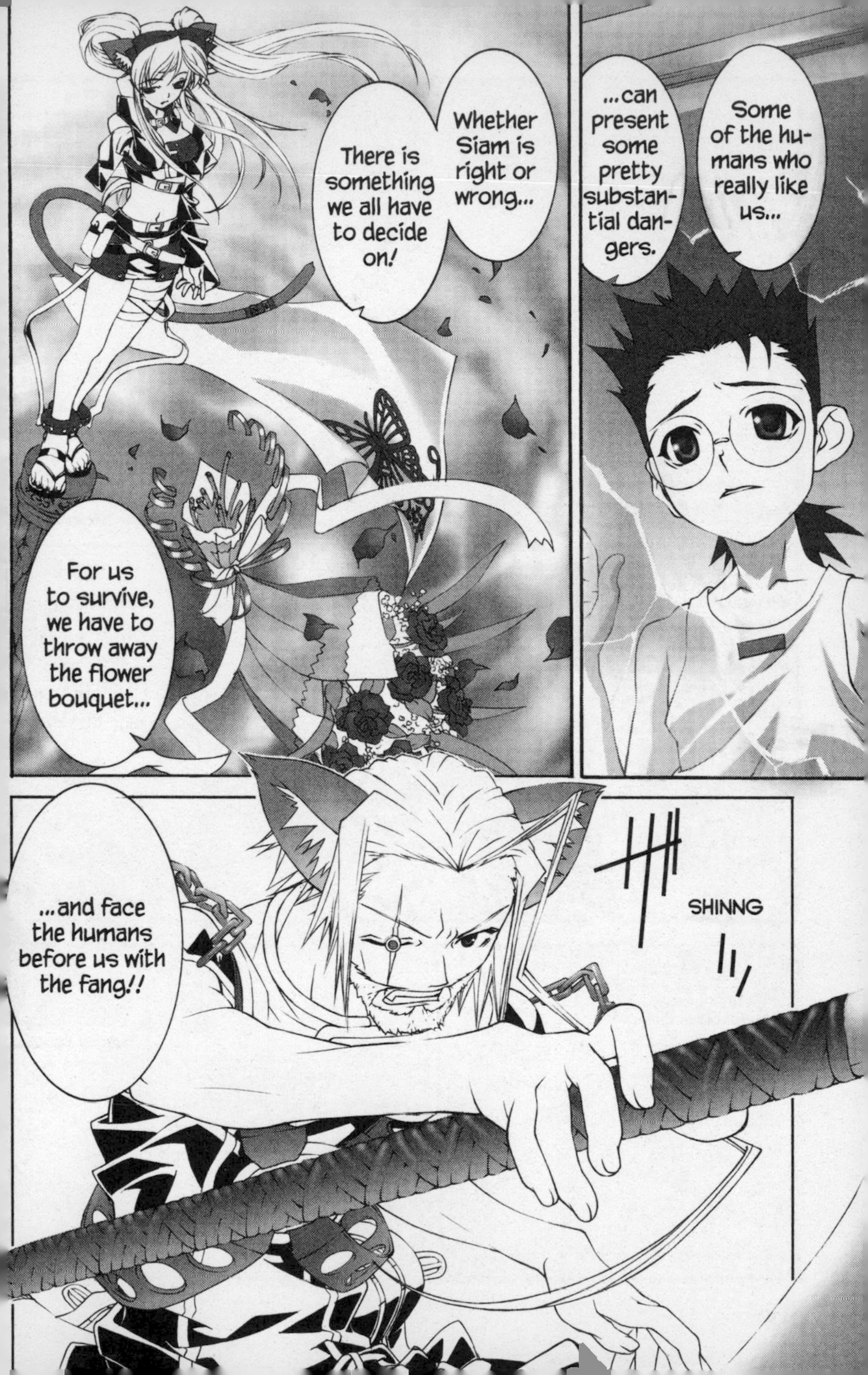
Some of the humans who really like us...
...can present some pretty substantial dangers.
Whether Siam is right or wrong...
There is something we all have to decide on!
For us to survive, we have to throw away the flower bouquet...
...and face the humans before us with the fang!!
SHINNG

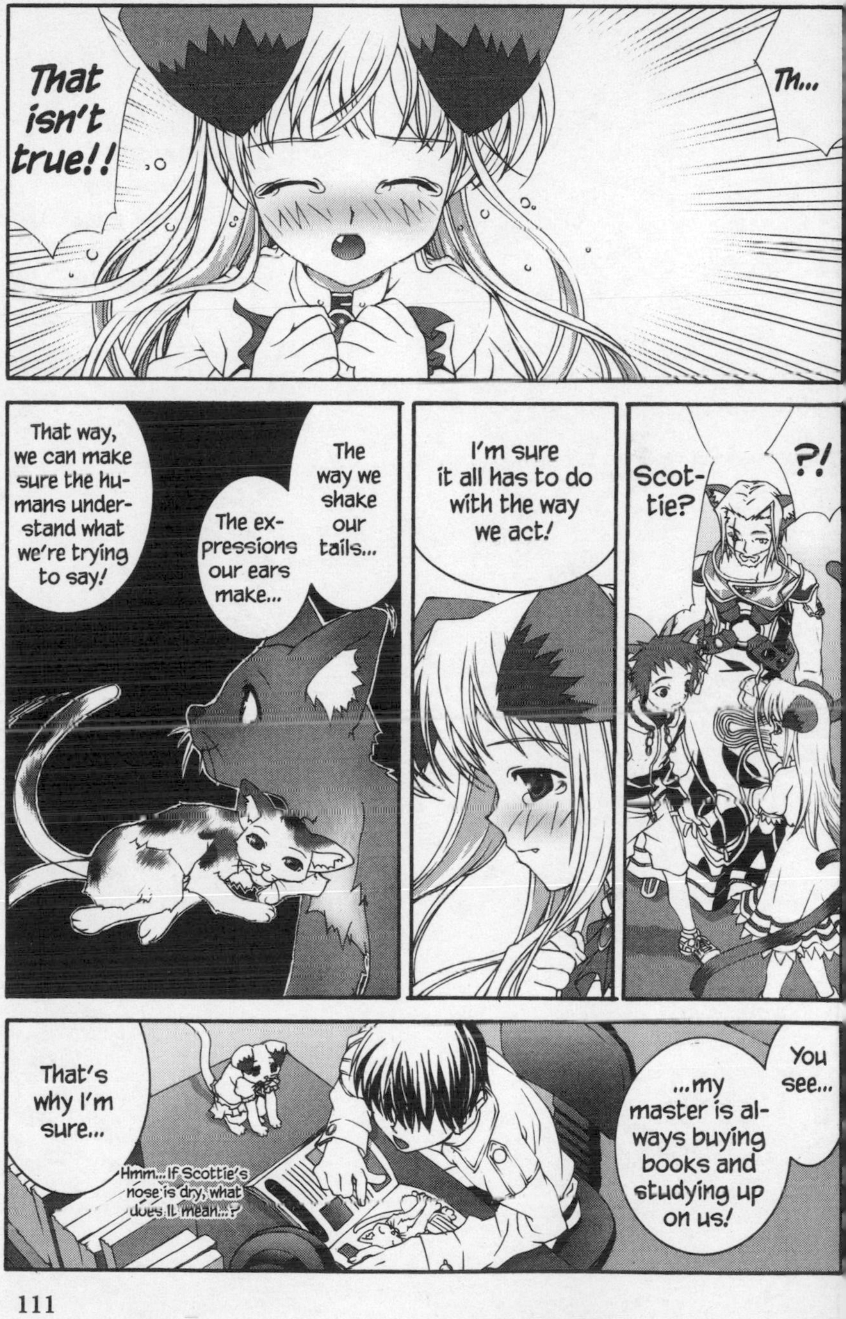
Th...
That isn't true!!
?!
Scottie?
I'm sure it all has to do with the way we act!
The way we shake our tails...
The expressions our ears make...
That way, we can make sure the humans understand what we're trying to say!
You see...
...my master is always buying books and studying up on us!
Hmm... If Scottie's nose is dry, what does it mean...?
That's why I'm sure...

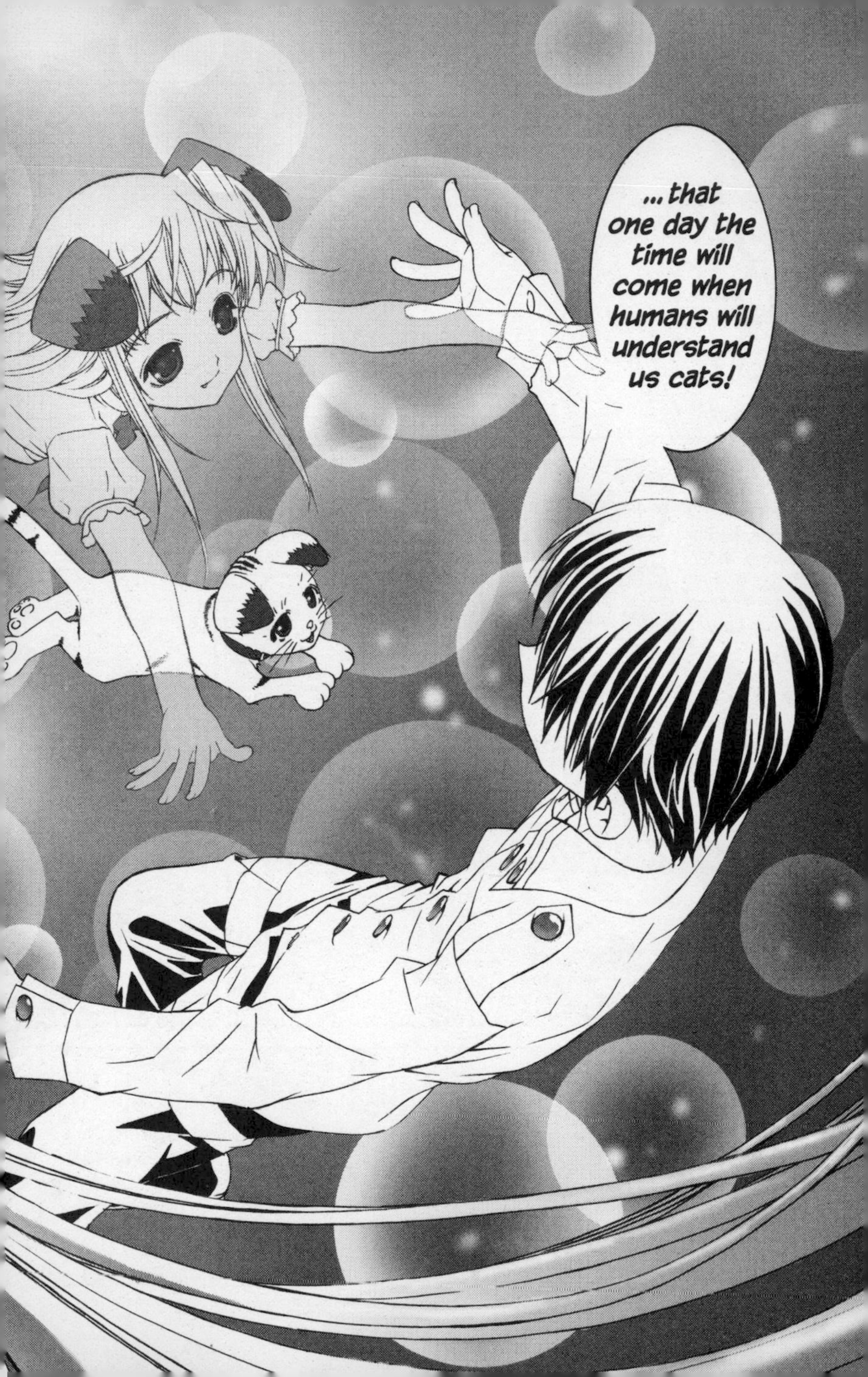
...that one day the time will come when humans will understand us cats!

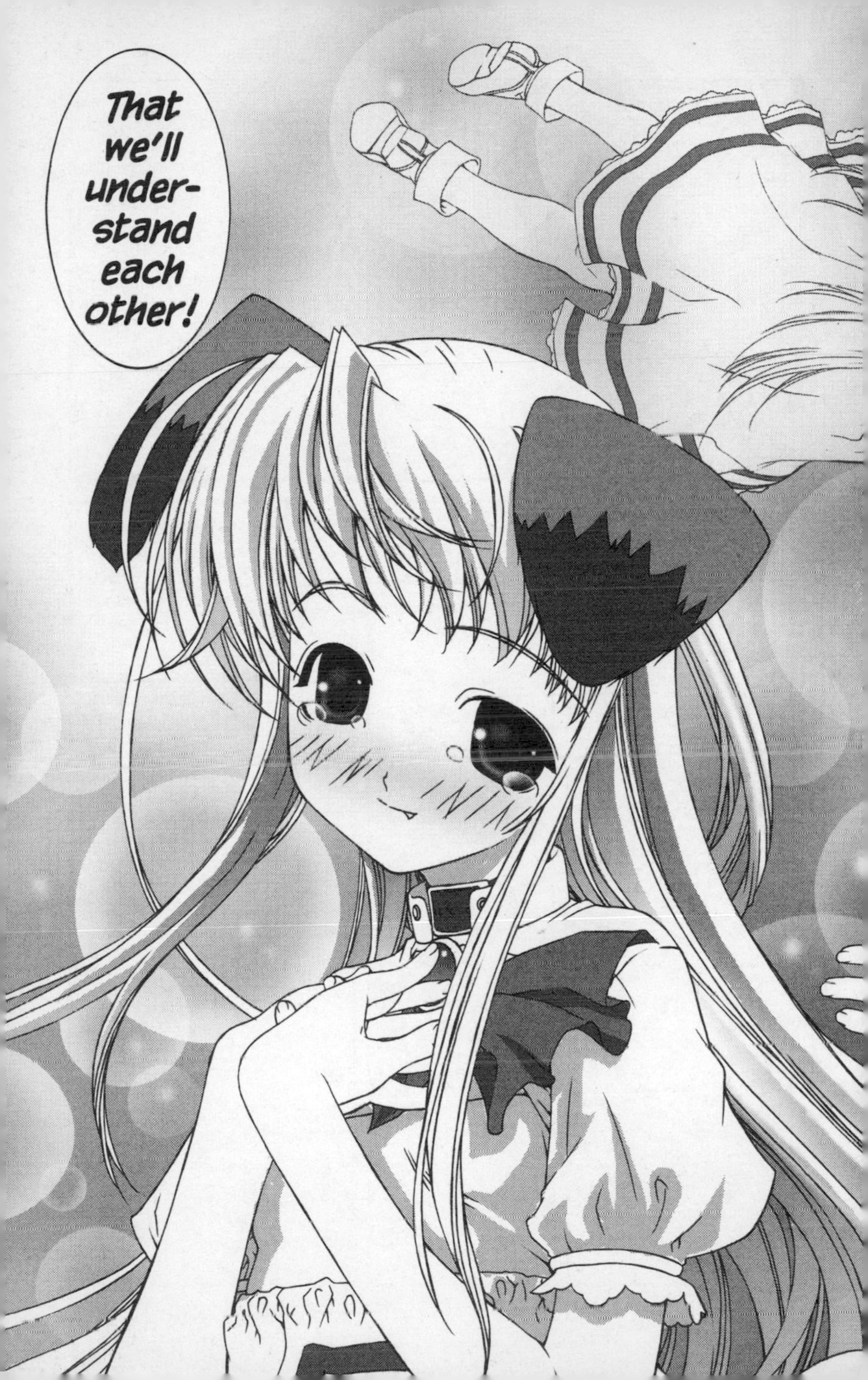
That we'll understand each other!

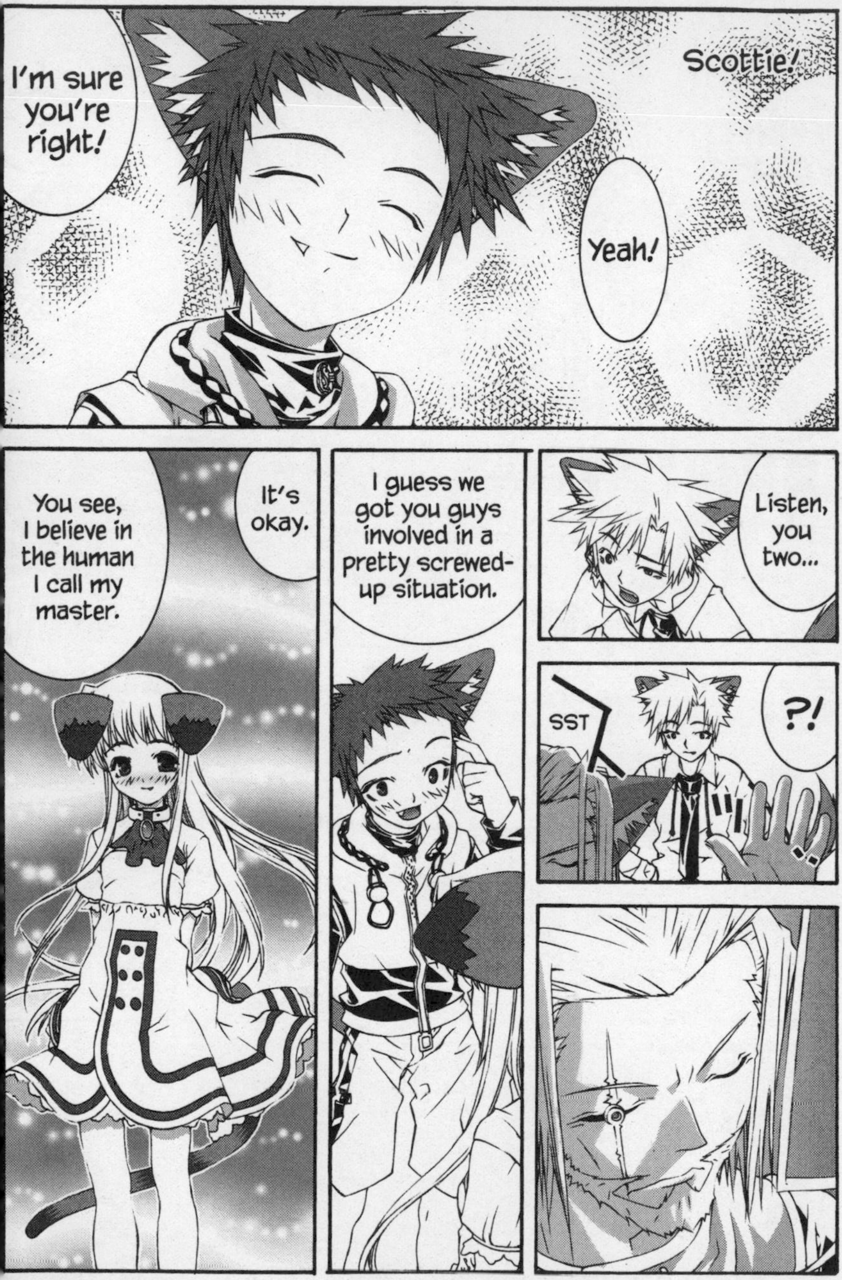
Scottie!
Yeah!
I'm sure you're right!
Listen, you two...
?!
SST
I guess we got you guys involved in a pretty screwed-up situation.
It's okay.
You see, I believe in the human I call my master.

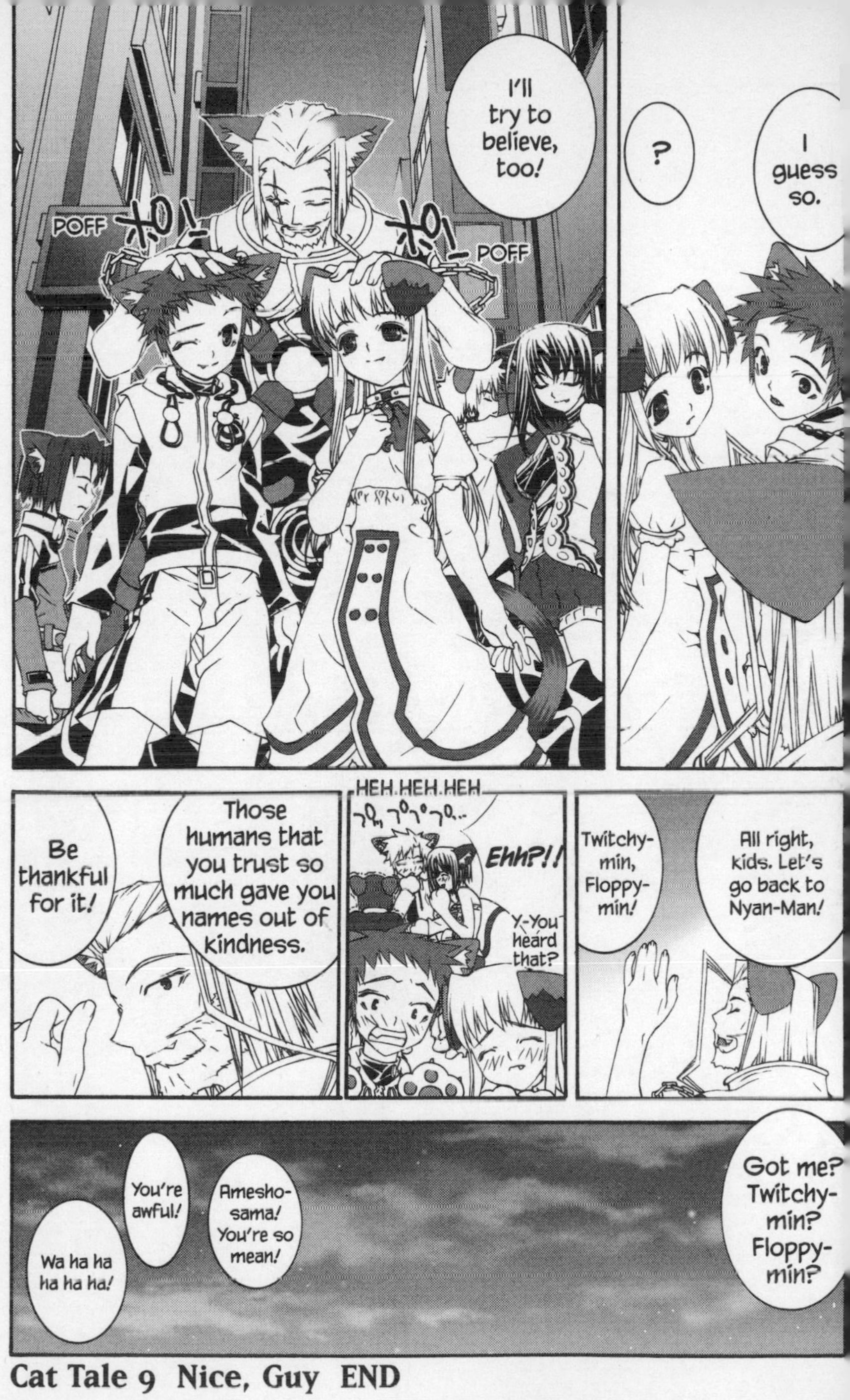
I guess so.
?
I'll try to believe, too!
POFF
POFF
All right, kids. Let's go back to Nyan-Man!
Twitchy-min, Floppy-min!
HEH HEH HEH
Ehh?!!
Y-You heard that?
Those humans that you trust so much gave you names out of kindness.
Be thankful for it!
Got me? Twitchy-min? Floppy-min?
Ameshosama! You're so mean!
You're awful!
Wa ha ha ha ha!

Cat Tale 9 Nice, Guy END

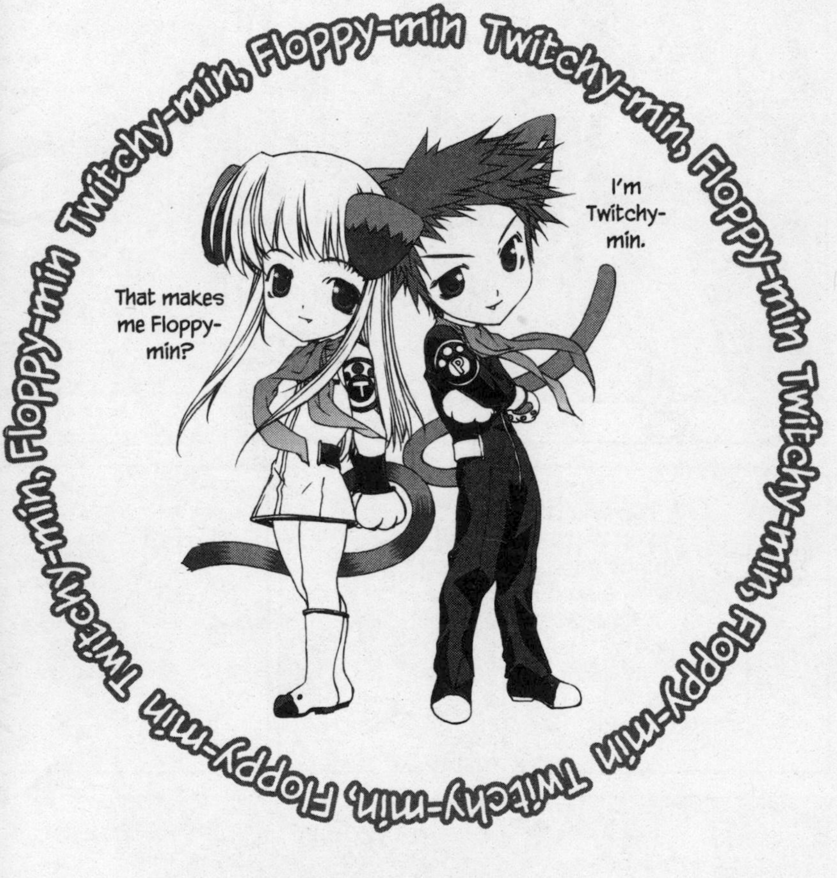
Twitchy-min, Floppy-min Twitchy-min, Floppy-min Twitchy-min, Floppy-min Twitchy-min, Floppy-min Twitchy-min, Floppy-min
I'm Twitchy-min.
That makes me Floppy-min?

Cat Tale 10 Round & Round, Fate Goes Around

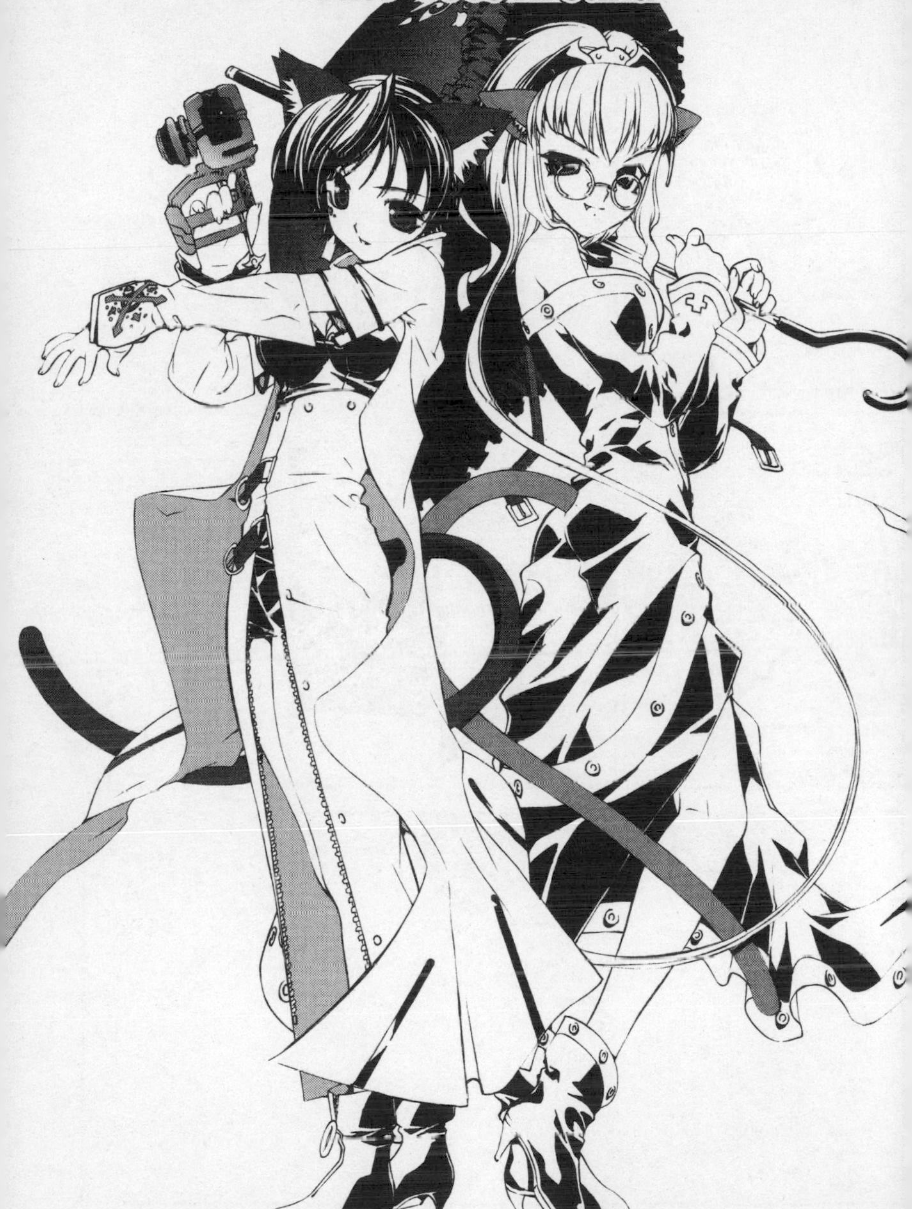

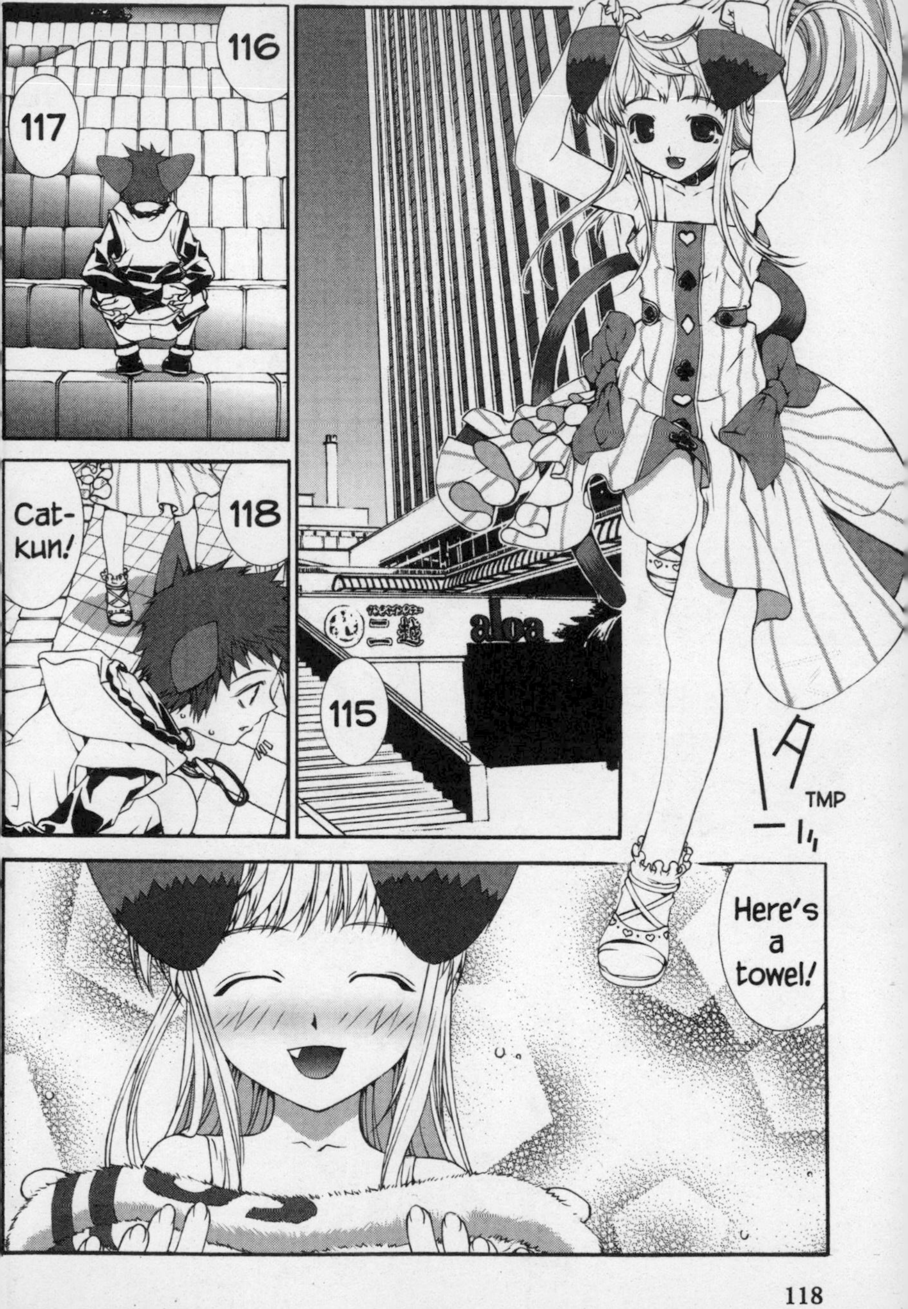
115
116
117
118
Cat-kun!
TMP
Here's a towel!

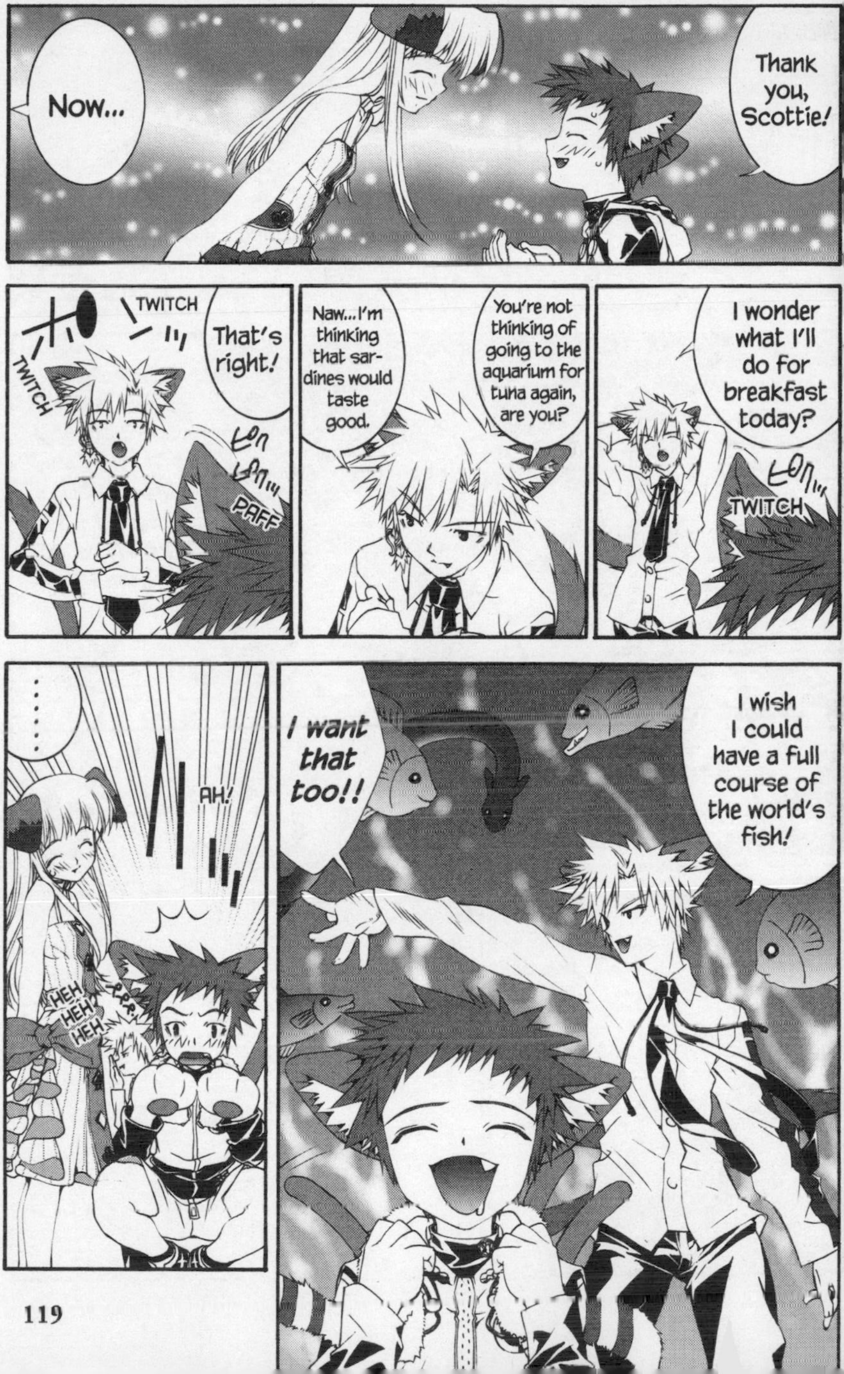
Thank you, Scottie!
Now...
I wonder what I'll do for breakfast today?
TWITCH
You're not thinking of going to the aquarium for tuna again, are you?
Naw...I'm thinking that sardines would taste good.
That's right!
TWITCH
TWITCH
PAFF
I wish I could have a full course of the world's fish!
I want that too!!
......
AH!
RRR!
HEH HEH HEH

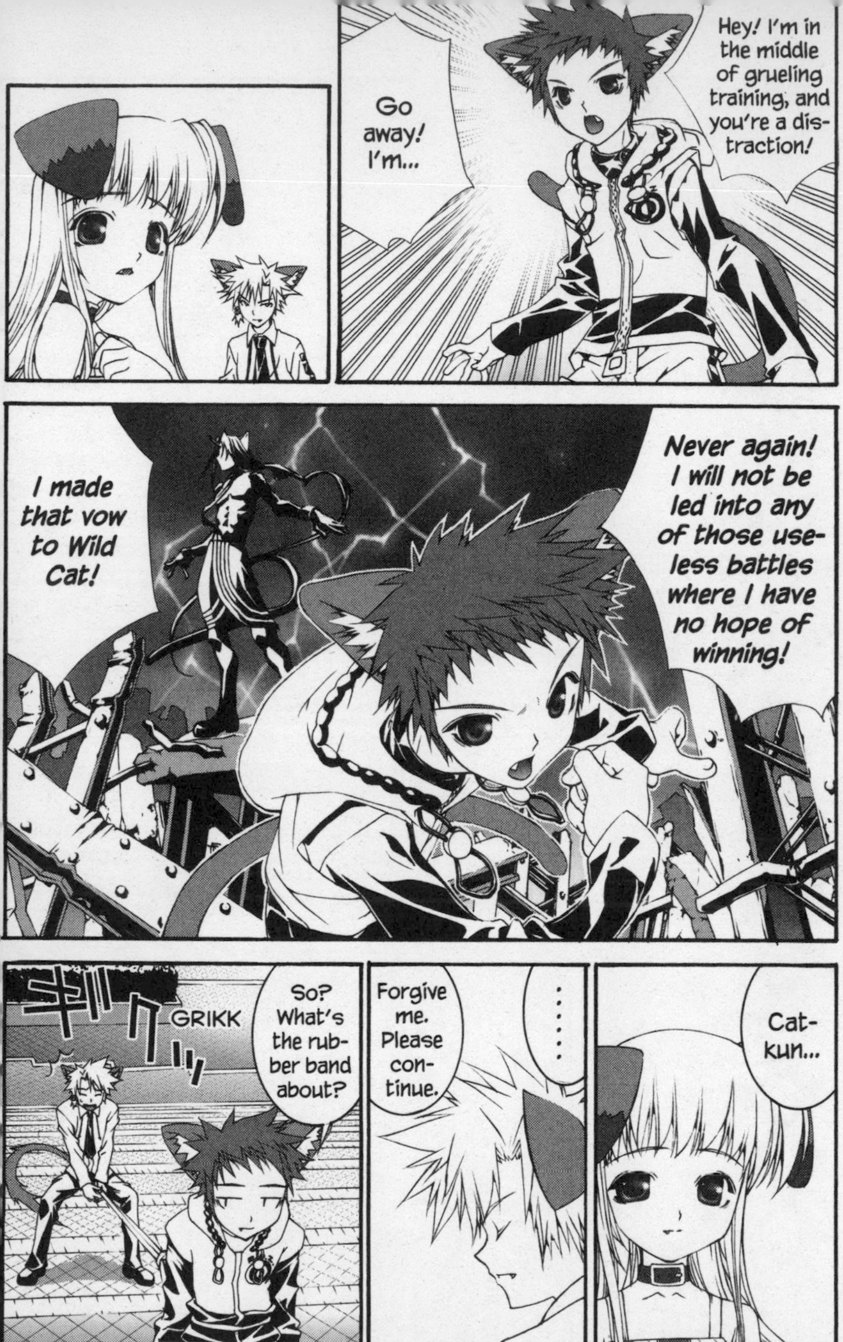
Hey! I'm in the middle of grueling training, and you're a distraction!
Go away! I'm...
Never again! I will not be led into any of those useless battles where I have no hope of winning!
I made that vow to Wild Cat!
Cat-kun...
......
Forgive me. Please continue.
So? What's the rubber band about?
GRIKK

You liar!

GWIM

GWIM

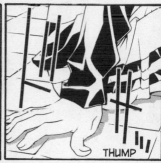

I attached it so you can build up your knee strength.

Here.

Okay, okay.

FWIP

VSSH

THUMP

Ah!

Oh, shut up!!!

FLAPPA

FLAPPA

Good idea! Let's go to that revolving sushi restaurant!

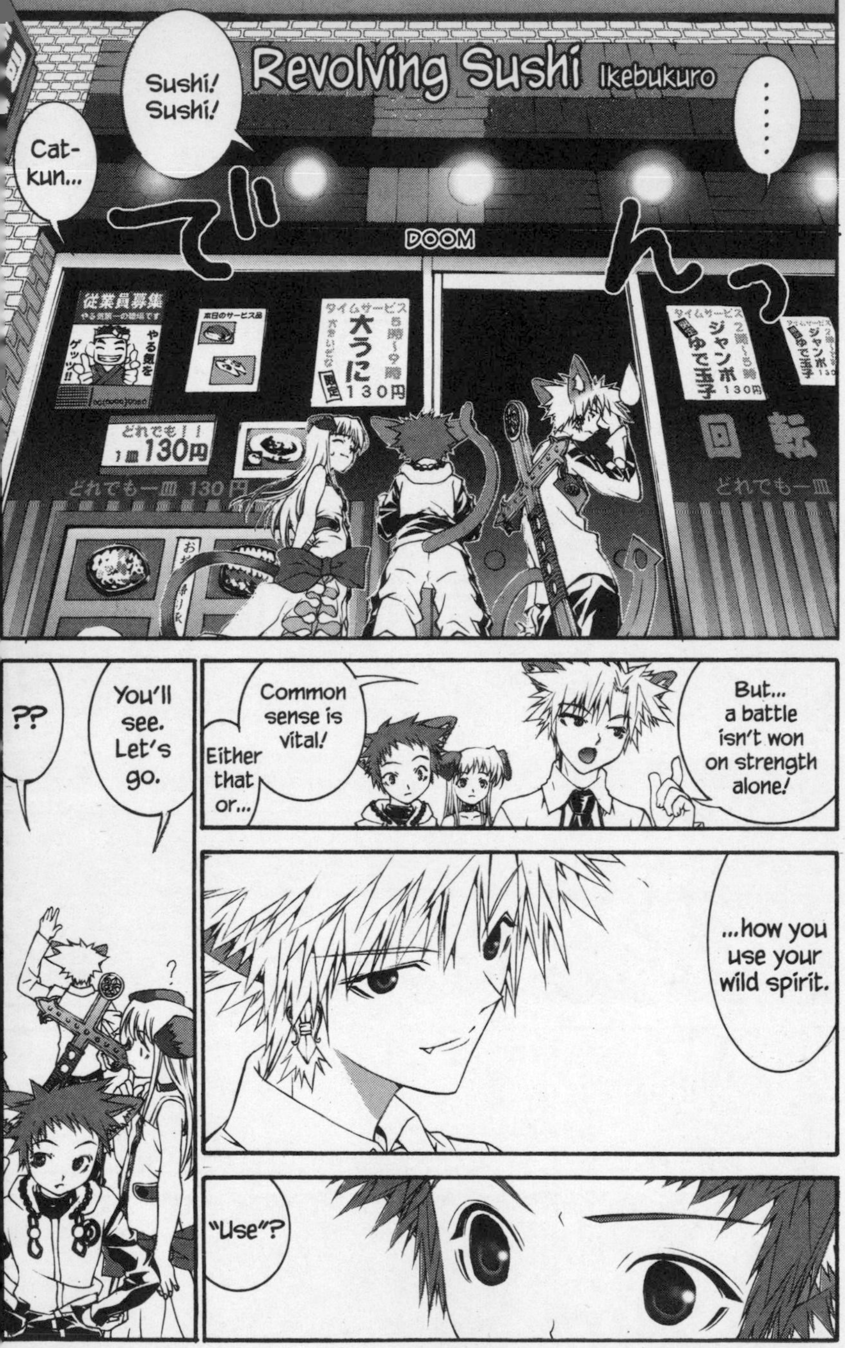
......
Revolving Sushi Ikebukuro
Sushi! Sushi!
Cat-kun...
でんっ
DOOM
タイムサービス 2時～5時 ジャンボ ゆで玉子 130円
回転
どれでも一皿
タイムサービス 5時～9時 大うに 限定 130円
本日のサービス品
従業員募集
やる気をゲッツ!!
どれでも!! 1皿130円
どれでも一皿 130円
But... a battle isn't won on strength alone!
Common sense is vital!
Either that or...
...how you use your wild spirit.
"Use"?
You'll see. Let's go.
??
?

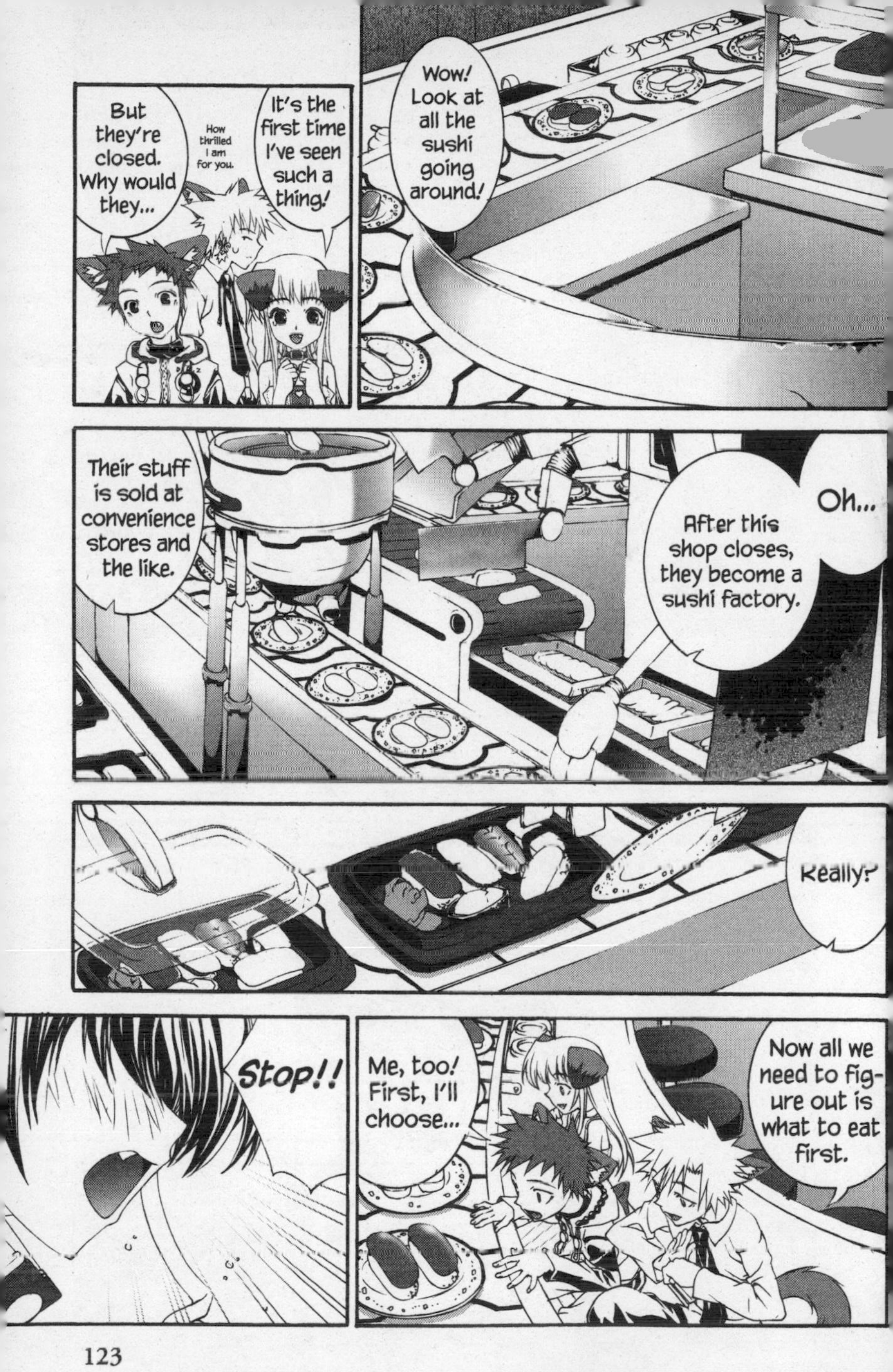
Wow! Look at all the sushi going around!
It's the first time I've seen such a thing!
How thrilled I am for you.
But they're closed. Why would they...
Oh...
After this shop closes, they become a sushi factory.
Their stuff is sold at convenience stores and the like.
Really?
Now all we need to fig-ure out is what to eat first.
Me, too! First, I'll choose...
Stop!!

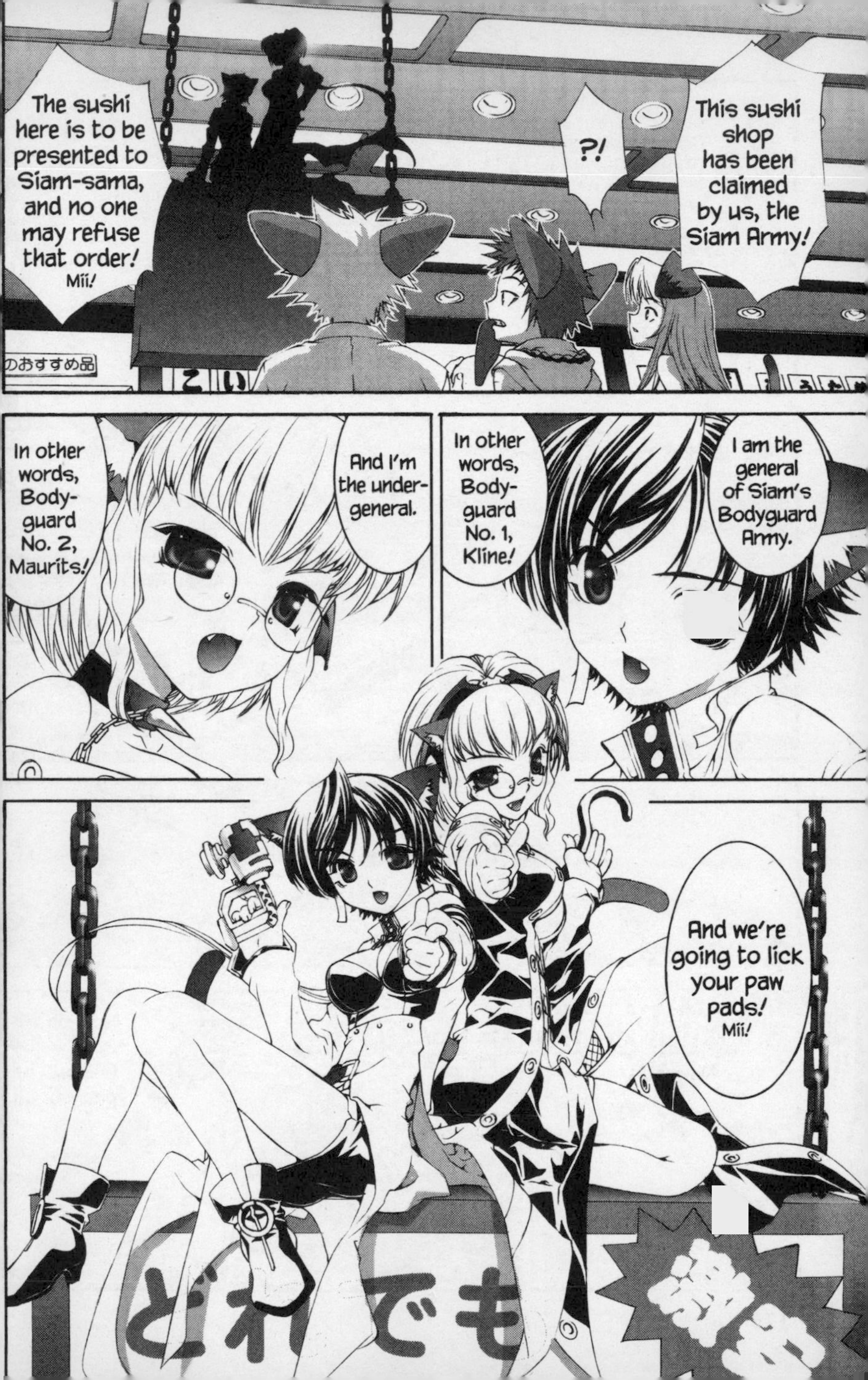
This sushi shop has been claimed by us, the Siam Army!
?!
The sushi here is to be presented to Siam-sama, and no one may refuse that order! Mii!
のおすすめ品
I am the general of Siam's Bodyguard Army.
In other words, Bodyguard No. 1, Kline!
And I'm the under-general.
In other words, Bodyguard No. 2, Maurits!
And we're going to lick your paw pads! Mii!

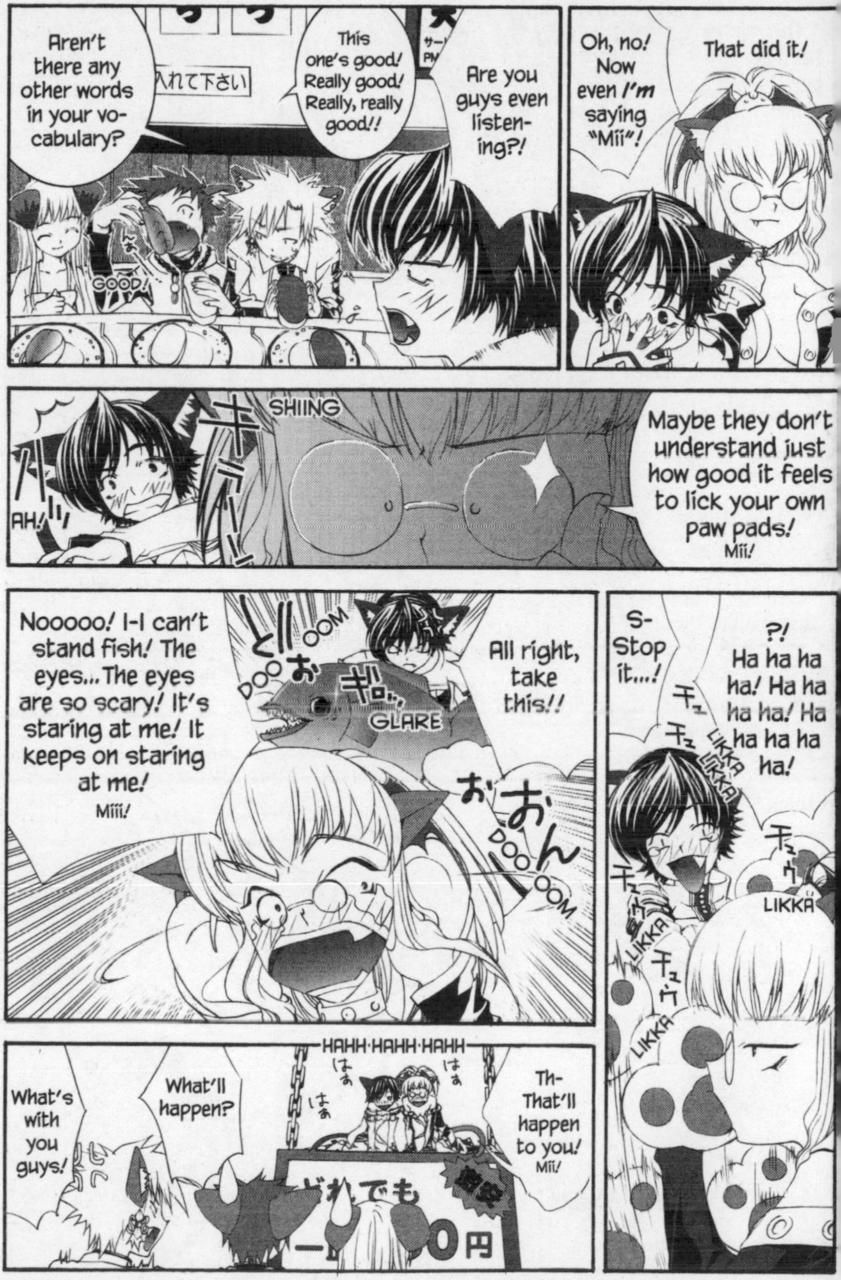

That did it!
Oh, no! Now even I'm saying "Mii"!
Are you guys even listen-ing?!
This one's good! Really good! Really, really good!!
Aren't there any other words in your vo-cabulary?
GOOD!
Maybe they don't understand just how good it feels to lick your own paw pads! Mii!
SHIING
AH!
?! Ha ha ha ha! Ha ha ha ha! Ha ha ha ha ha!
S-Stop it...!
LIKKA LIKKA
LIKKA
LIKKA
LIKKA
All right, take this!!
DOOOOM
GLARE
Noooo! I-I can't stand fish! The eyes... The eyes are so scary! It's staring at me! It keeps on staring at me! Miii!
DOOOOOM
Th-That'll happen to you! Mii!
HAHH·HAHH·HAHH
What'll happen?
What's with you guys!

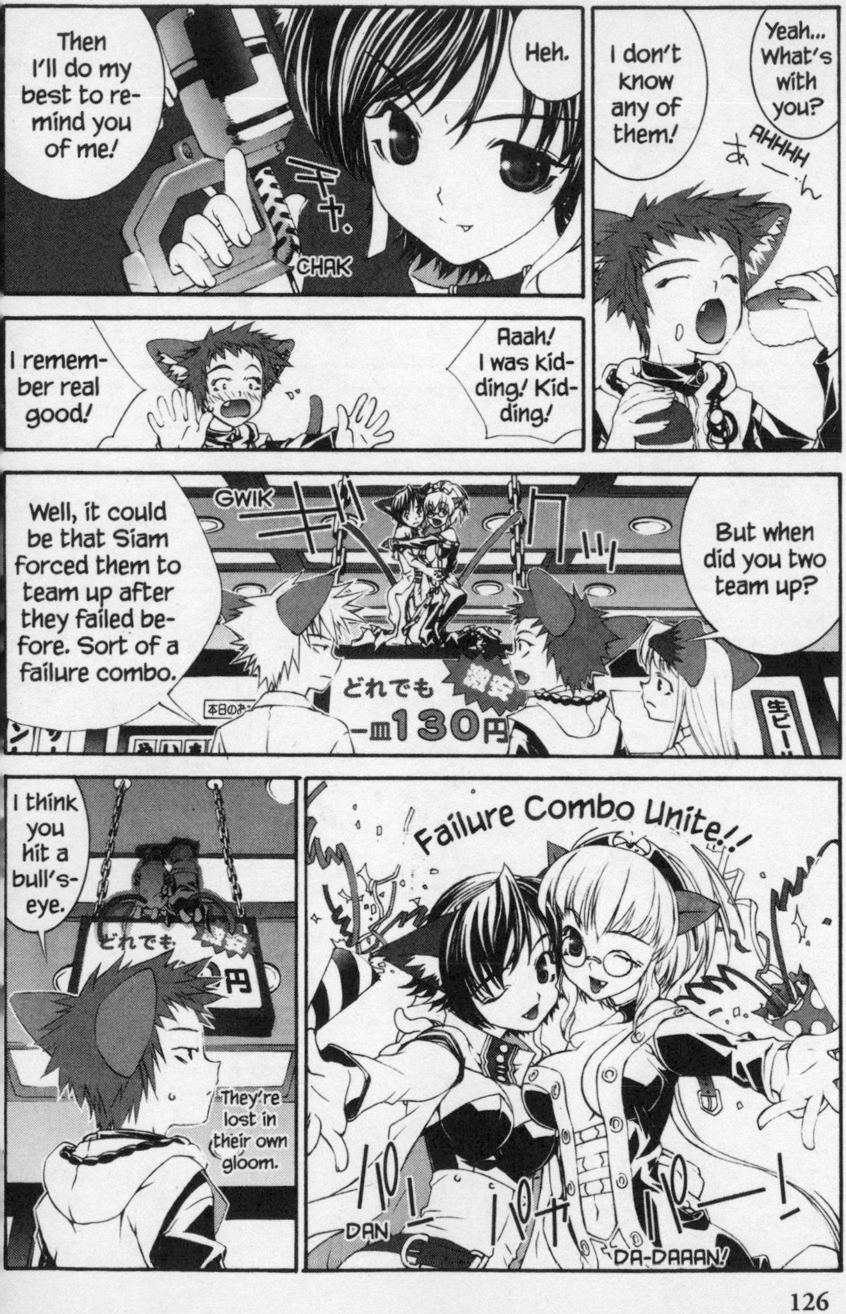
Yeah... What's with you?
I don't know any of them!
AHHHH
Heh.
Then I'll do my best to re-mind you of me!
CHAK
Aaah! I was kid-ding! Kid-ding!
I remem-ber real good!
But when did you two team up?
Well, it could be that Siam forced them to team up after they failed be-fore. Sort of a failure combo.
GWIK
どれでも
一皿130円
Failure Combo Unite!!
DAN
DA-DAAAN!
I think you hit a bull's-eye.
They're lost in their own gloom.

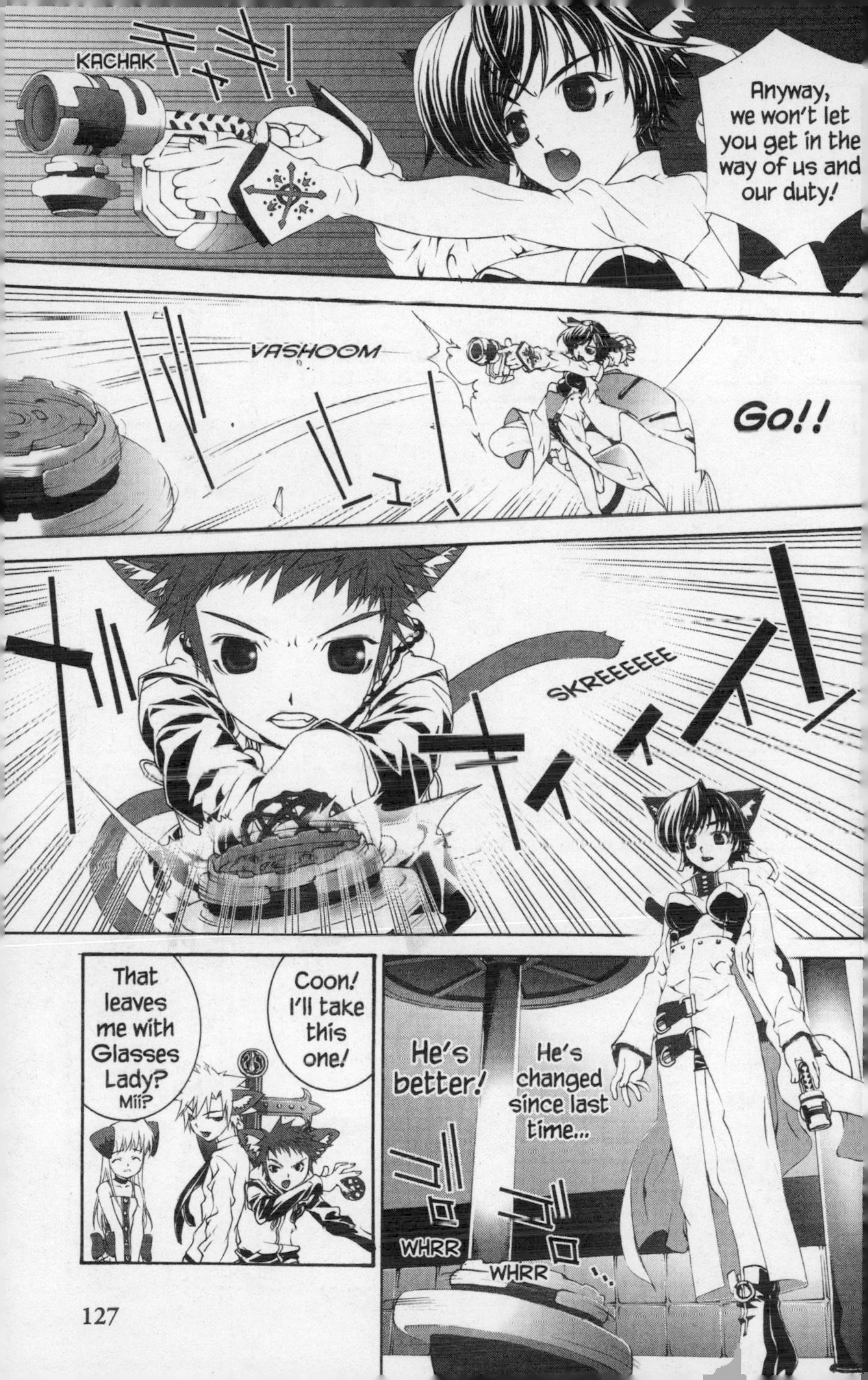
Anyway, we won't let you get in the way of us and our duty!
KACHAK
Go!!
VASHOOM
SKREEEEEE
He's changed since last time...
He's better!
WHRR
WHRR
Coon! I'll take this one!
That leaves me with Glasses Lady?
Mii?

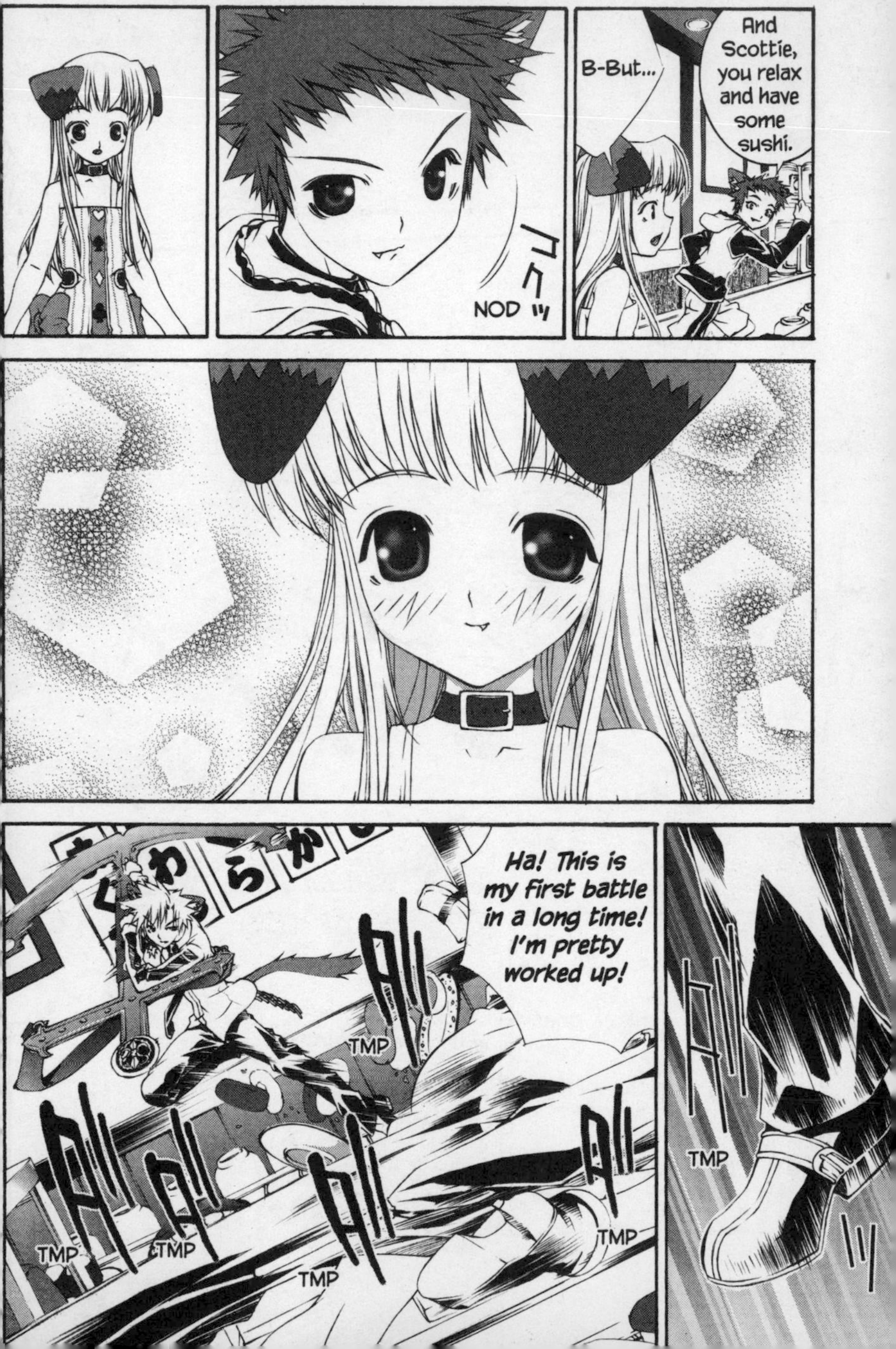
And Scottie, you relax and have some sushi.
B-But...
NOD
コクッ
TMP
Ha! This is my first battle in a long time! I'm pretty worked up!
TMP
TMP
TMP
TMP
TMP

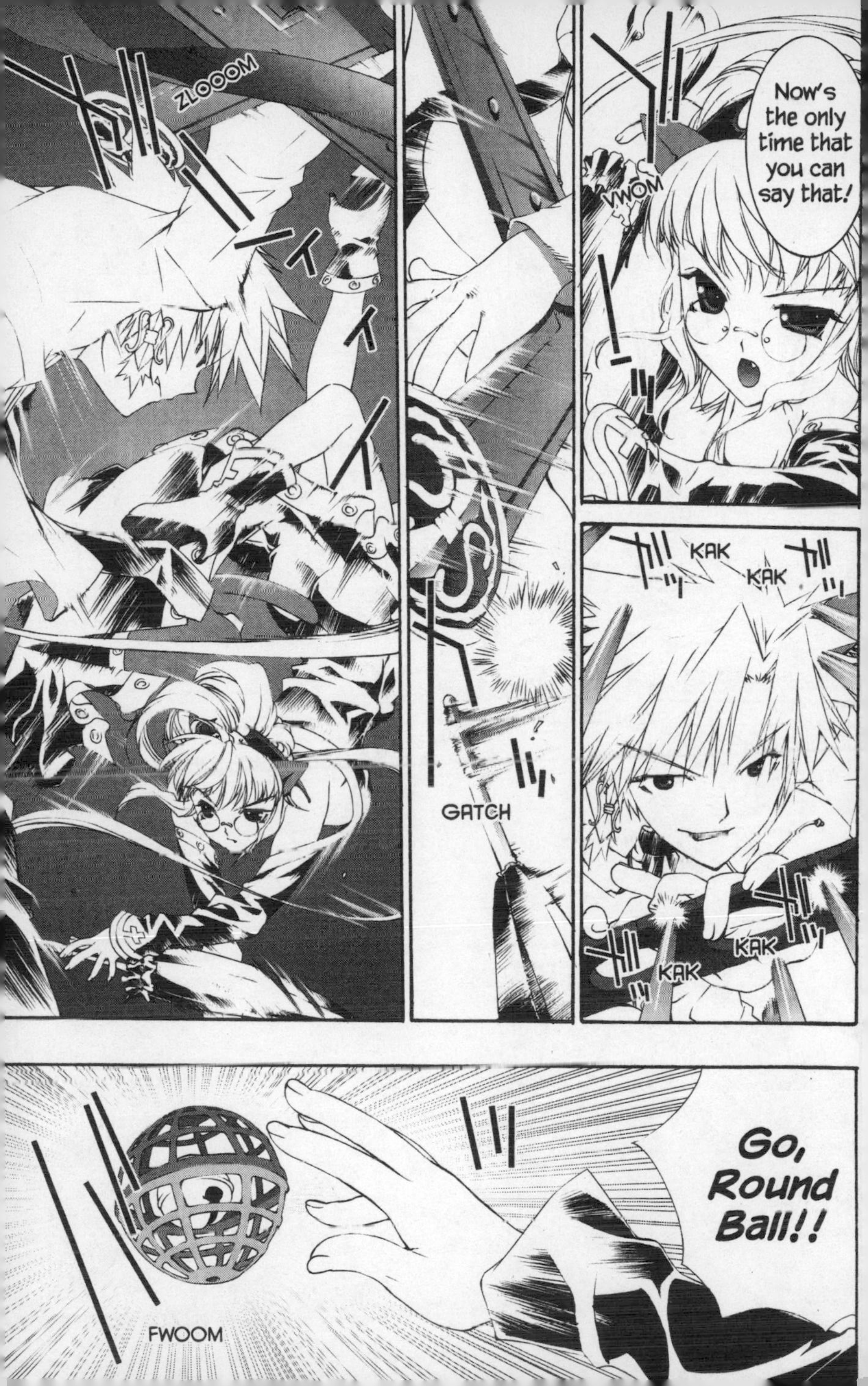
Now's the only time that you can say that!
VWOM
KAK
KAK
KAK
KAK
GATCH
ZLOOOM
Go, Round Ball!!
FWOOM

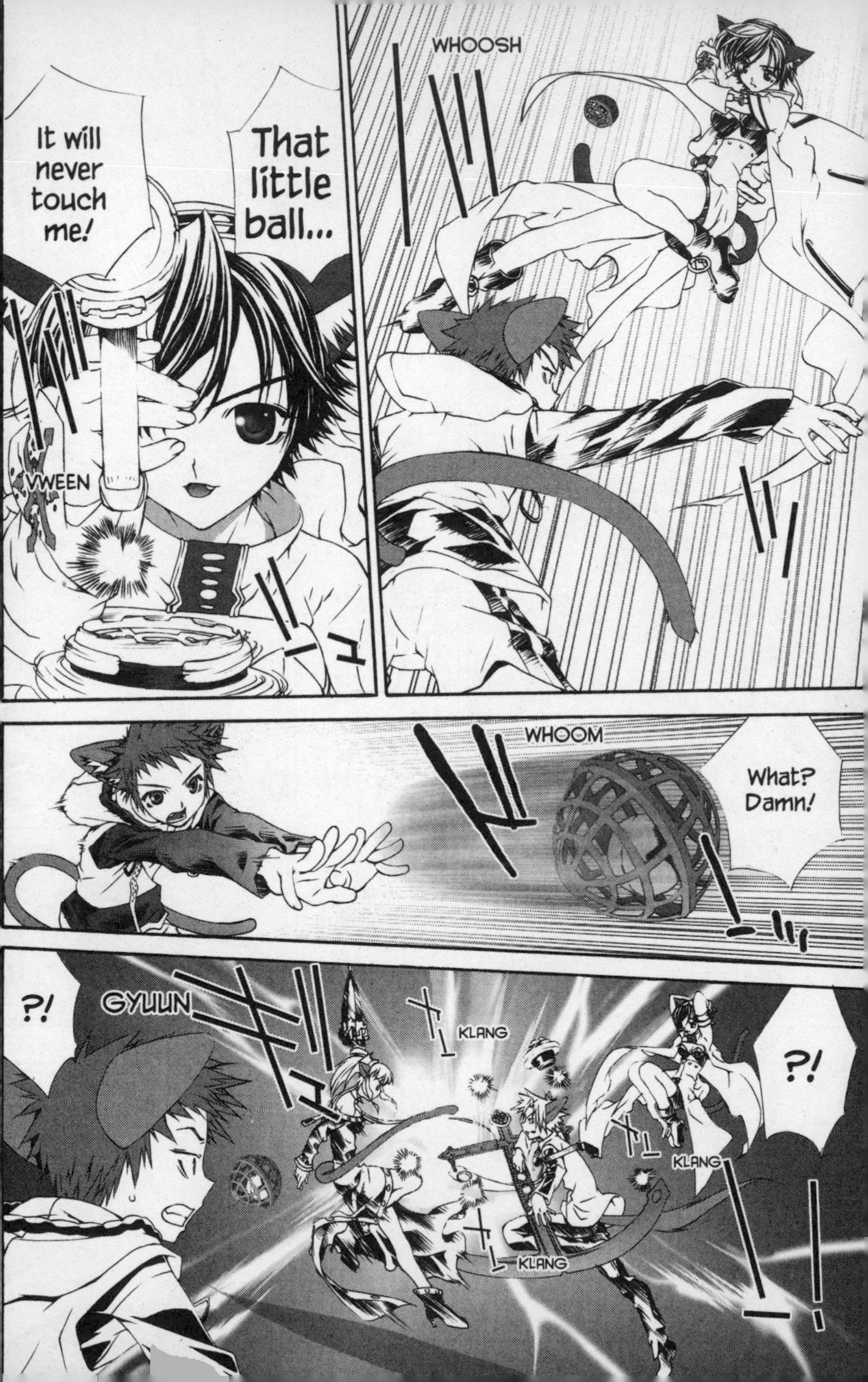
WHOOSH
That little ball...
It will never touch me!
VWEEN
WHOOM
What? Damn!
?!
KLANG
KLANG
GYUUN
?!
KLANG

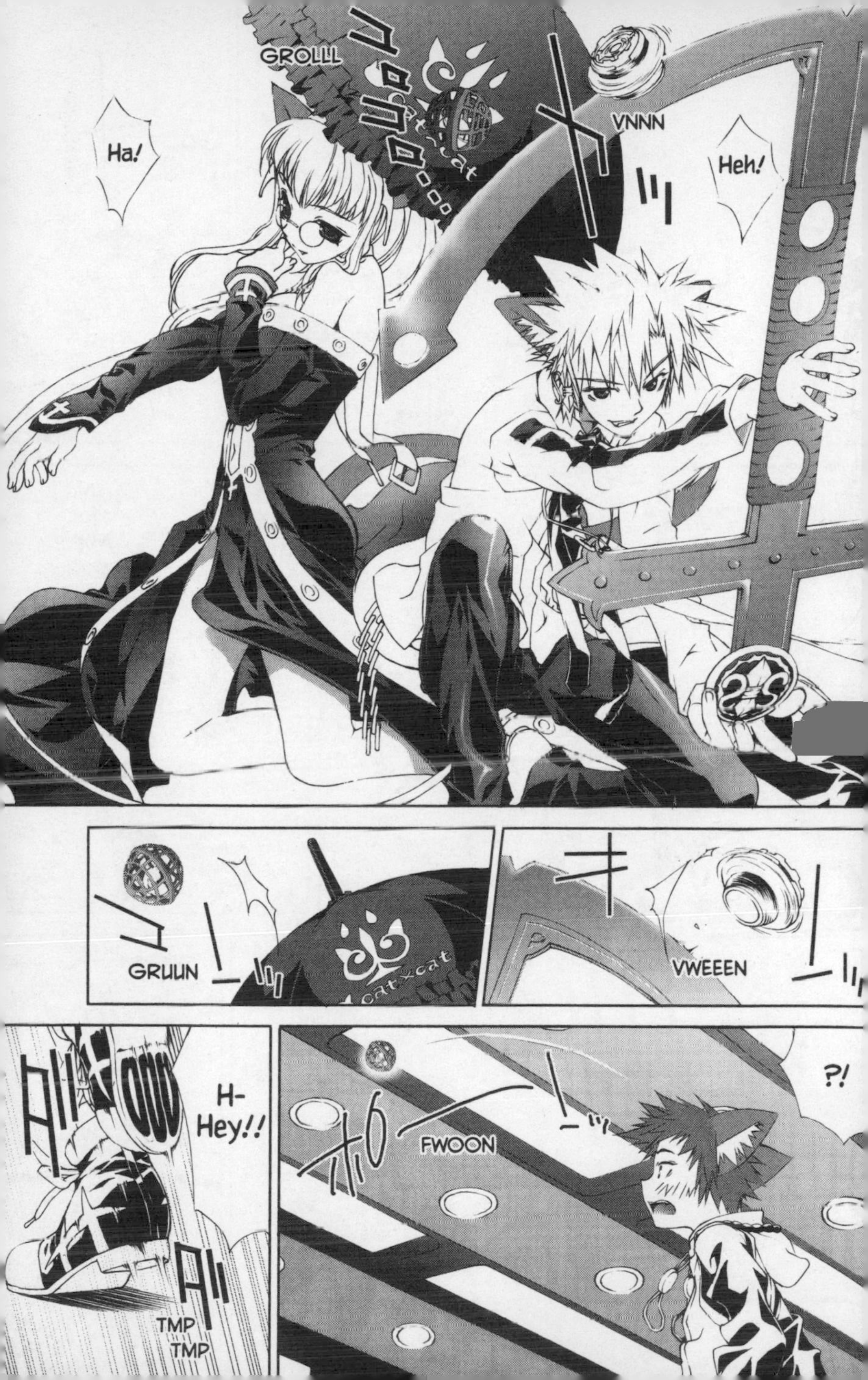
Heh!
VNNN
GROLLL
Ha!
VWEEEN
GRUUN
?!
FWOON
H-Hey!!
TMP TMP

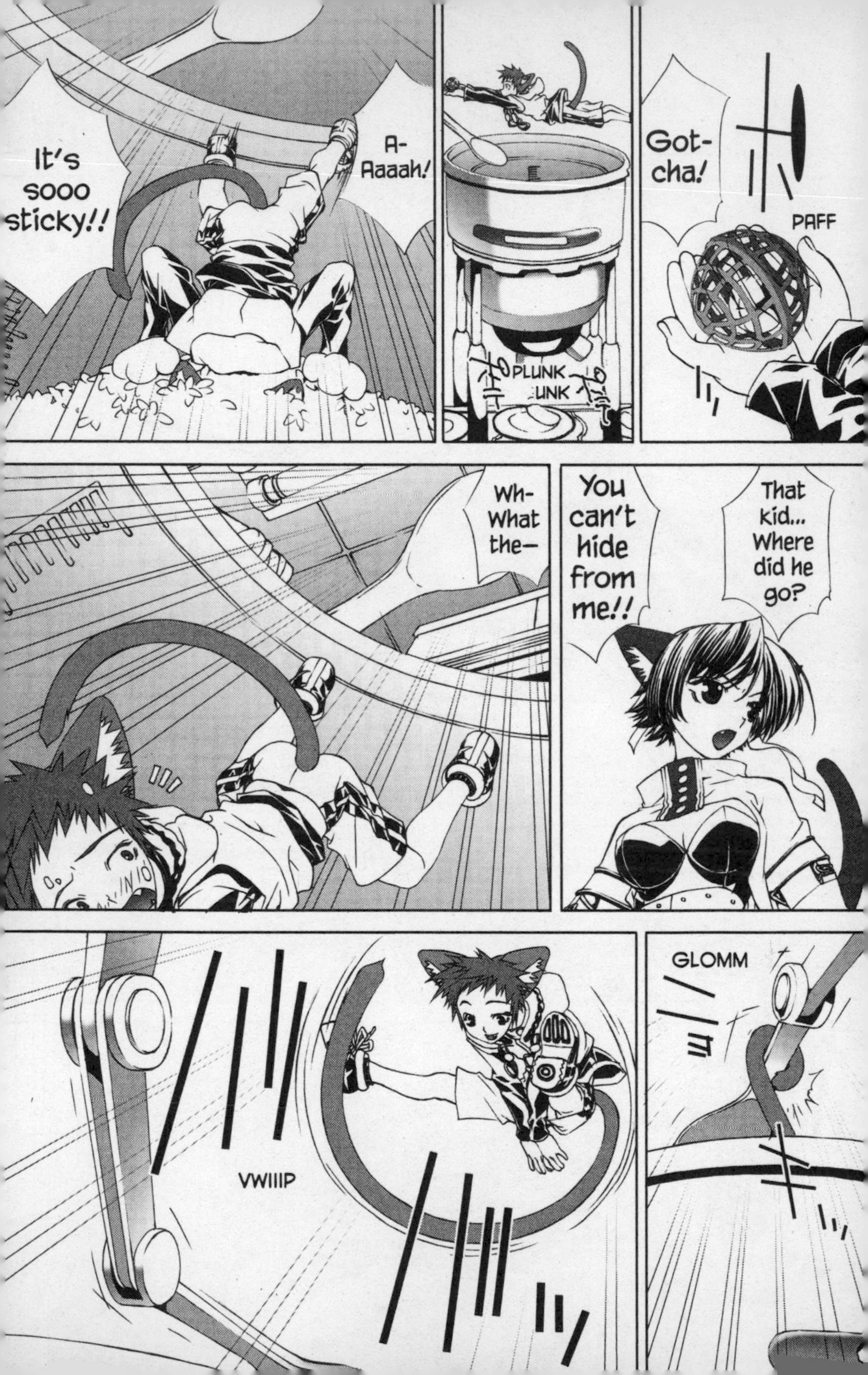
Got-cha!
PAFF
PLUNK
UNK
A-Aaaah!
It's sooo sticky!!
That kid... Where did he go?
You can't hide from me!!
Wh-What the–
GLOMM
VWIIIP

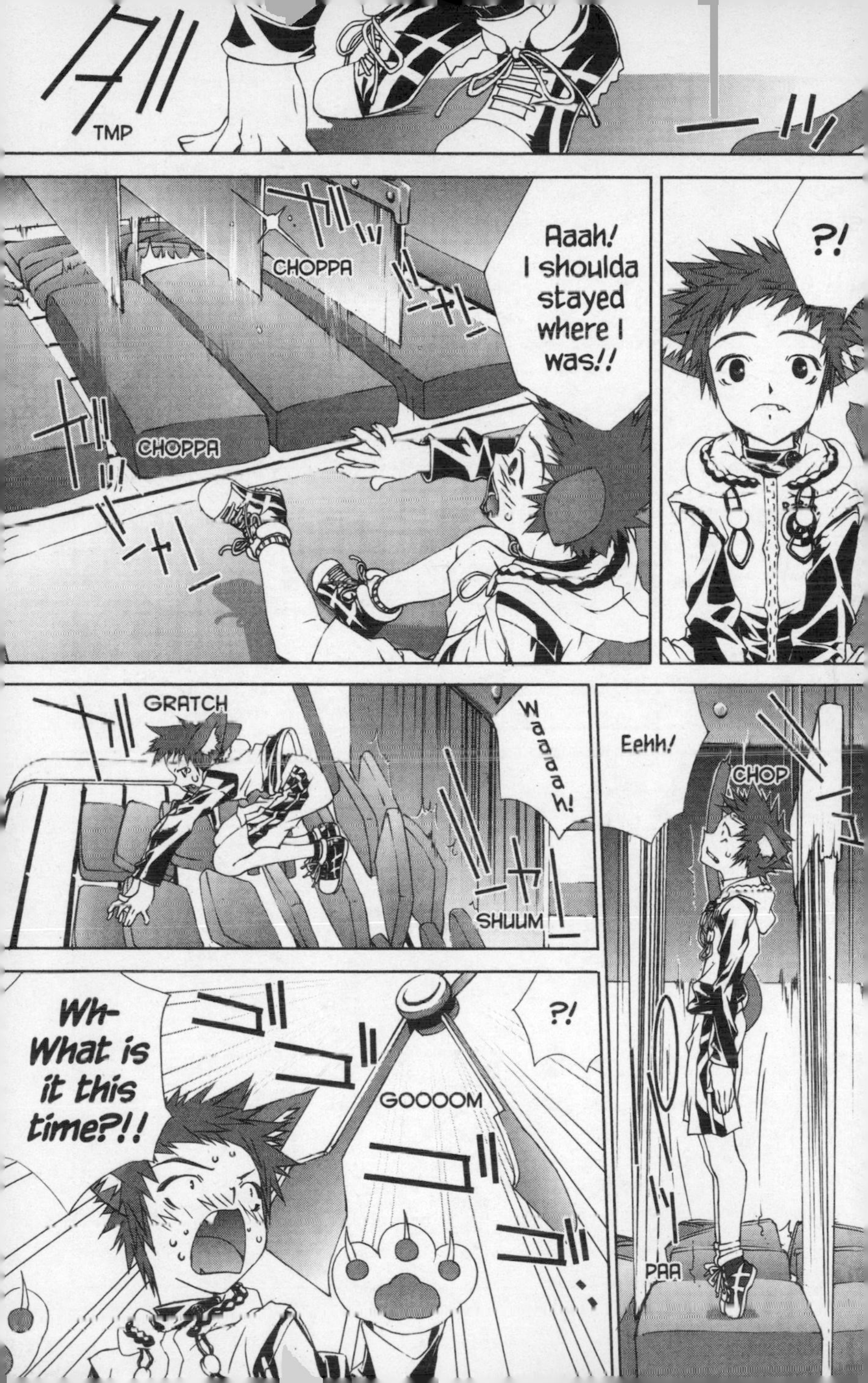
TMP
?!
Aaah! I shoulda stayed where I was!!
CHOPPA
CHOPPA
Eehh!
CHOP
PAA
Waaaah!
GRATCH
SHUUM
?!
Wh- What is it this time?!!
GOOOOM

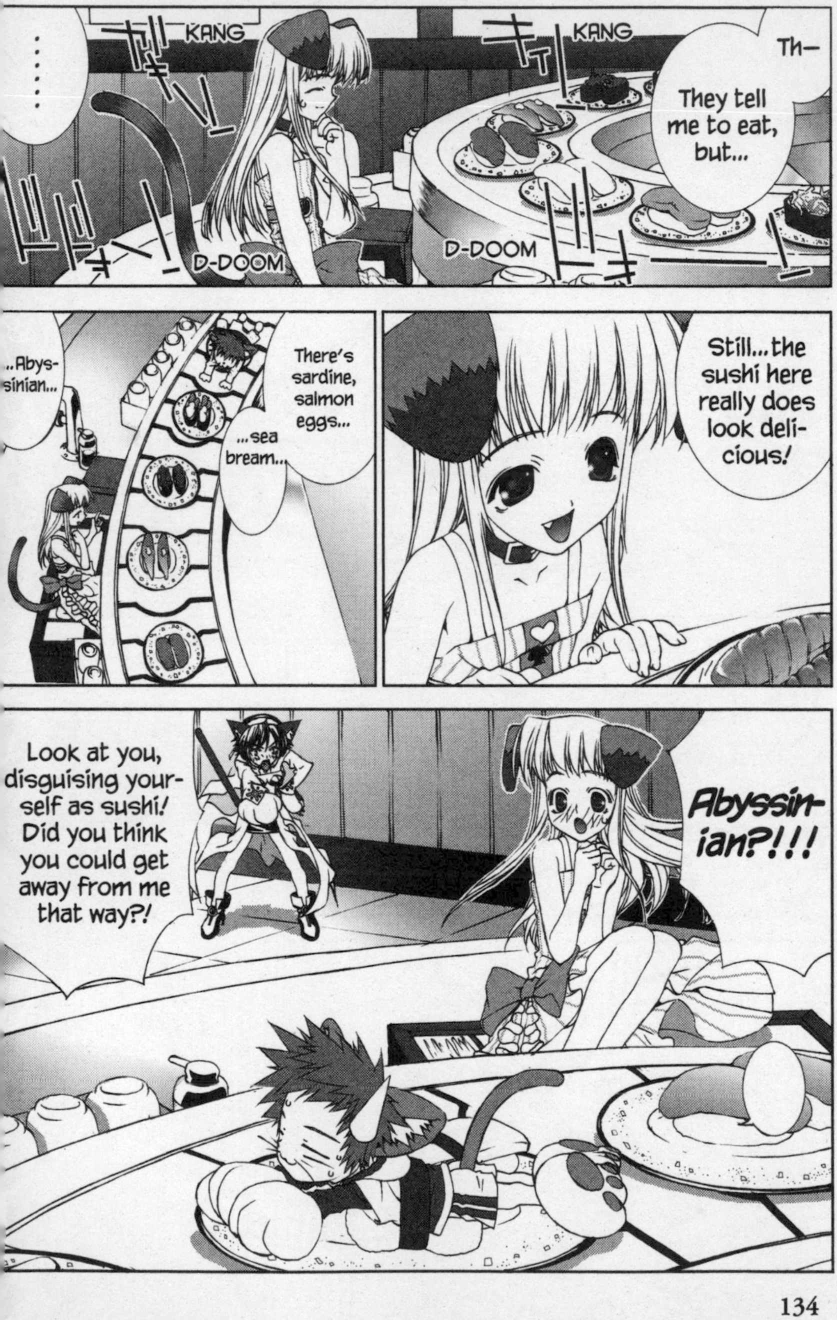
Th—
They tell me to eat, but...
KANG
KANG
......
D-DOOM
D-DOOM
Still...the sushi here really does look deli-cious!
There's sardine, salmon eggs...
...sea bream...
...Abys-sinian...
Abyssin-ian?!!!
Look at you, disguising your-self as sushi! Did you think you could get away from me that way?!

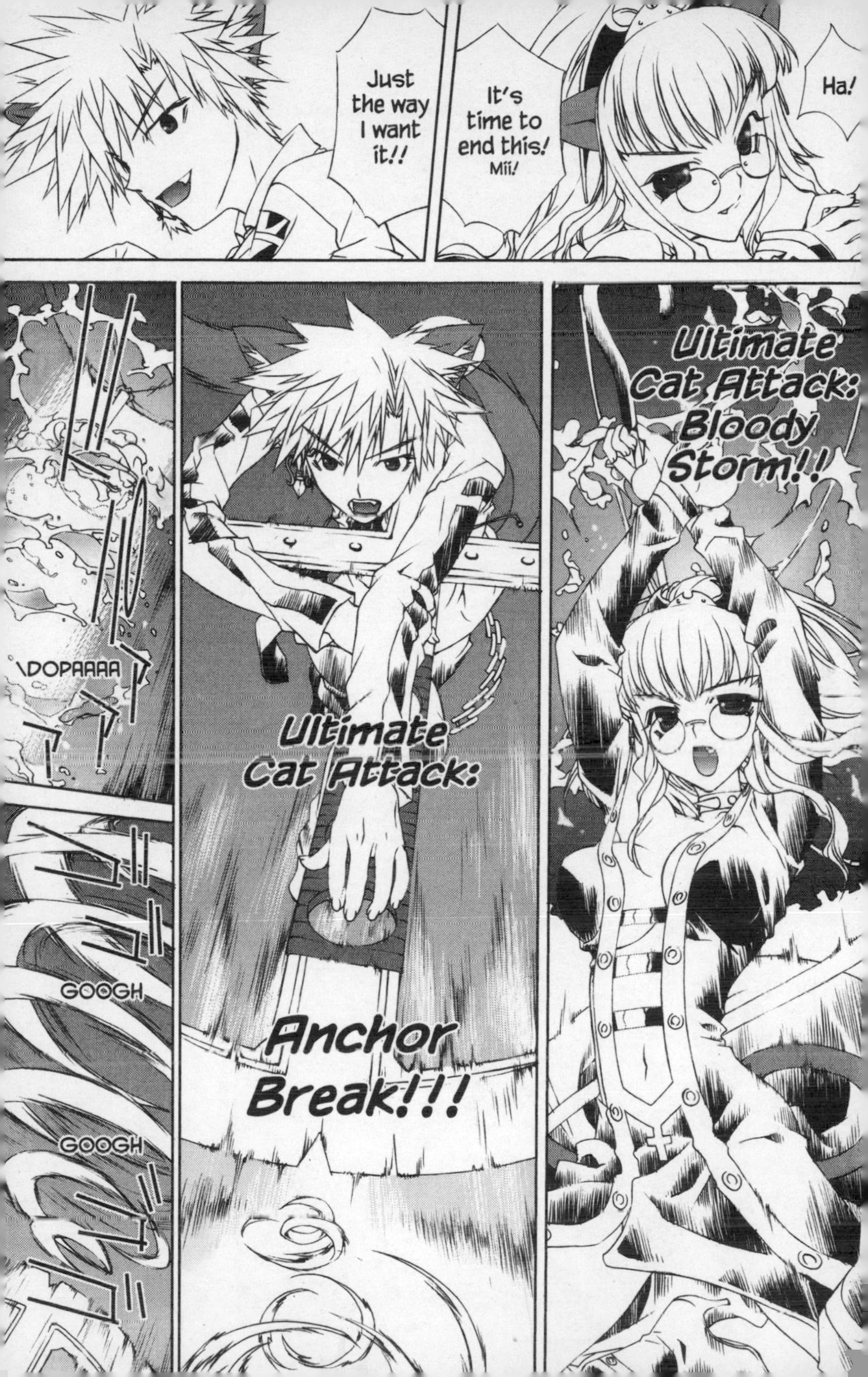

Ha!
It's time to end this! Mii!
Just the way I want it!!
Ultimate Cat Attack: Bloody Storm!!
Ultimate Cat Attack:
Anchor Break!!!
DOPAAAA
GOOGH
GOOGH

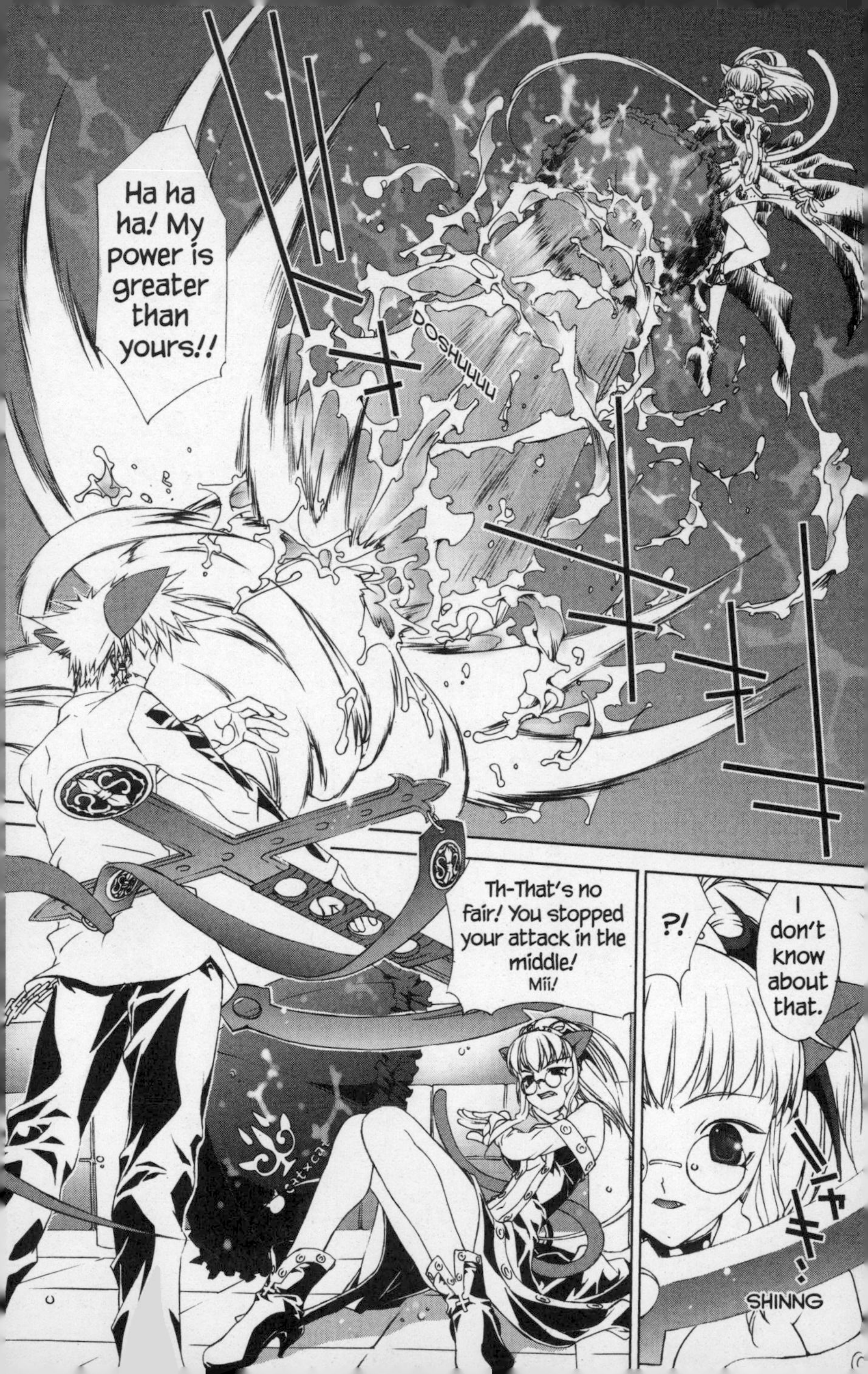
Ha ha ha! My power is greater than yours!!
DOSHUUUU
I don't know about that.
?!
SHINNG
Th-That's no fair! You stopped your attack in the middle!
Mii!

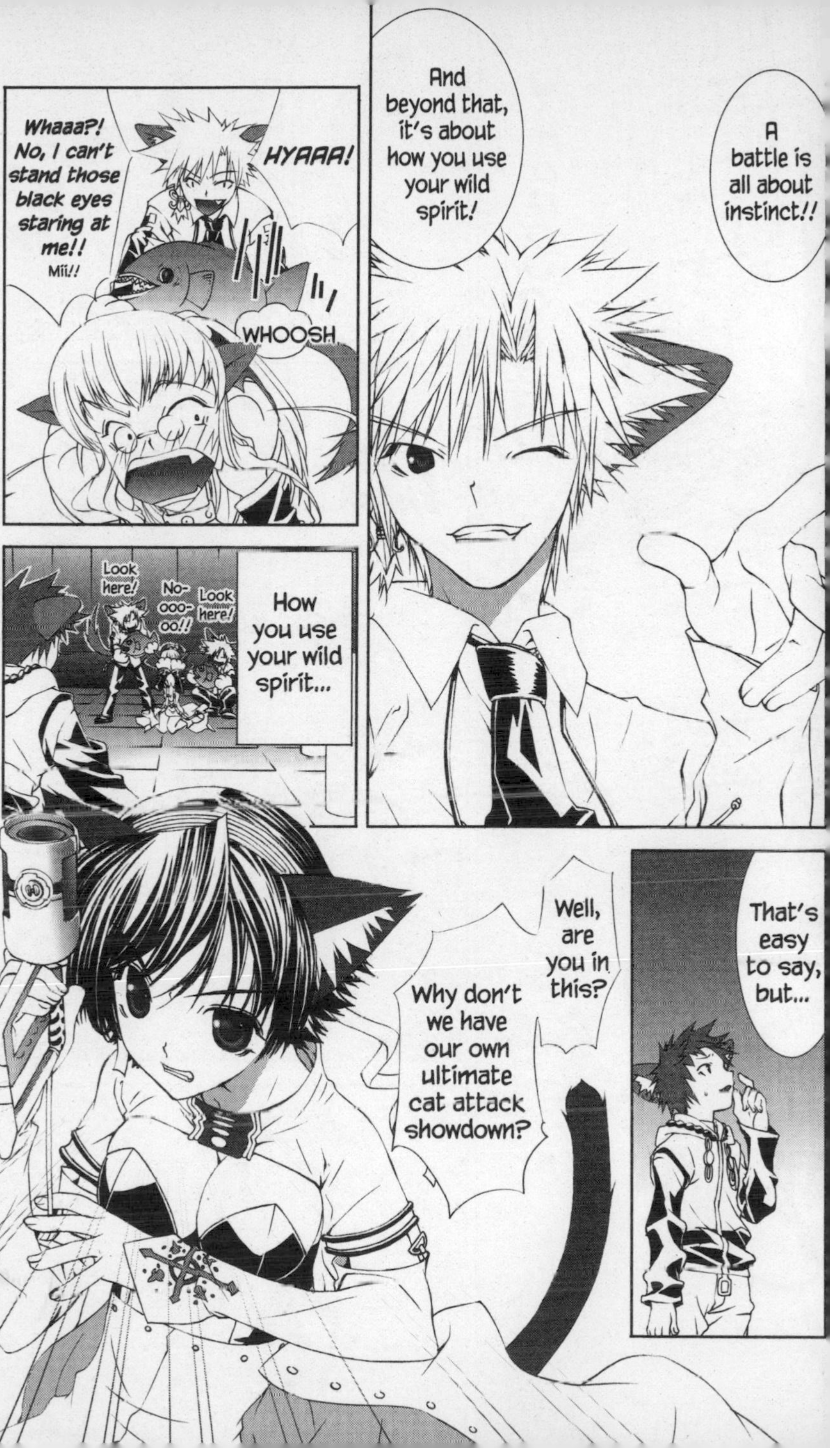
A battle is all about instinct!!
And beyond that, it's about how you use your wild spirit!
HYAAA!
Whaaa?! No, I can't stand those black eyes staring at me!!
Mii!!
WHOOSH
How you use your wild spirit...
Look here!
No-ooo-oo!!
Look here!
That's easy to say, but...
Well, are you in this?
Why don't we have our own ultimate cat attack showdown?

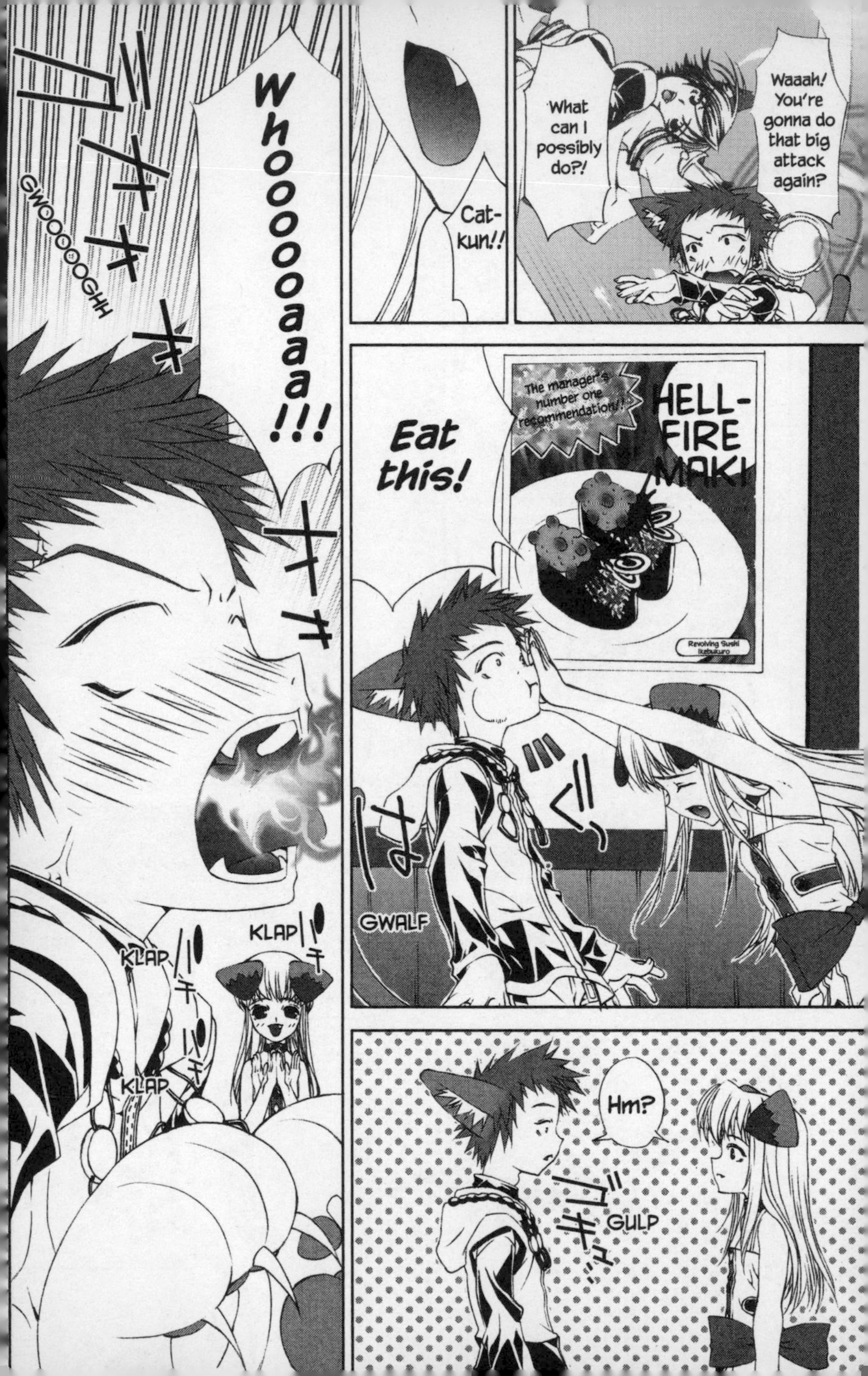
Waaah! You're gonna do that big attack again?
What can I possibly do?!
Cat-kun!!
The manager's number one recommendation!!
HELL-FIRE MAKI
Revolving Sushi Ikebukuro
Eat this!
GWALF
Hm?
GULP
Whoooooaaa!!!
GWOOOOOGHH
KLAP
KLAP
KLAP

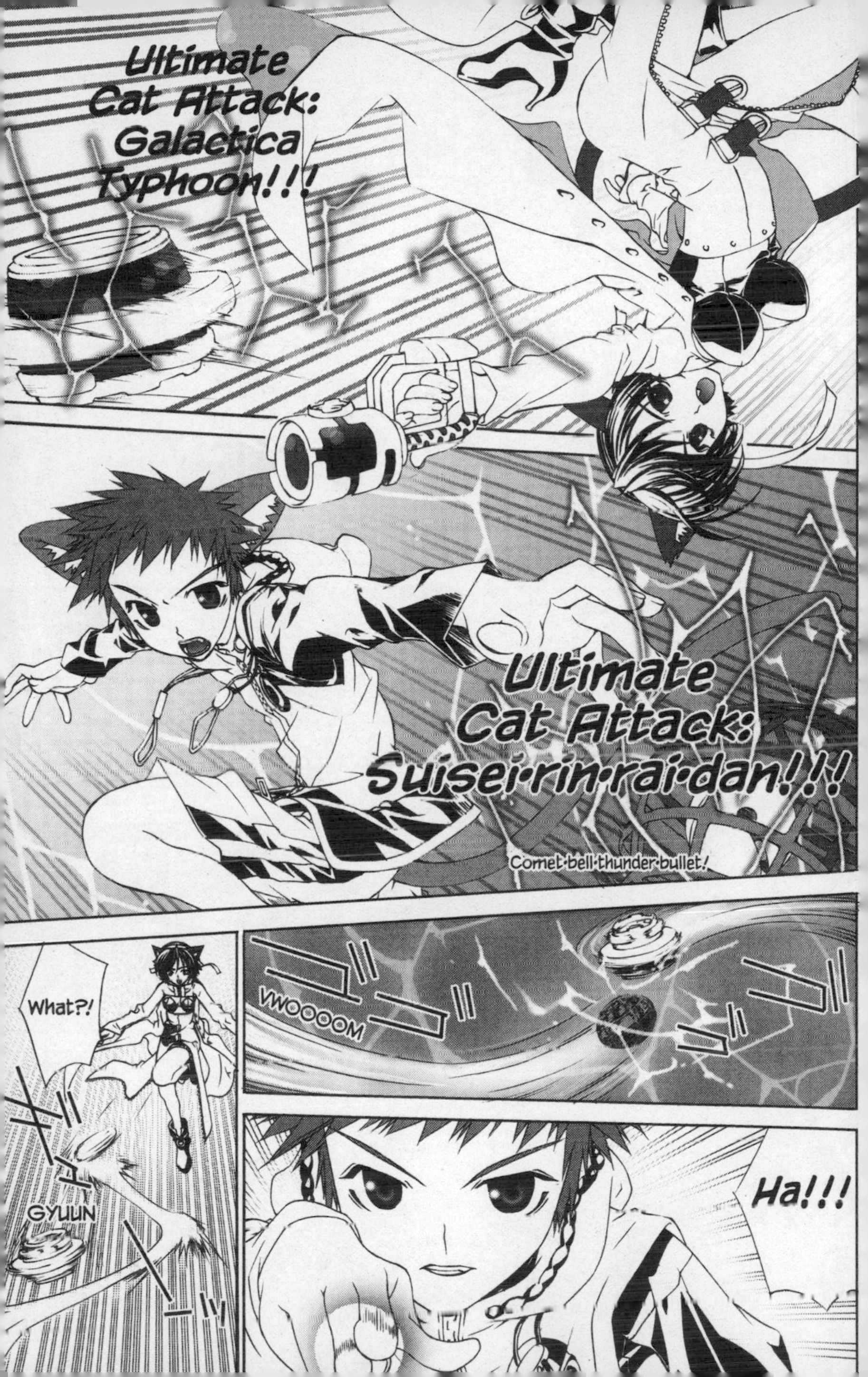
Ultimate Cat Attack: Galactica Typhoon!!!
Ultimate Cat Attack: Suisei-rin-rai-dan!!!
Comet-bell-thunder-bullet!
VWOOOOM
Ha!!!
What?!
GYUUN

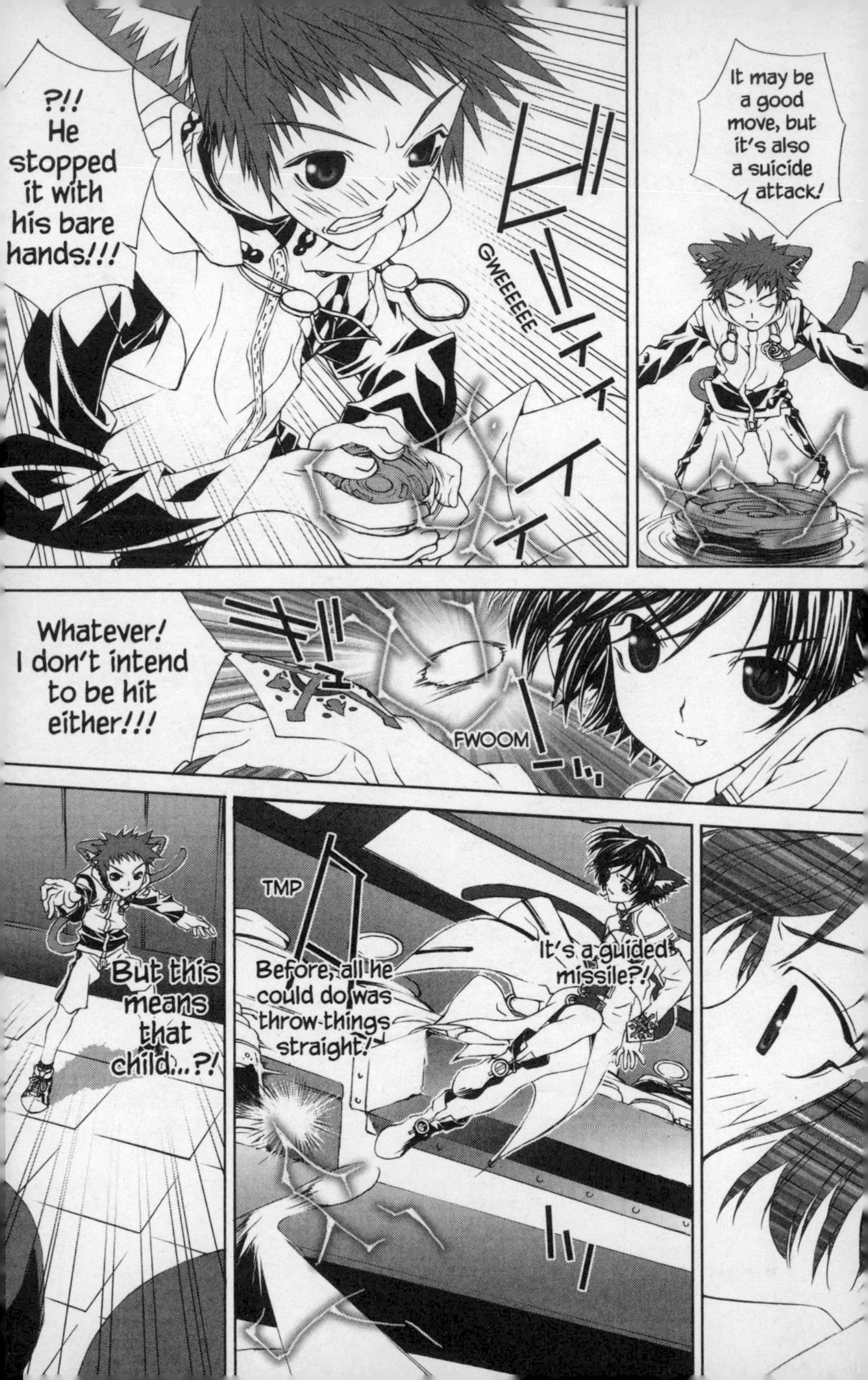
It may be a good move, but it's also a suicide attack!
GWEEEEEEE
?!! He stopped it with his bare hands!!!
FWOOM
Whatever! I don't intend to be hit either!!!
It's a guided missile?!
TMP
Before, all he could do was throw things straight!
But this means that child...?!

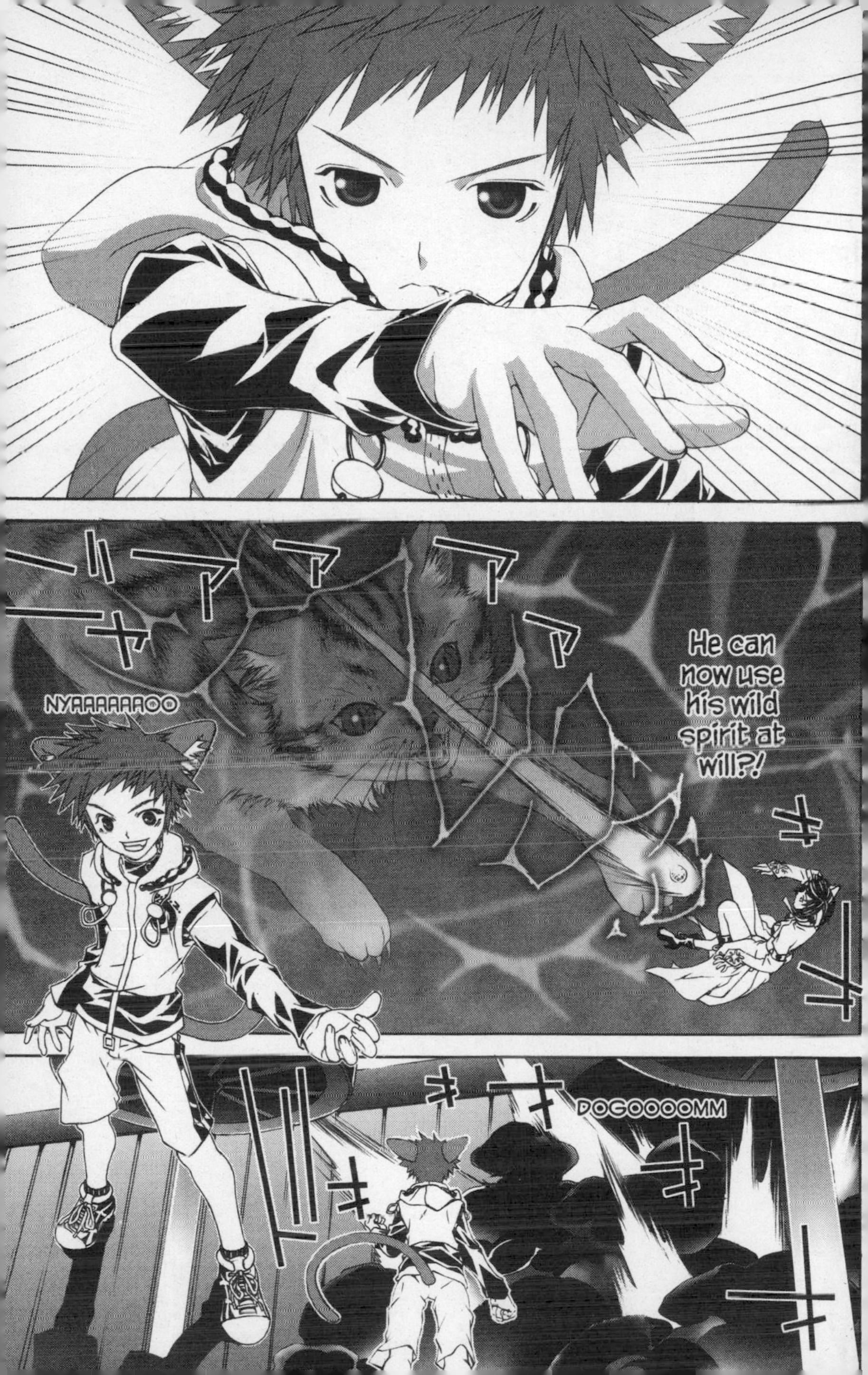
He can now use his wild spirit at will?!
NYAAAAAAOO
DOGOOOOMM

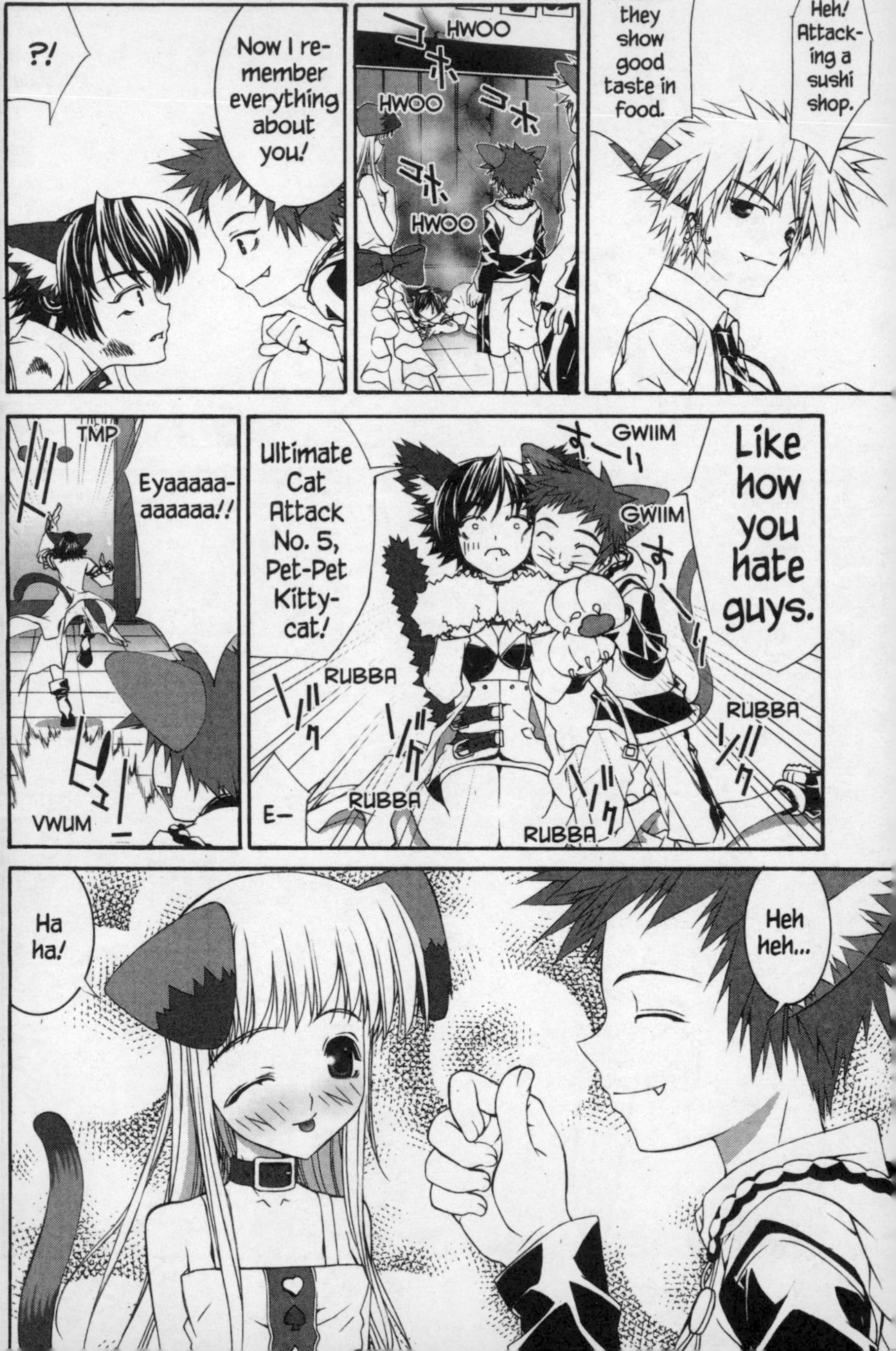

Heh! Attack-ing a sushi shop.
At least they show good taste in food.
HWOO
HWOO
HWOO
Now I re-member everything about you!
?!
Like how you hate guys.
GWIIM
GWIIM
Ultimate Cat Attack No. 5, Pet-Pet Kitty-cat!
RUBBA
RUBBA
RUBBA
RUBBA
E–
TMP
Eyaaaaa-aaaaaa!!
VWUM
Heh heh...
Ha ha!

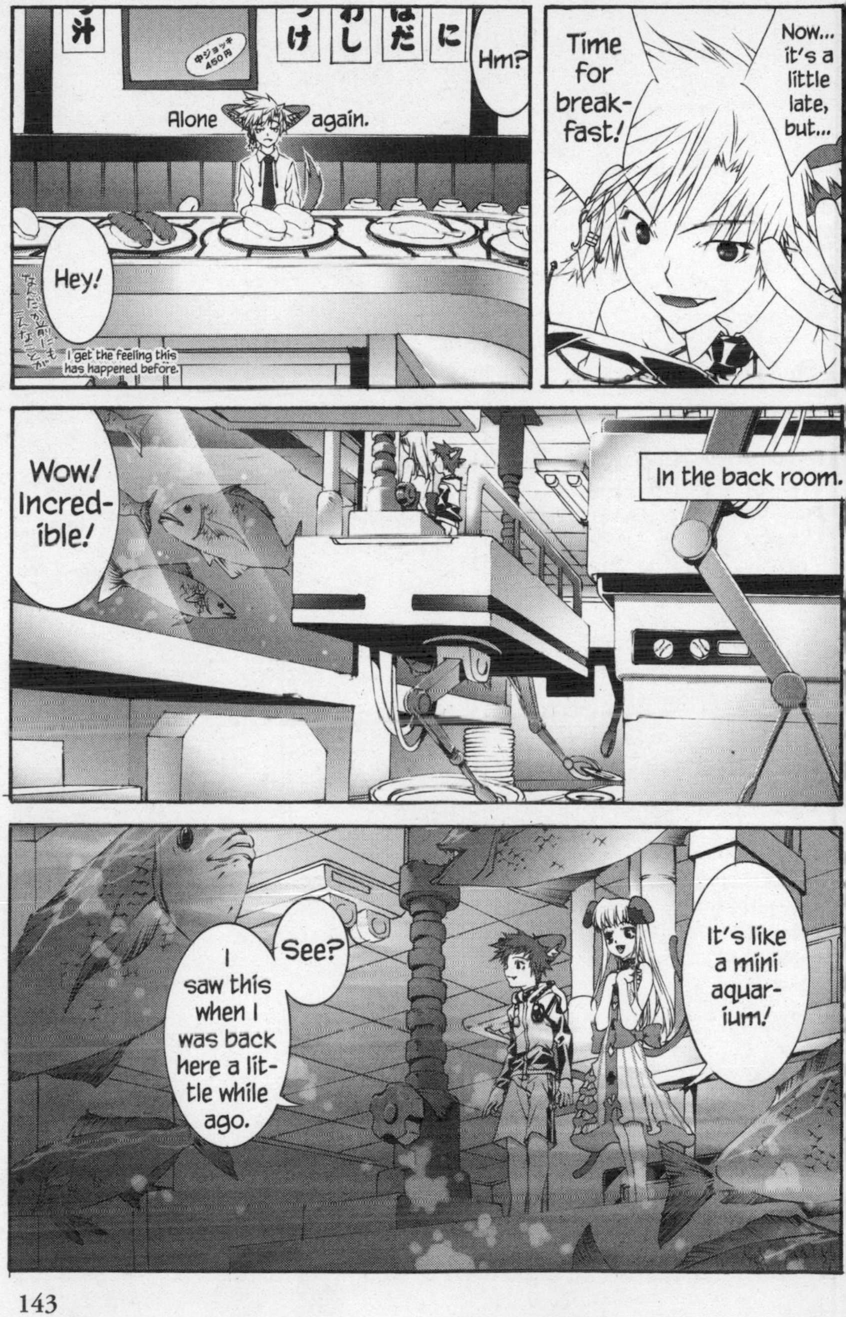
Now... it's a little late, but...
Time for break-fast!
Hm?
中ジョッキ 450円
Alone again.
Hey!
I get the feeling this has happened before.
In the back room.
Wow! Incred-ible!
It's like a mini aquar-ium!
See?
I saw this when I was back here a lit-tle while ago.

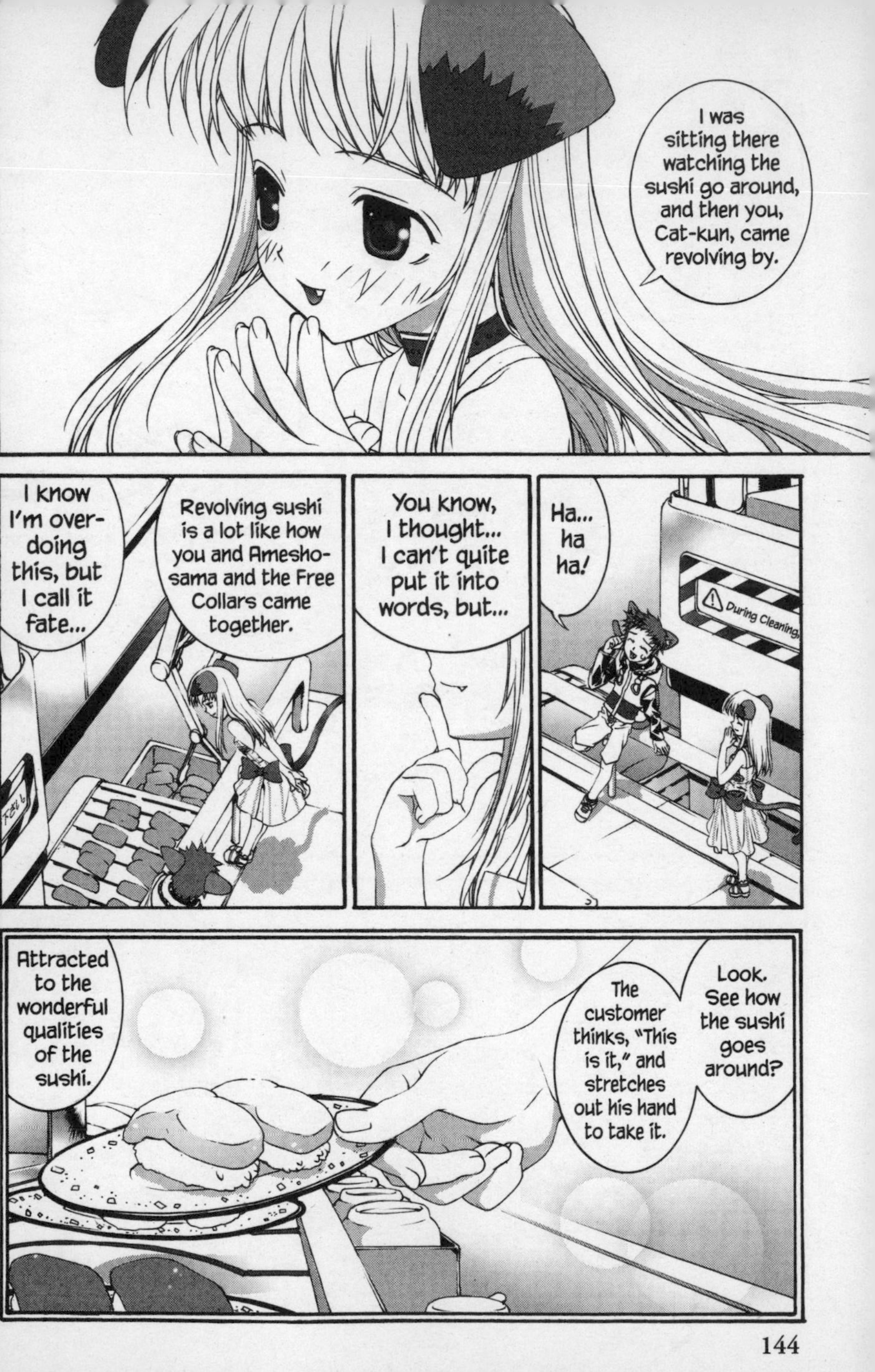
I was sitting there watching the sushi go around, and then you, Cat-kun, came revolving by.
Ha... ha ha!
During Cleaning
You know, I thought... I can't quite put it into words, but...
Revolving sushi is a lot like how you and Amesho-sama and the Free Collars came together.
I know I'm over-doing this, but I call it fate...
Look. See how the sushi goes around?
The customer thinks, "This is it," and stretches out his hand to take it.
Attracted to the wonderful qualities of the sushi.

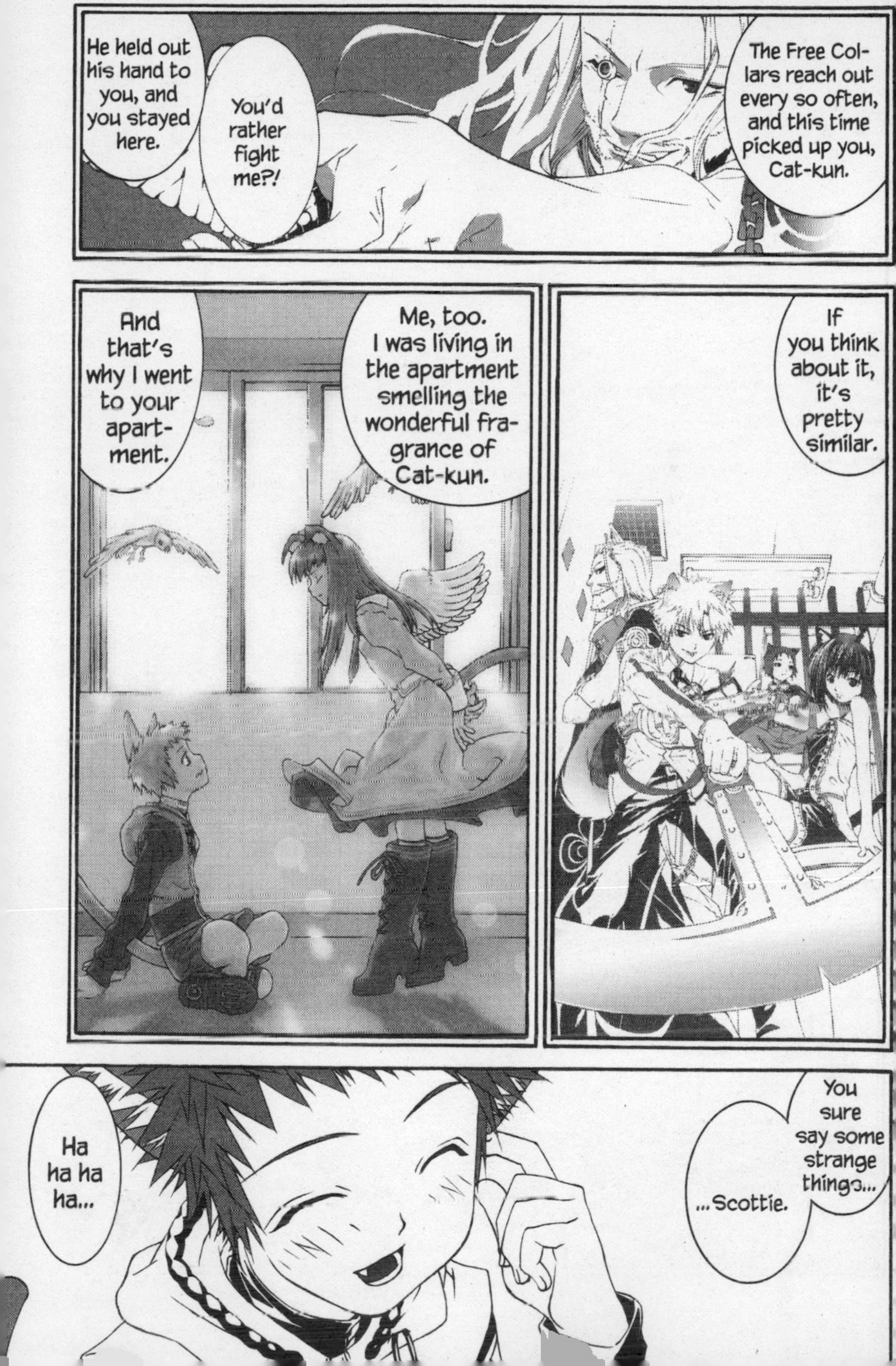

The Free Collars reach out every so often, and this time picked up you, Cat-kun.
He held out his hand to you, and you stayed here.
You'd rather fight me?!
If you think about it, it's pretty similar.
Me, too. I was living in the apartment smelling the wonderful fragrance of Cat-kun.
And that's why I went to your apartment.
You sure say some strange things...
...Scottie.
Ha ha ha ha...

Yep!
I'm sure it's
fate!

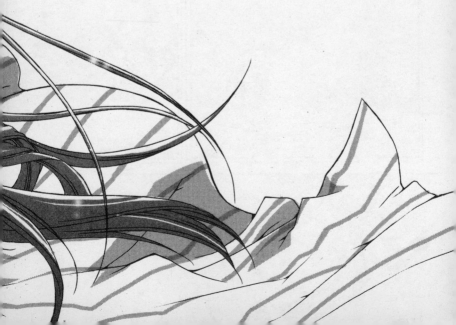

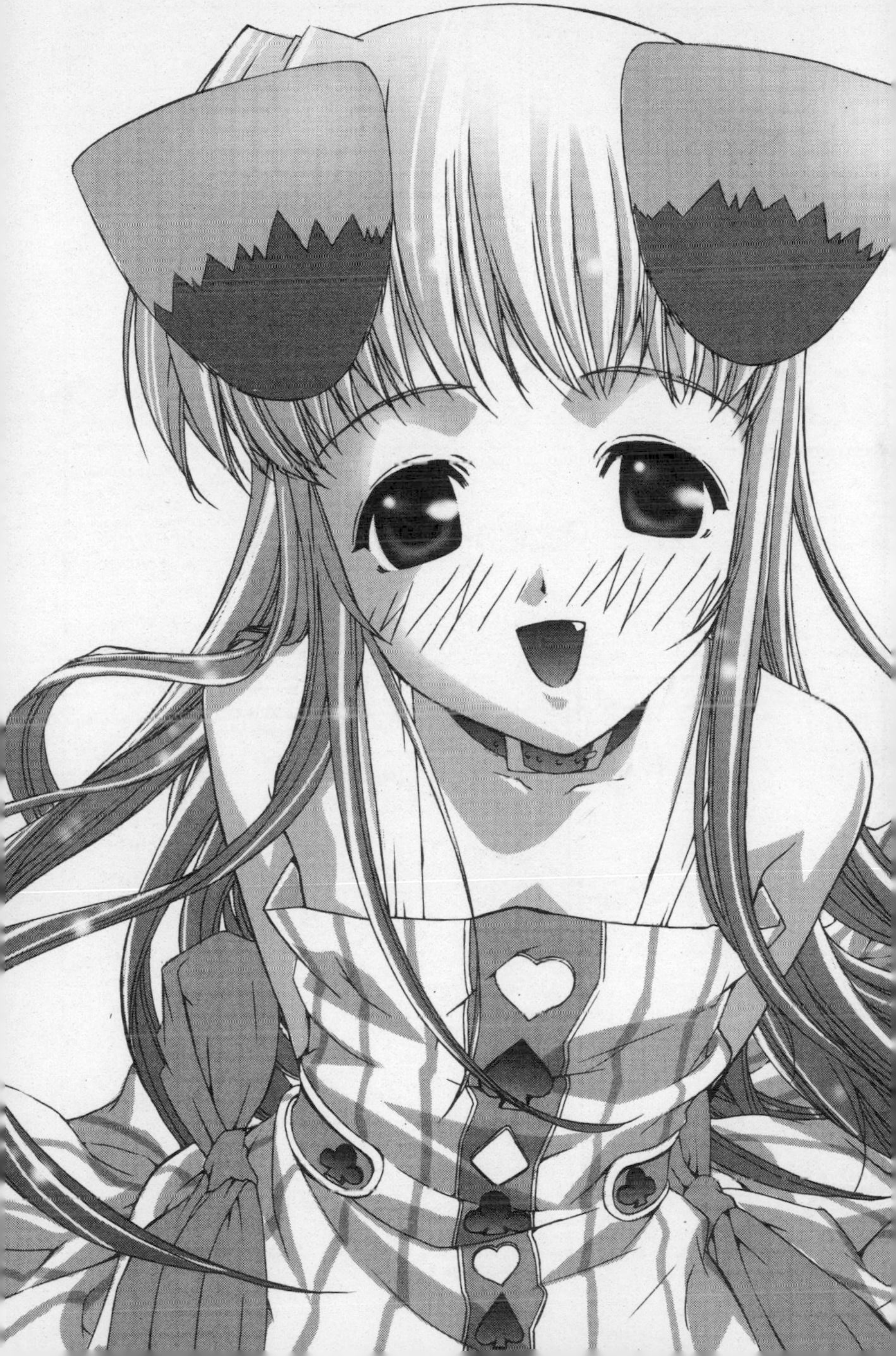

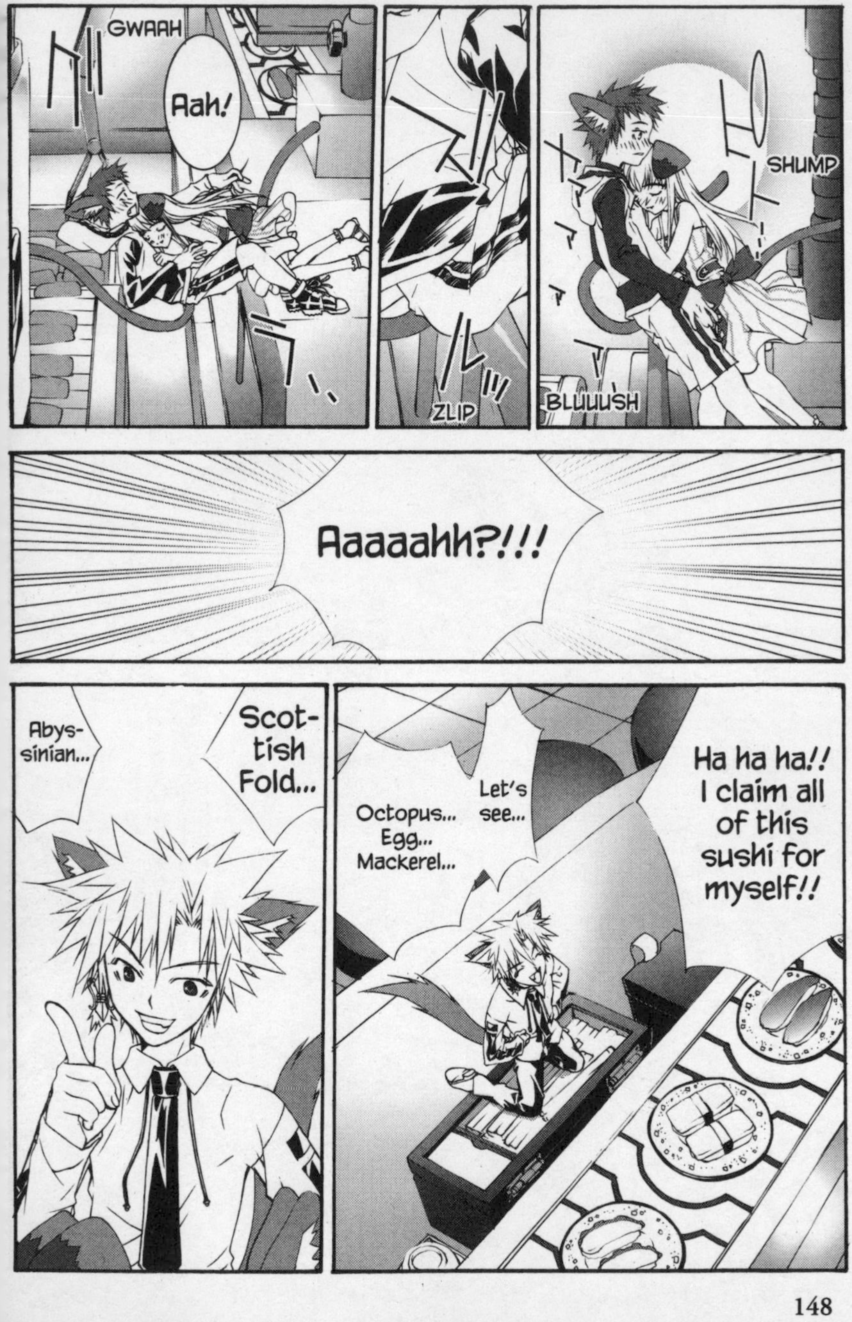
SHUMP
BLUUUSH
ZLIP
GWAAH
Aah!
Aaaaahh?!!!
Ha ha ha!! I claim all of this sushi for myself!!
Let's see...
Octopus... Egg... Mackerel...
Scot-tish Fold...
Abys-sinian...

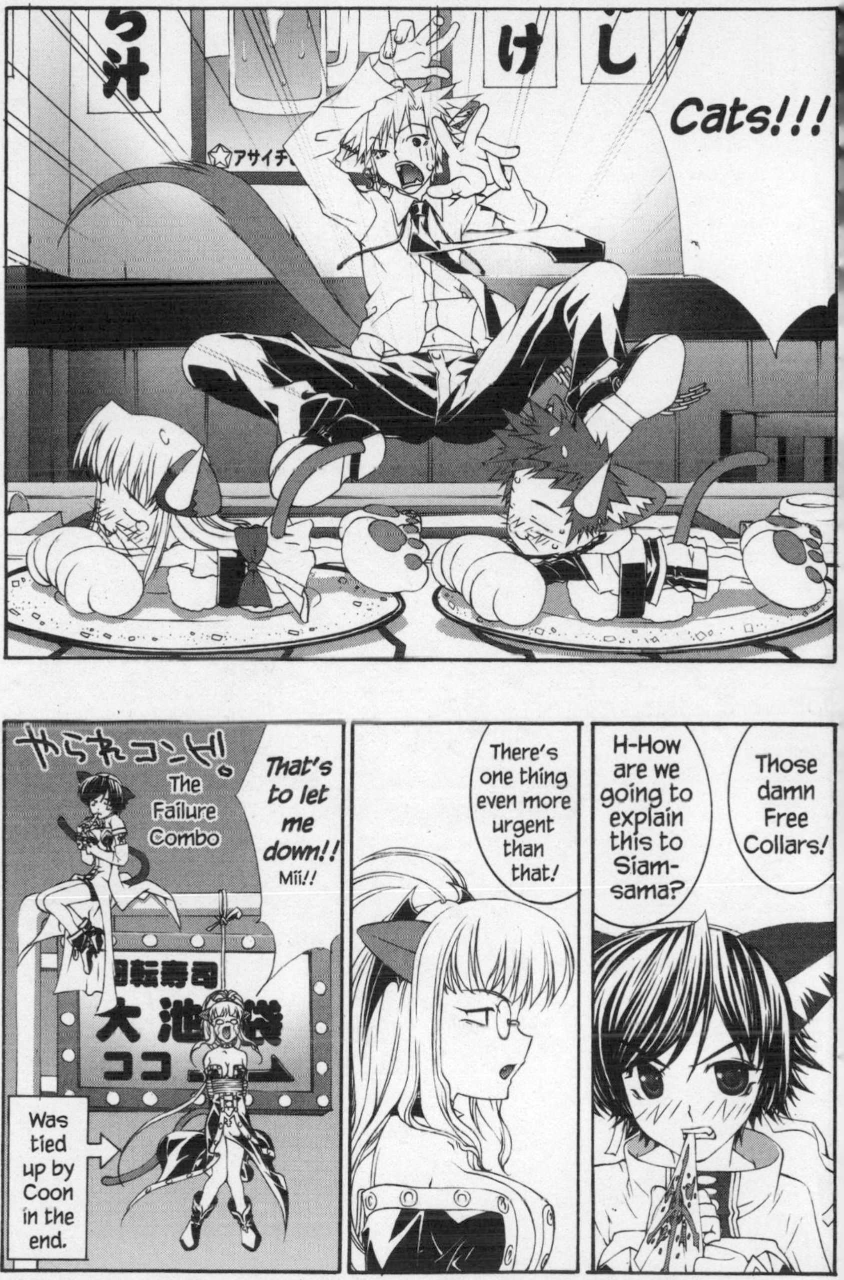
Cats!!!
Those damn Free Collars!
H-How are we going to explain this to Siam-sama?
There's one thing even more urgent than that!
That's to let me down!!
Mii!!
やられコンビ。
The Failure Combo
回転寿司
大池袋
ココ
Was tied up by Coon in the end.

Cat Tale 10 Round & Round, Fate Goes Around END

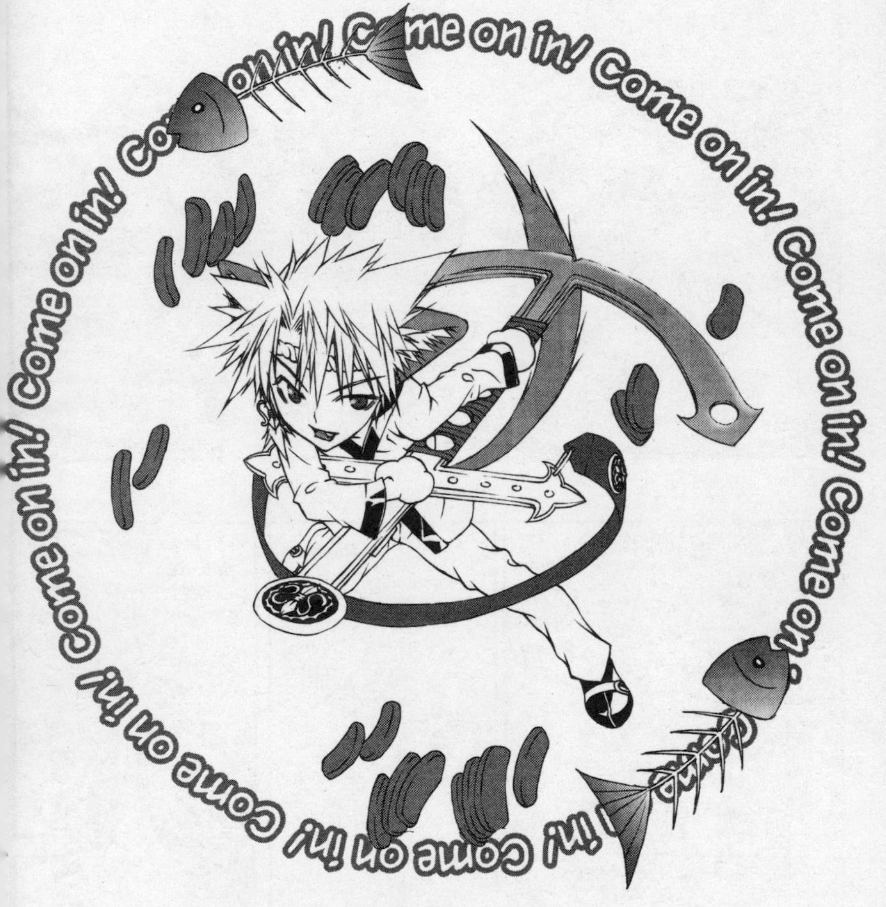
Come on in! Come on in! Come on in! Come on in! Come on in! Come on in! Come on in! Come on in!

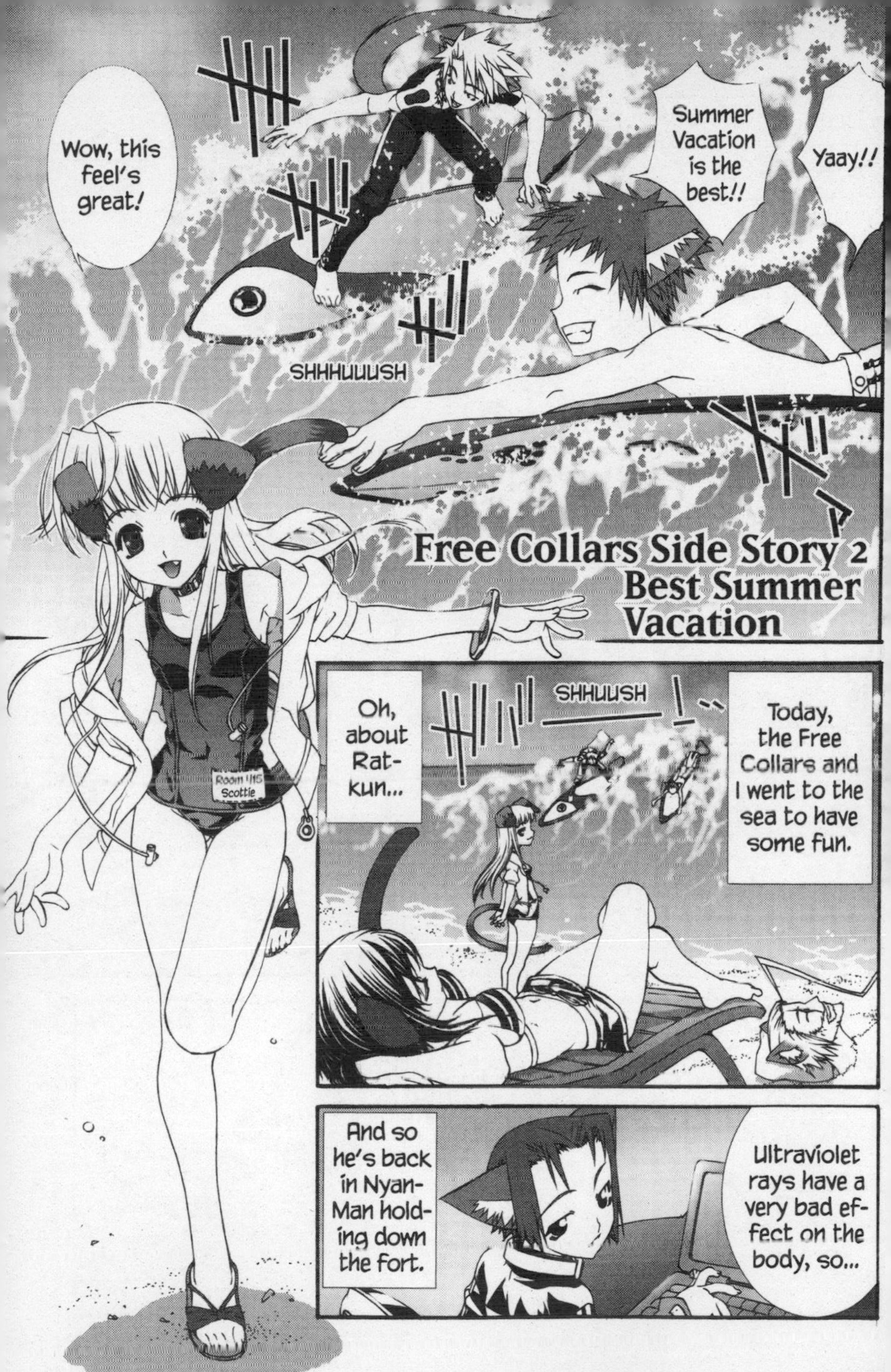
Yaay!!
Summer Vacation is the best!!
Wow, this feel's great!
SHHHUUUSH
Free Collars Side Story 2
Best Summer Vacation
Room 1/15 Scottie
Today, the Free Collars and I went to the sea to have some fun.
SHHUUSH
Oh, about Rat-kun...
Ultraviolet rays have a very bad effect on the body, so...
And so he's back in Nyan-Man holding down the fort.

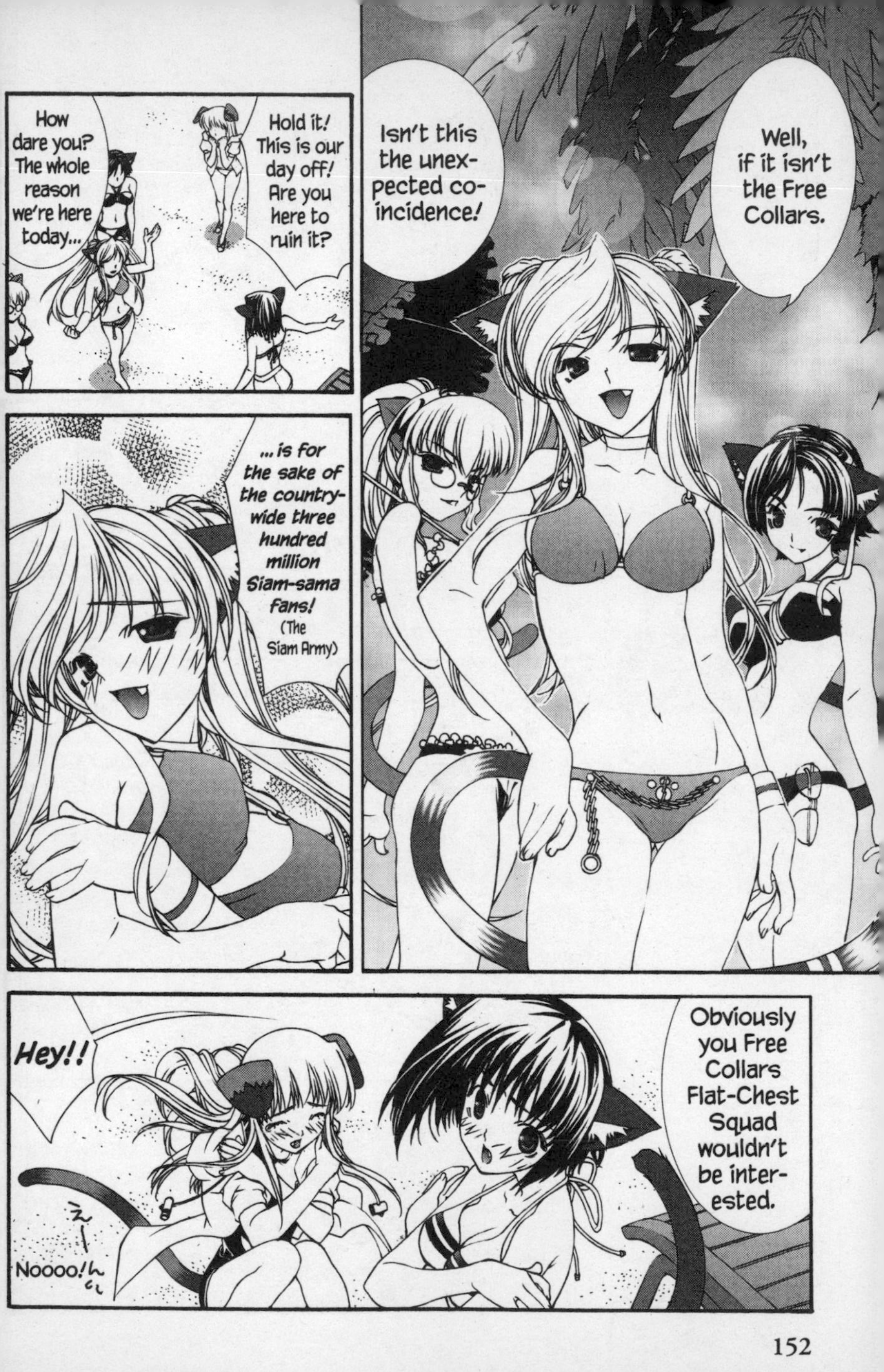
Well, if it isn't the Free Collars.
Isn't this the unexpected coincidence!
Hold it! This is our day off! Are you here to ruin it?
How dare you? The whole reason we're here today...
...is for the sake of the country-wide three hundred million Siam-sama fans!
(The Siam Army)
Obviously you Free Collars Flat-Chest Squad wouldn't be interested.
Hey!!
Noooo!

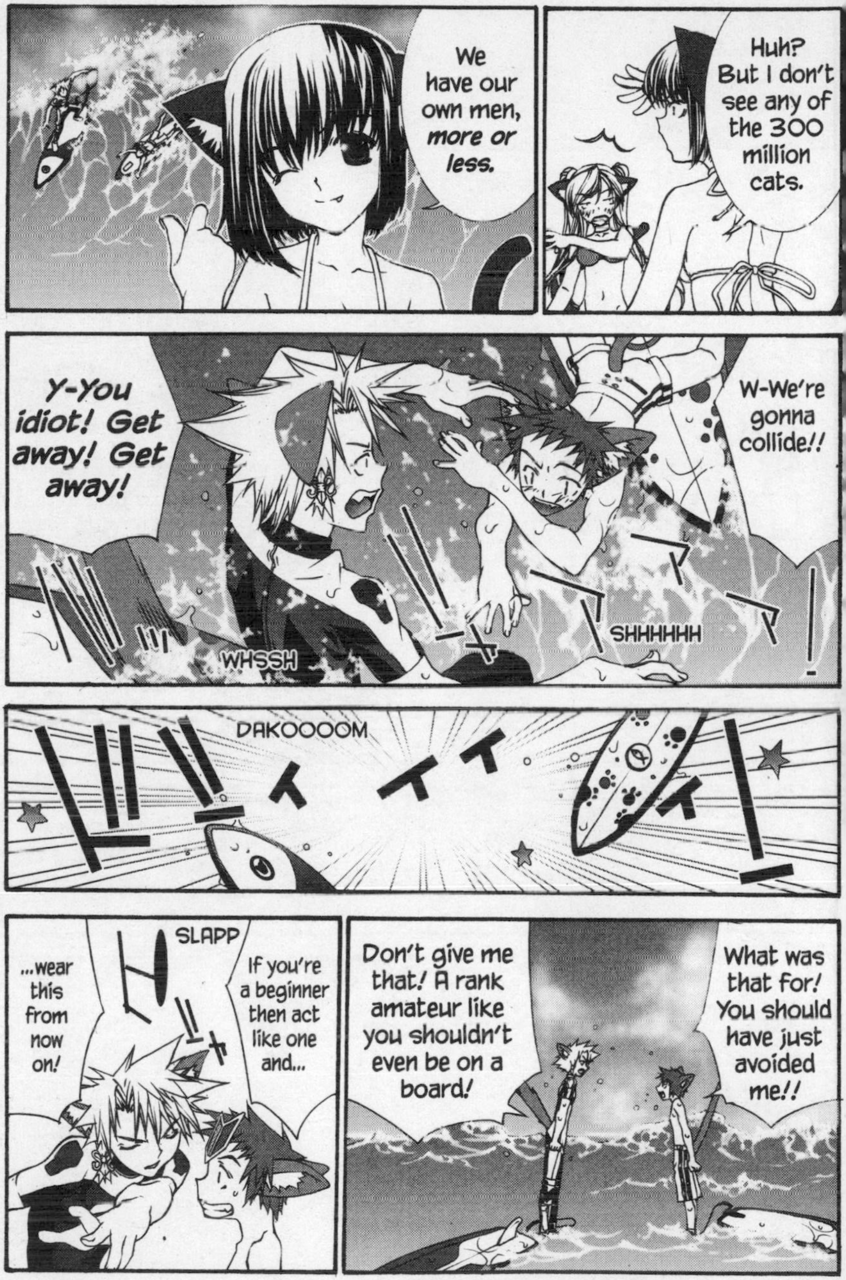
Huh? But I don't see any of the 300 million cats.
We have our own men, *more or less.*
W-We're gonna collide!!
Y-You idiot! Get away! Get away!
SHHHHHH
WHSSH
DAKOOOOM
What was that for! You should have just avoided me!!
Don't give me that! A rank amateur like you shouldn't even be on a board!
SLAPP
If you're a beginner then act like one and...
...wear this from now on!

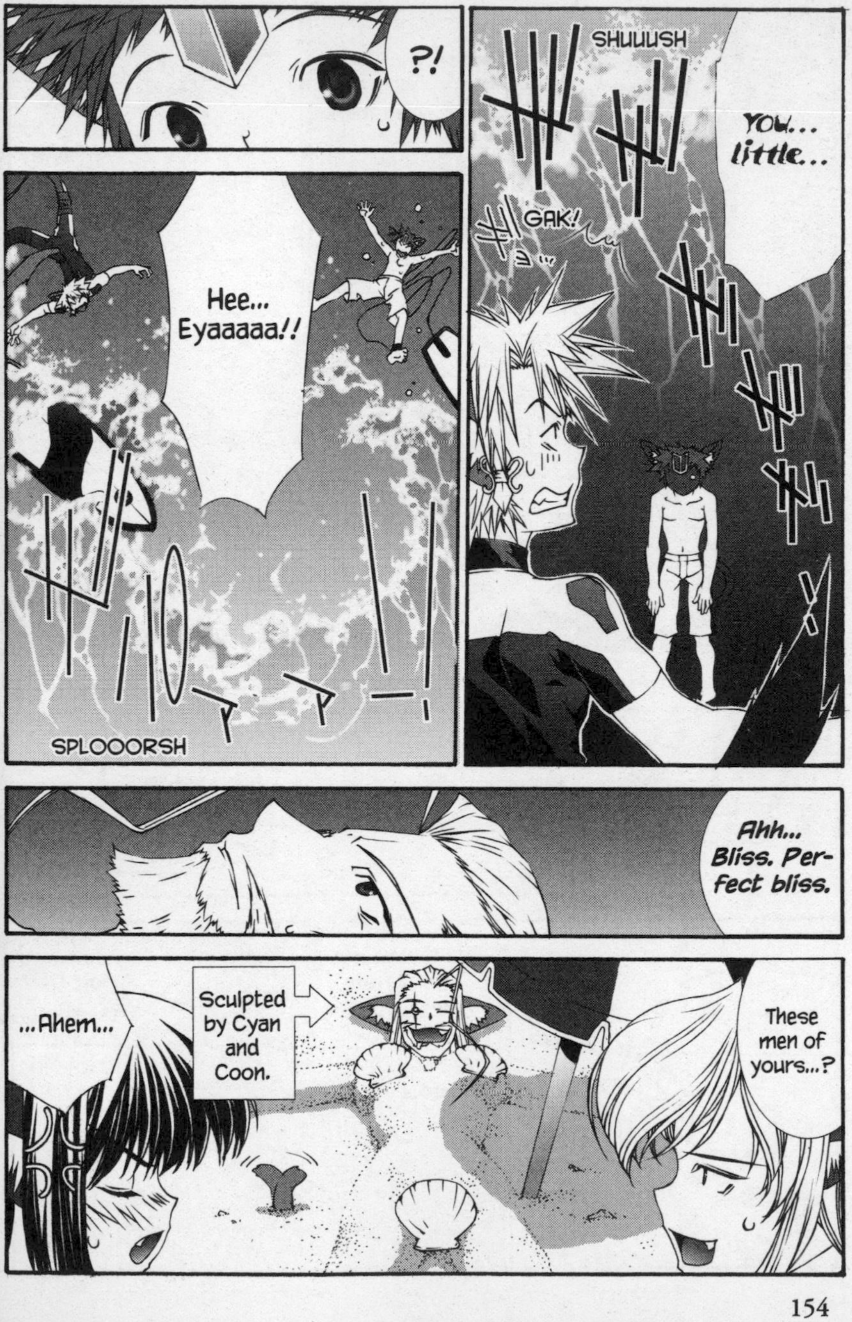
SHUUUSH
YOU... little...
GAK!
?!
Hee... Eyaaaaa!!
SPLOOORSH
Ahh... Bliss. Per-fect bliss.
These men of yours...?
Sculpted by Cyan and Coon.
...Ahem...

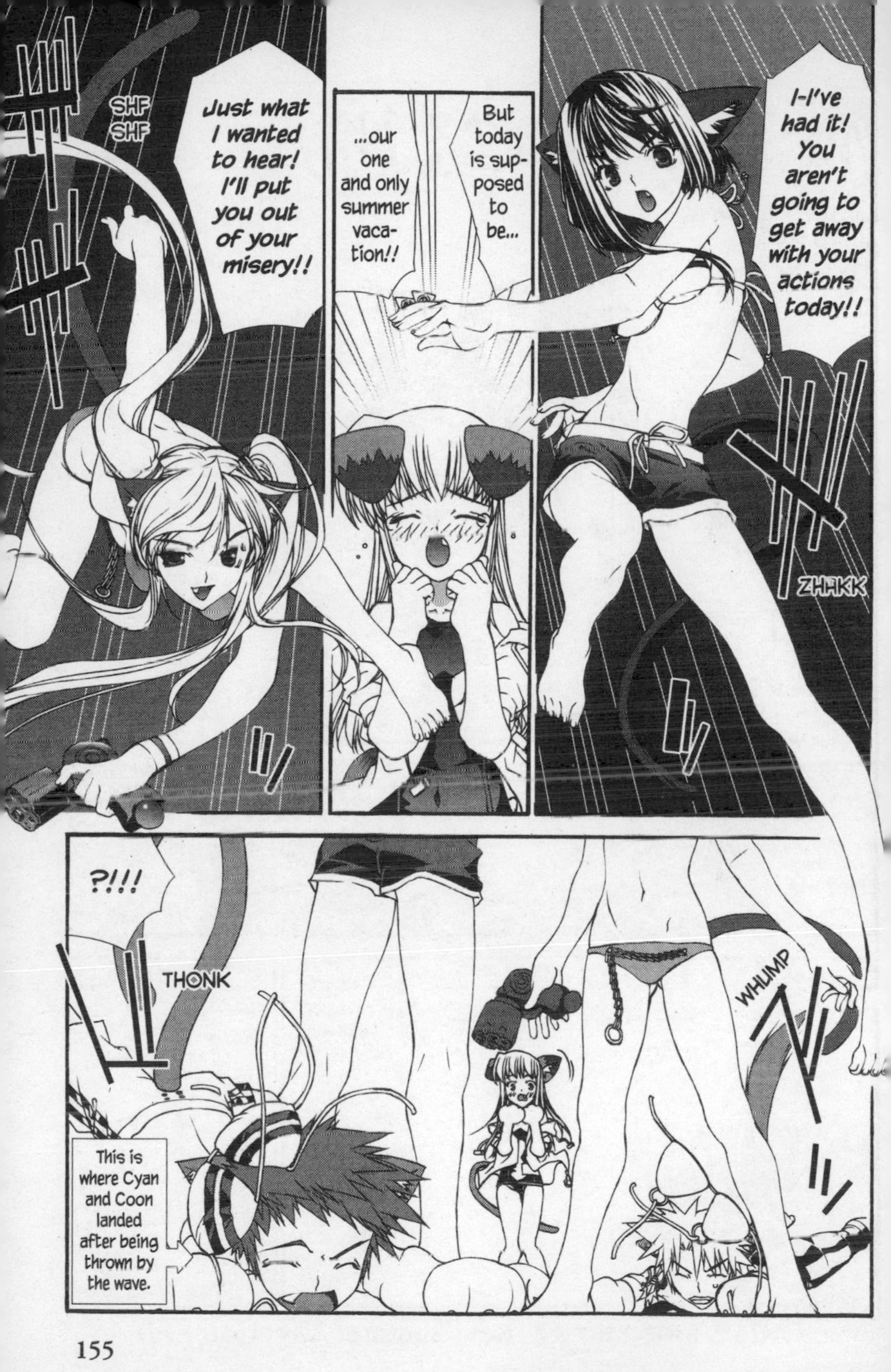
I-I've had it! You aren't going to get away with your actions today!!
ZHAKK
But today is supposed to be...
...our one and only summer vacation!!
Just what I wanted to hear! I'll put you out of your misery!!
SHF SHF
WHUMP
THONK
?!!!
This is where Cyan and Coon landed after being thrown by the wave.

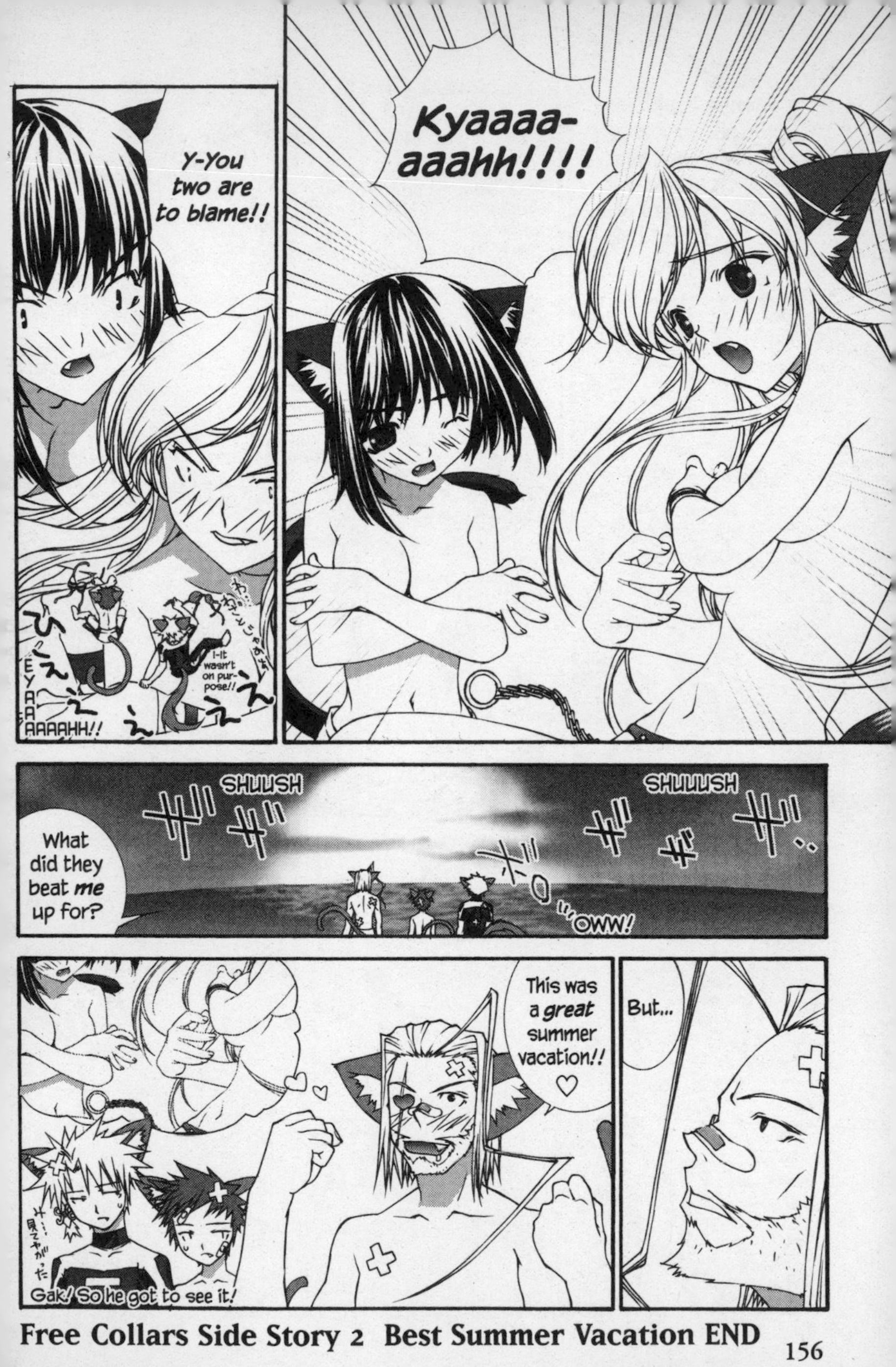
Kyaaaa-aaaahh!!!!
Y-You two are to blame!!
I-It wasn't on pur-pose!!
EYAAAAAAHH!!
SHUUSH
SHUUSH
What did they beat *me* up for?
OWW!
But...
This was a *great* summer vacation!! ♡
Gak! So he got to see it!

Free Collars Side Story 2 Best Summer Vacation END

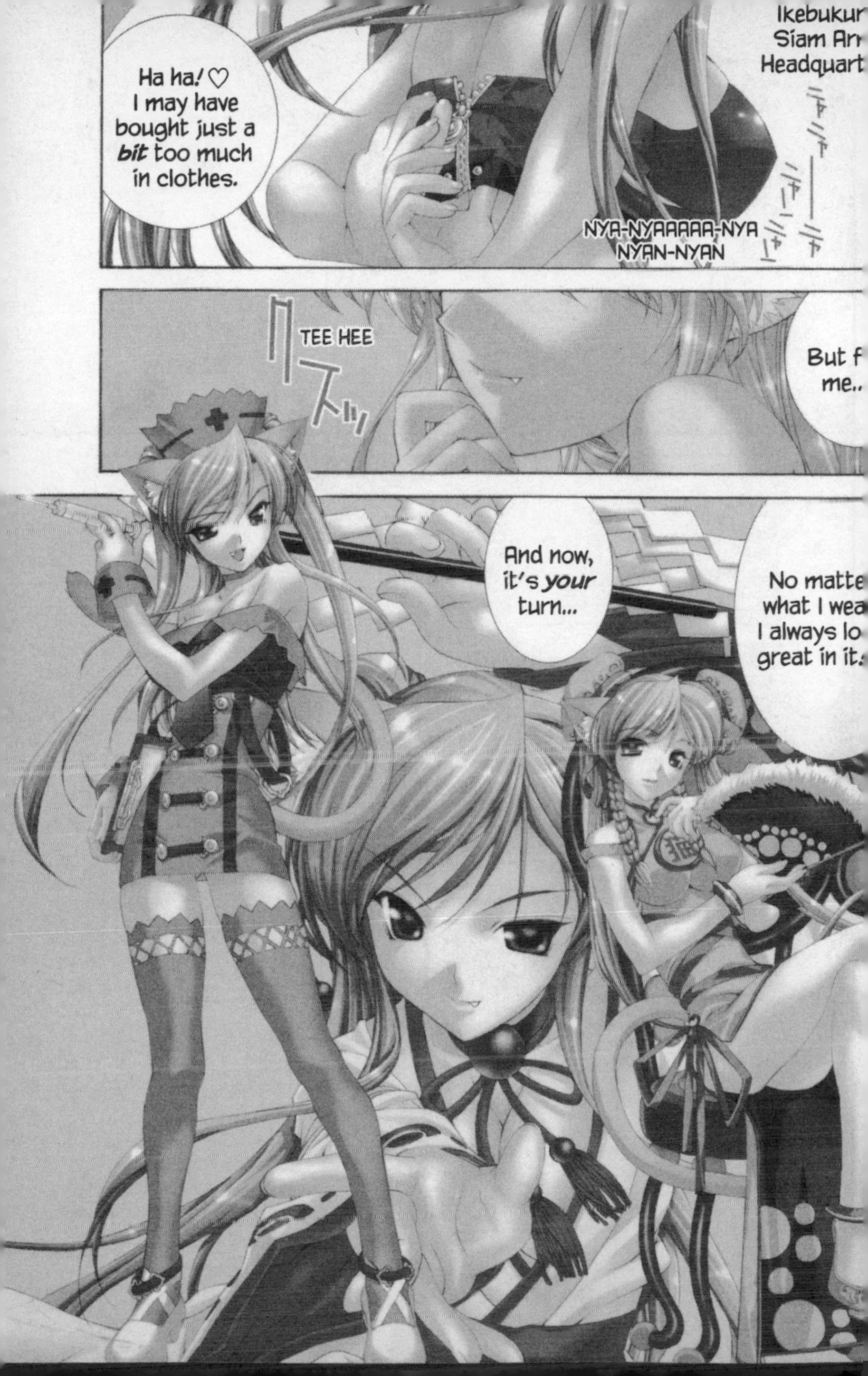
Ikebukur
Siam Arr
Headquart
NYA-NYAAAAA-NYA NYAN-NYAN
Ha ha! ♡ I may have bought just a *bit* too much in clothes.
But f me..
TEE HEE
No matte what I wea I always lo great in it.
And now, it's *your* turn...

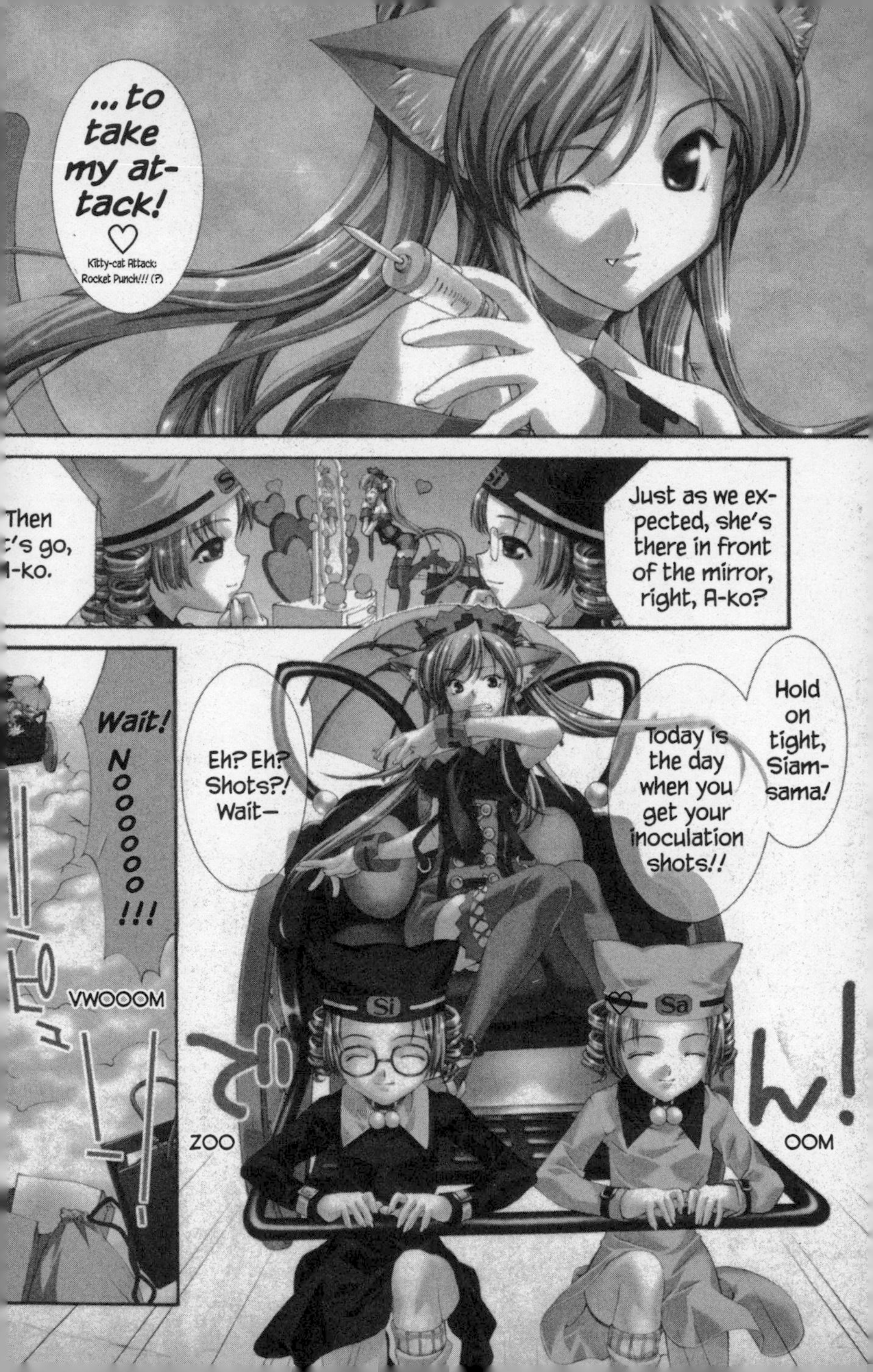
...to take my at-tack! ♡
Kitty-cat Attack: Rocket Punch!!! (?)
Just as we ex-pected, she's there in front of the mirror, right, A-ko?
Then 's go, -ko.
Hold on tight, Siam-sama!
Today is the day when you get your inoculation shots!!
Eh? Eh? Shots?! Wait—
ZOO
OOM
Wait!
Noooooooo!!!
VWOOOM

Cat Tale II An Injection for a Certain Special Someone

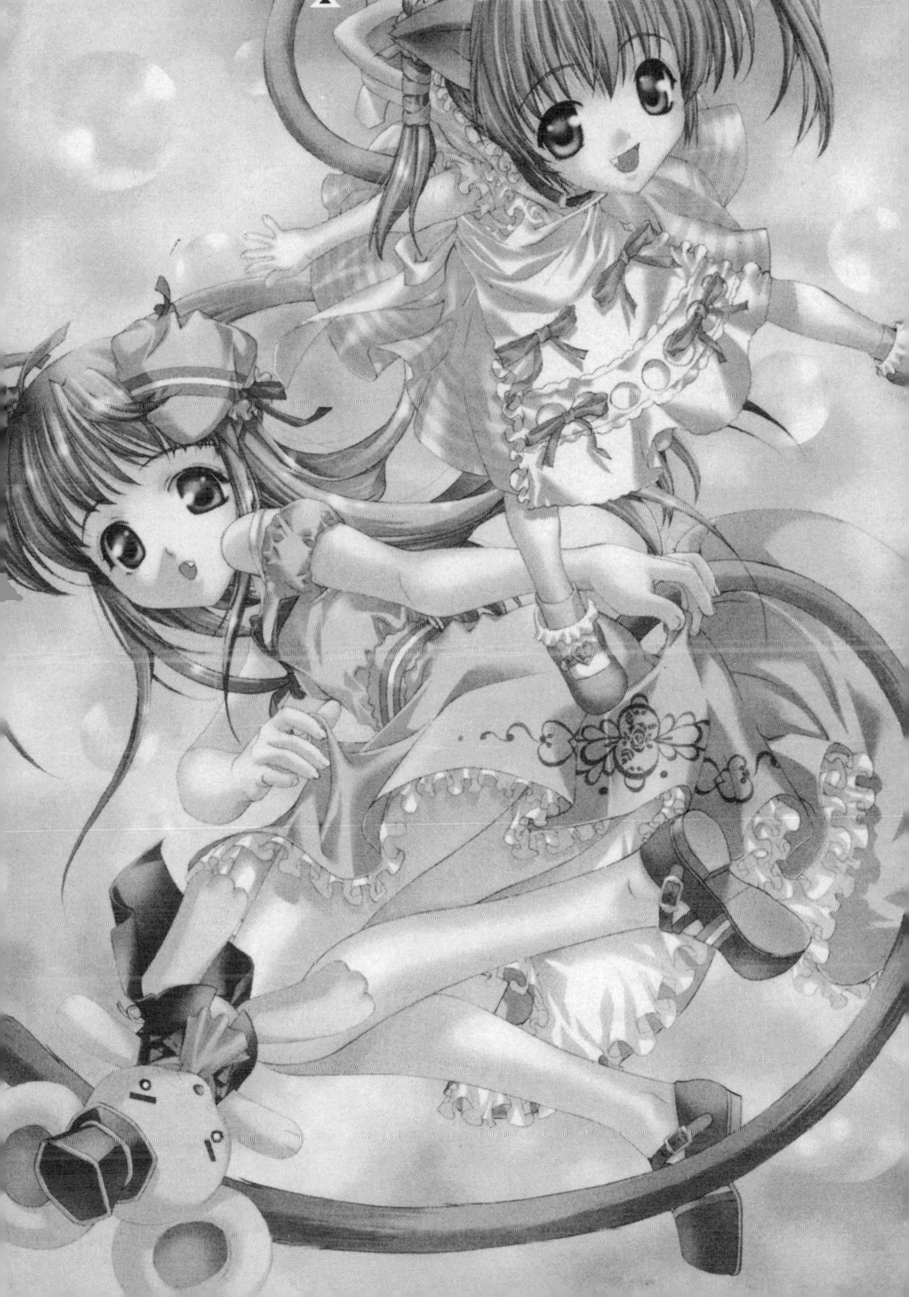

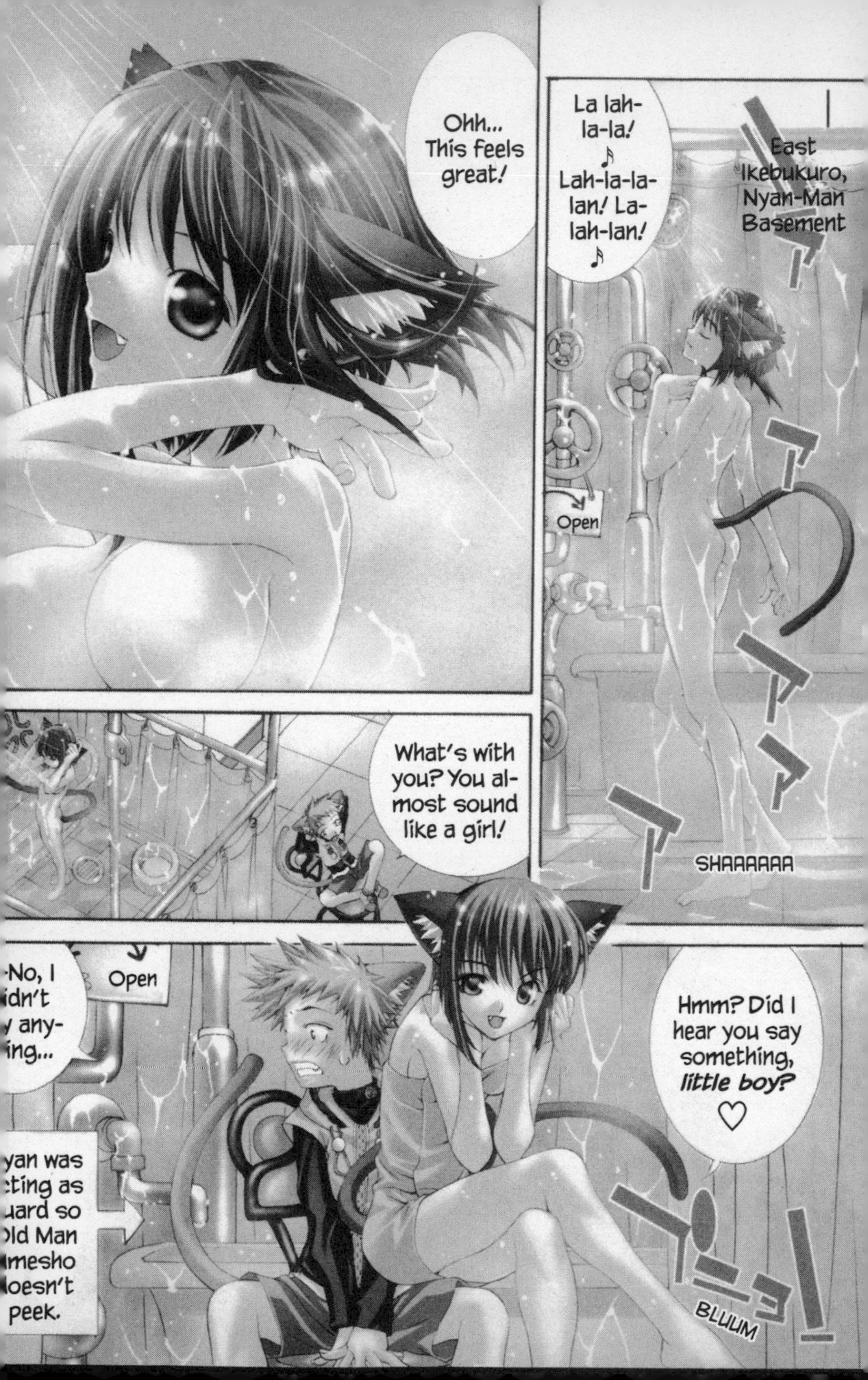
East Ikebukuro, Nyan-Man Basement
La lah-la-la! ♪ Lah-la-la-lan! La-lah-lan! ♪
Open
SHAAAAAA
Ohh... This feels great!
What's with you? You almost sound like a girl!
Hmm? Did I hear you say something, little boy? ♡
BLUUM
Open
-No, I idn't y any- ing...
yan was cting as uard so Old Man mesho oesn't peek.

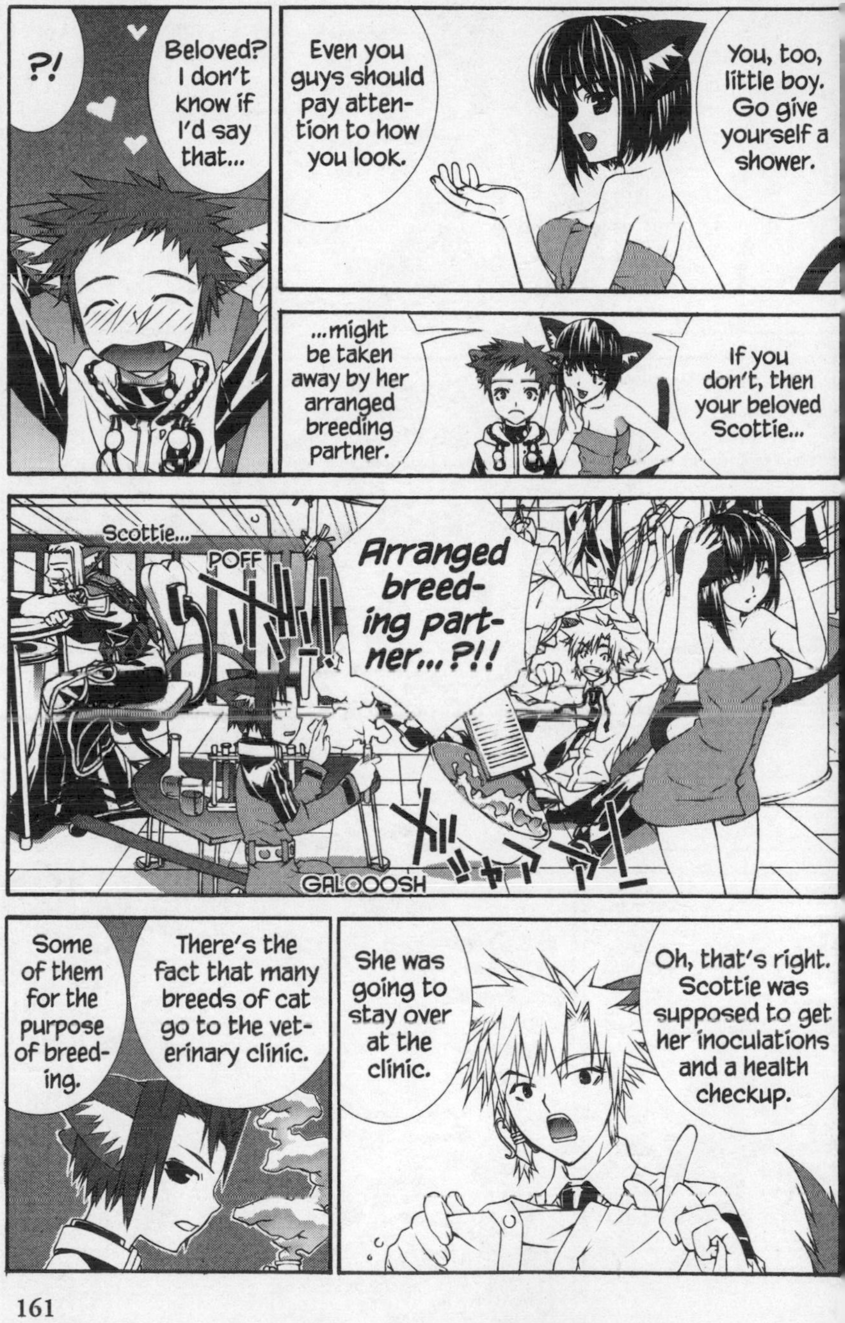
You, too, little boy. Go give yourself a shower.
Even you guys should pay attention to how you look.
If you don't, then your beloved Scottie...
...might be taken away by her arranged breeding partner.
Beloved? I don't know if I'd say that...
?!
Arranged breeding partner...?!!
Scottie...
POFF
GALOOOSH
Oh, that's right. Scottie was supposed to get her inoculations and a health checkup.
She was going to stay over at the clinic.
There's the fact that many breeds of cat go to the veterinary clinic.
Some of them for the purpose of breeding.

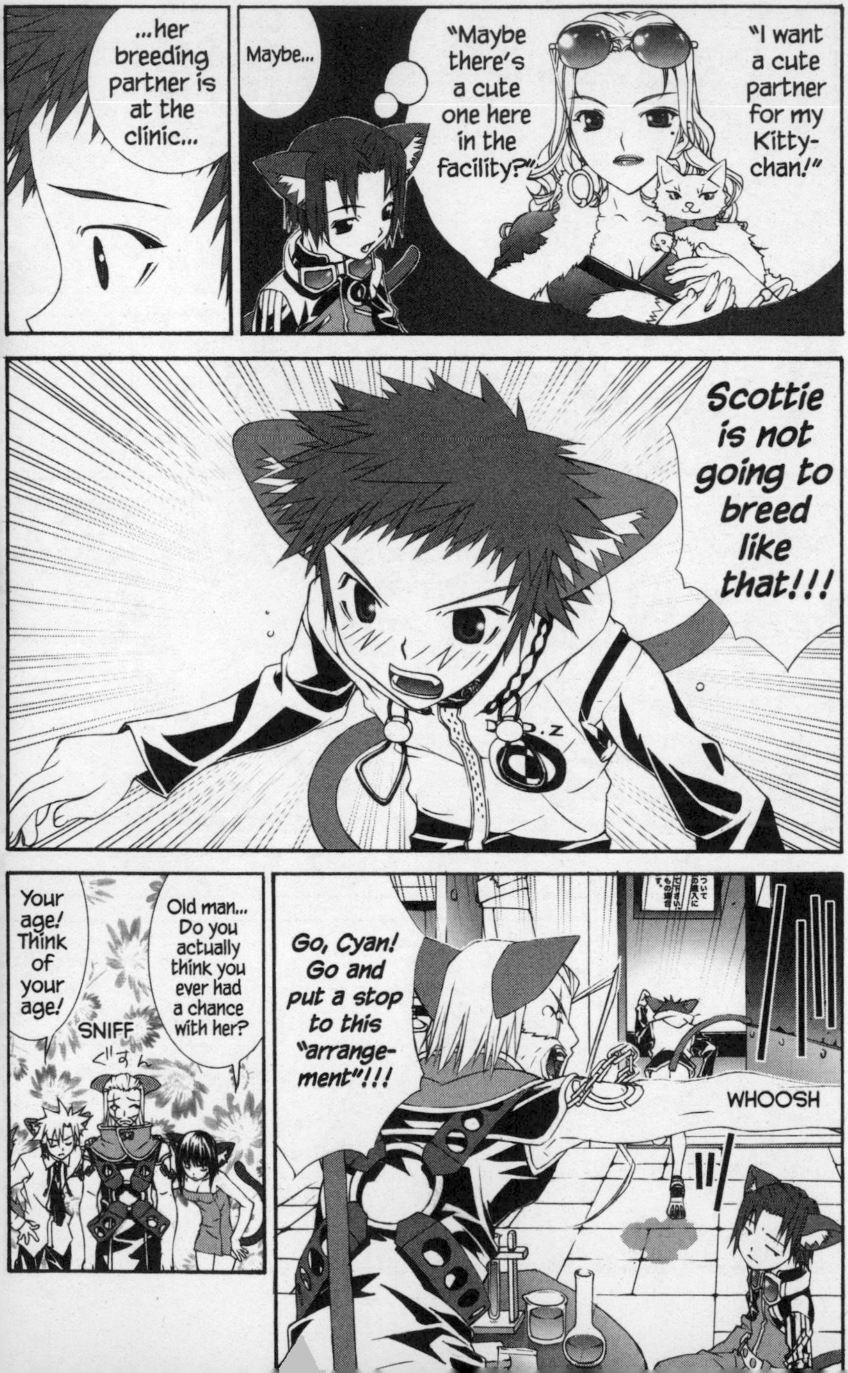
"I want a cute partner for my Kitty-chan!"
"Maybe there's a cute one here in the facility?"
Maybe...
...her breeding partner is at the clinic...
Scottie is not going to breed like that!!!
Go, Cyan! Go and put a stop to this "arrangement"!!!
WHOOSH
Old man... Do you actually think you ever had a chance with her?
Your age! Think of your age!
SNIFF
ぐすん

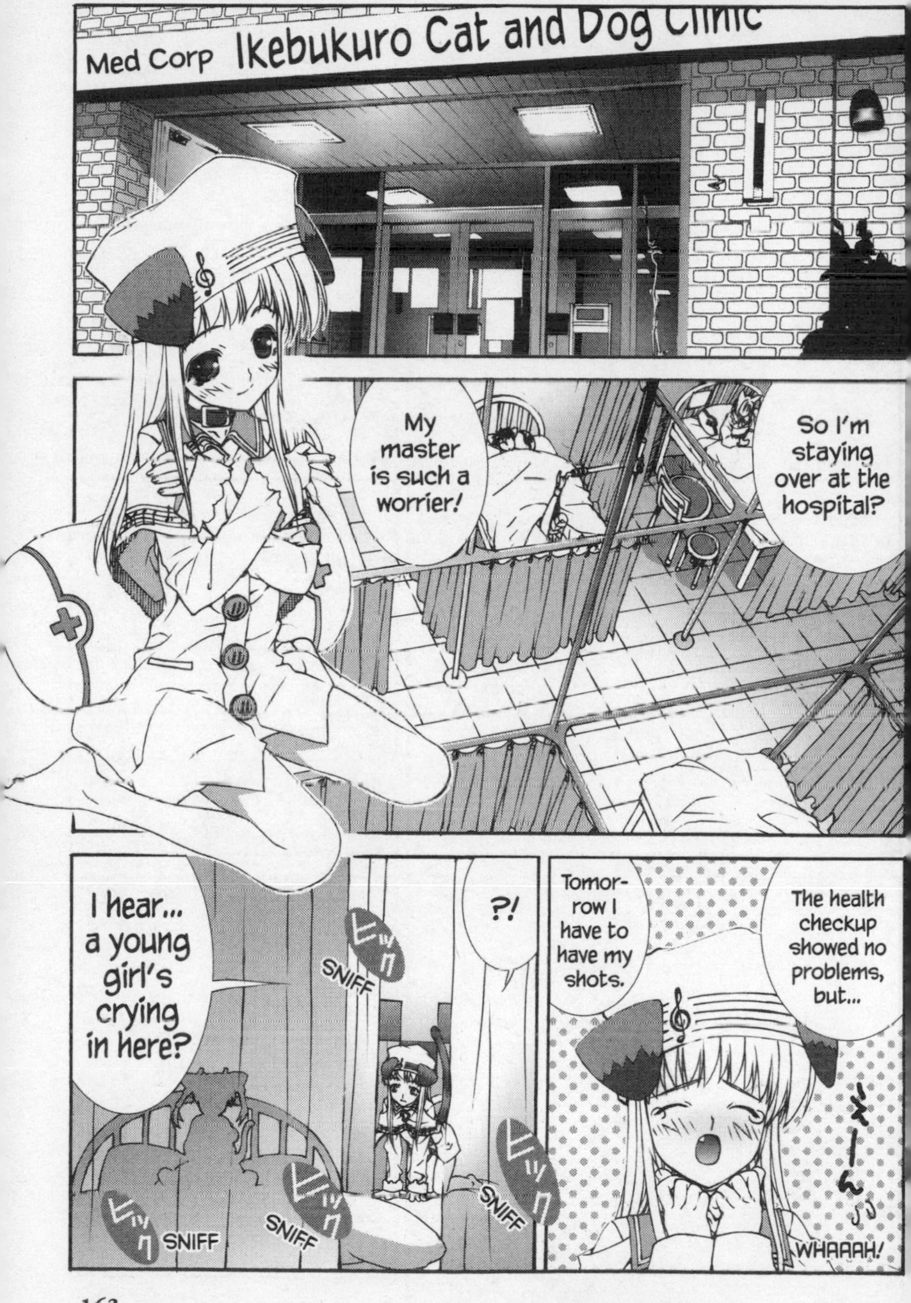
Med Corp Ikebukuro Cat and Dog Clinic
So I'm staying over at the hospital?
My master is such a worrier!
The health checkup showed no problems, but...
Tomorrow I have to have my shots.
WHAAAH!
?!
SNIFF
SNIFF
I hear... a young girl's crying in here?
SNIFF
SNIFF

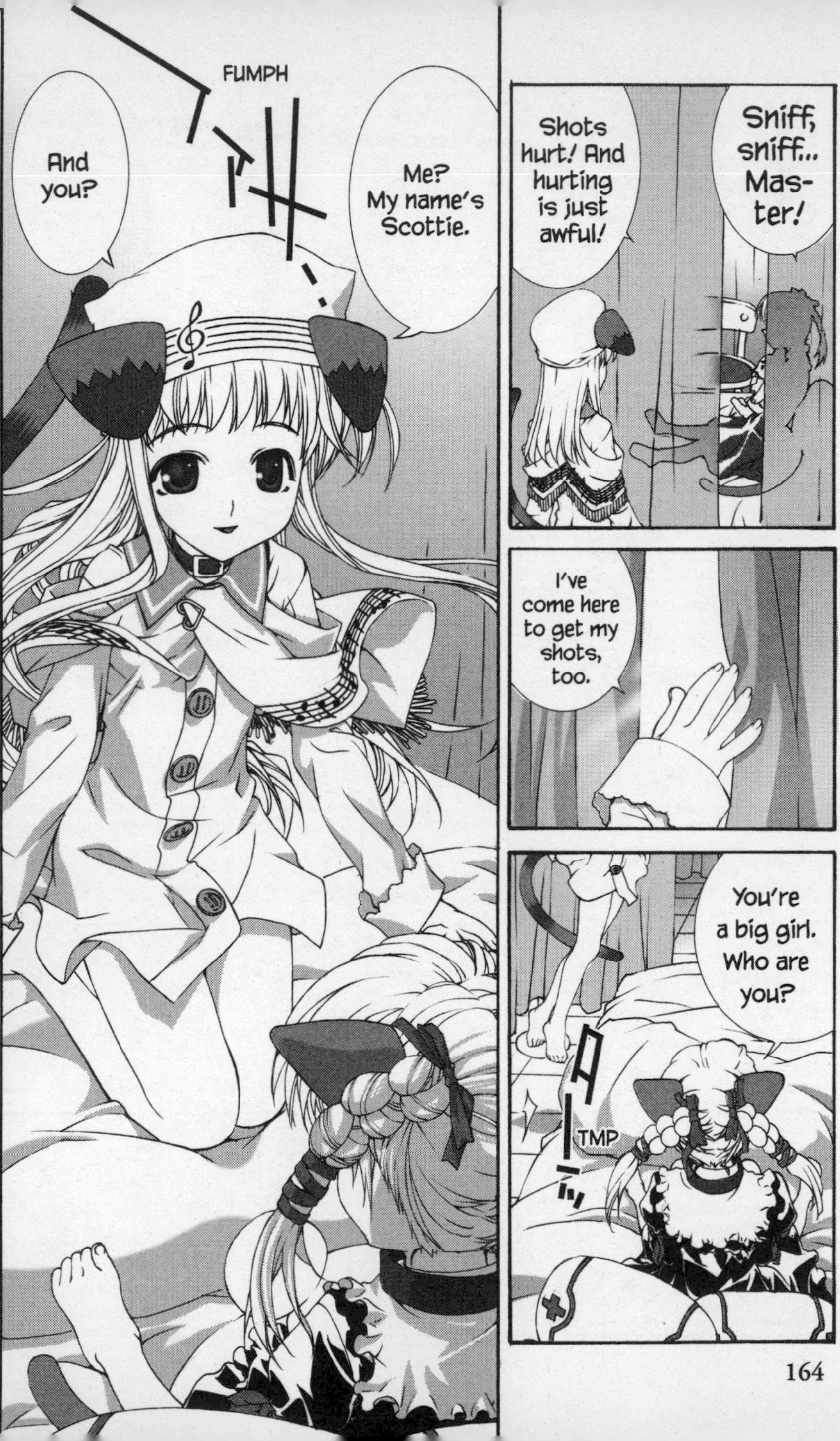
Sniff, sniff... Mas-ter!
Shots hurt! And hurting is just awful!
I've come here to get my shots, too.
You're a big girl. Who are you?
TMP
Me? My name's Scottie.
FUMPH
And you?

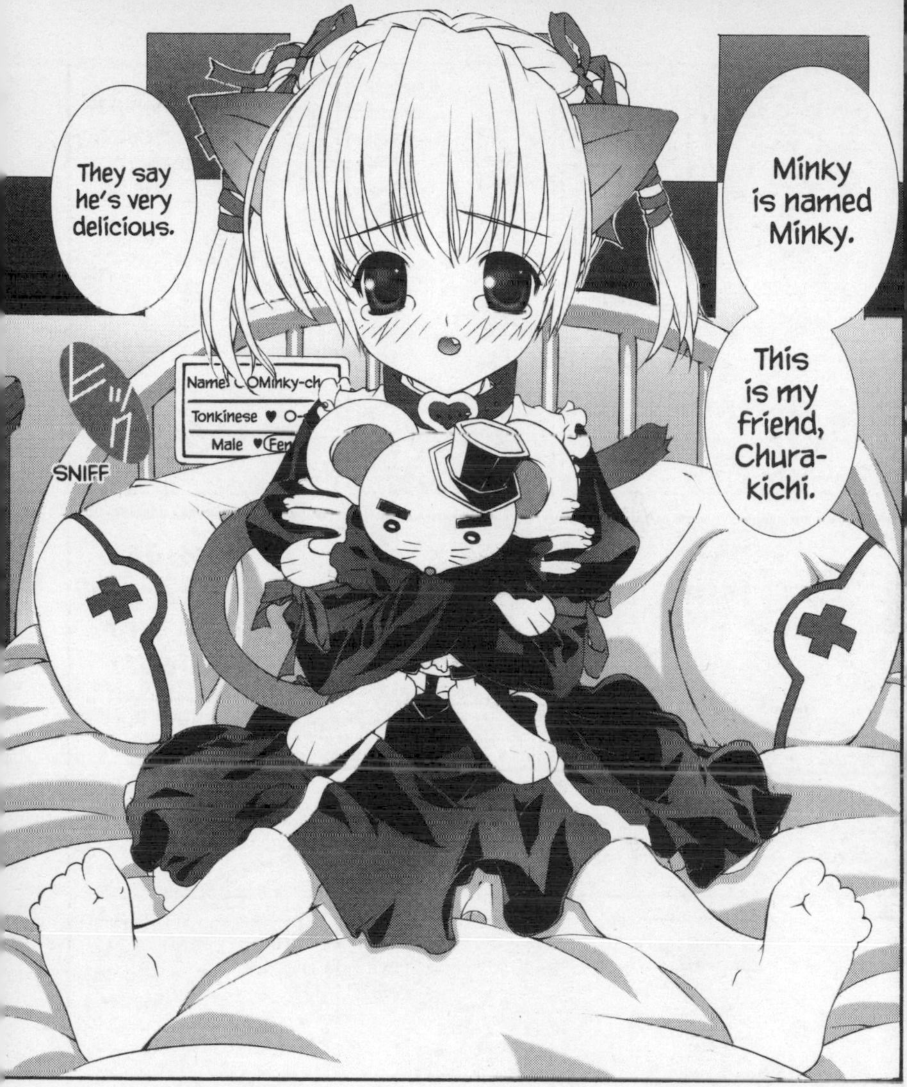
Minky is named Minky.
This is my friend, Chura-kichi.
They say he's very delicious.
SNIFF

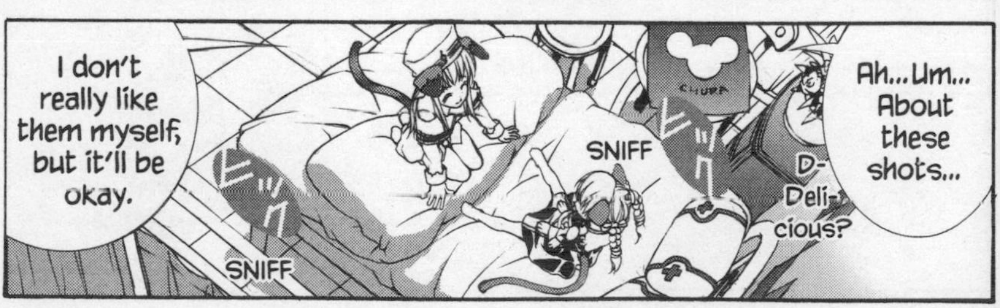
Ah...Um... About these shots...
D-Deli-cious?
SNIFF
I don't really like them myself, but it'll be okay.
SNIFF

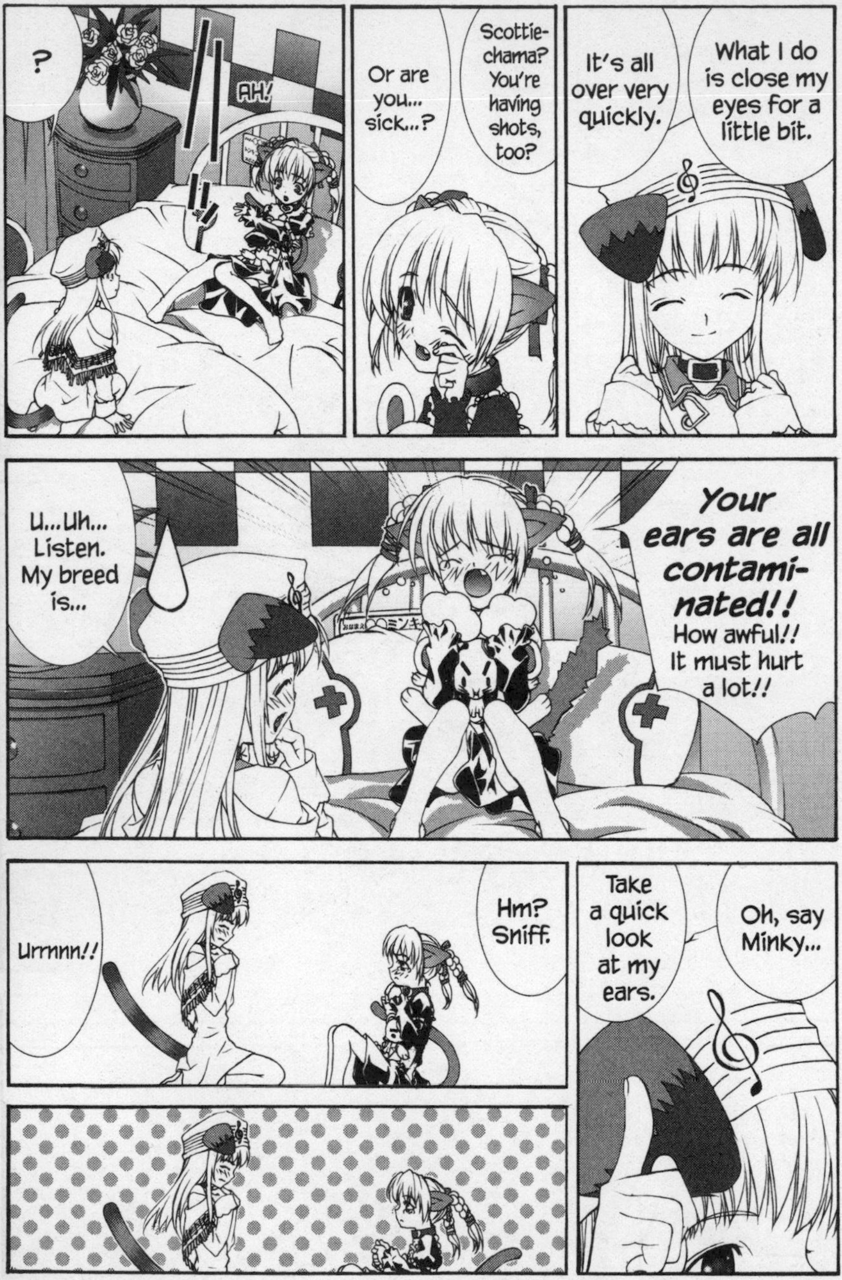
What I do is close my eyes for a little bit.
It's all over very quickly.
Scottie-chama? You're having shots, too?
Or are you... sick...?
AH!
?
Your ears are all contami-nated!! How awful!! It must hurt a lot!!
U...uh... Listen. My breed is...
Oh, say Minky...
Take a quick look at my ears.
Hm? Sniff.
Urrnnn!!

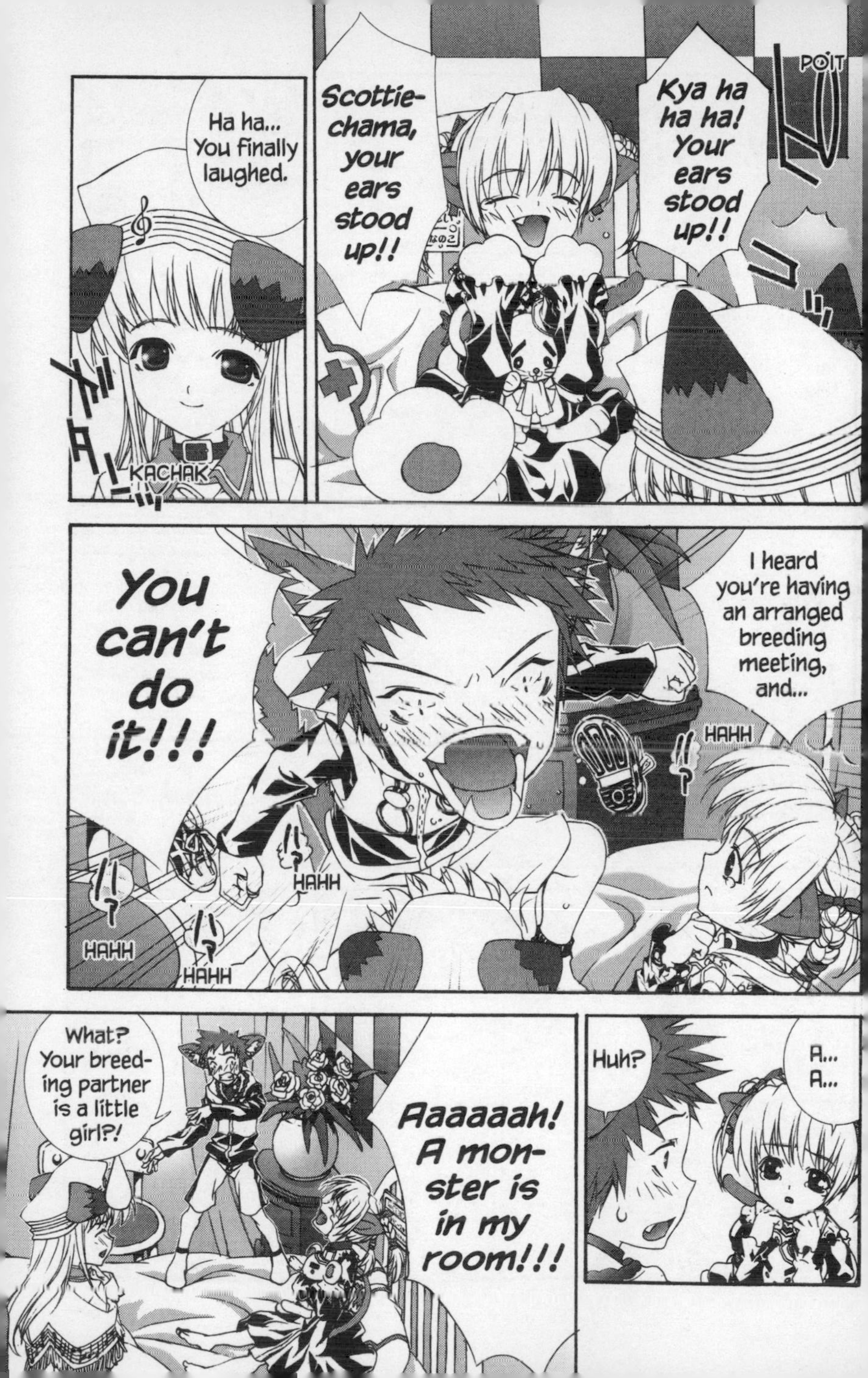
POIT
Kya ha ha ha! Your ears stood up!!
Scottie-chama, your ears stood up!!
Ha ha... You finally laughed.
KACHAK
I heard you're having an arranged breeding meeting, and...
HAHH
You can't do it!!!
HAHH
HAHH
HAHH
A... A...
Huh?
Aaaaaah! A monster is in my room!!!
What? Your breeding partner is a little girl?!

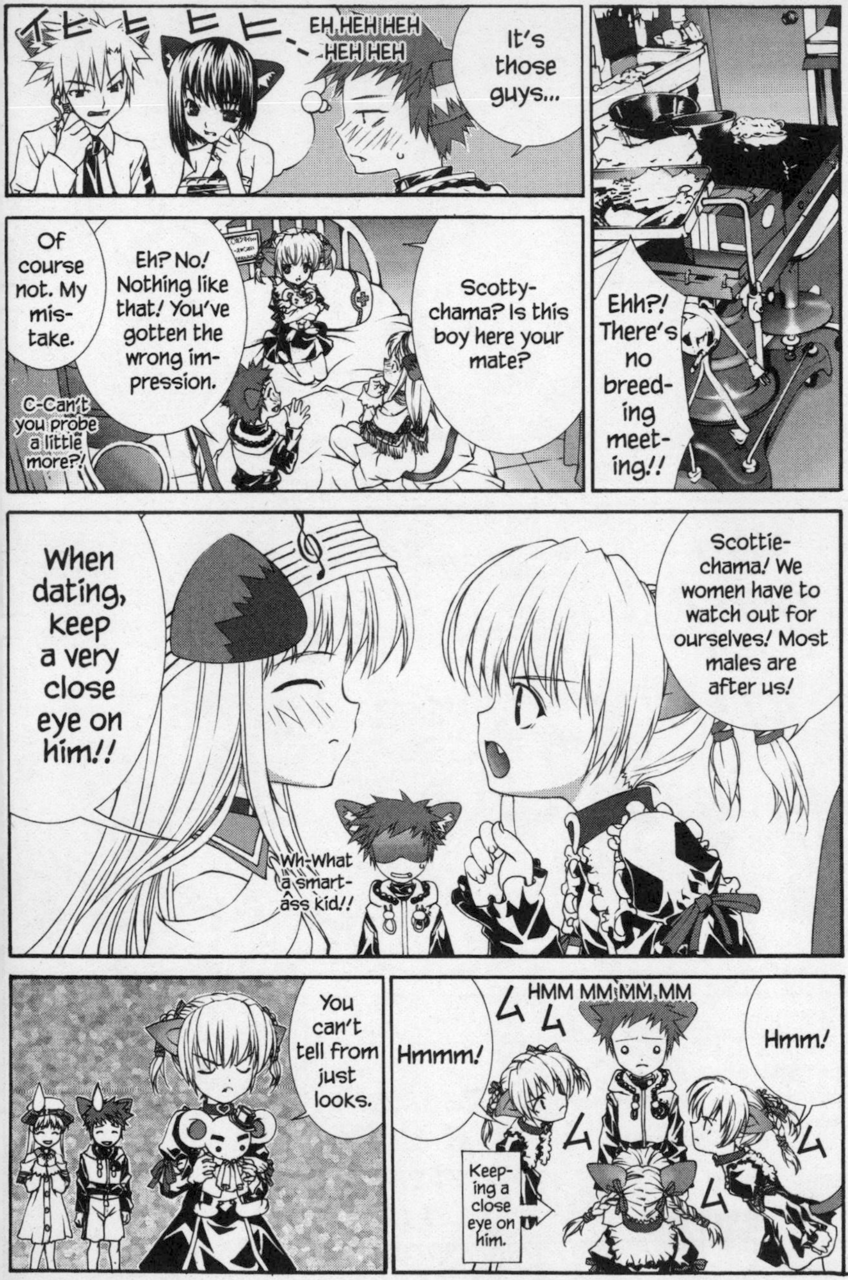
Ehh?! There's no breed-ing meet-ing!!
It's those guys...
EH HEH HEH HEH HEH
Scotty-chama? Is this boy here your mate?
Eh? No! Nothing like that! You've gotten the wrong im-pression.
Of course not. My mis-take.
C-Can't you probe a little more?!
Scottie-chama! We women have to watch out for ourselves! Most males are after us!
When dating, keep a very close eye on him!!
Wh-What a smart-ass kid!!
Hmm!
HMM MM MM MM
Hmmm!
Keep-ing a close eye on him.
You can't tell from just looks.

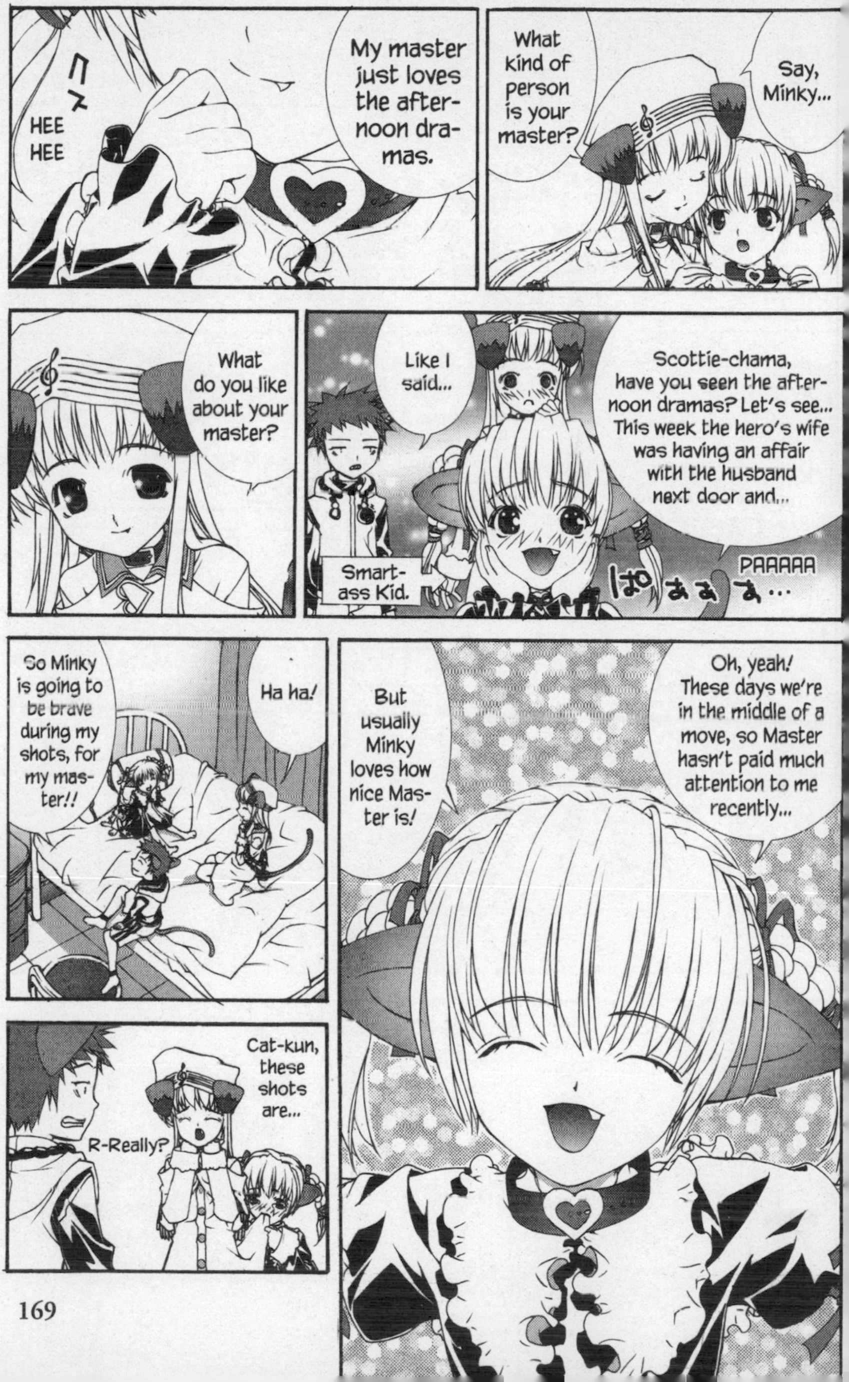
Say, Minky...
What kind of person is your master?
My master just loves the after-noon dra-mas.
HEE HEE
Scottie-chama, have you seen the after-noon dramas? Let's see... This week the hero's wife was having an affair with the husband next door and...
PAAAAA
ぱあああ...
Like I said...
Smart-ass Kid.
What do you like about your master?
Oh, yeah! These days we're in the middle of a move, so Master hasn't paid much attention to me recently...
But usually Minky loves how nice Mas-ter is!
Ha ha!
So Minky is going to be brave during my shots, for my mas-ter!!
Cat-kun, these shots are...
R-Really?

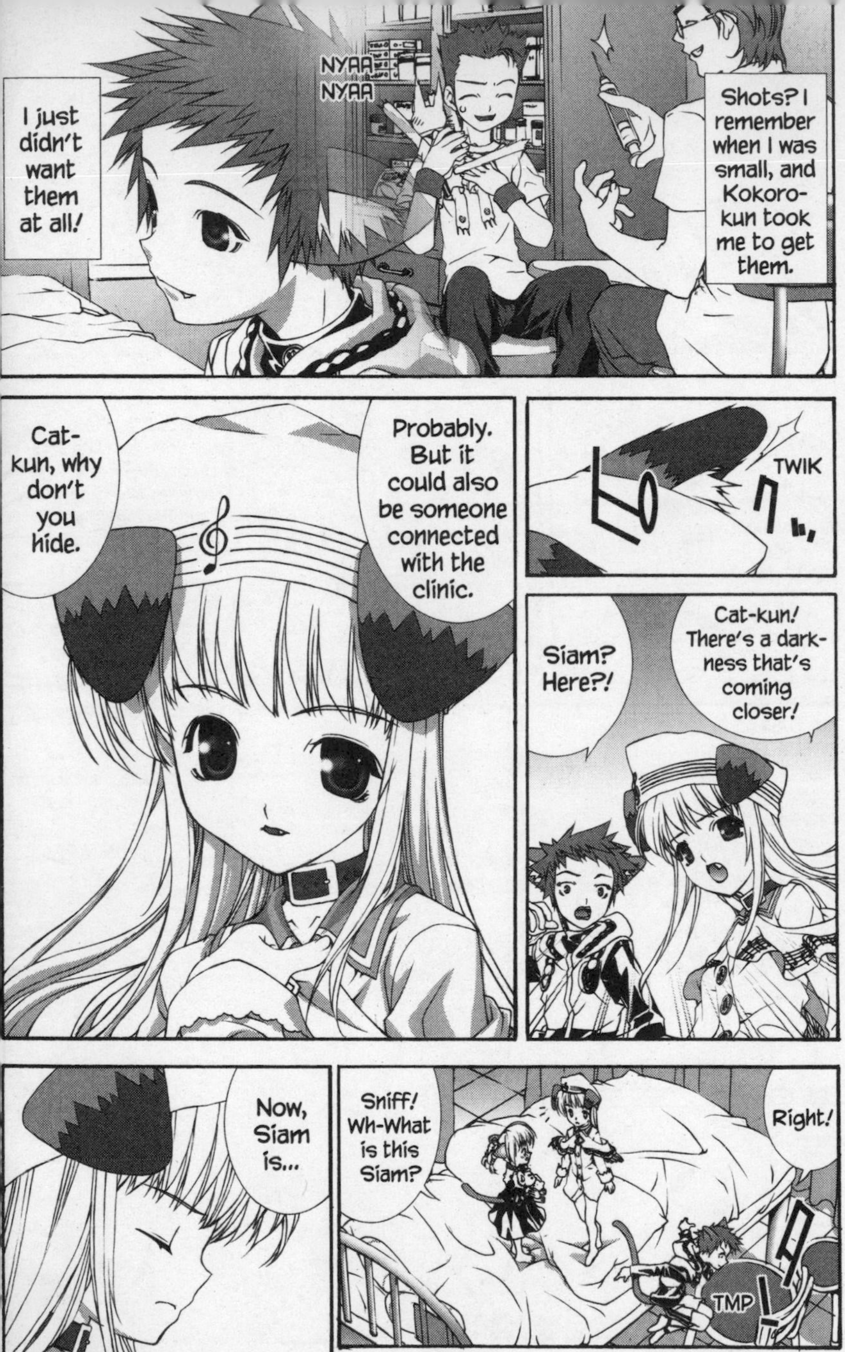
Shots? I remember when I was small, and Kokoro-kun took me to get them.
NYAA NYAA
I just didn't want them at all!
TWIK
Cat-kun! There's a darkness that's coming closer!
Siam? Here?!
Probably. But it could also be someone connected with the clinic.
Cat-kun, why don't you hide.
Right!
Sniff! Wh-What is this Siam?
TMP
Now, Siam is...

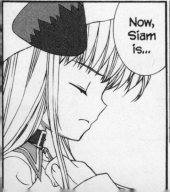

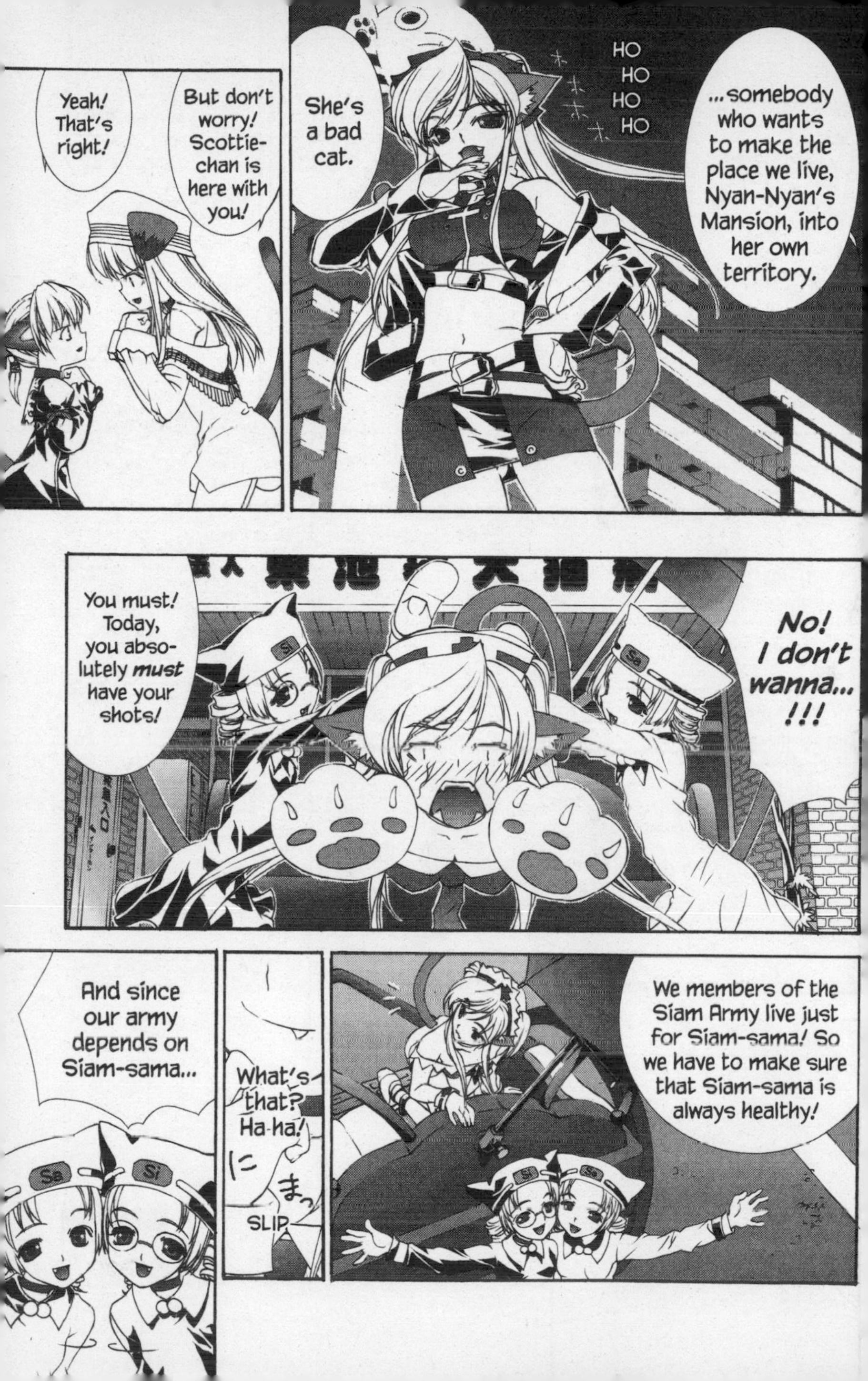
...somebody who wants to make the place we live, Nyan-Nyan's Mansion, into her own territory.
HO HO HO HO
She's a bad cat.
But don't worry! Scottie-chan is here with you!
Yeah! That's right!
No! I don't wanna...!!!
You must! Today, you absolutely must have your shots!
We members of the Siam Army live just for Siam-sama! So we have to make sure that Siam-sama is always healthy!
What's that? Ha-ha!
にまっ
SLIP
And since our army depends on Siam-sama...

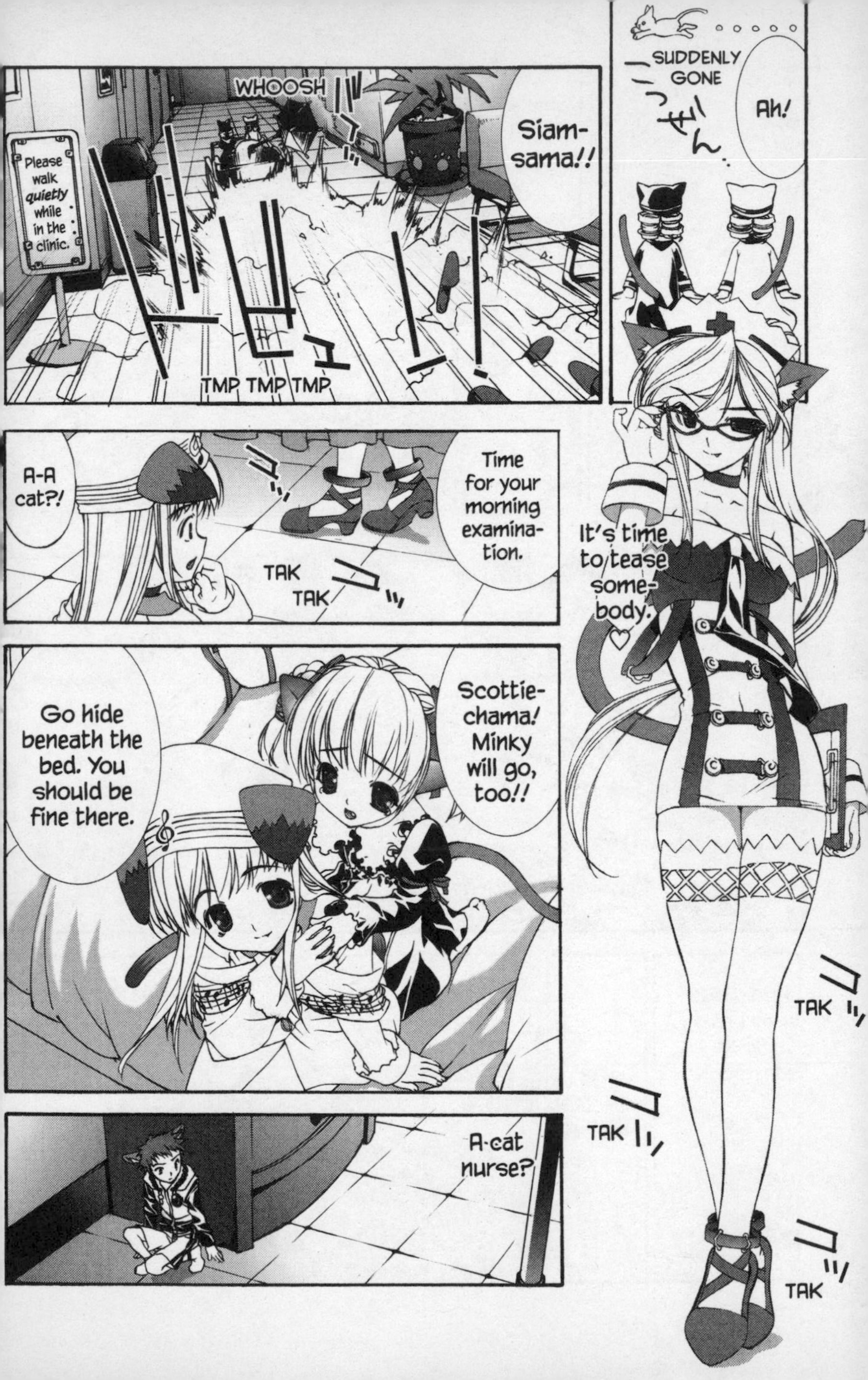
Ah!
SUDDENLY GONE
Siam-sama!!
WHOOSH
Please walk quietly while in the clinic.
TMP TMP TMP
It's time to tease somebody. ♡
TAK
TAK
TAK
Time for your morning examination.
A-A cat?!
TAK TAK
Scottie-chama! Minky will go, too!!
Go hide beneath the bed. You should be fine there.
A-cat nurse?

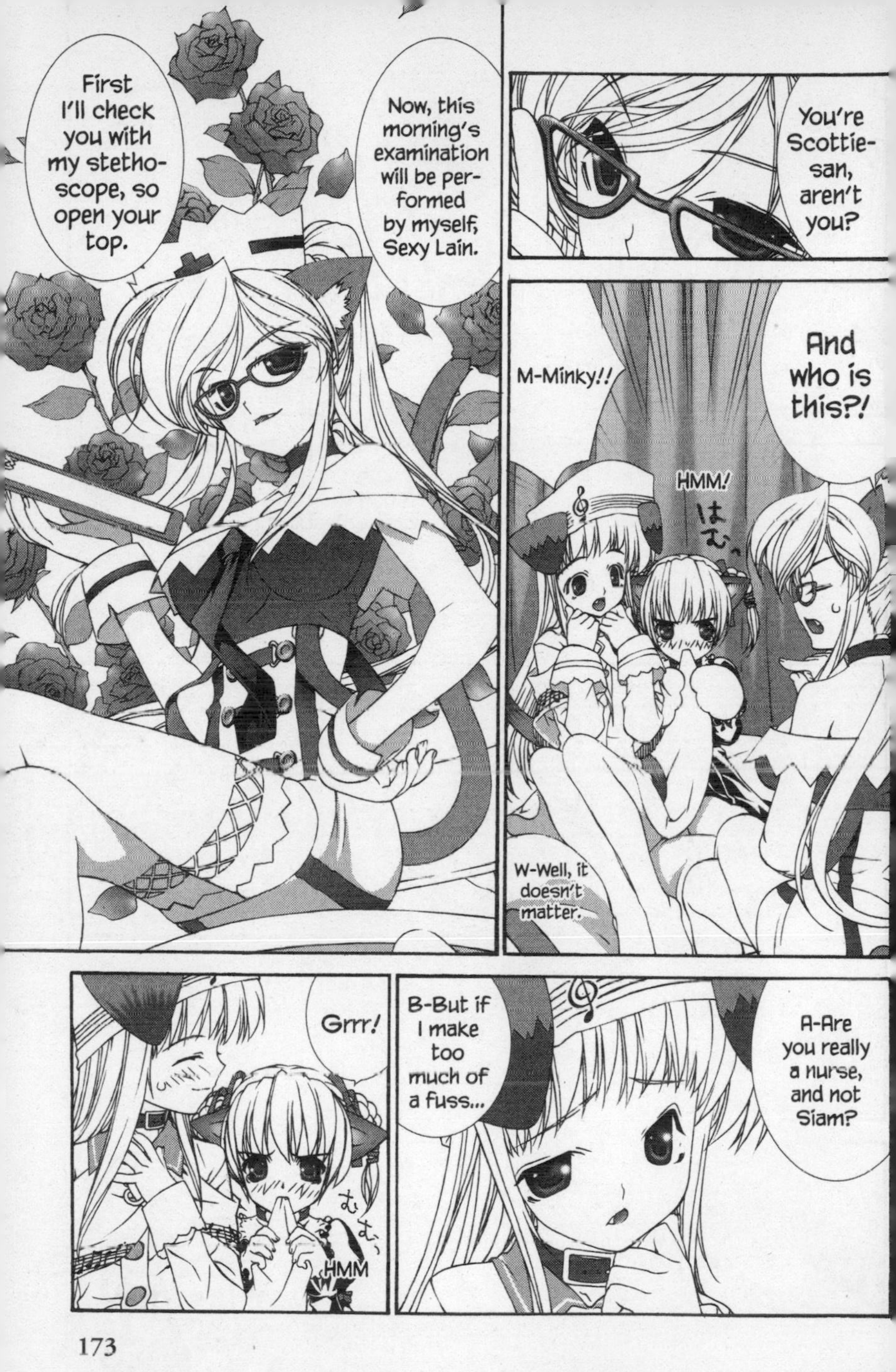
You're Scottie-san, aren't you?
And who is this?!
M-Minky!!
HMM!
W-Well, it doesn't matter.
Now, this morning's examination will be performed by myself, Sexy Lain.
First I'll check you with my stethoscope, so open your top.
A-Are you really a nurse, and not Siam?
B-But if I make too much of a fuss...
Grrr!
HMM

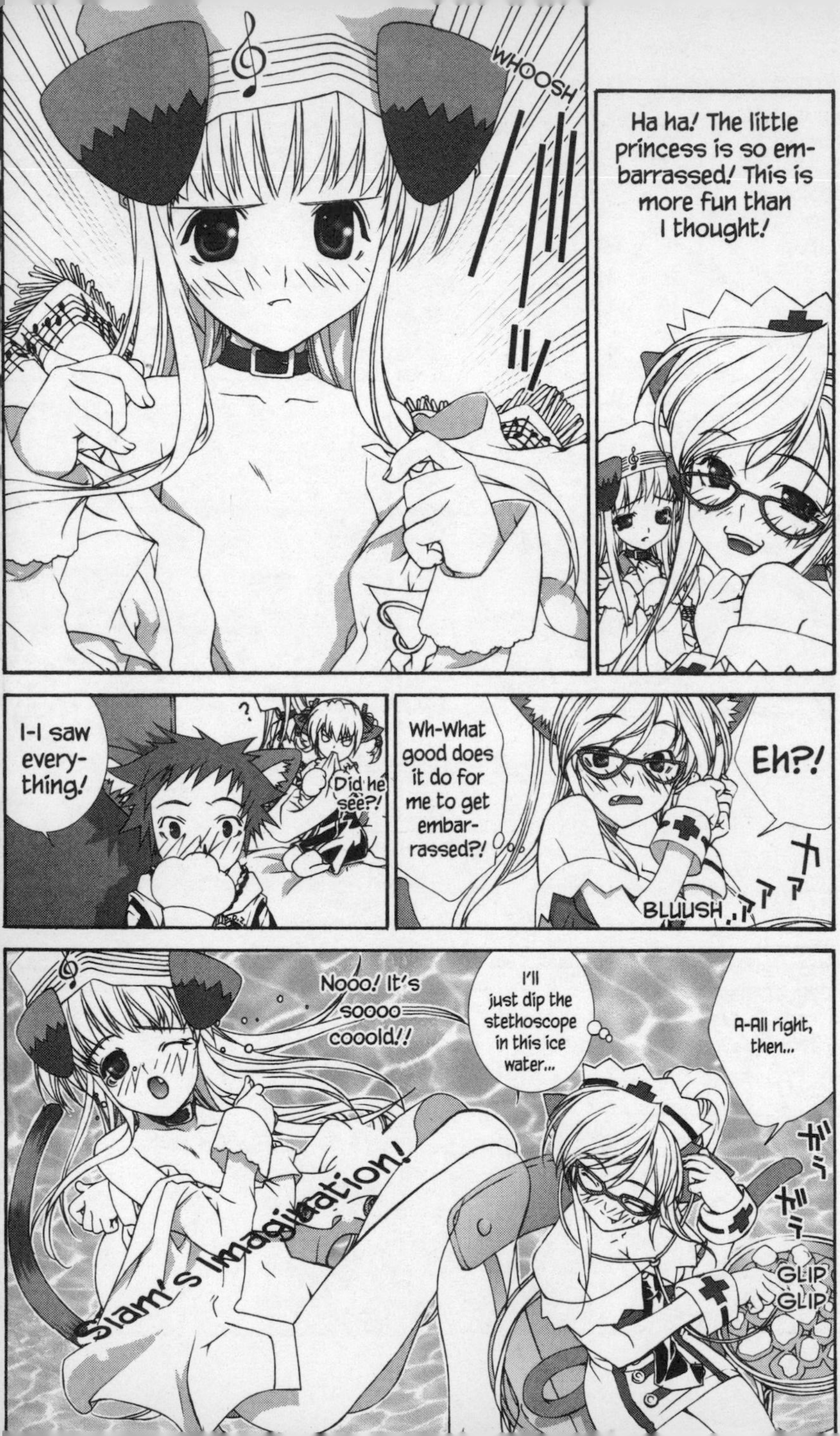
Ha ha! The little princess is so embarrassed! This is more fun than I thought!
WHOOSH
Eh?!
Wh-What good does it do for me to get embarrassed?!
BLUUSH
?
Did he see?!
I-I saw everything!
A-All right, then...
I'll just dip the stethoscope in this ice water...
Nooo! It's soooo cooold!!
GLIP GLIP
Siam's Imagination!

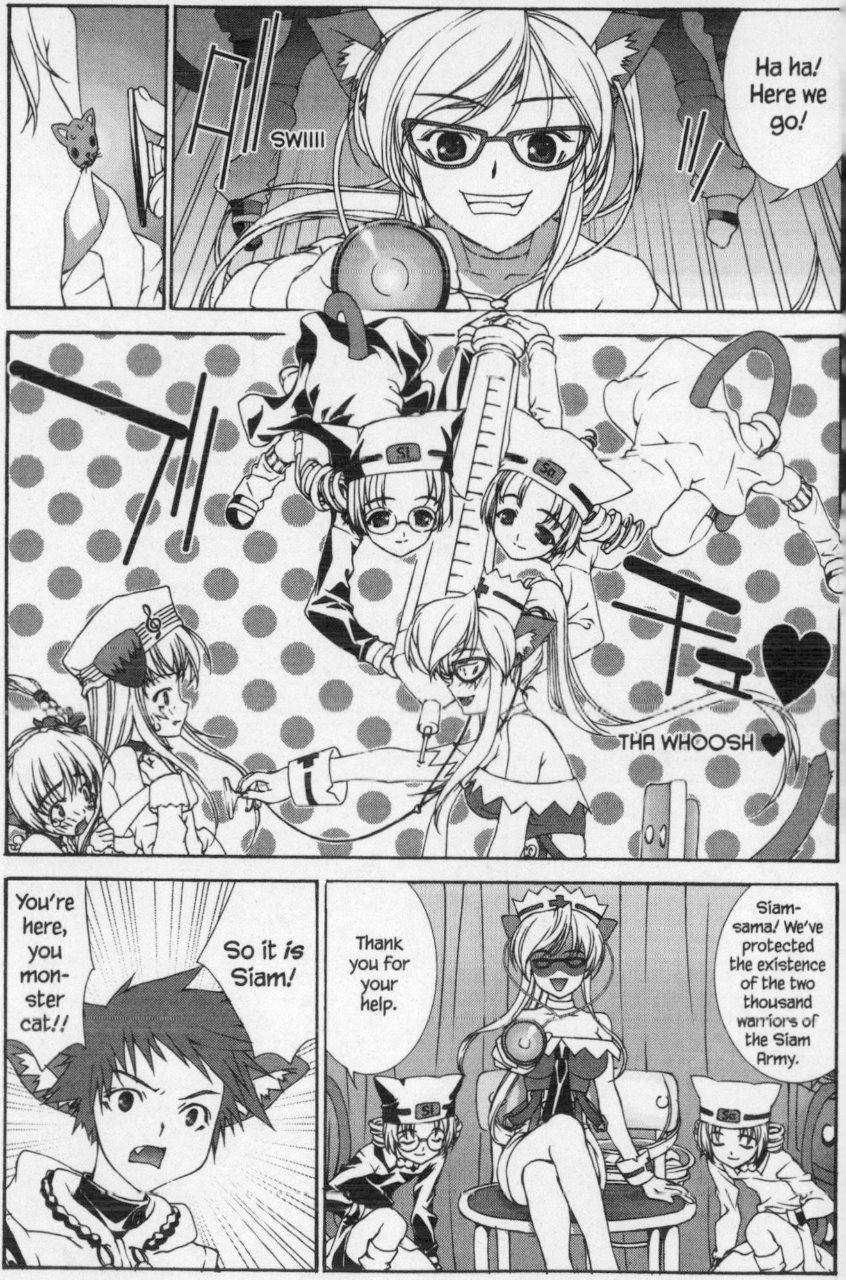
Ha ha! Here we go!
SWIIII
THA WHOOSH ♥
Siam-sama! We've protected the existence of the two thousand warriors of the Siam Army.
Thank you for your help.
So it *is* Siam!
You're here, you mon-ster cat!!

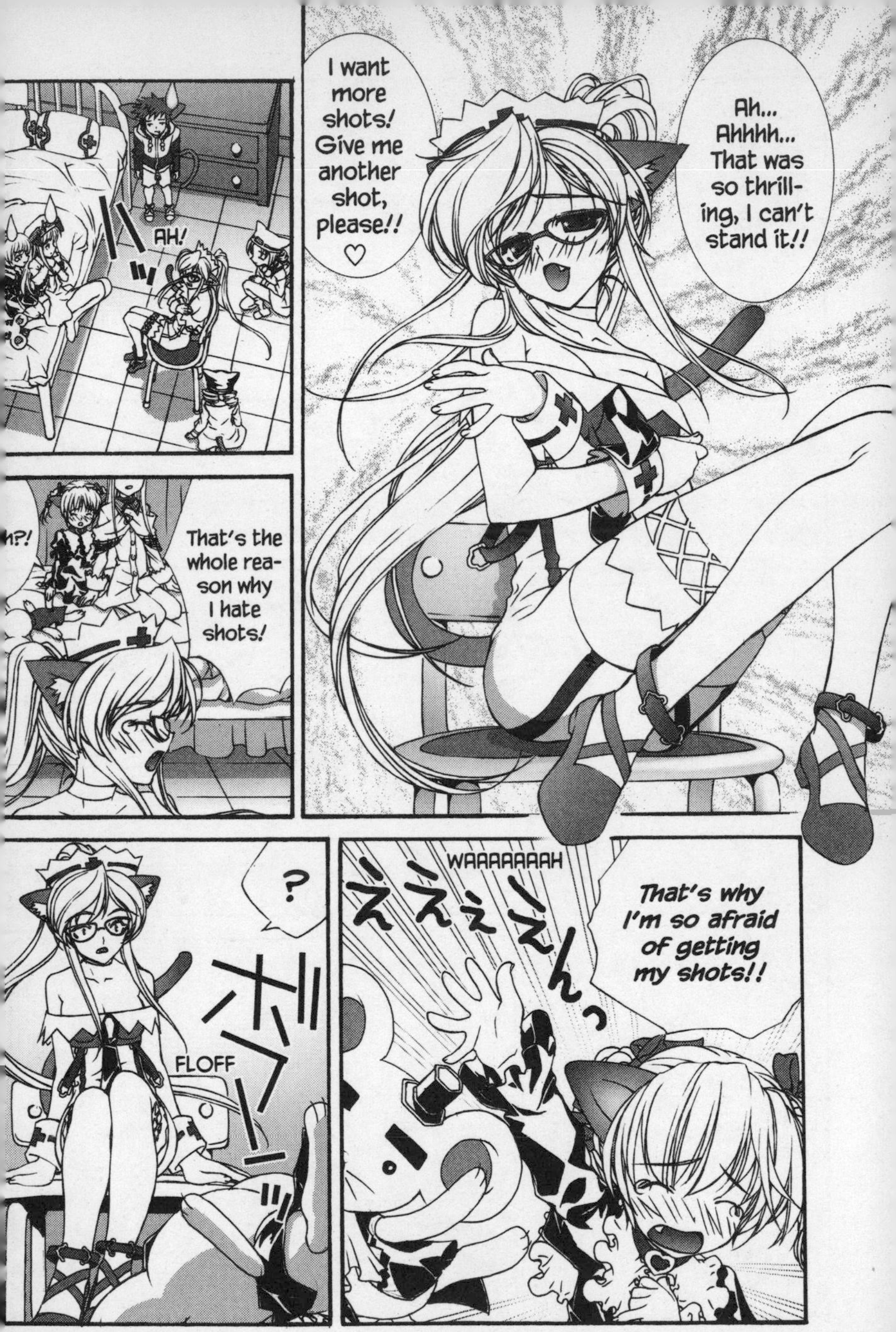
Ah... Ahhhh... That was so thrill-ing, I can't stand it!!
I want more shots! Give me another shot, please!! ♡
AH!
n?!
That's the whole rea-son why I hate shots!
WAAAAAAAAH
ええええんっ
That's why I'm so afraid of getting my shots!!
?
FLOFF

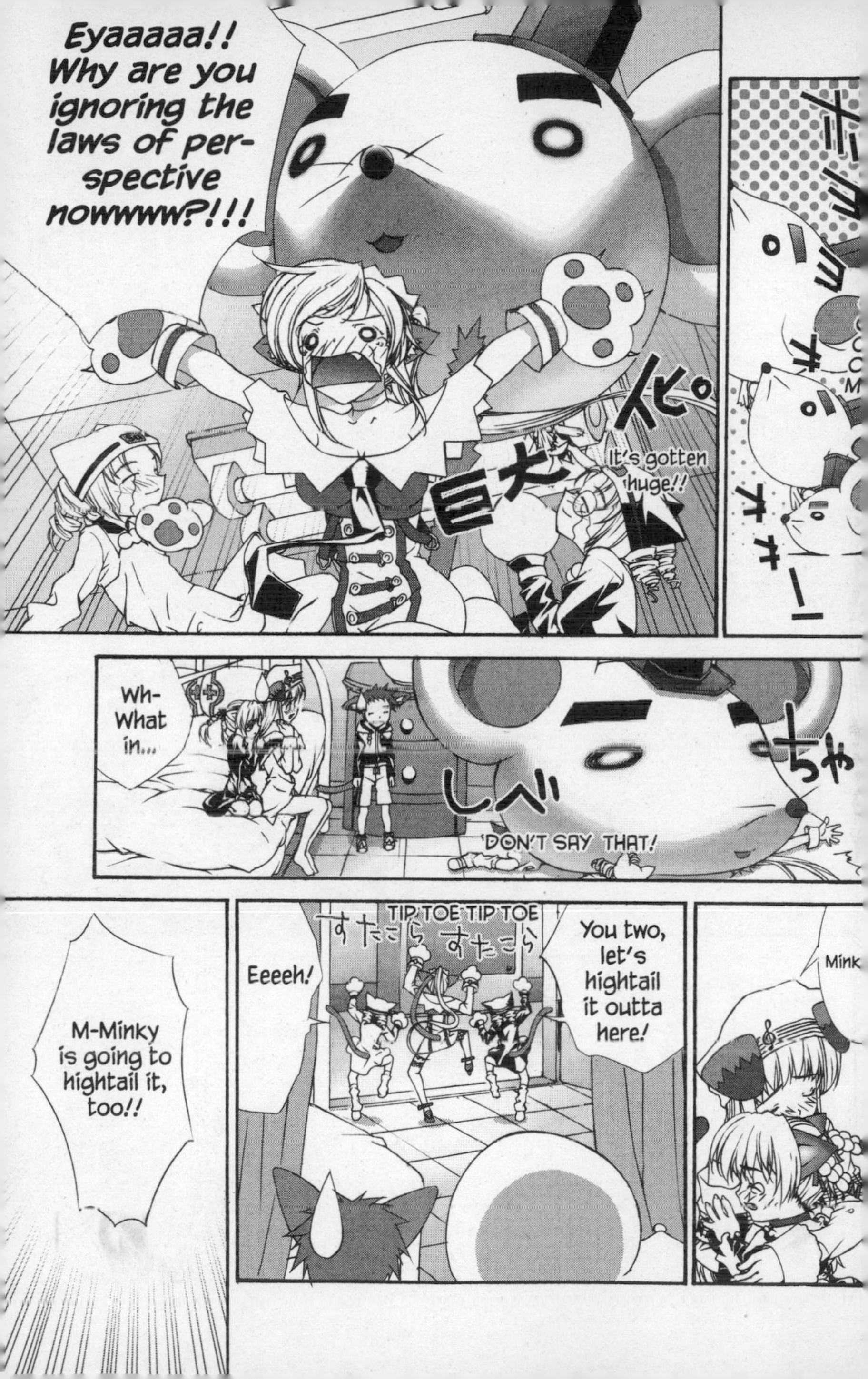
Eyaaaaa!! Why are you ignoring the laws of per-spective nowwww?!!!
巨大
It's gotten huge!!
ちゃ
しべ
'DON'T SAY THAT!
Wh- What in...
Mink
You two, let's hightail it outta here!
TIP TOE TIP TOE
すたこら すたこら
Eeeeh!
M-Minky is going to hightail it, too!!

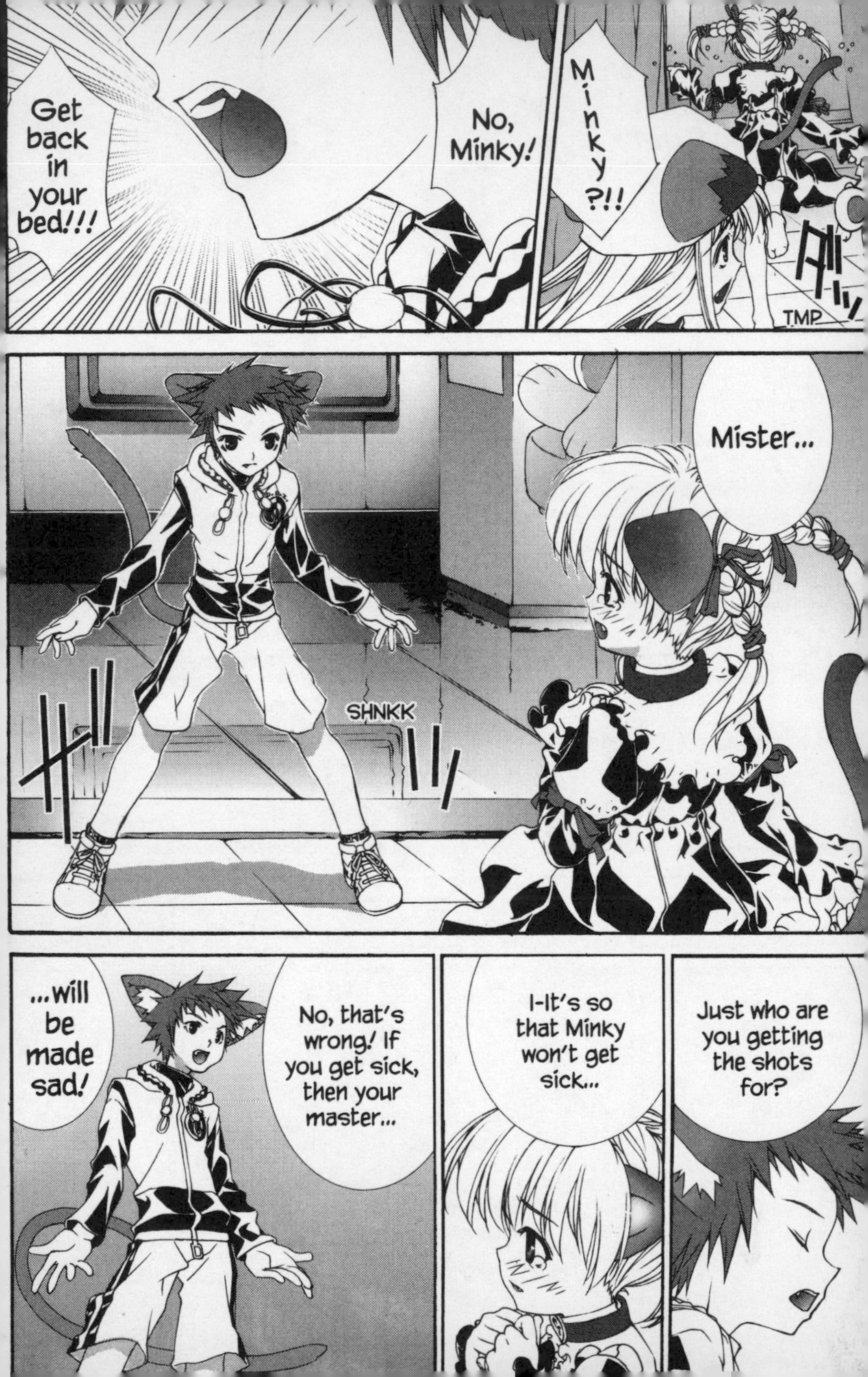
Minky?!!
TMP
No, Minky!
Get back in your bed!!!
Mister...
SHNKK
Just who are you getting the shots for?
I-It's so that Minky won't get sick...
No, that's wrong! If you get sick, then your master...
...will be made sad!

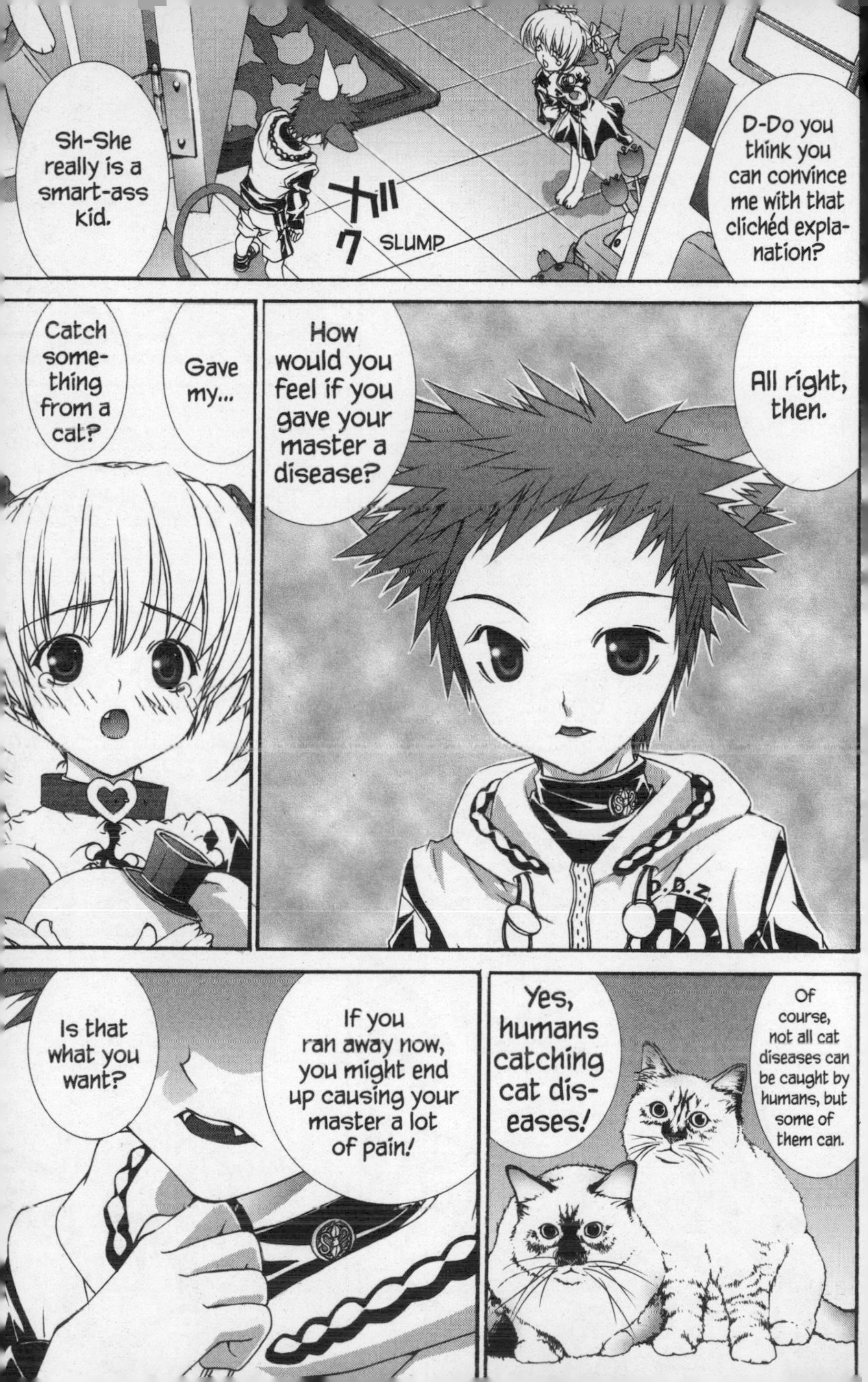
D-Do you think you can convince me with that clichéd explanation?
SLUMP
Sh-She really is a smart-ass kid.
All right, then.
How would you feel if you gave your master a disease?
Gave my...
Catch something from a cat?
Of course, not all cat diseases can be caught by humans, but some of them can.
Yes, humans catching cat diseases!
If you ran away now, you might end up causing your master a lot of pain!
Is that what you want?

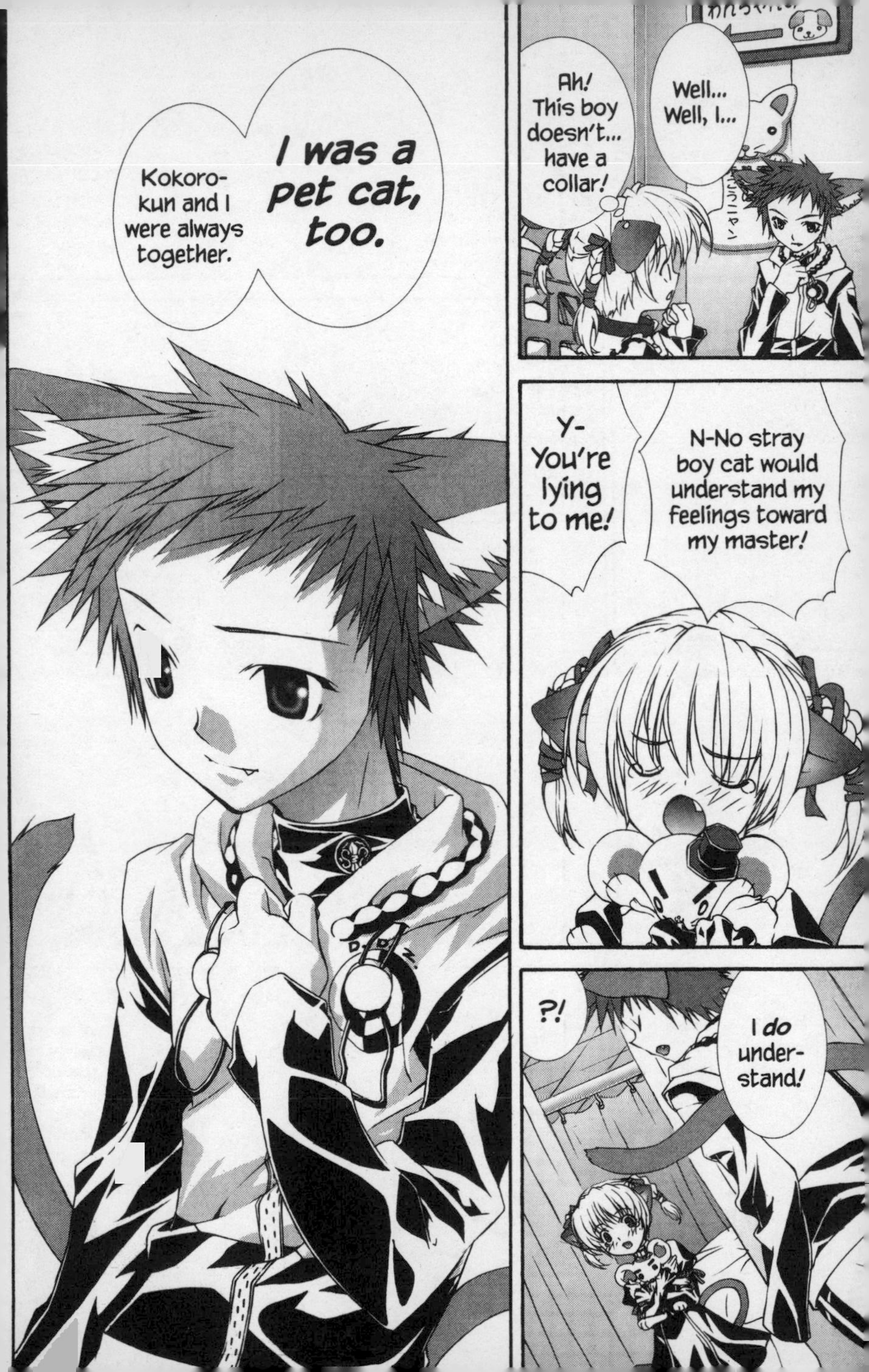
Well... Well, I...
Ah! This boy doesn't... have a collar!
N-No stray boy cat would understand my feelings toward my master!
Y- You're lying to me!
I *do* understand!
?!
I was a pet cat, too.
Kokoro-kun and I were always together.

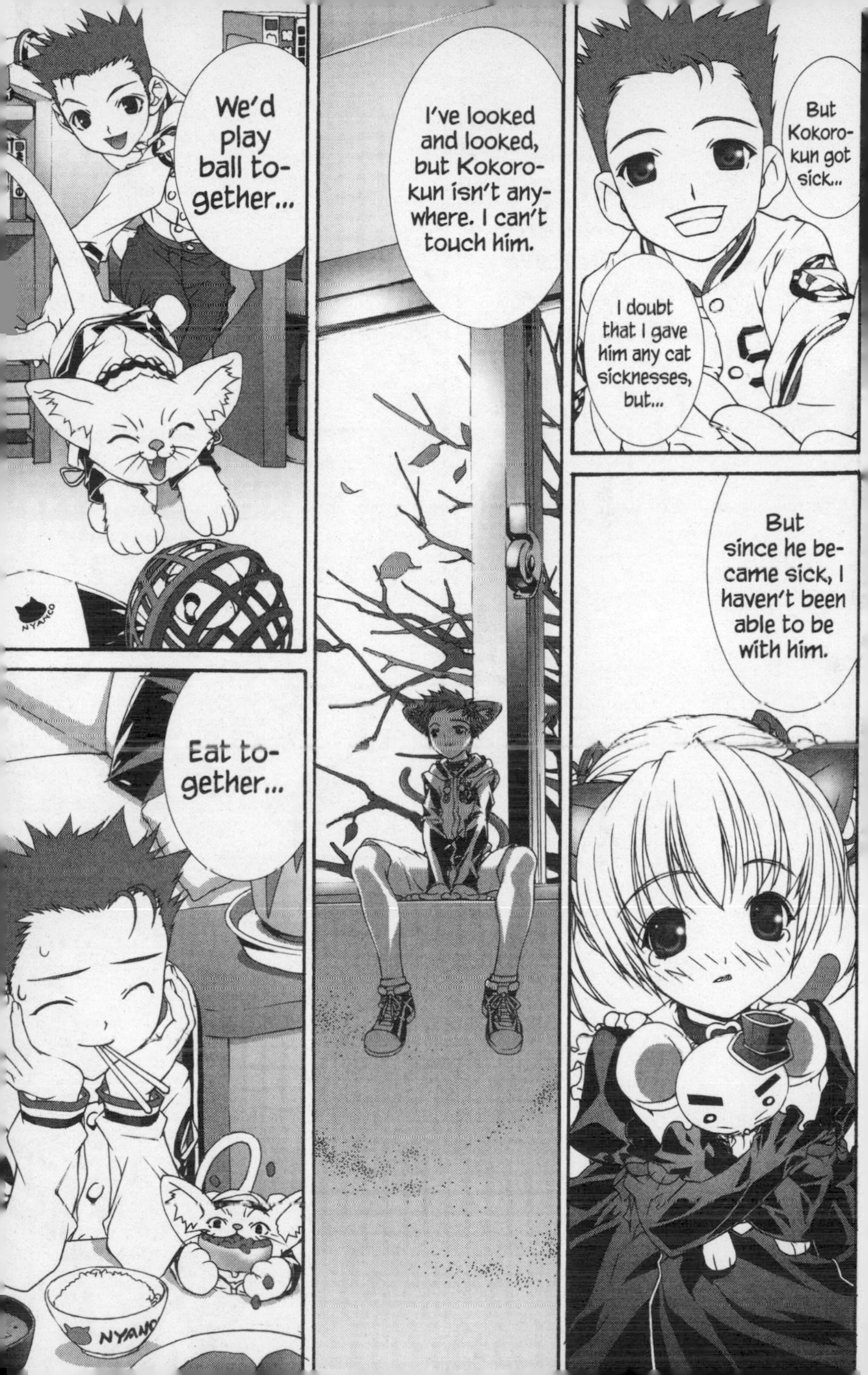
But Kokoro-kun got sick...
I doubt that I gave him any cat sicknesses, but...
But since he became sick, I haven't been able to be with him.
I've looked and looked, but Kokoro-kun isn't anywhere. I can't touch him.
We'd play ball together...
NYANCO
Eat together...
NYANCO

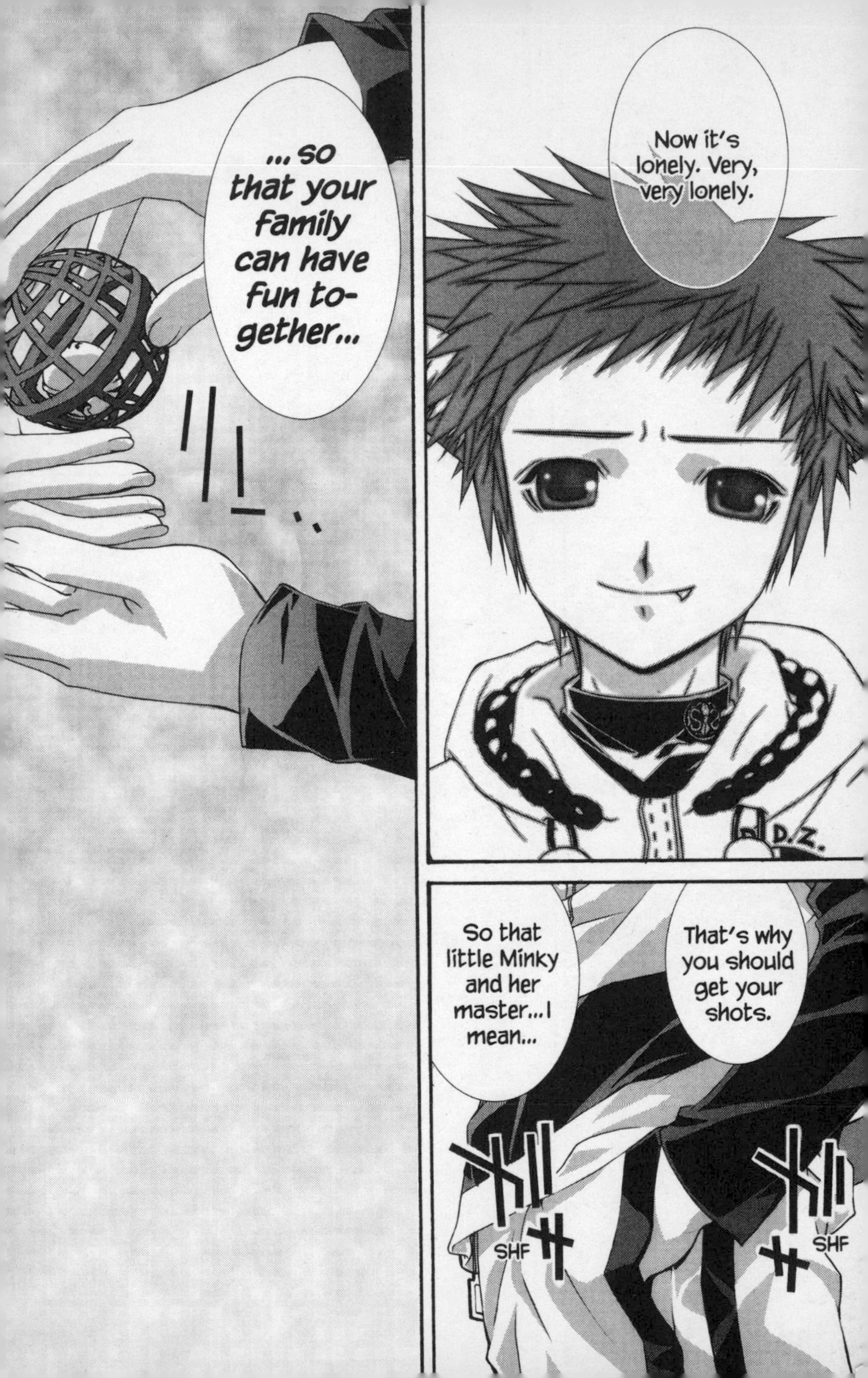
Now it's lonely. Very, very lonely.
D.Z.
That's why you should get your shots.
So that little Minky and her master...I mean...
SHF
SHF
...so that your family can have fun to-gether...

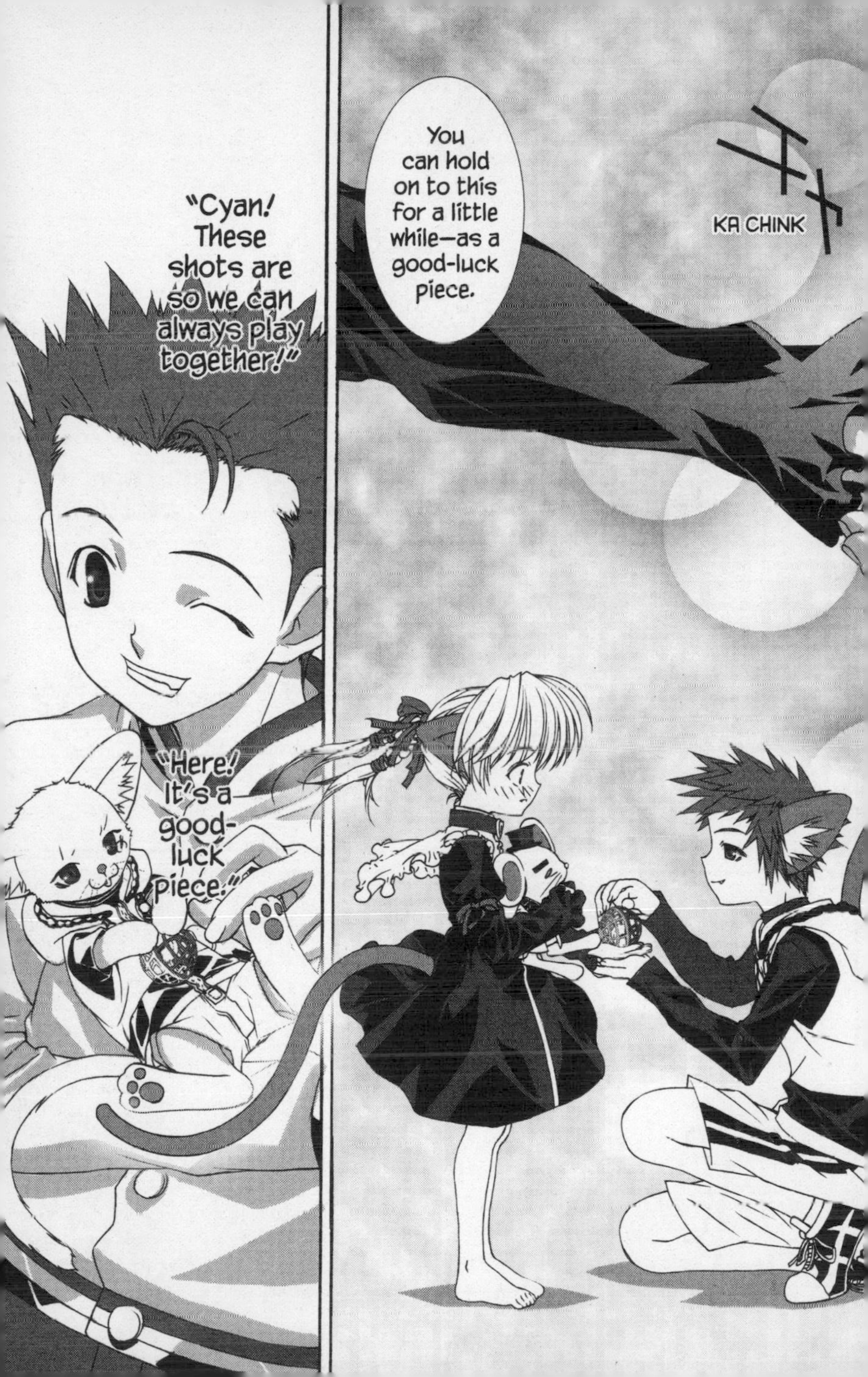
KA CHINK
You can hold on to this for a little while—as a good-luck piece.
"Cyan! These shots are so we can always play together!"
"Here! It's a good-luck piece."

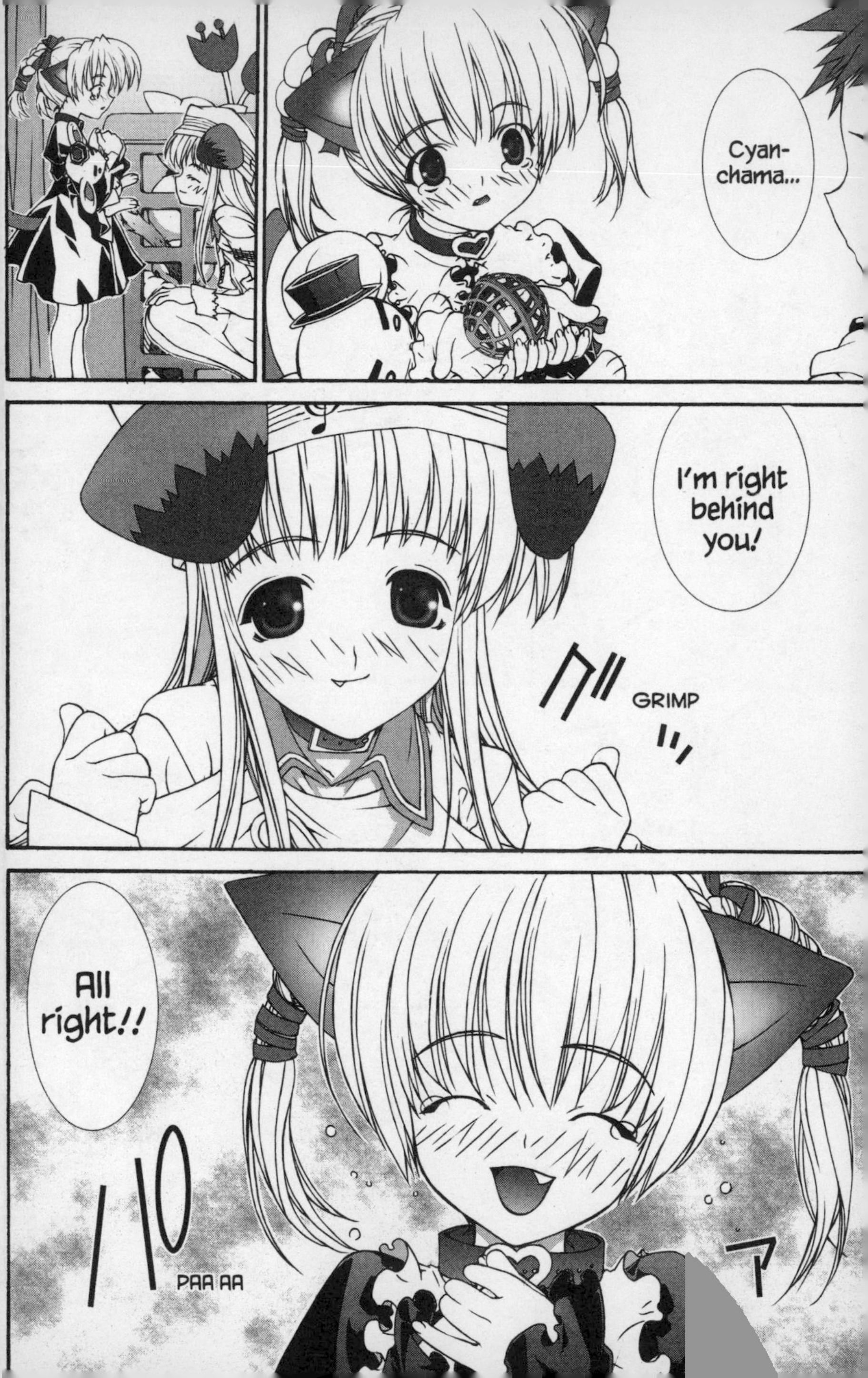
Cyan-chama...
I'm right behind you!
GRIMP
All right!!
PAA AA

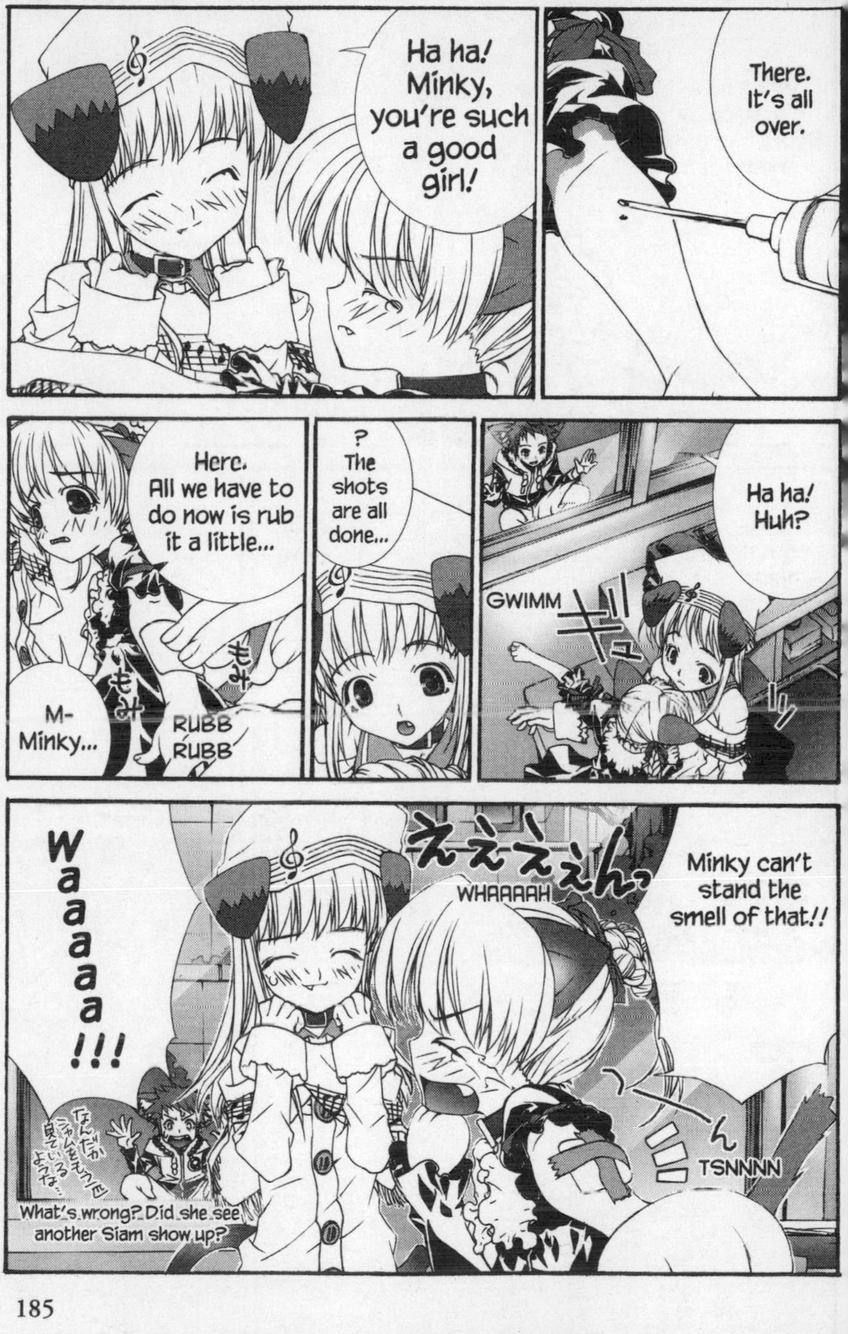
There. It's all over.
Ha ha! Minky, you're such a good girl!
Ha ha! Huh?
GWIMM
? The shots are all done...
Here. All we have to do now is rub it a little...
M- Minky...
RUBB RUBB
Minky can't stand the smell of that!!
WHAAAAH
Waaaaa!!!
TSNNNN
What's wrong? Did she see another Siam show up?

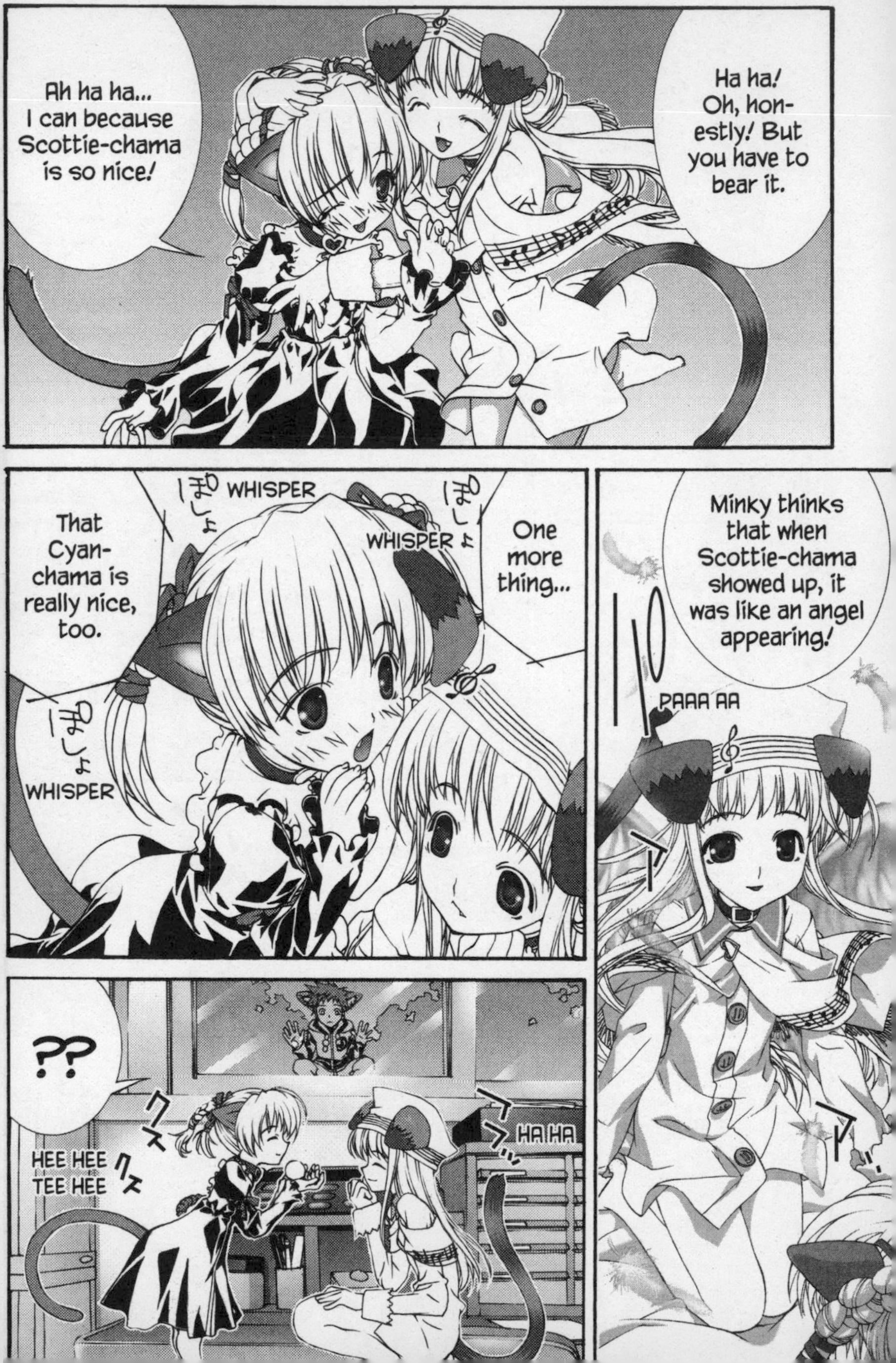
Ha ha! Oh, hon-estly! But you have to bear it.
Ah ha ha... I can because Scottie-chama is so nice!
Minky thinks that when Scottie-chama showed up, it was like an angel appearing!
PAAA AA
WHISPER
One more thing...
WHISPER
WHISPER
That Cyan-chama is really nice, too.
??
HA HA
HEE HEE TEE HEE

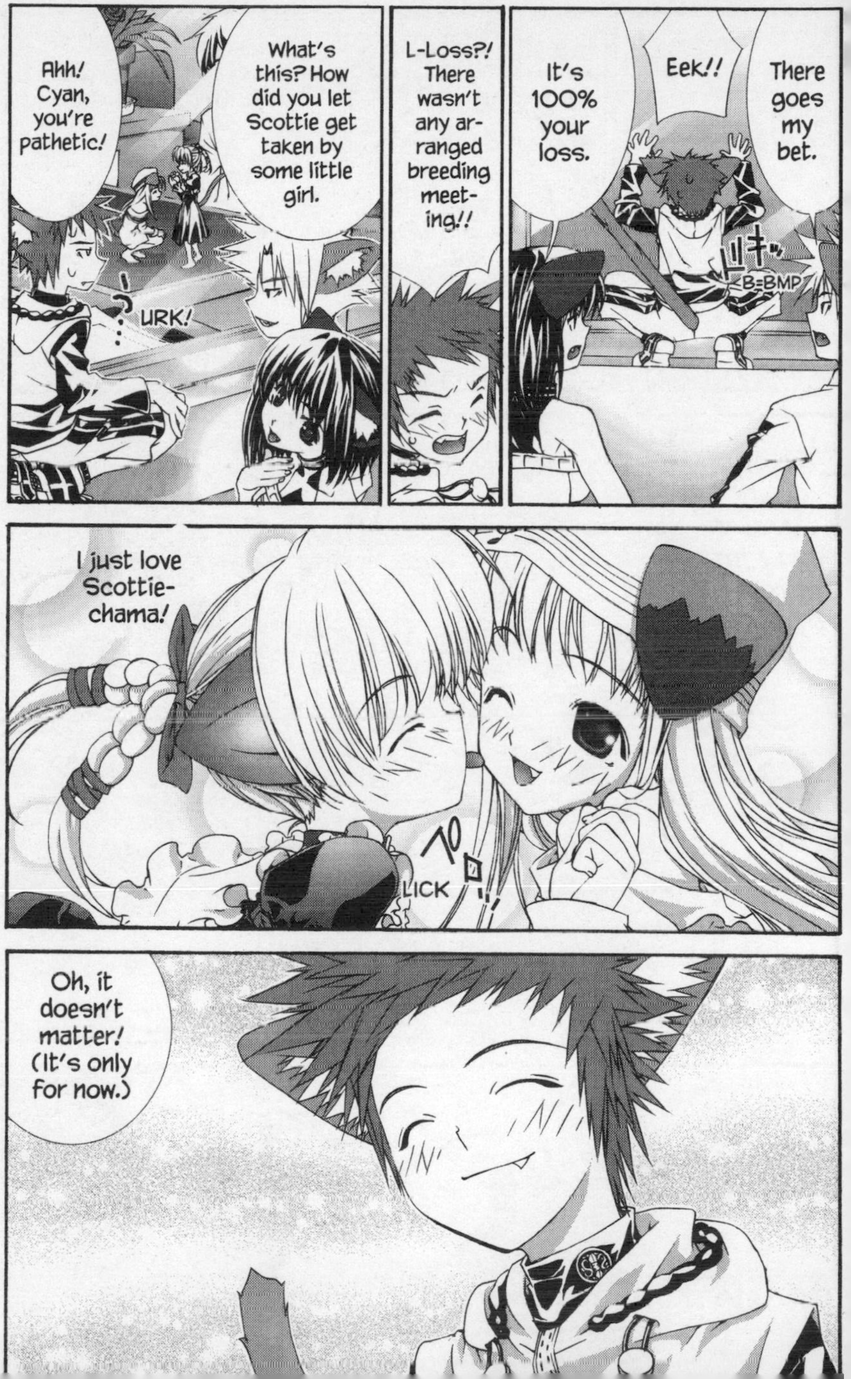
There goes my bet.
Eek!!
It's 100% your loss.
B-BMP
L-Loss?! There wasn't any arranged breeding meeting!!
What's this? How did you let Scottie get taken by some little girl.
Ahh! Cyan, you're pathetic!
URK!
I just love Scottie-chama!
LICK
Oh, it doesn't matter! (It's only for now.)

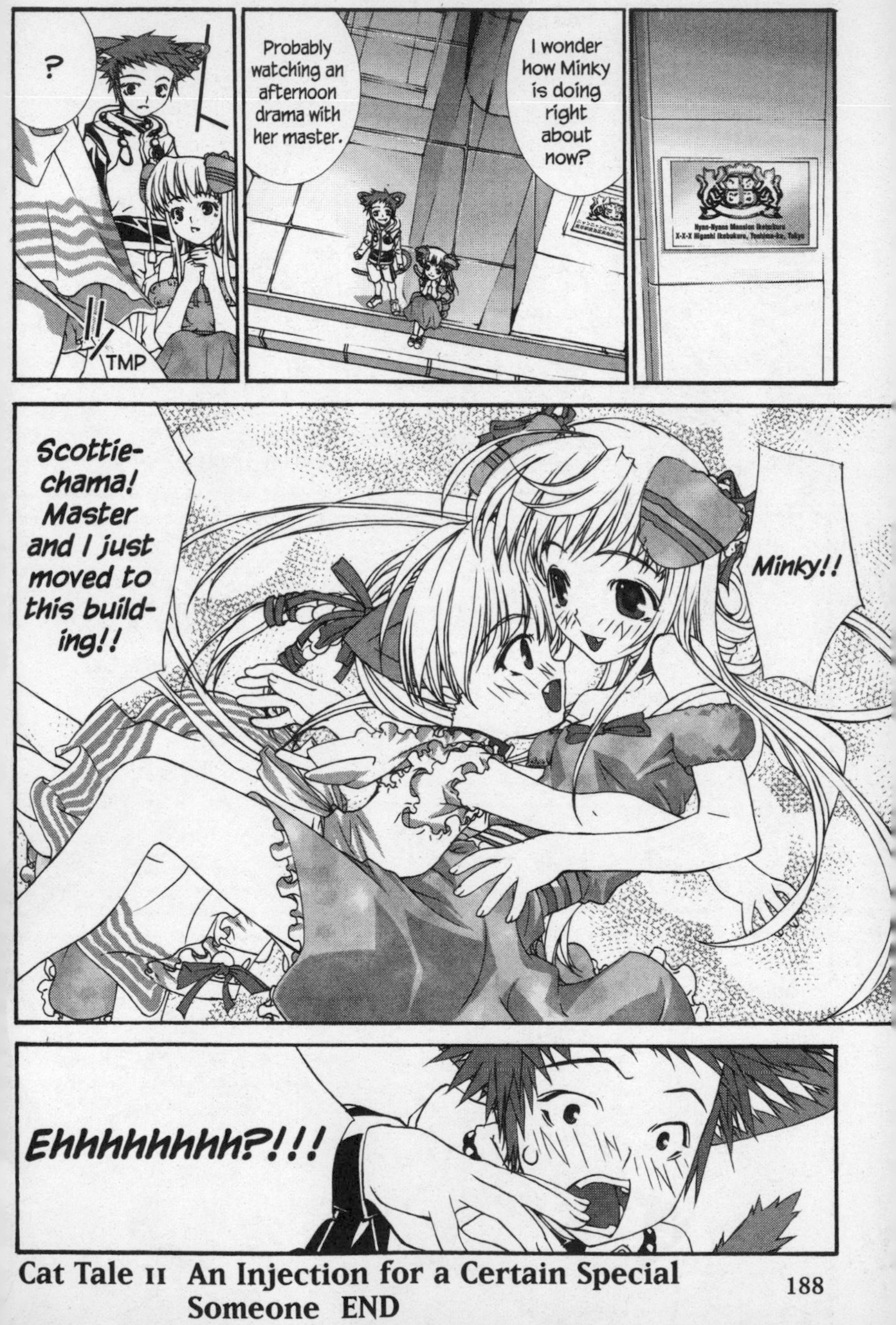
Nyan-Nyans Mansion Ikebukuro
X-X-X Higashi Ikebukuro, Toshima-ku, Tokyo
I wonder how Minky is doing right about now?
Probably watching an afternoon drama with her master.
?
TMP
Minky!!
Scottie-chama! Master and I just moved to this build-ing!!
Ehhhhhhhh?!!!

Cat Tale II An Injection for a Certain Special Someone END

Cat Tale 12 Collar of Love

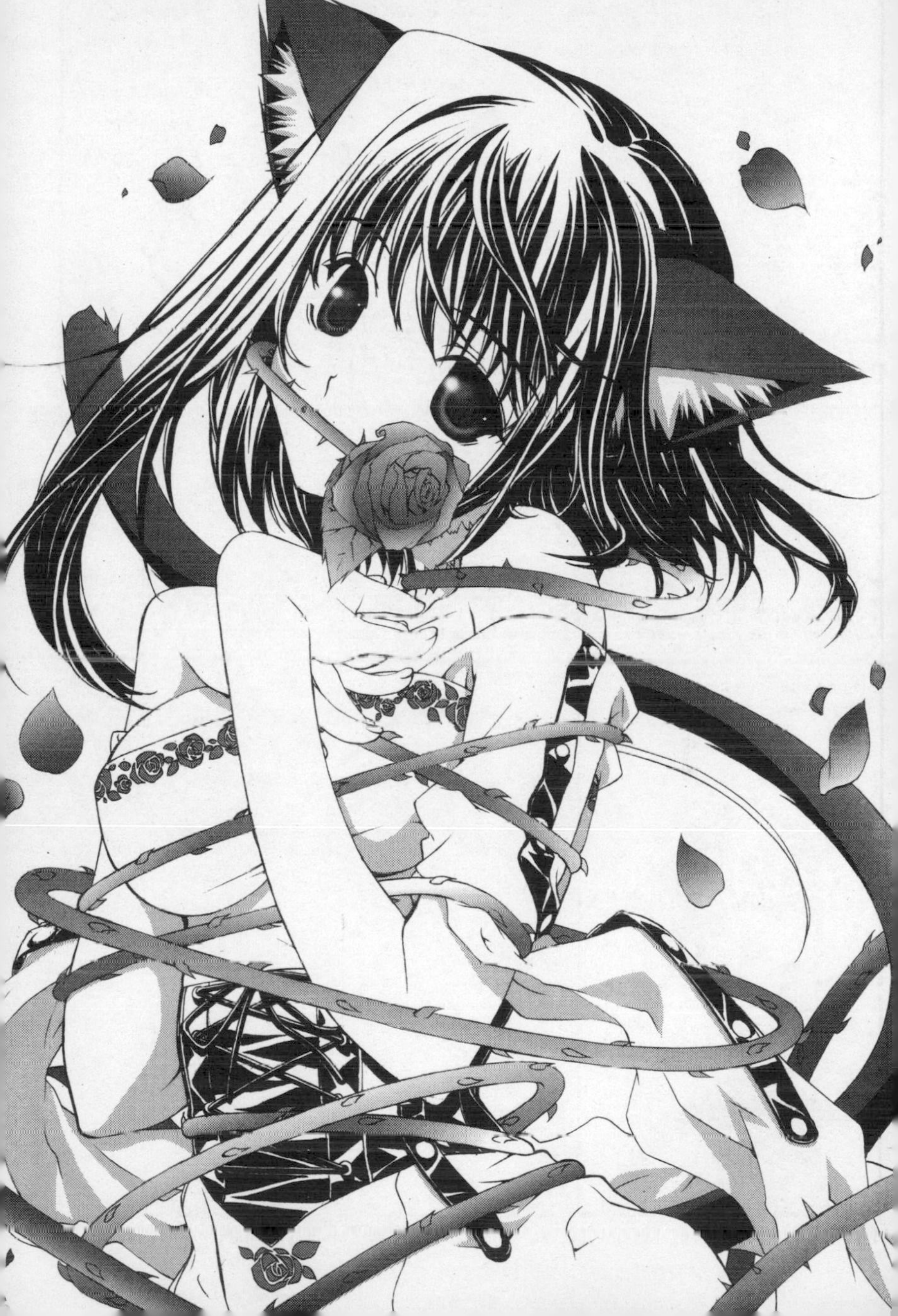

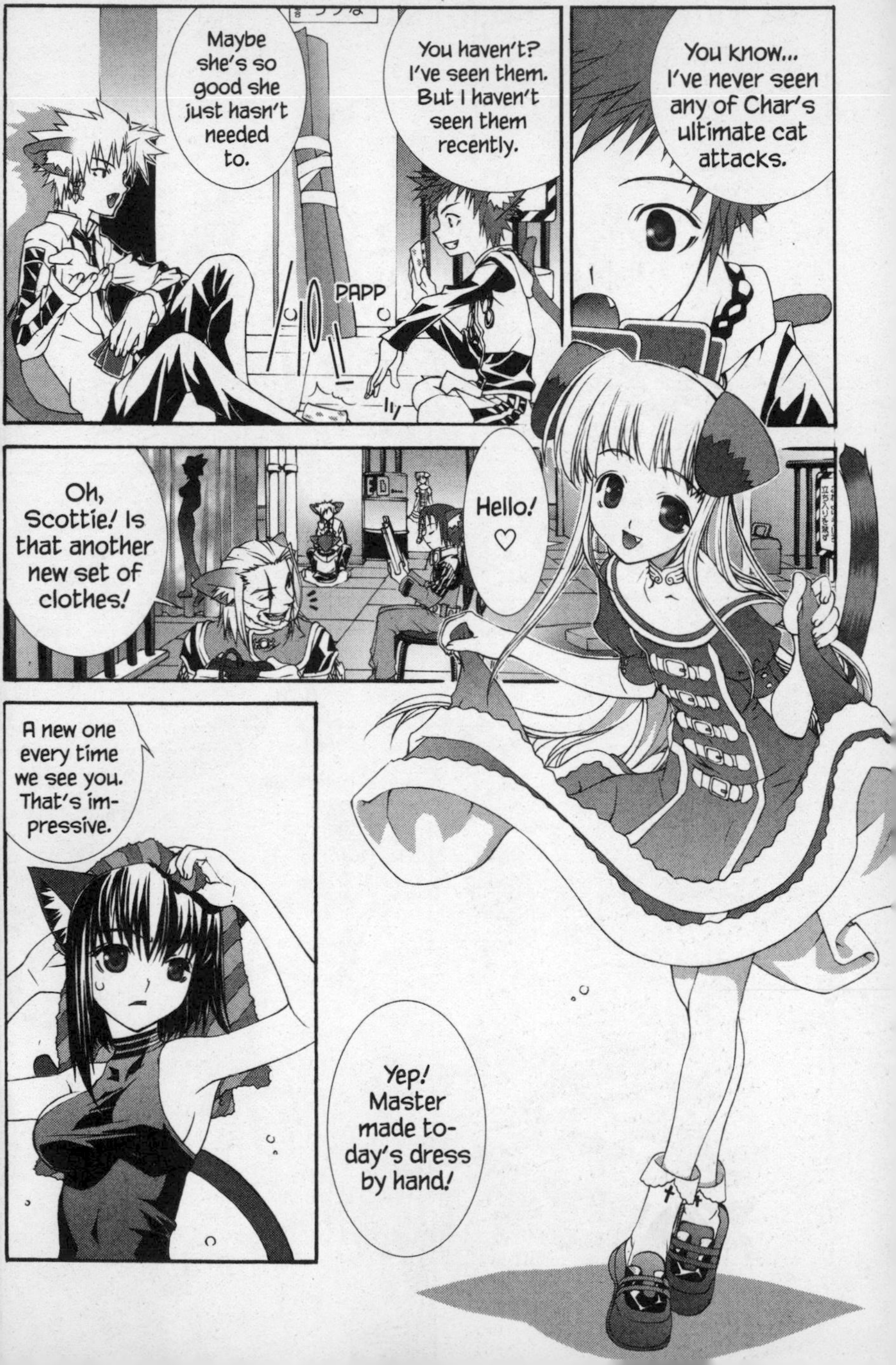

You know... I've never seen any of Char's ultimate cat attacks.
You haven't? I've seen them. But I haven't seen them recently.
PAPP
Maybe she's so good she just hasn't needed to.
Hello! ♡
Yep! Master made to-day's dress by hand!
Oh, Scottie! Is that another new set of clothes!
A new one every time we see you. That's im-pressive.

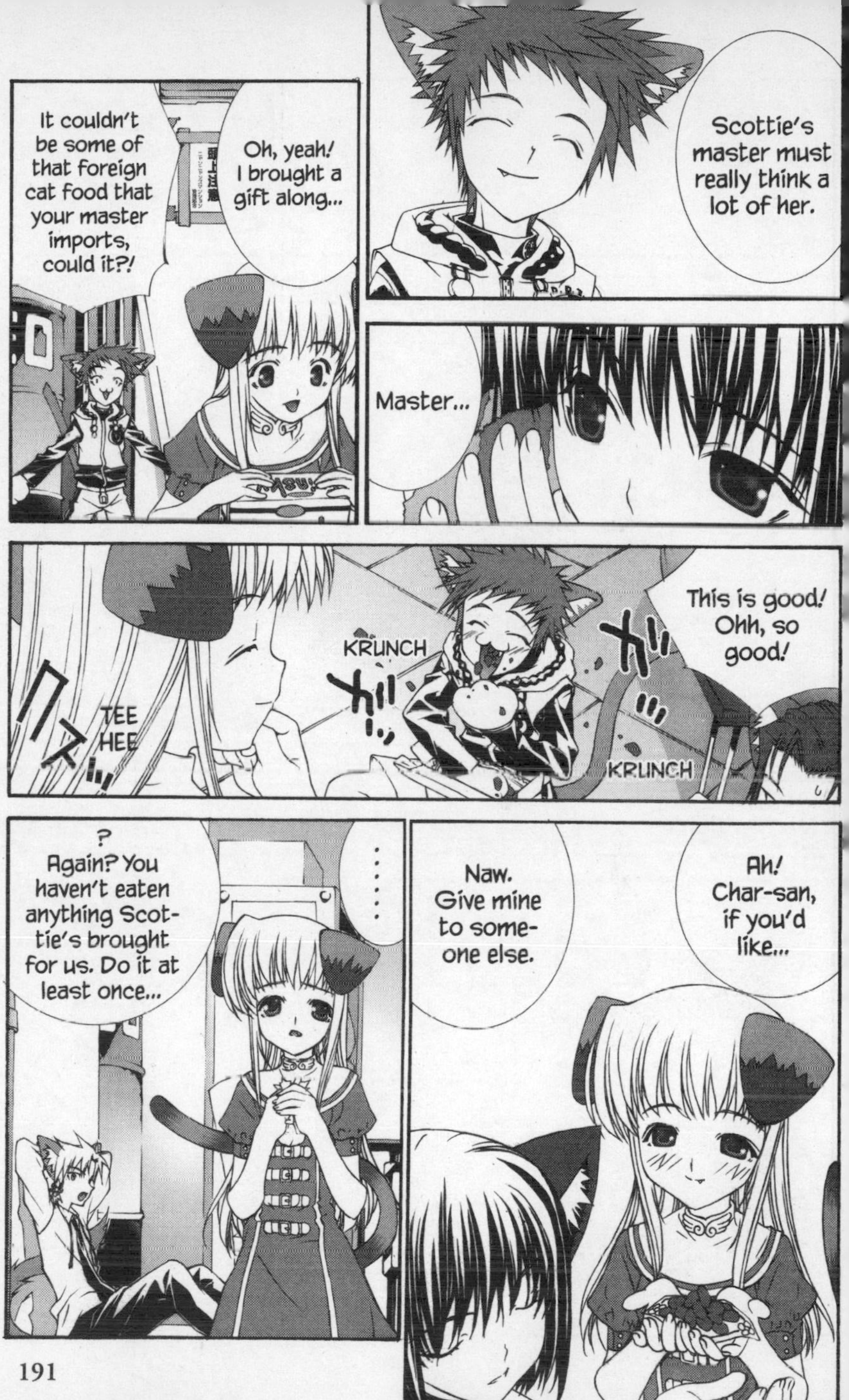
Scottie's master must really think a lot of her.
Master...
Oh, yeah! I brought a gift along...
It couldn't be some of that foreign cat food that your master imports, could it?!
This is good! Ohh, so good!
KRUNCH
KRUNCH
TEE HEE
Ah! Char-san, if you'd like...
Naw. Give mine to some-one else.
......
? Again? You haven't eaten anything Scot-tie's brought for us. Do it at least once...

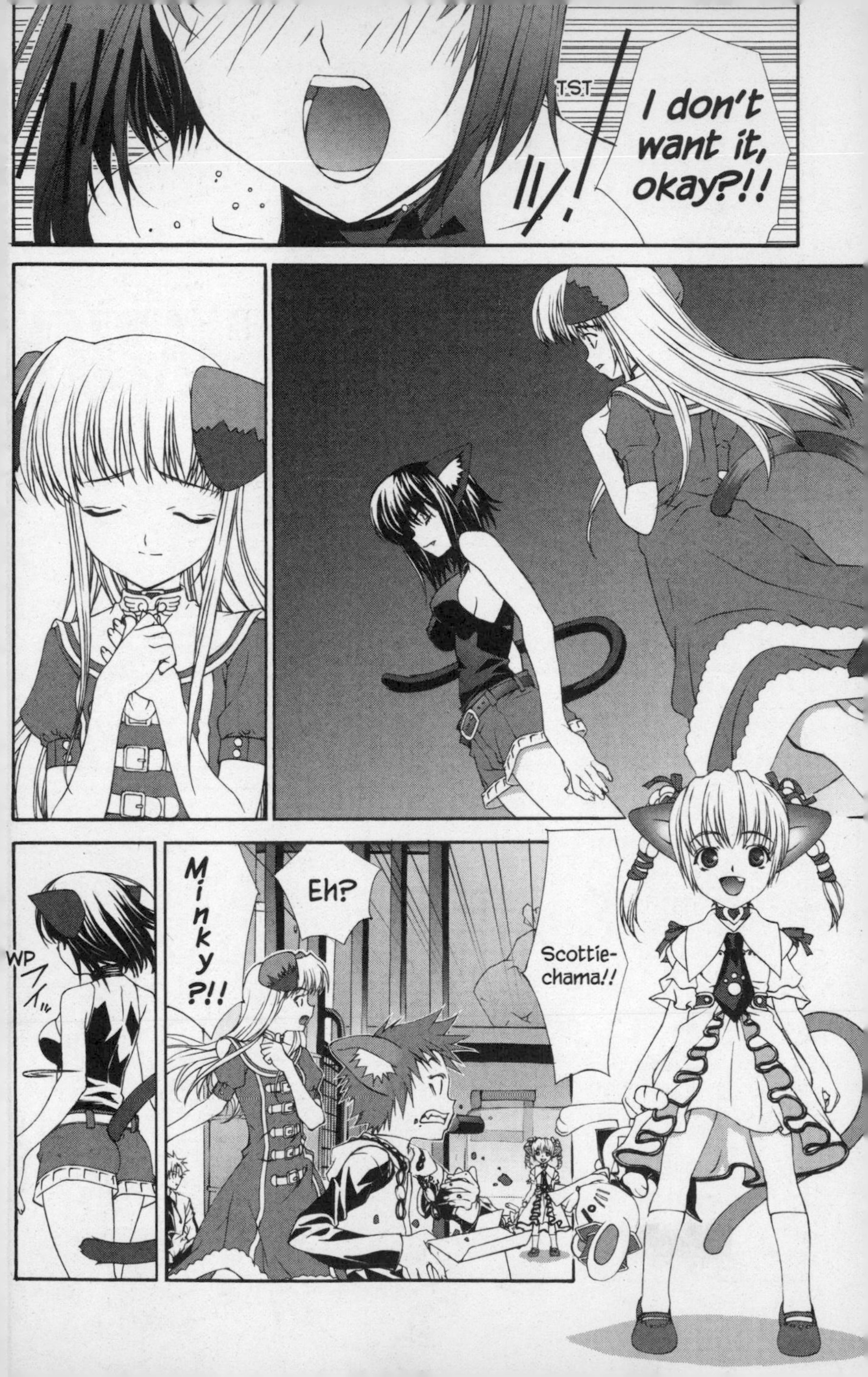
TST
I don't want it, okay?!!
Scottie-chama!!
Eh?
Minky?!!
WP

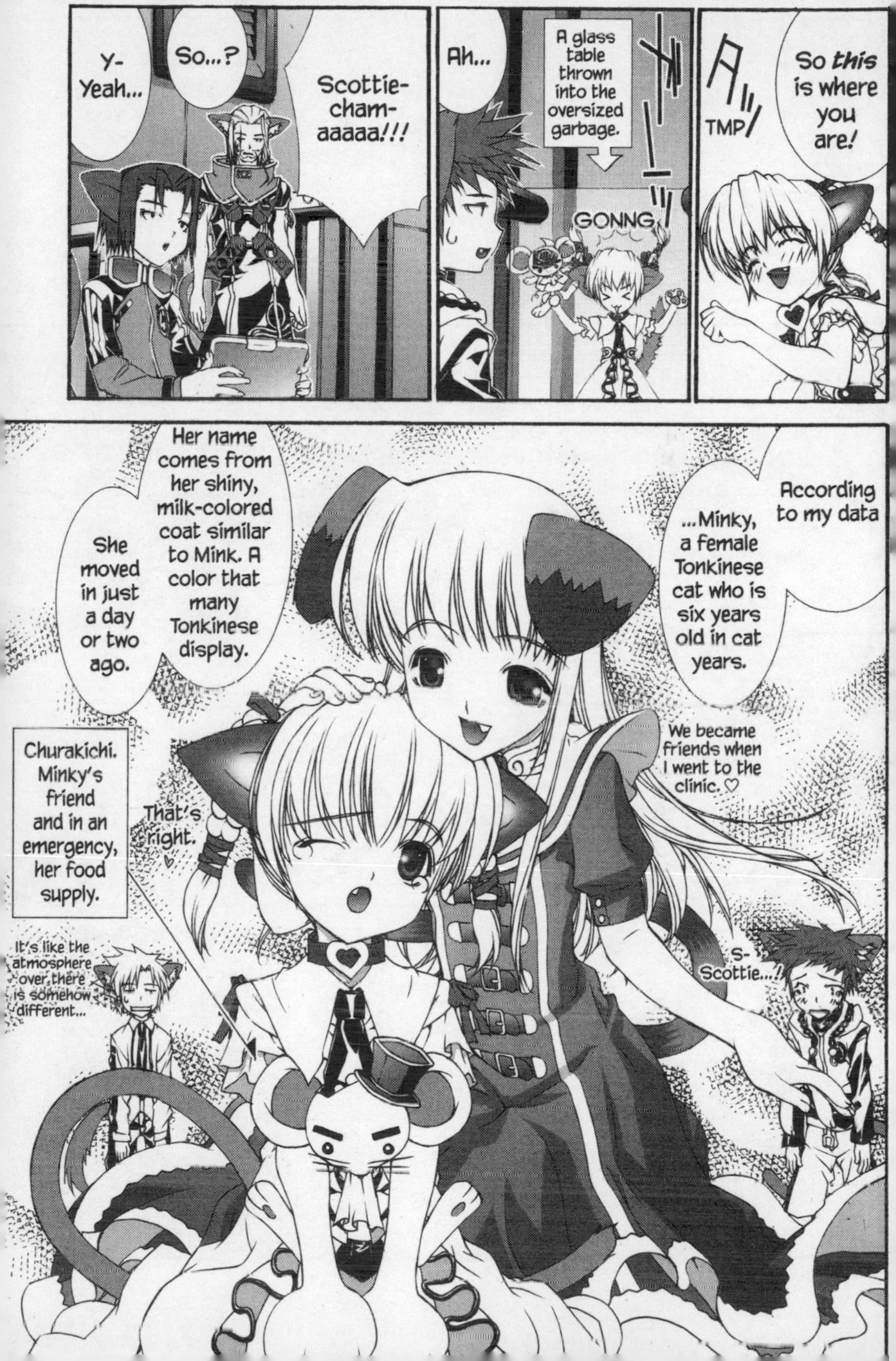
So *this* is where you are!
TMP
A glass table thrown into the oversized garbage.
Ah...
GONNG
Scottie-cham-aaaaa!!!
So...?
Y-Yeah...
According to my data
...Minky, a female Tonkinese cat who is six years old in cat years.
Her name comes from her shiny, milk-colored coat similar to Mink. A color that many Tonkinese display.
She moved in just a day or two ago.
We became friends when I went to the clinic. ♡
That's right. ♡
Churakichi. Minky's friend and in an emergency, her food supply.
S-Scottie...!
It's like the atmosphere over there is somehow different...

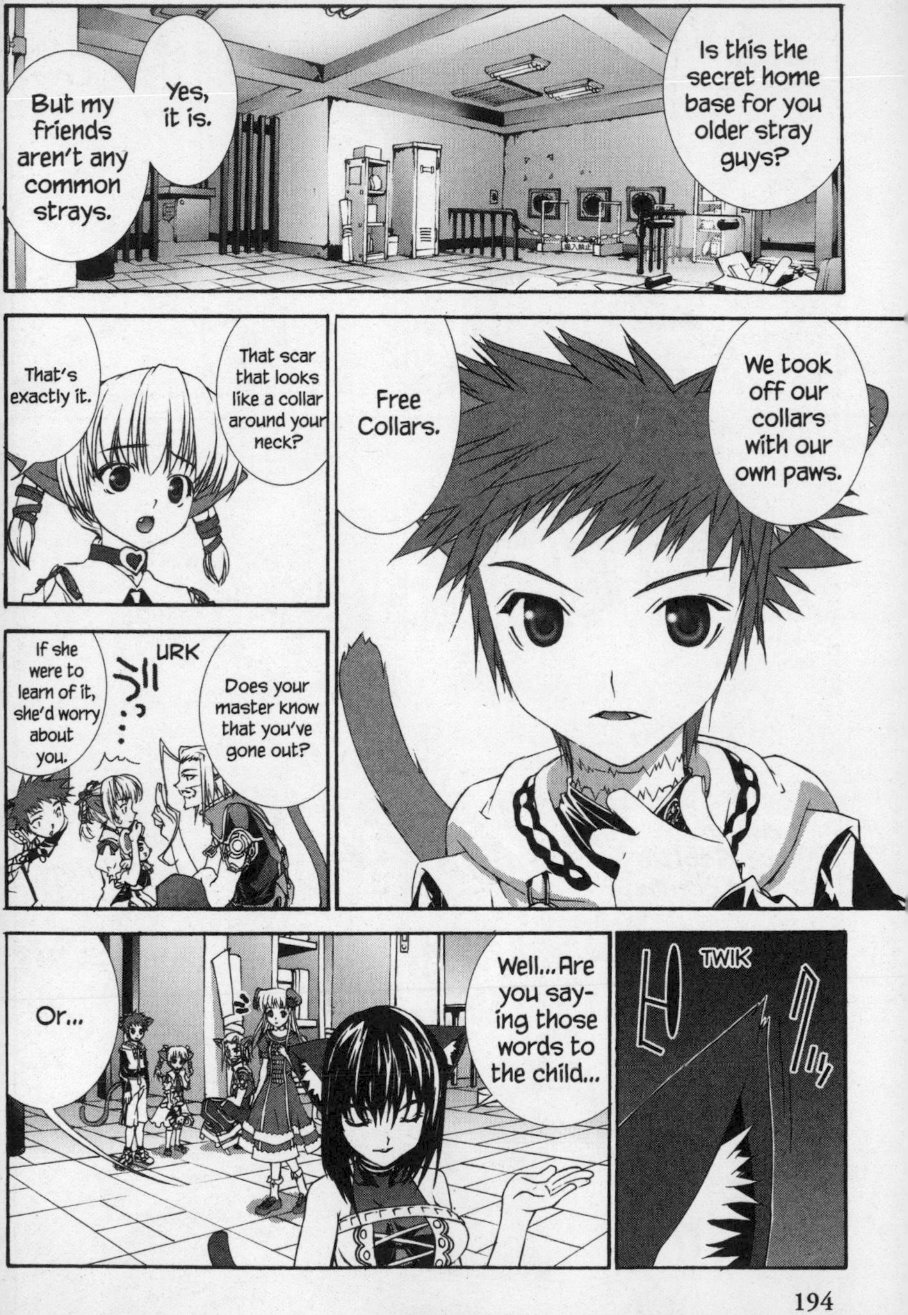
Is this the secret home base for you older stray guys?
Yes, it is.
But my friends aren't any common strays.
We took off our collars with our own paws.
Free Collars.
That scar that looks like a collar around your neck?
That's exactly it.
Does your master know that you've gone out?
URK
If she were to learn of it, she'd worry about you.
TWIK
Well... Are you say-ing those words to the child...
Or...

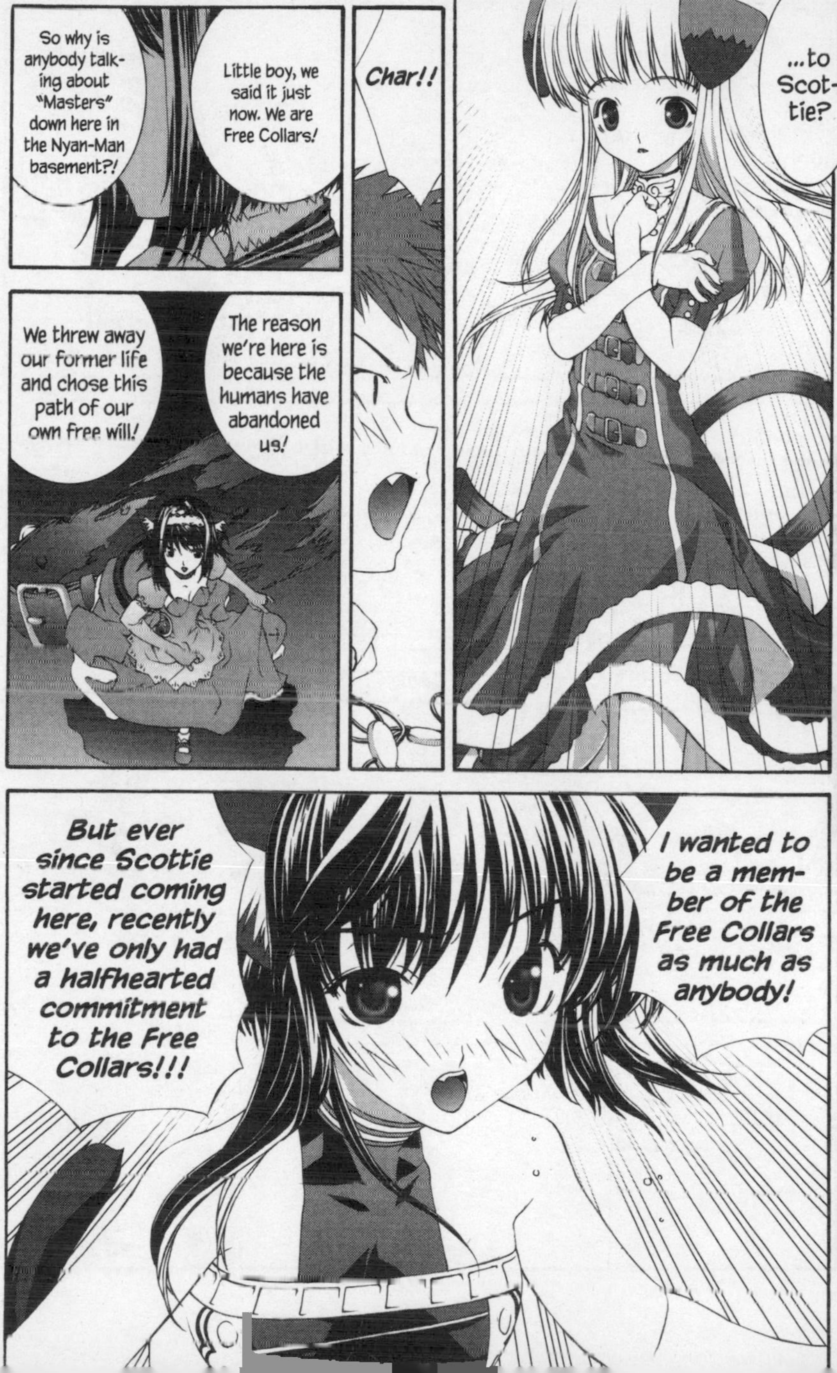
...to Scottie?
Char!!
Little boy, we said it just now. We are Free Collars!
So why is anybody talking about "Masters" down here in the Nyan-Man basement?!
The reason we're here is because the humans have abandoned us!
We threw away our former life and chose this path of our own free will!
I wanted to be a member of the Free Collars as much as anybody!
But ever since Scottie started coming here, recently we've only had a halfhearted commitment to the Free Collars!!!

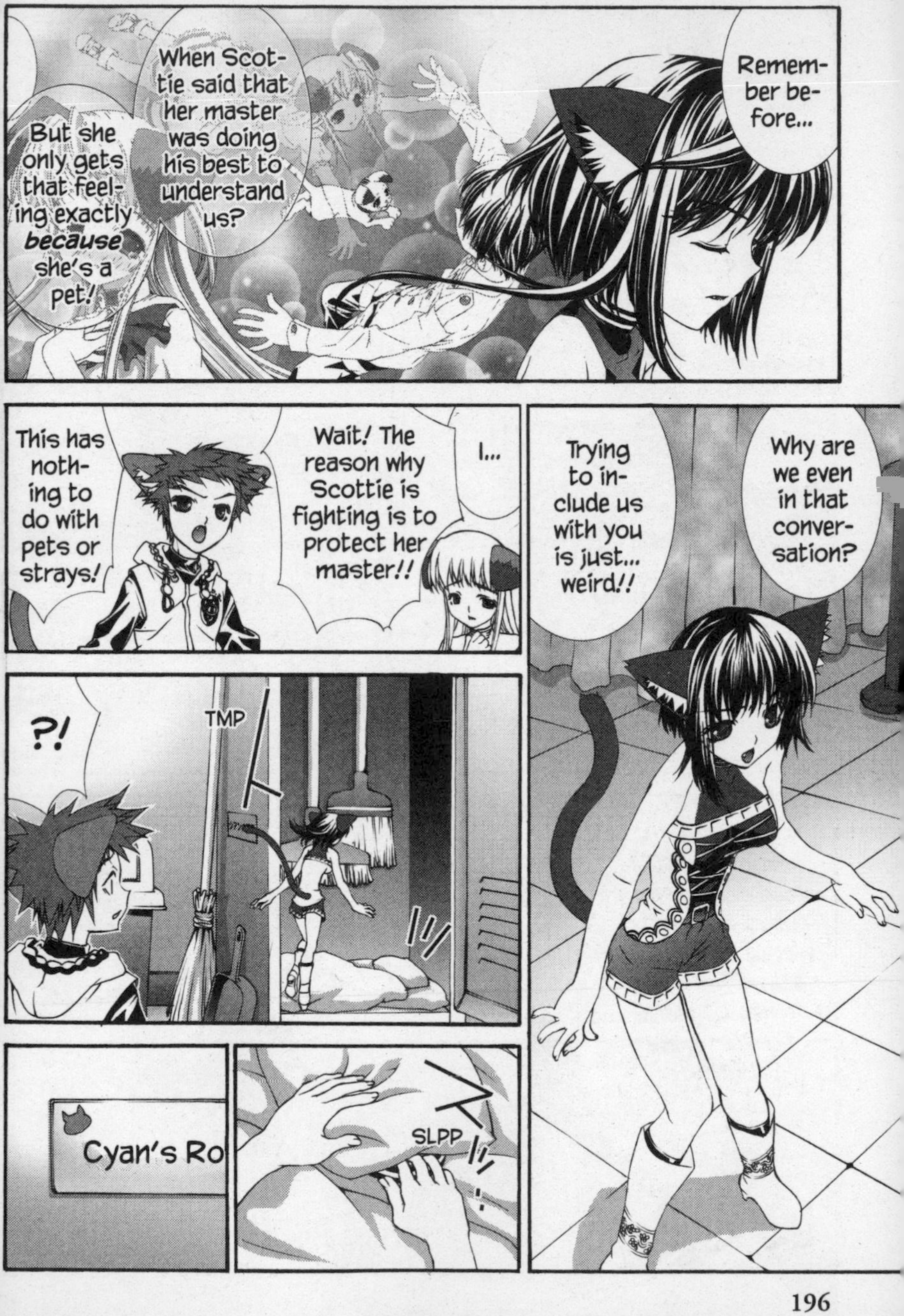
Remember before...
When Scottie said that her master was doing his best to understand us?
But she only gets that feeling exactly *because* she's a pet!
Why are we even in that conversation?
Trying to include us with you is just... weird!!
I...
Wait! The reason why Scottie is fighting is to protect her master!!
This has nothing to do with pets or strays!
TMP
?!
SLPP
Cyan's Ro

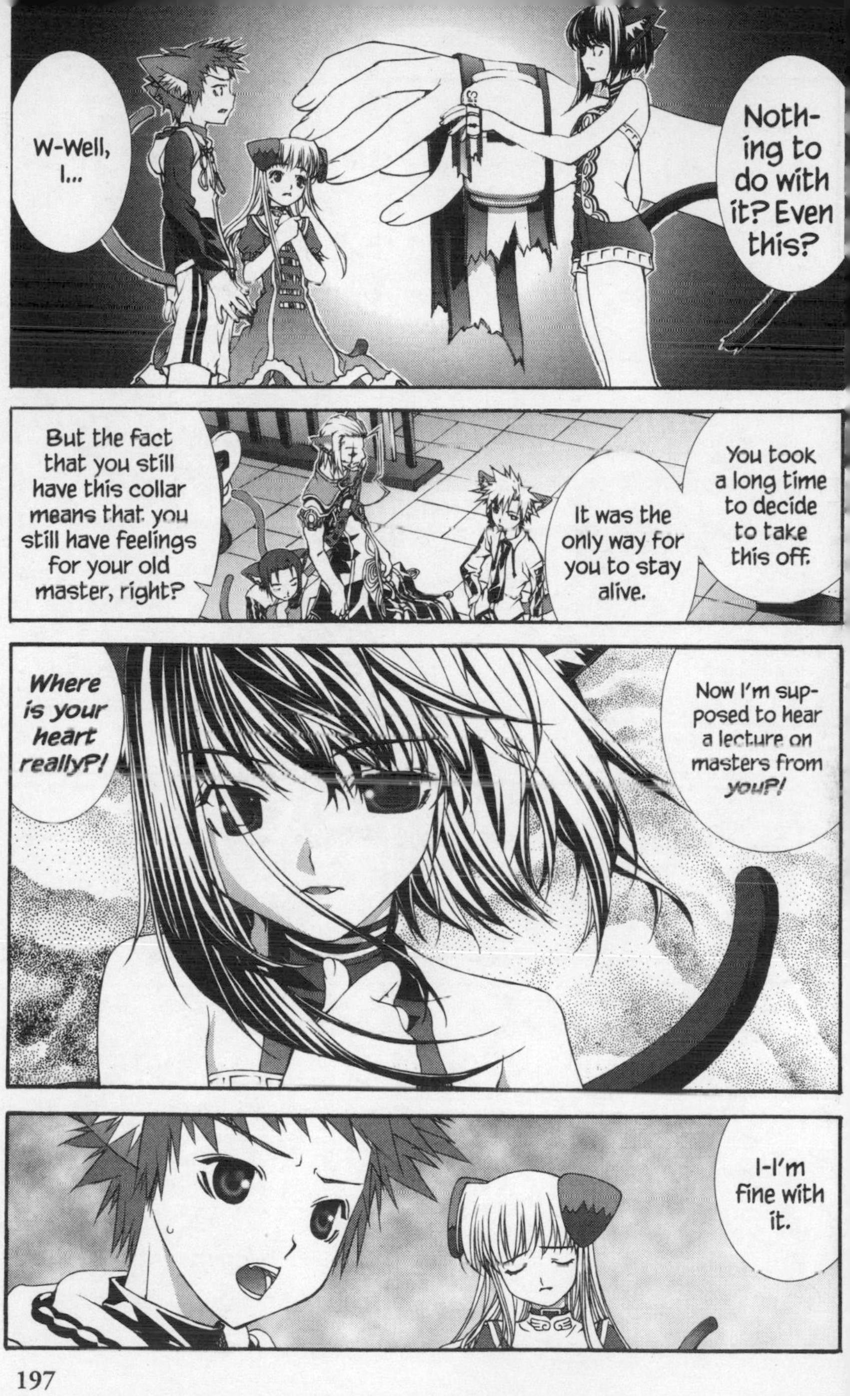
Noth-ing to do with it? Even this?
W-Well, I...
You took a long time to decide to take this off.
It was the only way for you to stay alive.
But the fact that you still have this collar means that you still have feelings for your old master, right?
Now I'm sup-posed to hear a lecture on masters from *you*?!
Where is your heart really?!
I-I'm fine with it.

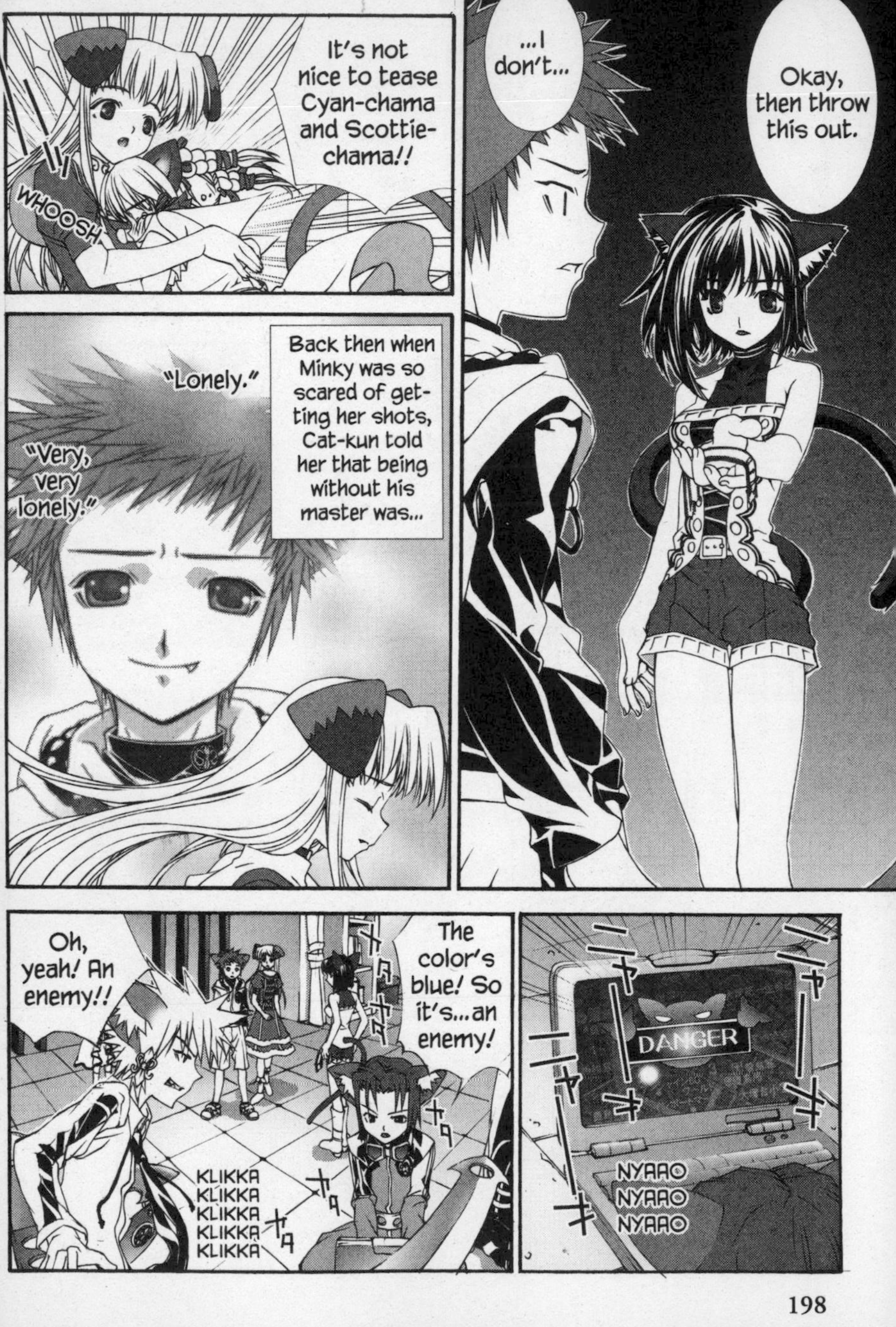
Okay, then throw this out.
...I don't...
It's not nice to tease Cyan-chama and Scottie-chama!!
WHOOSH
Back then when Minky was so scared of getting her shots, Cat-kun told her that being without his master was...
"Lonely."
"Very, very lonely."
DANGER
NYAAO
NYAAO
NYAAO
The color's blue! So it's...an enemy!
Oh, yeah! An enemy!!
KLIKKA
KLIKKA
KLIKKA
KLIKKA
KLIKKA

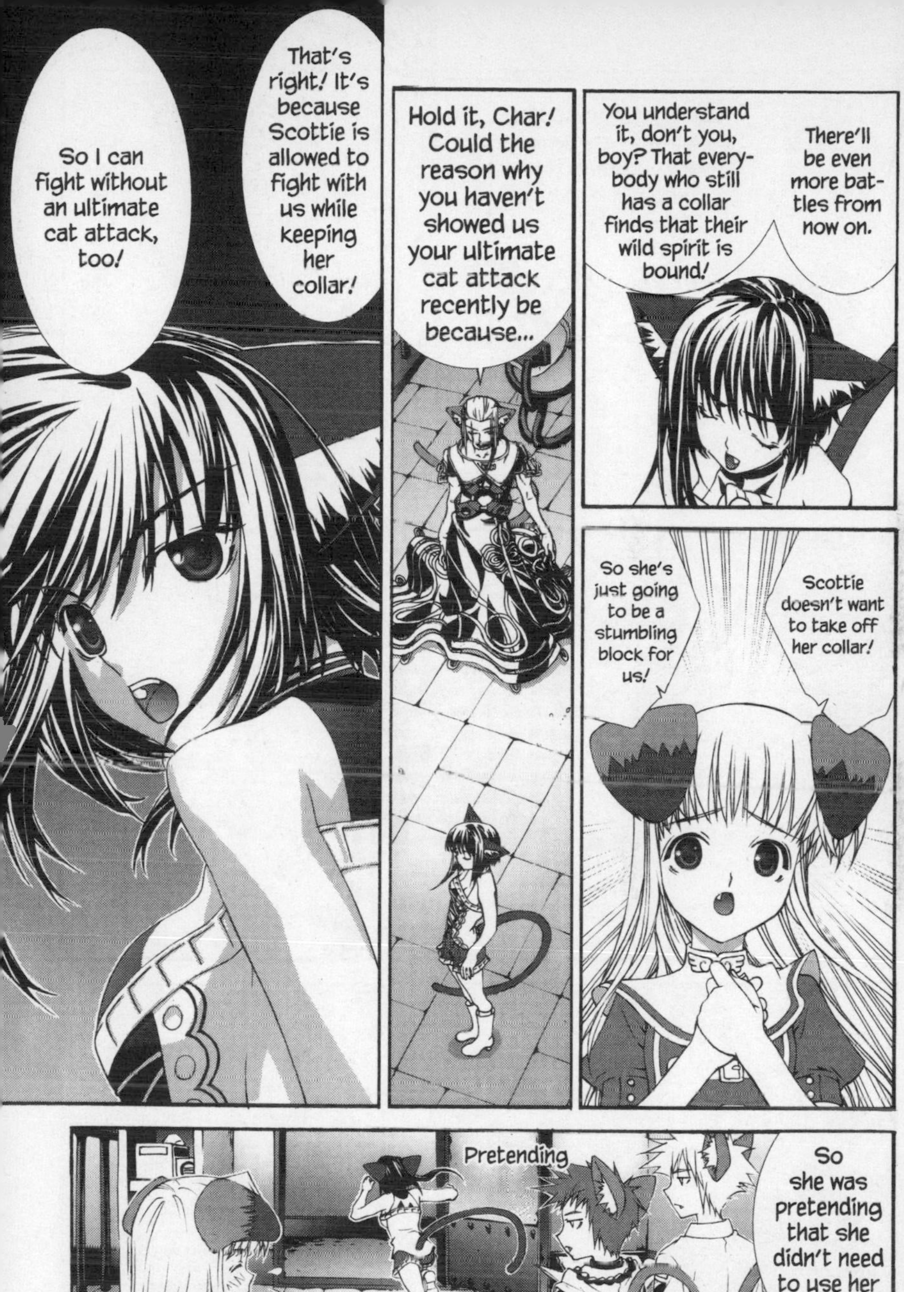
There'll be even more bat-tles from now on.
You understand it, don't you, boy? That every-body who still has a collar finds that their wild spirit is bound!
Scottie doesn't want to take off her collar!
So she's just going to be a stumbling block for us!
Hold it, Char! Could the reason why you haven't showed us your ultimate cat attack recently be because...
That's right! It's because Scottie is allowed to fight with us while keeping her collar!
So I can fight without an ultimate cat attack, too!
So she was pretending that she didn't need to use her attack.
Pretending

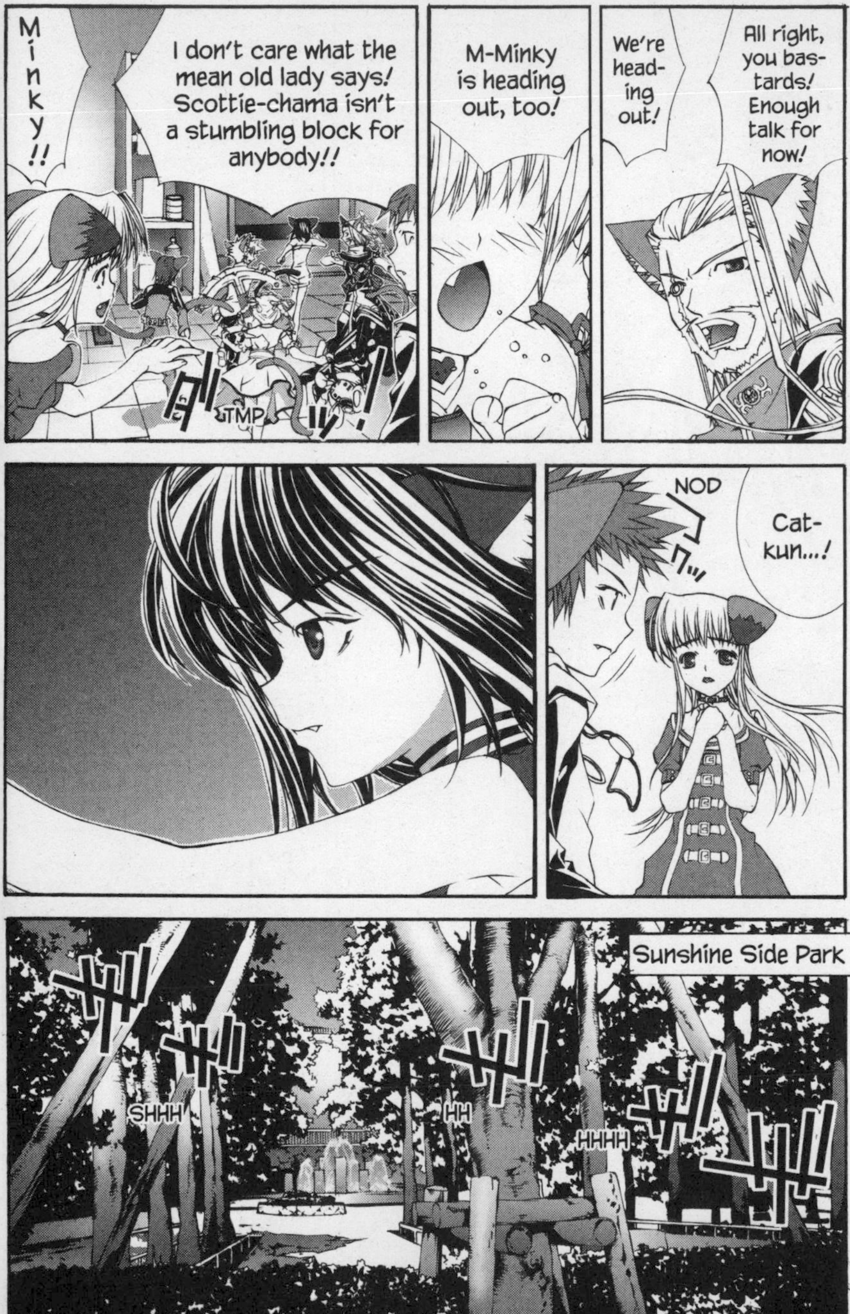
All right, you bastards! Enough talk for now!
We're heading out!
M-Minky is heading out, too!
I don't care what the mean old lady says! Scottie-chama isn't a stumbling block for anybody!!
Minky!!
TMP
NOD
Cat-kun...!
Sunshine Side Park
HHHH
HH
SHHH

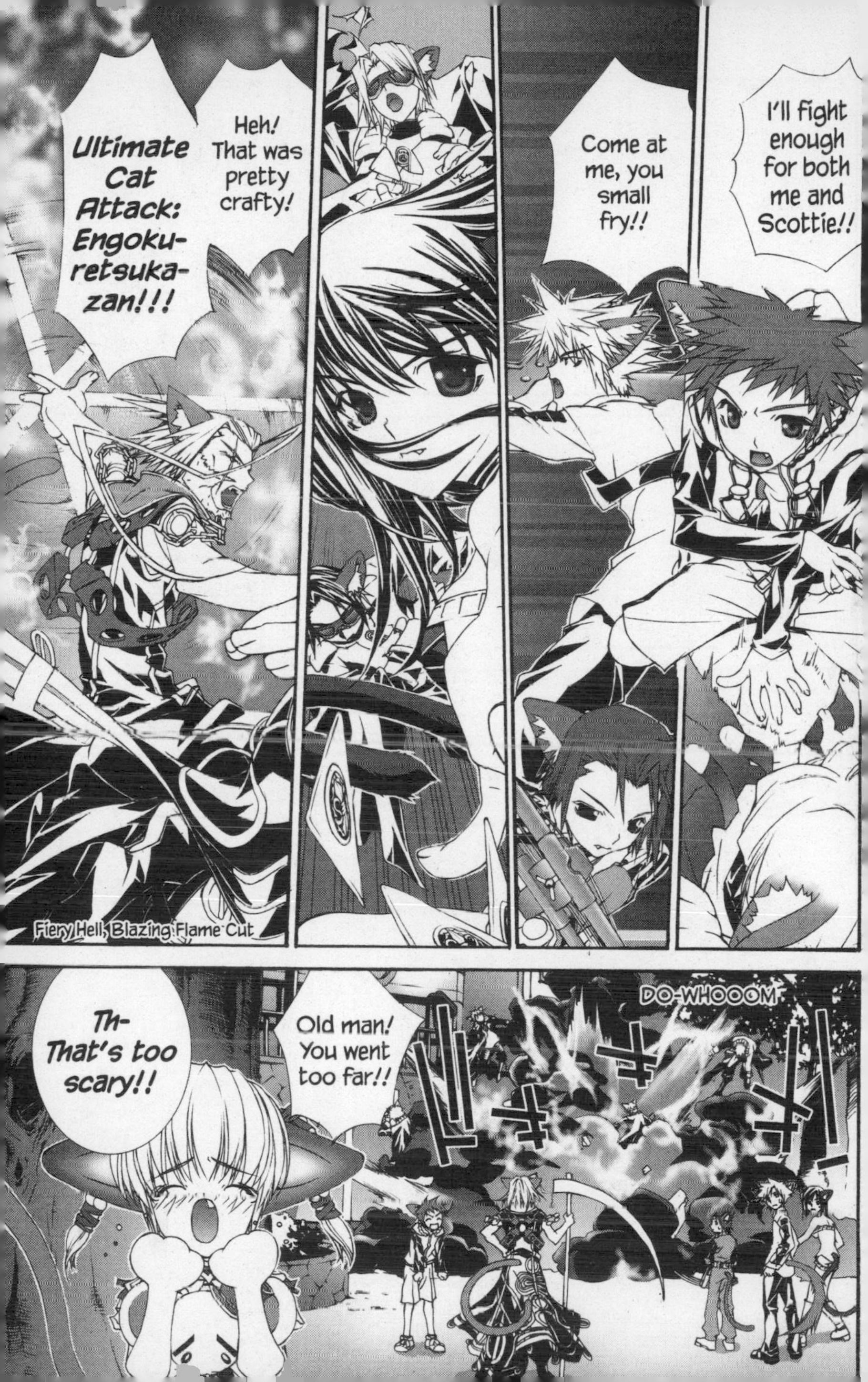
I'll fight enough for both me and Scottie!!
Come at me, you small fry!!
Heh! That was pretty crafty!
Ultimate Cat Attack: Engoku-retsuka-zan!!!
Fiery Hell, Blazing Flame Cut
DO-WHOOOM
Old man! You went too far!!
Th- That's too scary!!

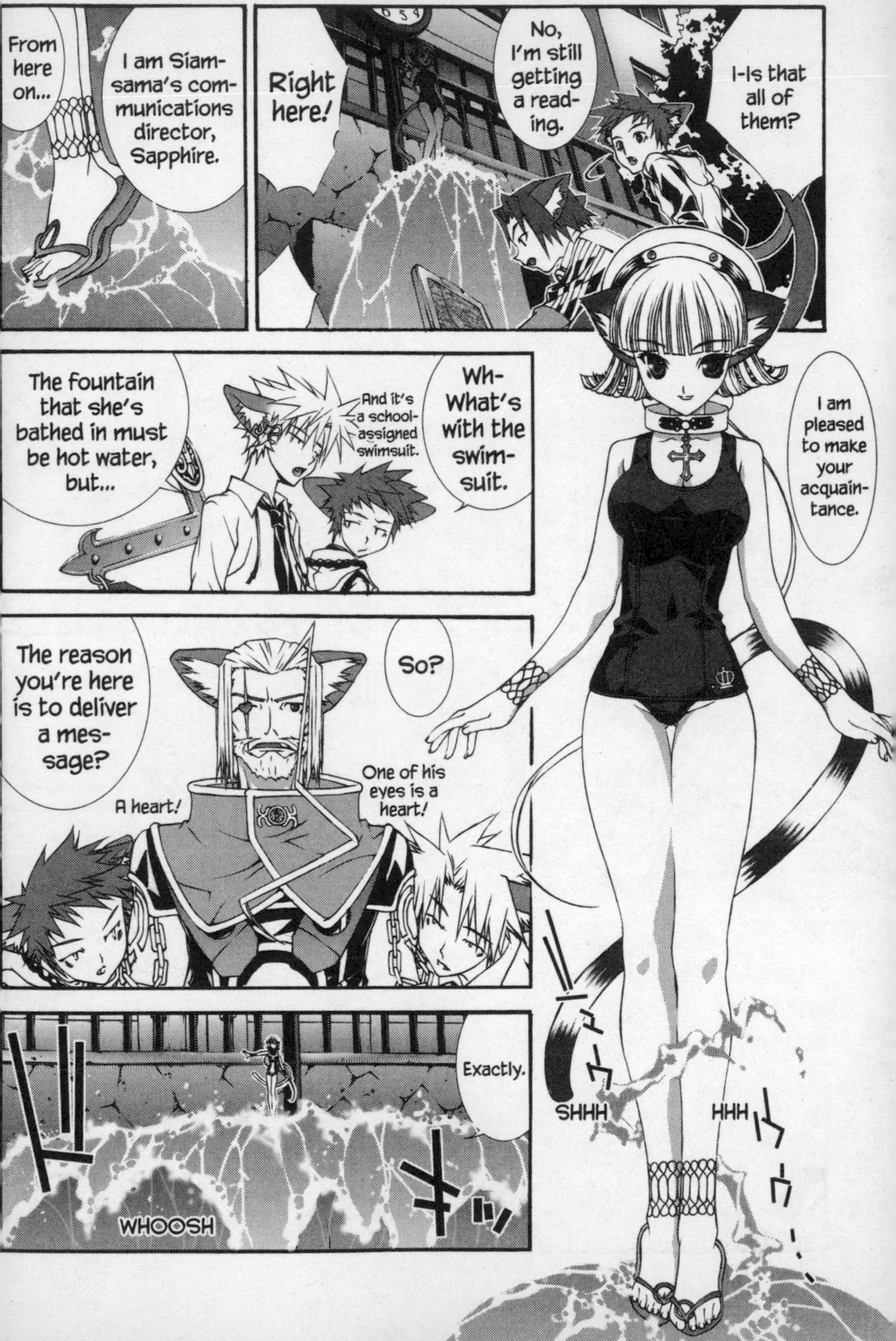
I-Is that all of them?
No, I'm still getting a reading.
Right here!
I am Siam-sama's communications director, Sapphire.
From here on...
I am pleased to make your acquaintance.
SHHH
HHH
Wh-What's with the swimsuit.
And it's a school-assigned swimsuit.
The fountain that she's bathed in must be hot water, but...
So?
The reason you're here is to deliver a message?
One of his eyes is a heart!
A heart!
Exactly.
WHOOSH

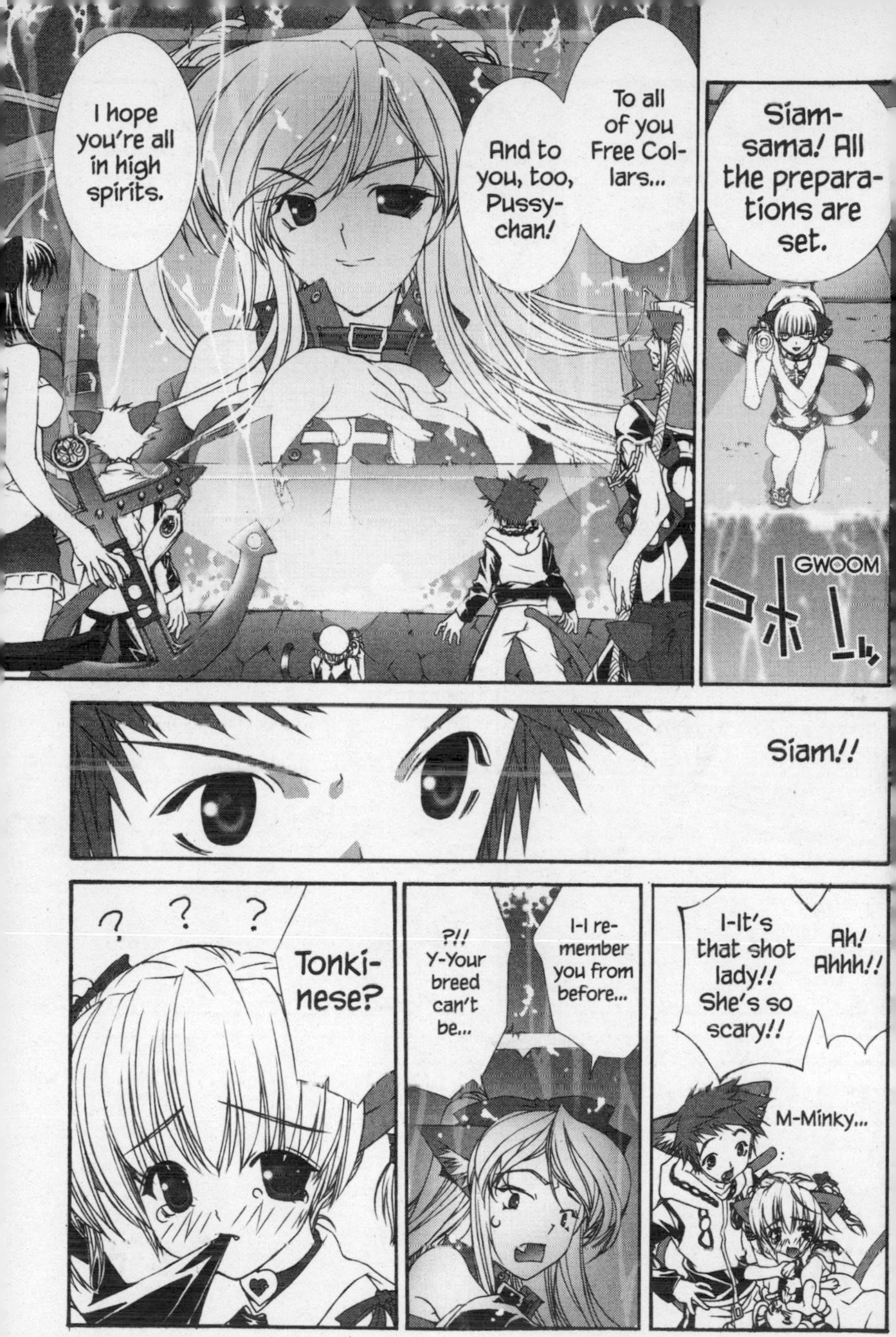
Siam-sama! All the prepara-tions are set.
GWOOM
To all of you Free Col-lars...
And to you, too, Pussy-chan!
I hope you're all in high spirits.
Siam!!
Ah! Ahhh!!
I-It's that shot lady!! She's so scary!!
M-Minky...
I-I re-member you from before...
?!! Y-Your breed can't be...
Tonki-nese?
? ? ?

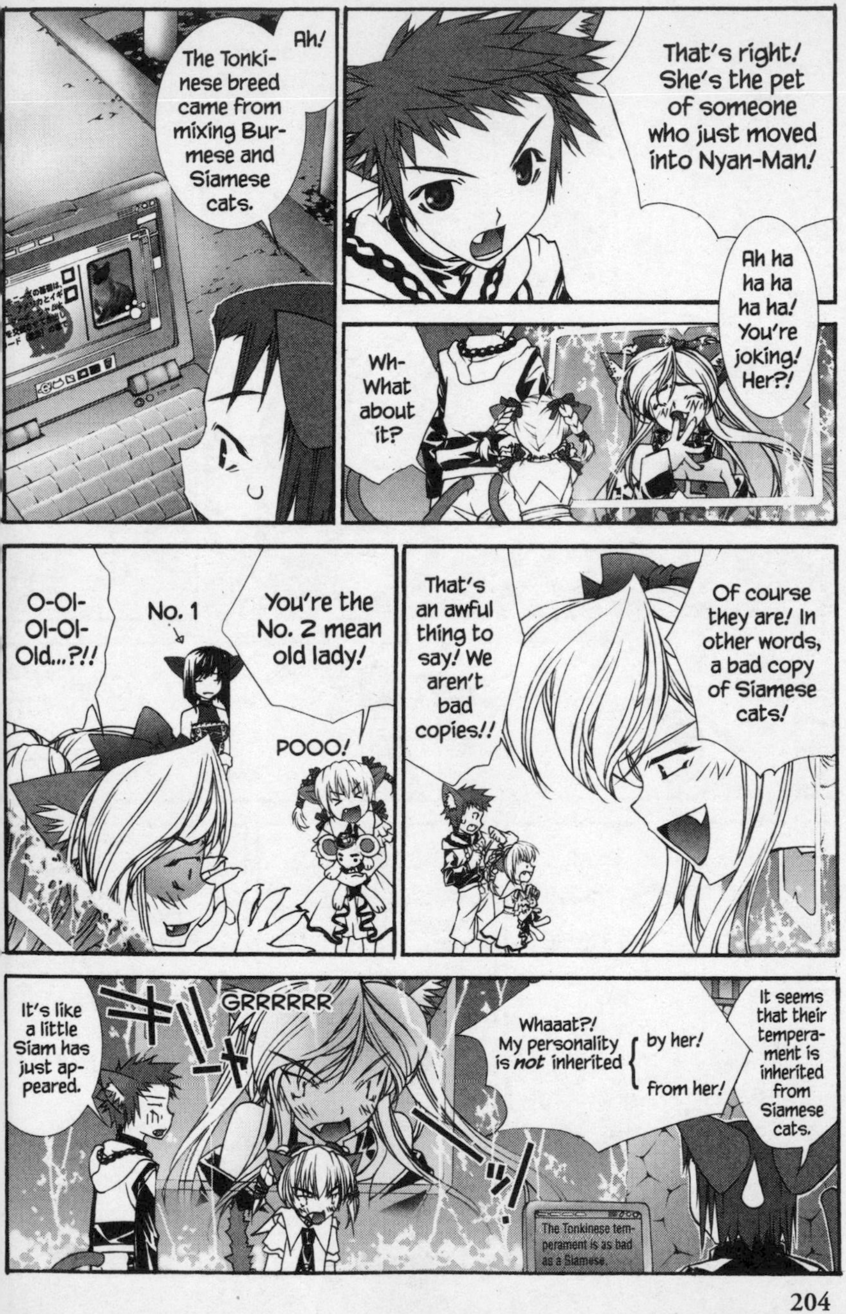
That's right! She's the pet of someone who just moved into Nyan-Man!
Ah ha ha ha ha! You're joking! Her?!
Wh-What about it?
Ah! The Tonkinese breed came from mixing Burmese and Siamese cats.
Of course they are! In other words, a bad copy of Siamese cats!
That's an awful thing to say! We aren't bad copies!!
You're the No. 2 mean old lady!
No. 1
POOO!
O-Ol-Ol-Ol-Old...?!!
It seems that their temperament is inherited from Siamese cats.
Whaaat?! My personality is *not* inherited by her! from her!
GRRRRRR
It's like a little Siam has just appeared.
The Tonkinese temperament is as bad as a Siamese.

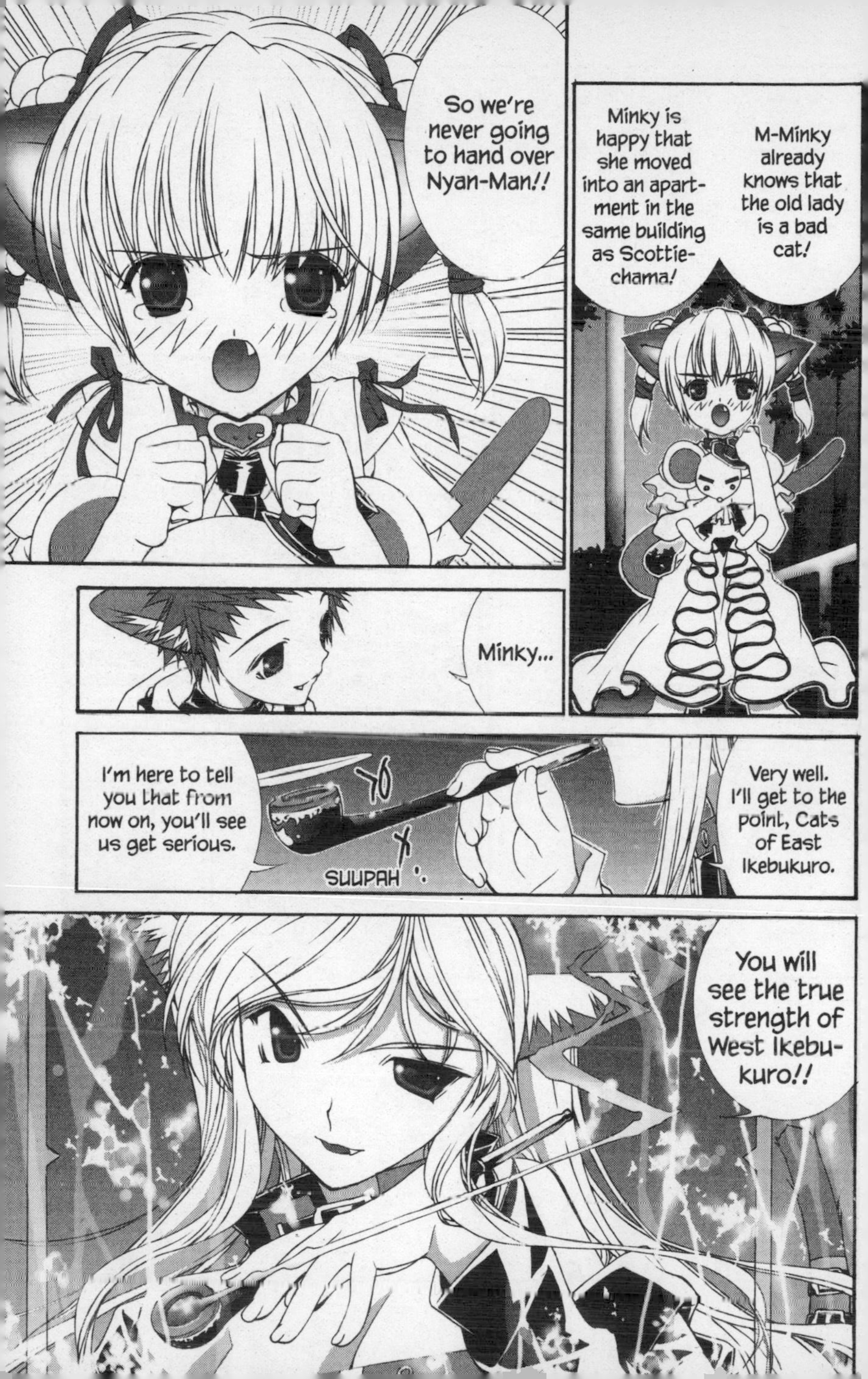
M-Minky already knows that the old lady is a bad cat!
Minky is happy that she moved into an apartment in the same building as Scottie-chama!
So we're never going to hand over Nyan-Man!!
Minky...
Very well. I'll get to the point, Cats of East Ikebukuro.
SUUPAH
I'm here to tell you that from now on, you'll see us get serious.
You will see the true strength of West Ikebukuro!!

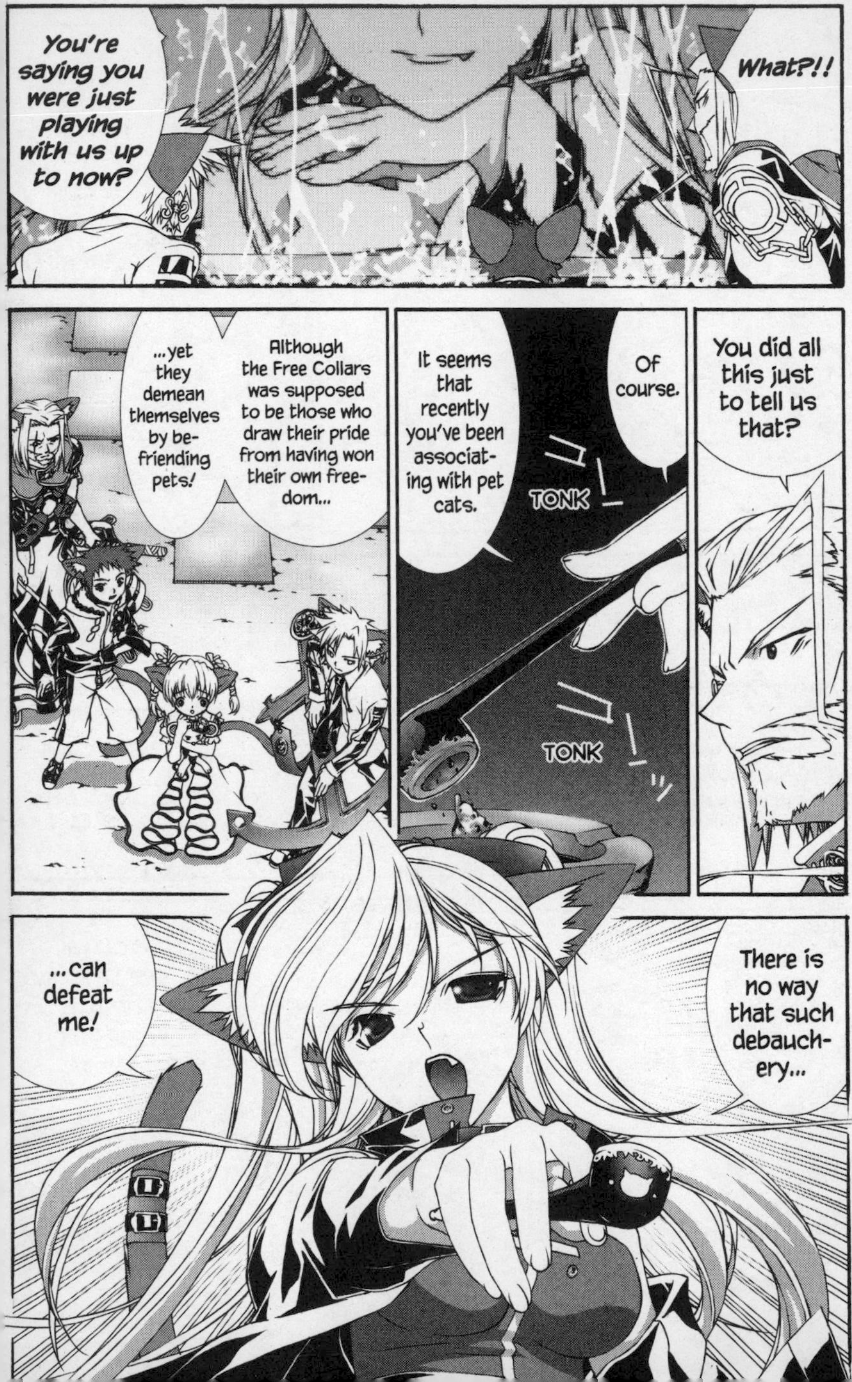
What?!!
You're saying you were just playing with us up to now?
You did all this just to tell us that?
Of course.
TONK
TONK
It seems that recently you've been associating with pet cats.
Although the Free Collars was supposed to be those who draw their pride from having won their own freedom...
...yet they demean themselves by befriending pets!
There is no way that such debauchery...
...can defeat me!

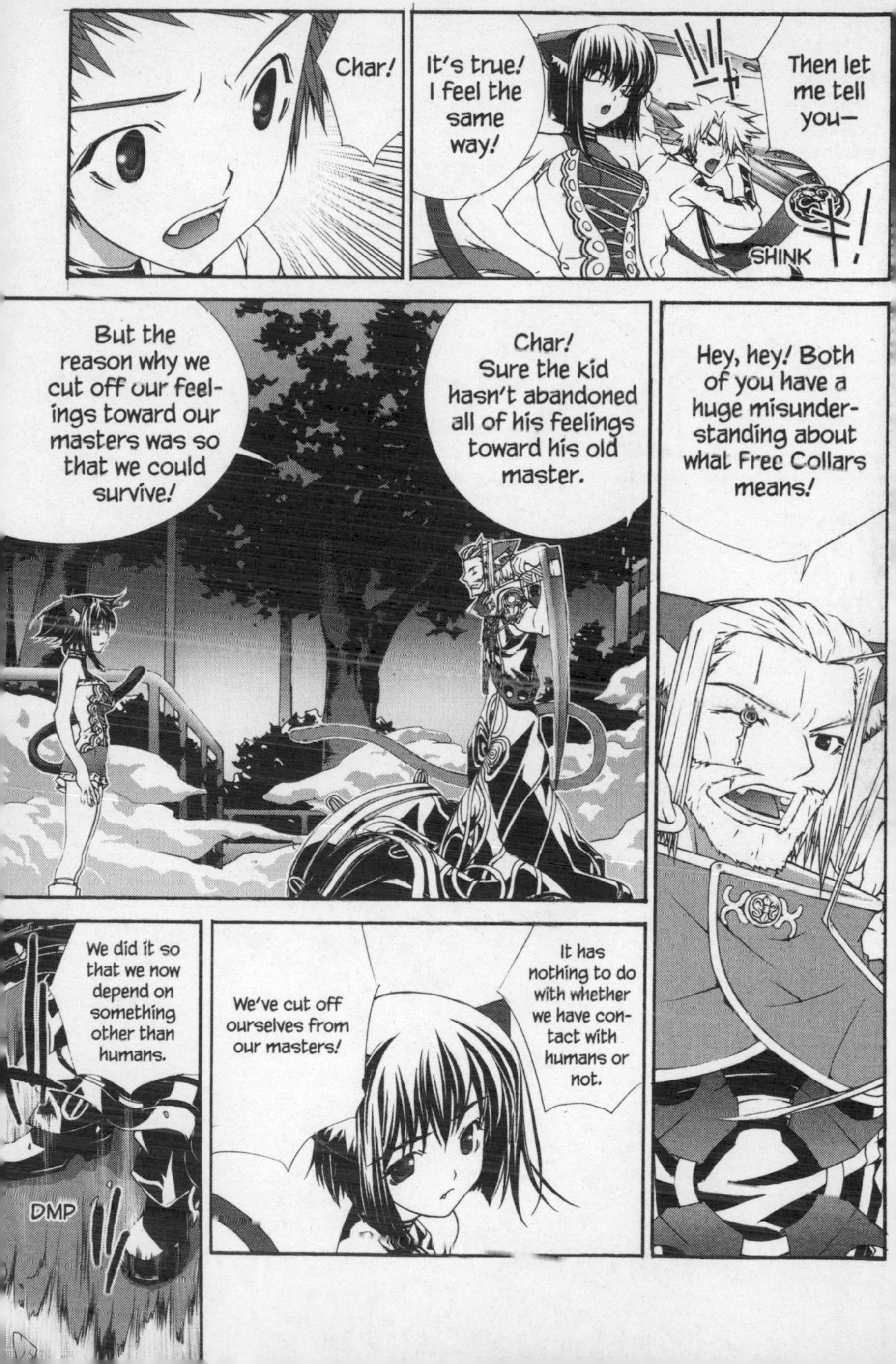
Then let me tell you—
It's true! I feel the same way!
SHINK
Char!
Hey, hey! Both of you have a huge misunder-standing about what Free Collars means!
Char! Sure the kid hasn't abandoned all of his feelings toward his old master.
But the reason why we cut off our feel-ings toward our masters was so that we could survive!
It has nothing to do with whether we have con-tact with humans or not.
We've cut off ourselves from our masters!
We did it so that we now depend on something other than humans.
DMP

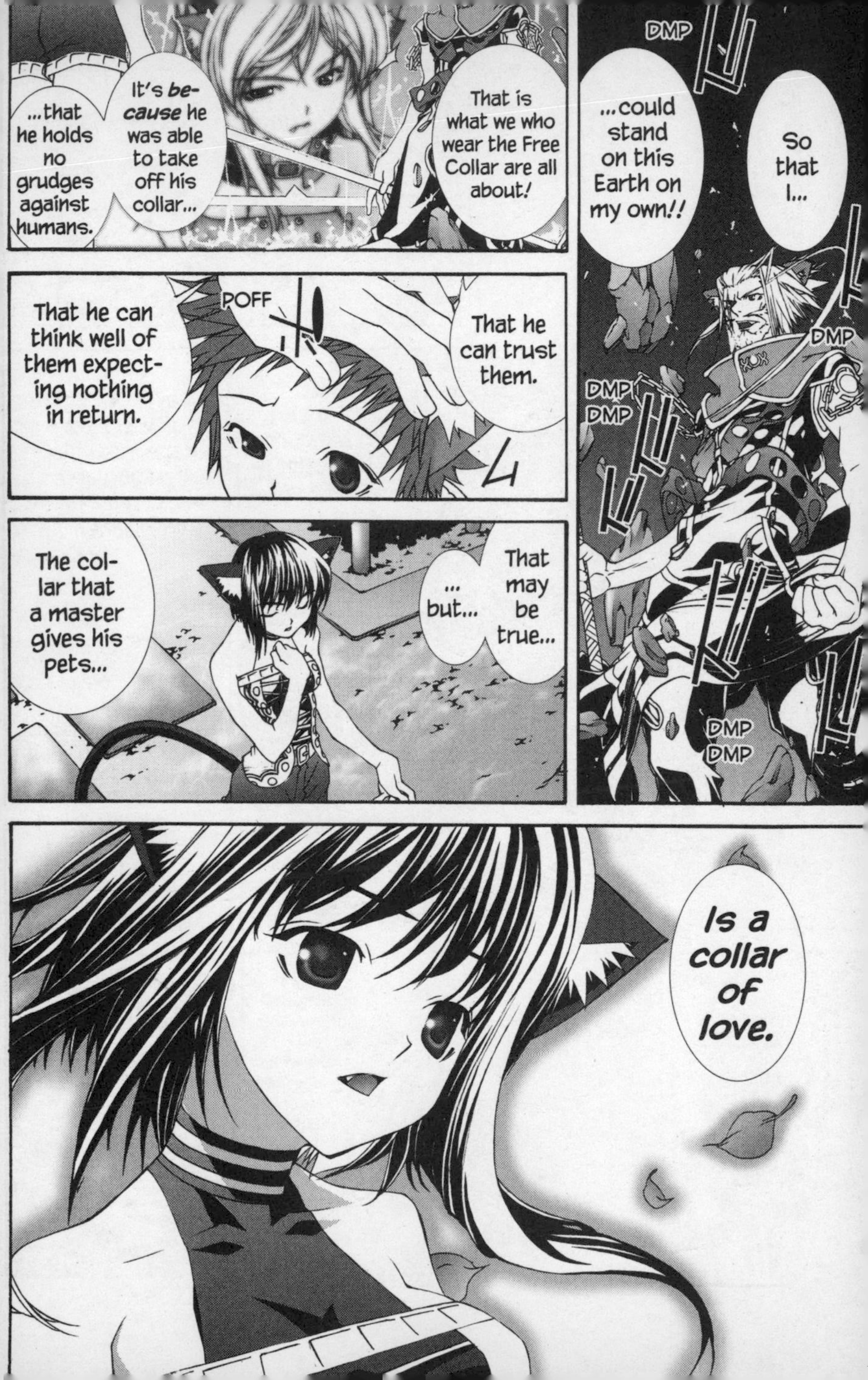
DMP
So that I...
...could stand on this Earth on my own!!
DMP
DMP DMP
DMP DMP
That is what we who wear the Free Collar are all about!
It's *because* he was able to take off his collar...
...that he holds no grudges against humans.
POFF
That he can trust them.
That he can think well of them expecting nothing in return.
That may be true...
... but...
The collar that a master gives his pets...
Is a collar of love.

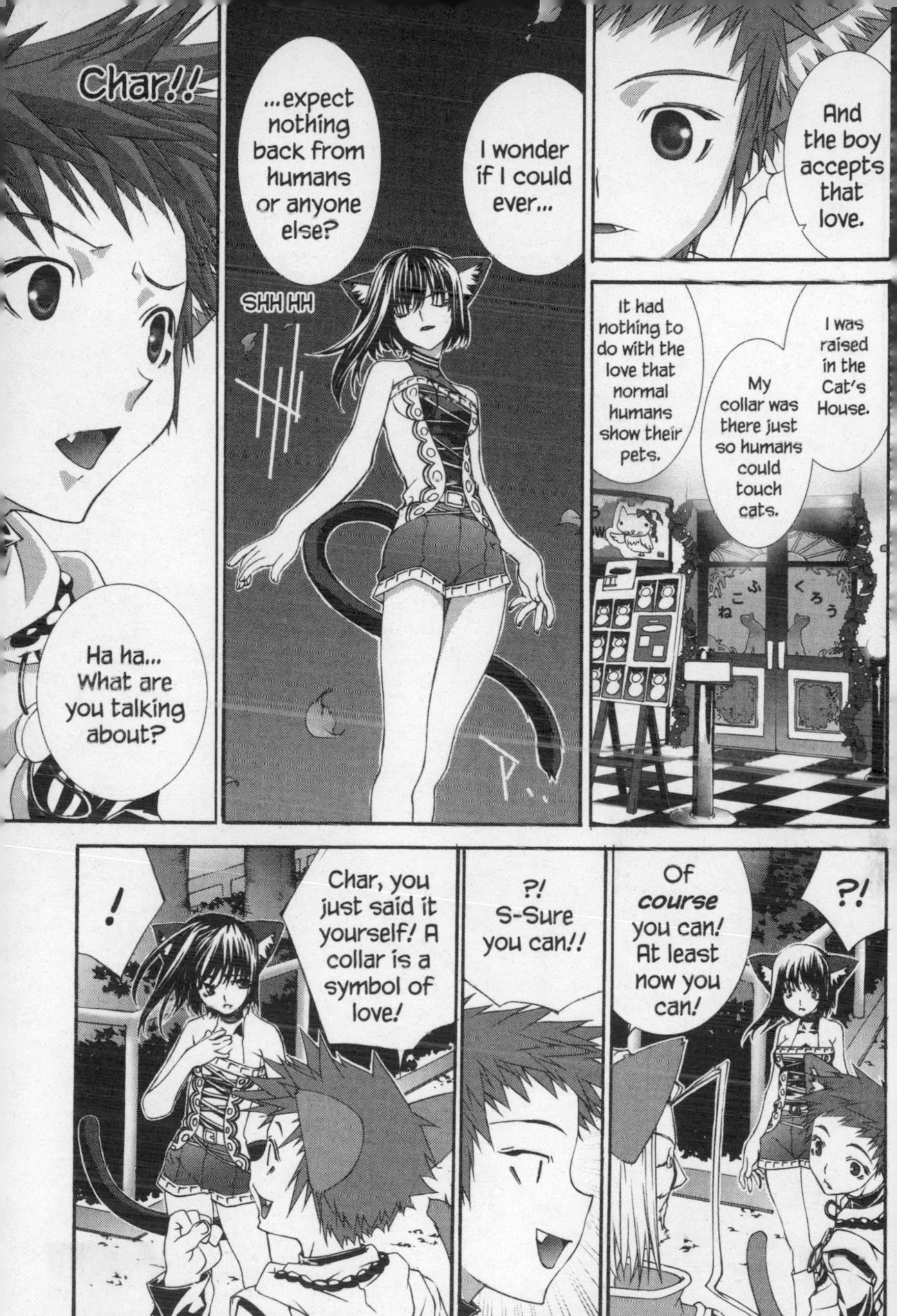
And the boy accepts that love.
I was raised in the Cat's House.
My collar was there just so humans could touch cats.
It had nothing to do with the love that normal humans show their pets.
I wonder if I could ever...
...expect nothing back from humans or anyone else?
SHH HH
Char!!
Ha ha... What are you talking about?
?!
Of *course* you can! At least now you can!
?! S-Sure you can!!
Char, you just said it yourself! A collar is a symbol of love!
!

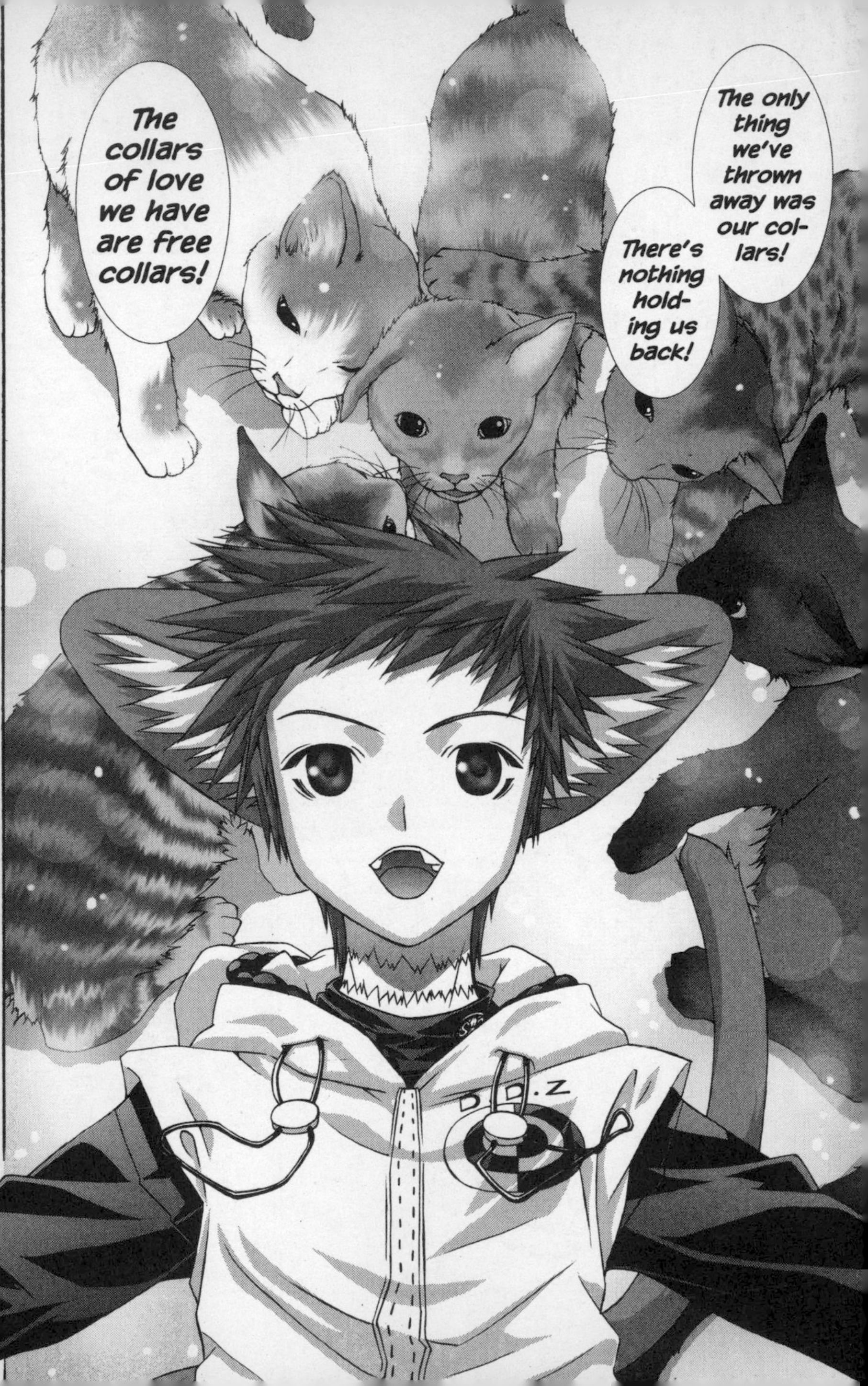
The only thing we've thrown away was our collars!
There's nothing holding us back!
The collars of love we have are free collars!
D.D.Z

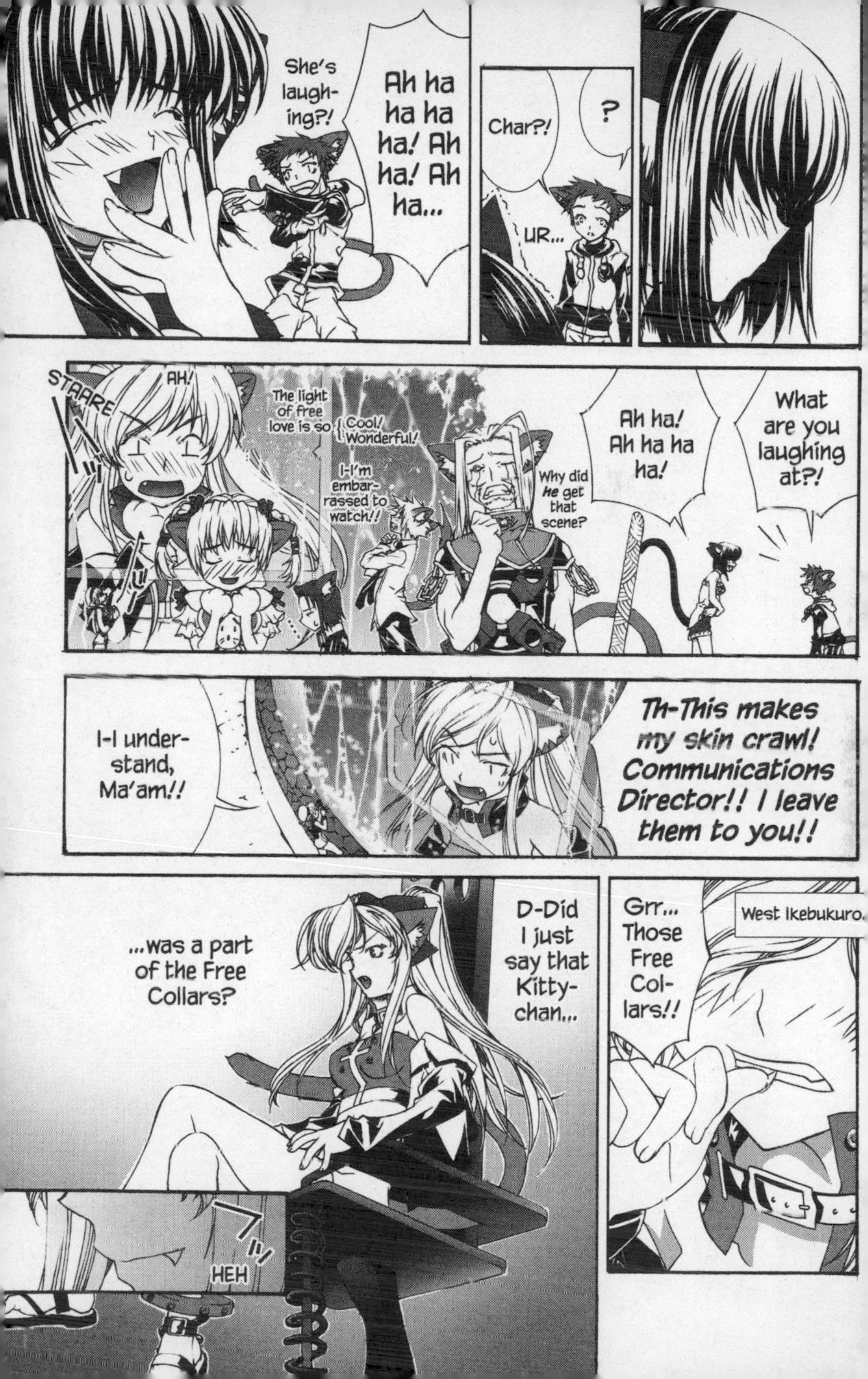
?
Char?!
UR...
Ah ha ha ha! Ah ha! Ah ha...
She's laughing?!
What are you laughing at?!
Ah ha! Ah ha ha ha!
Why did he get that scene?
I-I'm embarrassed to watch!!
Cool! Wonderful!
The light of free love is so
AH!
STAARE
Th-This makes my skin crawl! Communications Director!! I leave them to you!!
I-I understand, Ma'am!!
West Ikebukuro.
Grr... Those Free Collars!!
D-Did I just say that Kitty-chan...
...was a part of the Free Collars?
HEH

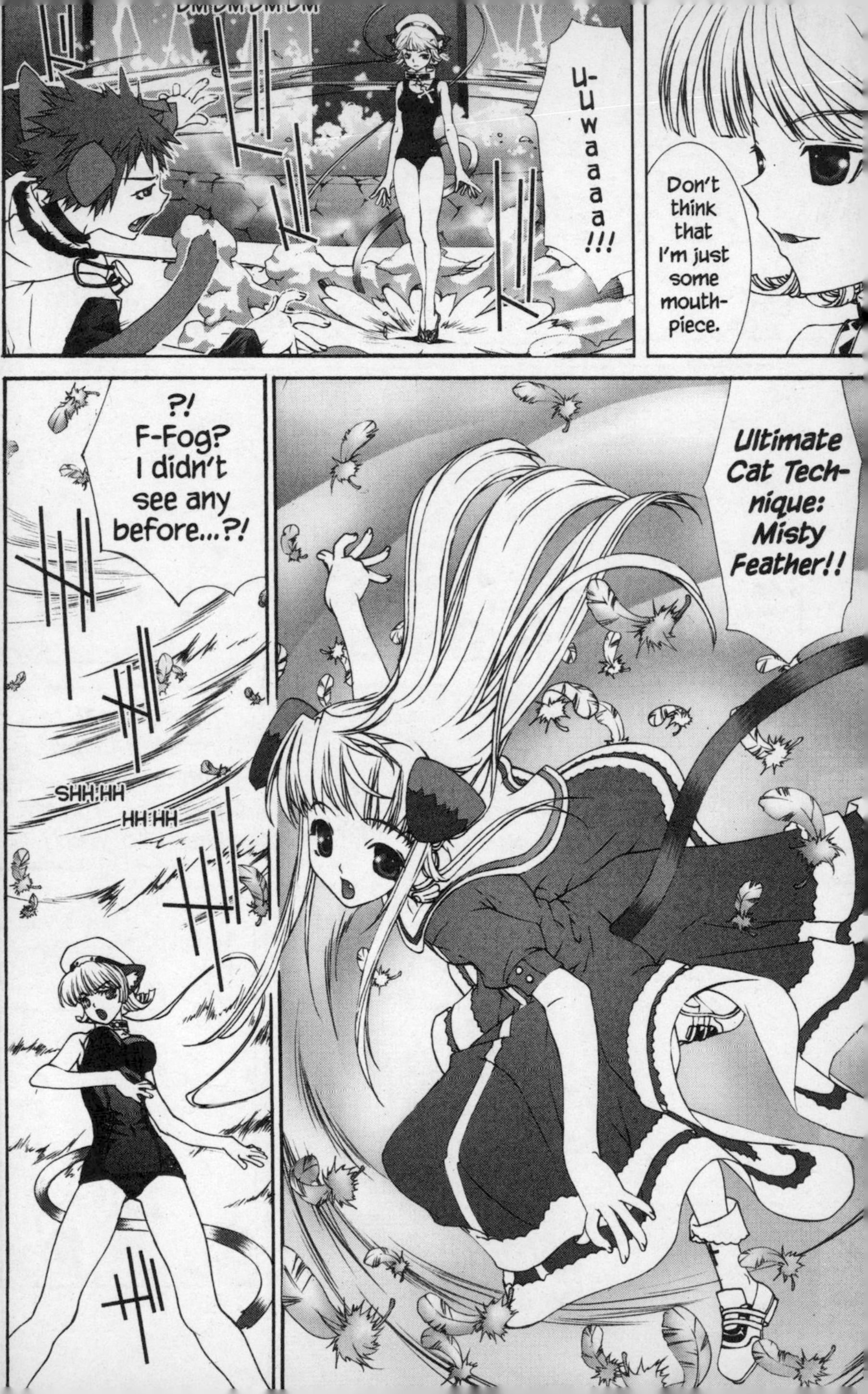
Don't think that I'm just some mouth-piece.
DM DM DM DM
U-uwaaaaa!!!
Ultimate Cat Tech-nique: Misty Feather!!
?! F-Fog? I didn't see any before...?!
SHH HH
HH HH

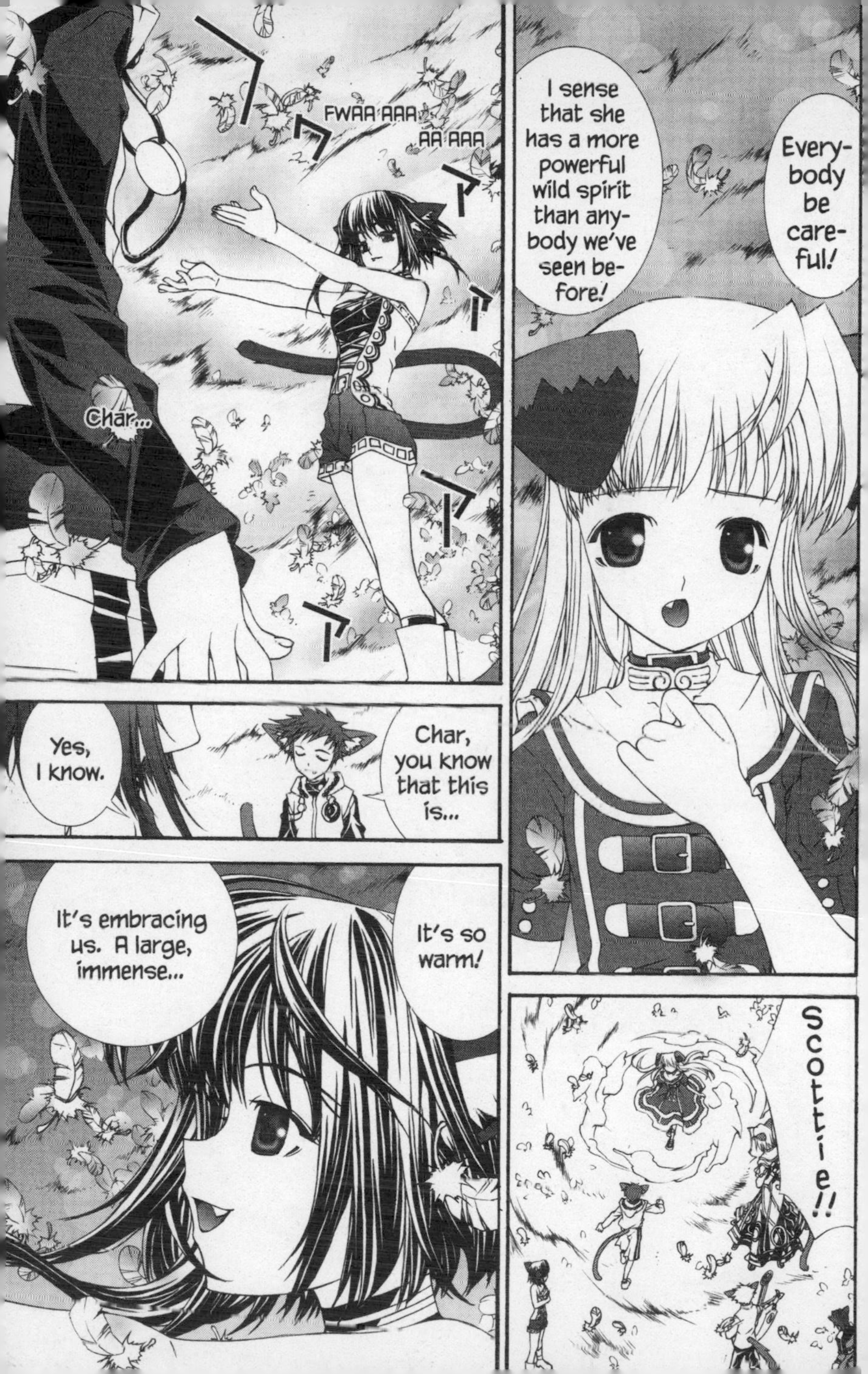
Every-body be care-ful!
I sense that she has a more powerful wild spirit than any-body we've seen be-fore!
FWAA AAA
AA AAA
Char...
Char, you know that this is...
Yes, I know.
It's so warm!
It's embracing us. A large, immense...
Scottie!!

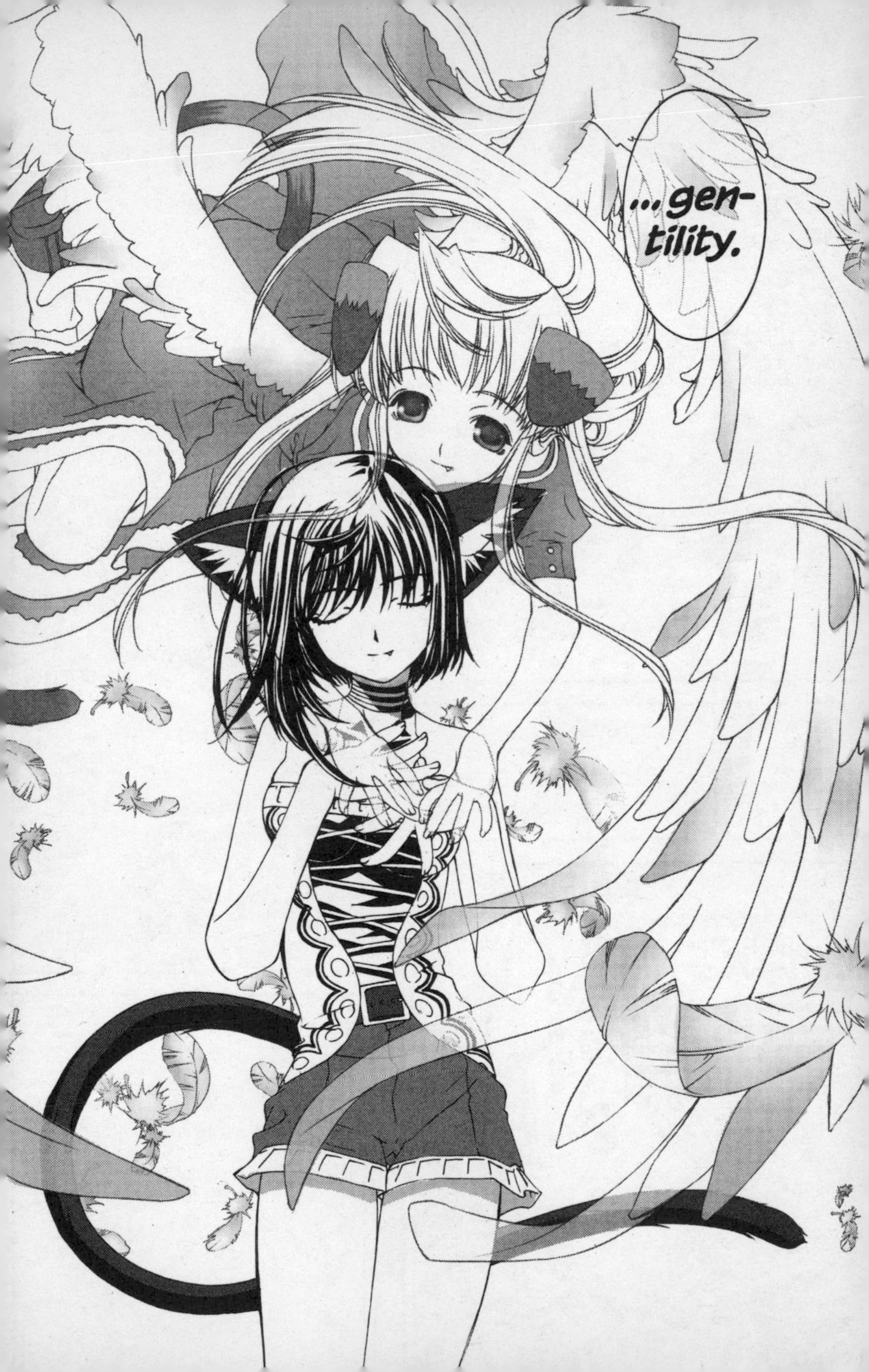
...gen-
tility.

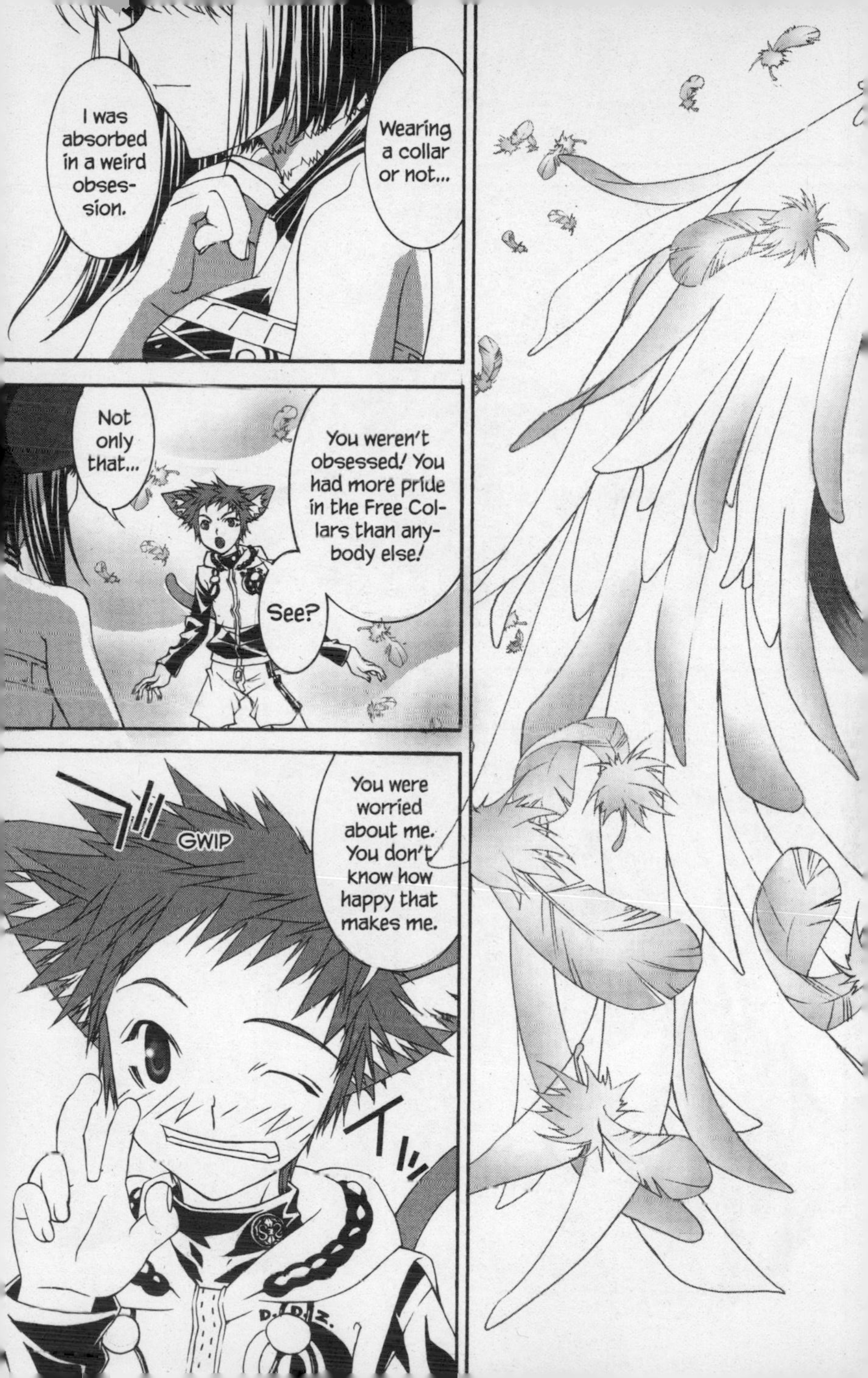
Wearing a collar or not...
I was absorbed in a weird obsession.
You weren't obsessed! You had more pride in the Free Collars than anybody else!
Not only that...
See?
You were worried about me. You don't know how happy that makes me.
GWIP
D.D.Z.

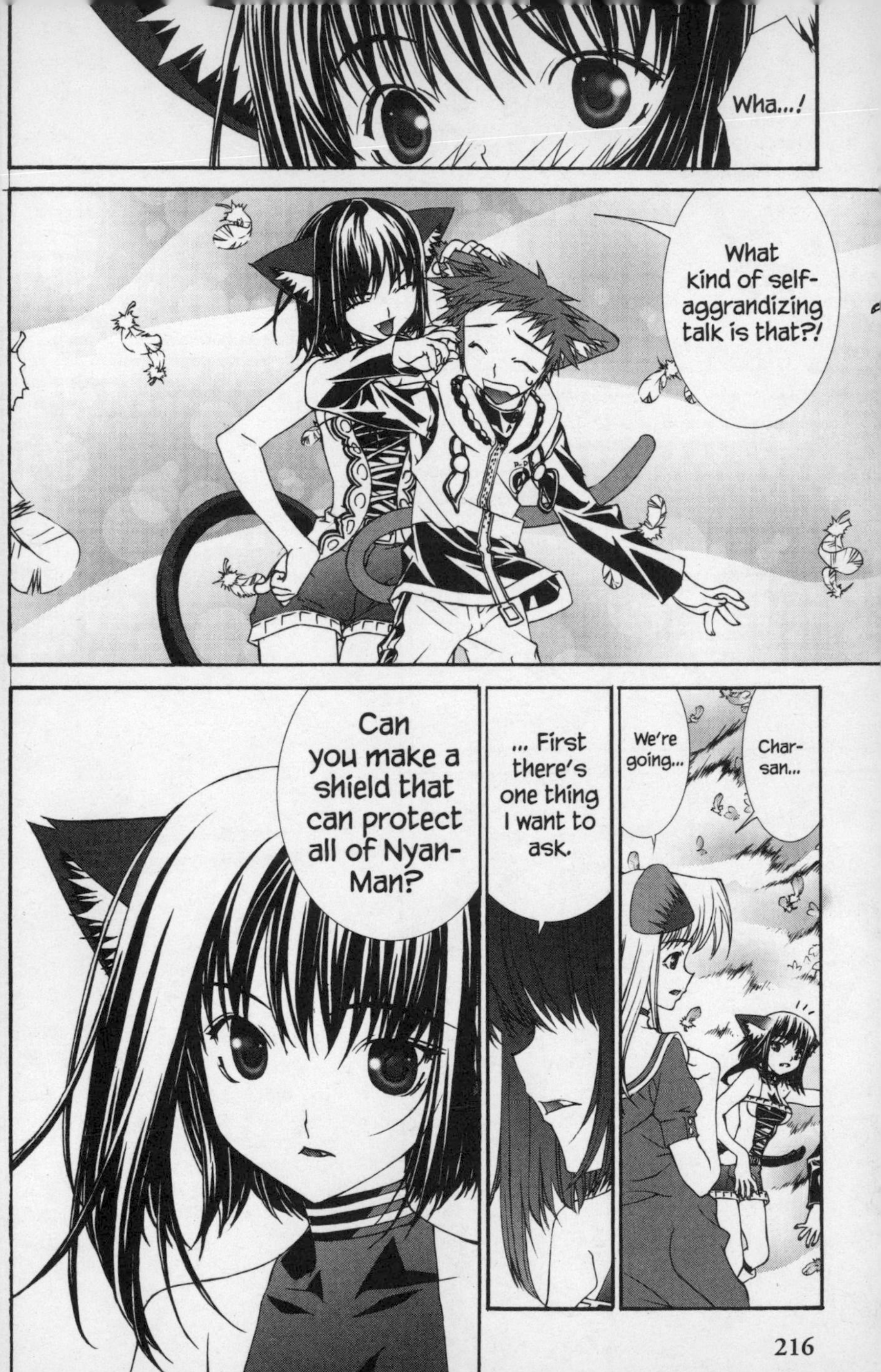
Wha...!
What kind of self-aggrandizing talk is that?!
Char-san...
We're going...
... First there's one thing I want to ask.
Can you make a shield that can protect all of Nyan-Man?

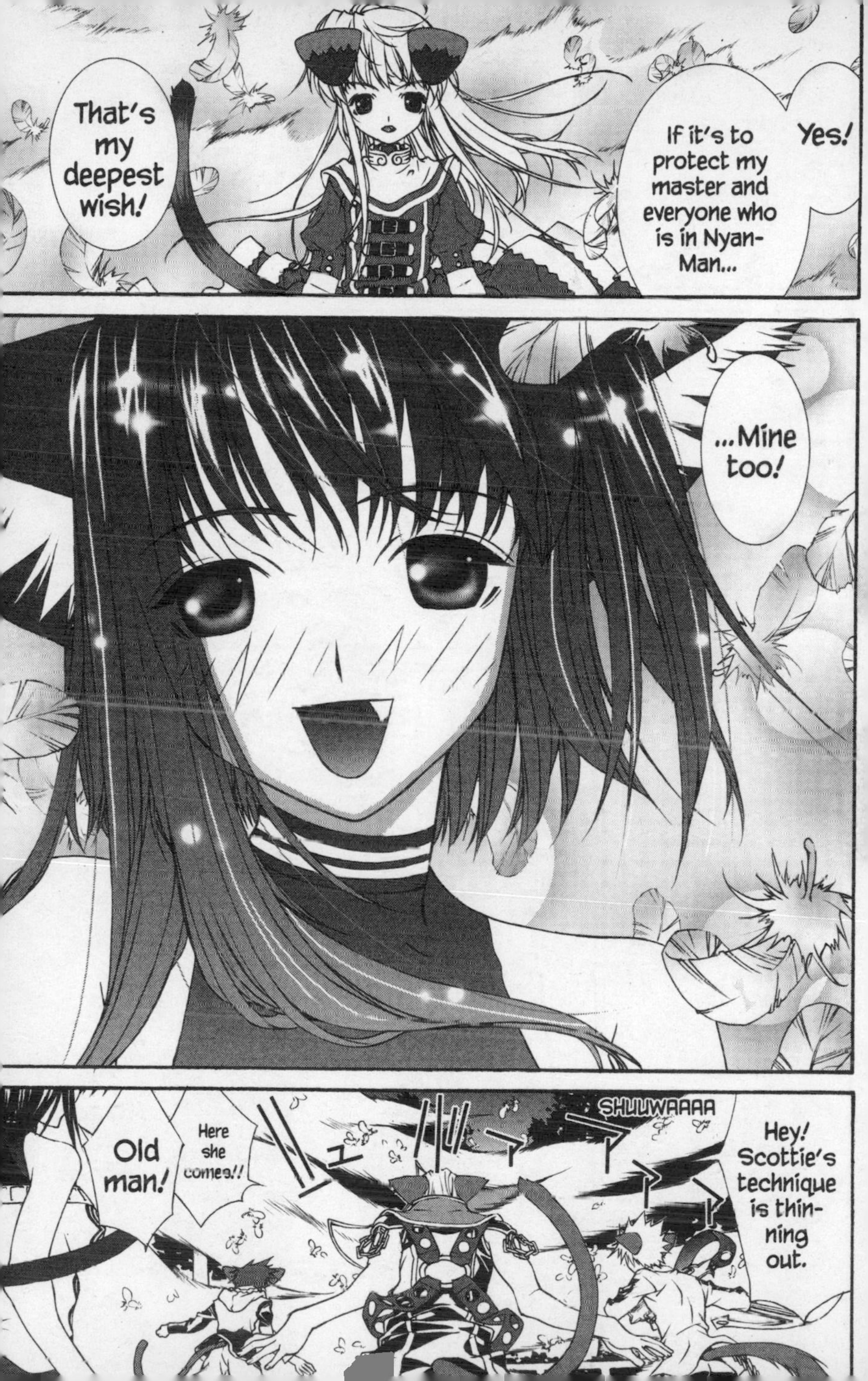
Yes!
If it's to protect my master and everyone who is in Nyan-Man...
That's my deepest wish!
...Mine too!
Hey! Scottie's technique is thin-ning out.
SHUUWAAAA
Here she comes!!
Old man!

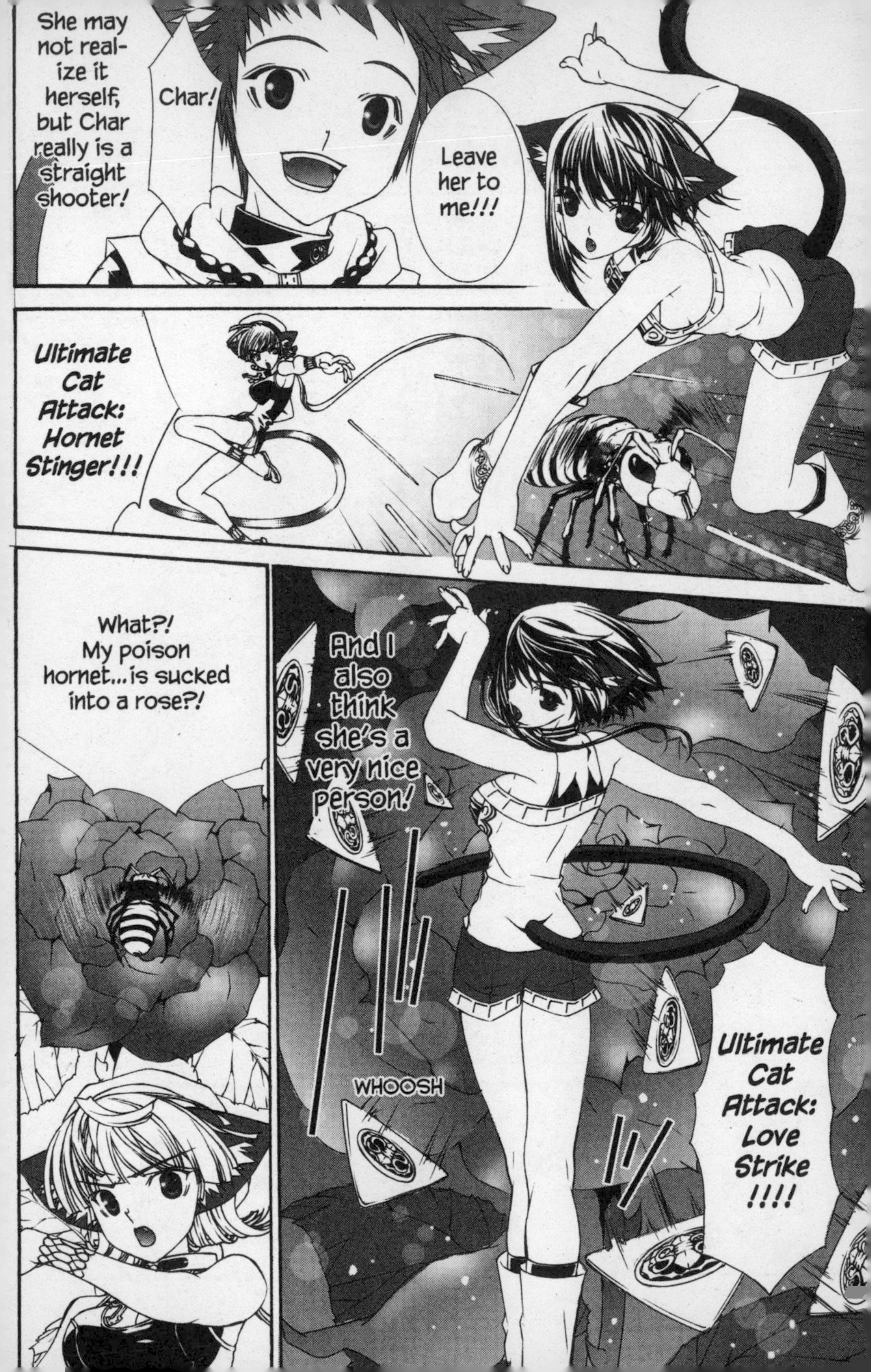
Char!
Leave her to me!!!
She may not realize it herself, but Char really is a straight shooter!
Ultimate Cat Attack: Hornet Stinger!!!
And I also think she's a very nice person!
Ultimate Cat Attack: Love Strike!!!!
WHOOSH
What?! My poison hornet...is sucked into a rose?!

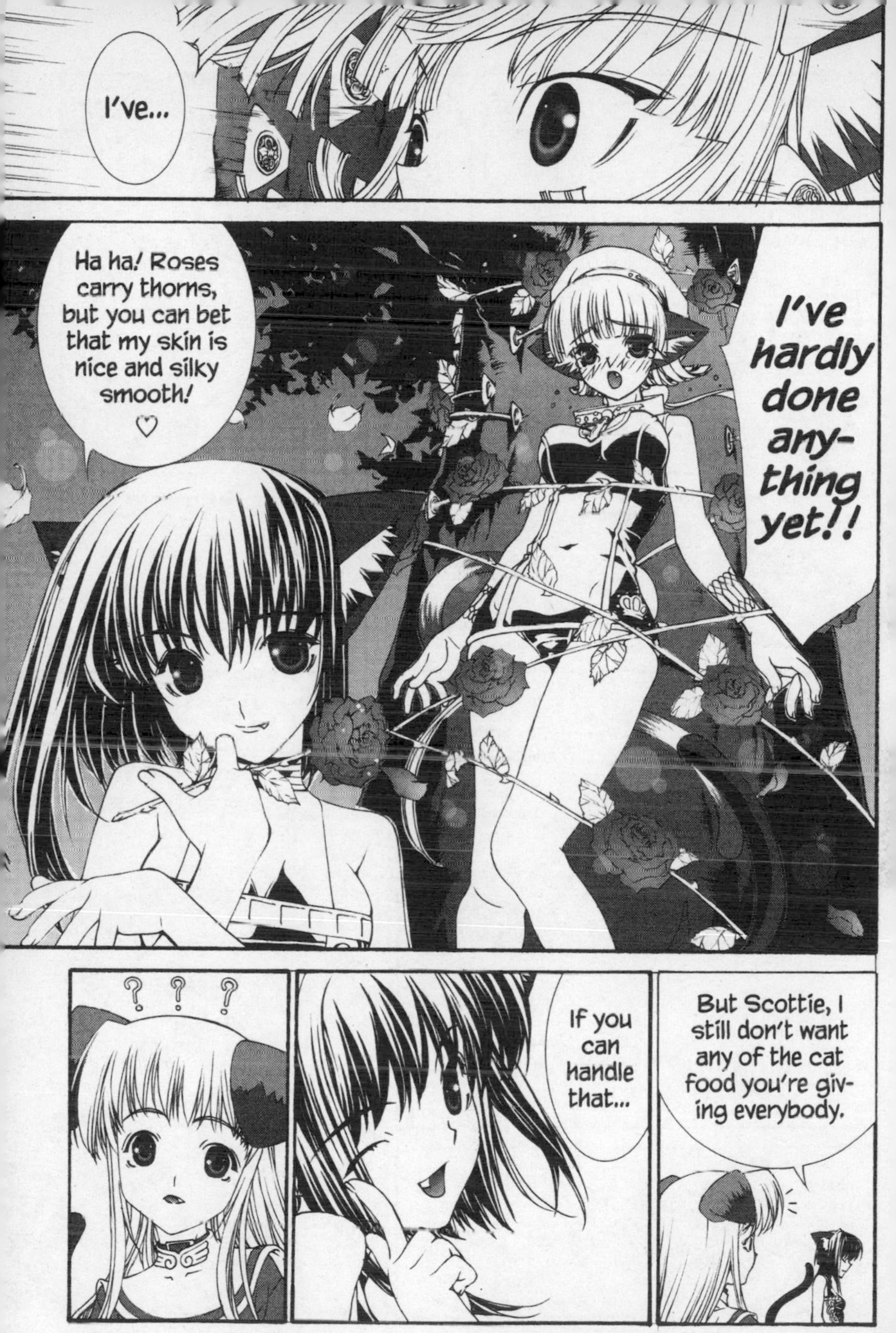
I've...
I've hardly done any-thing yet!!
Ha ha! Roses carry thorns, but you can bet that my skin is nice and silky smooth! ♡
But Scottie, I still don't want any of the cat food you're giv-ing everybody.
If you can handle that...
? ? ?

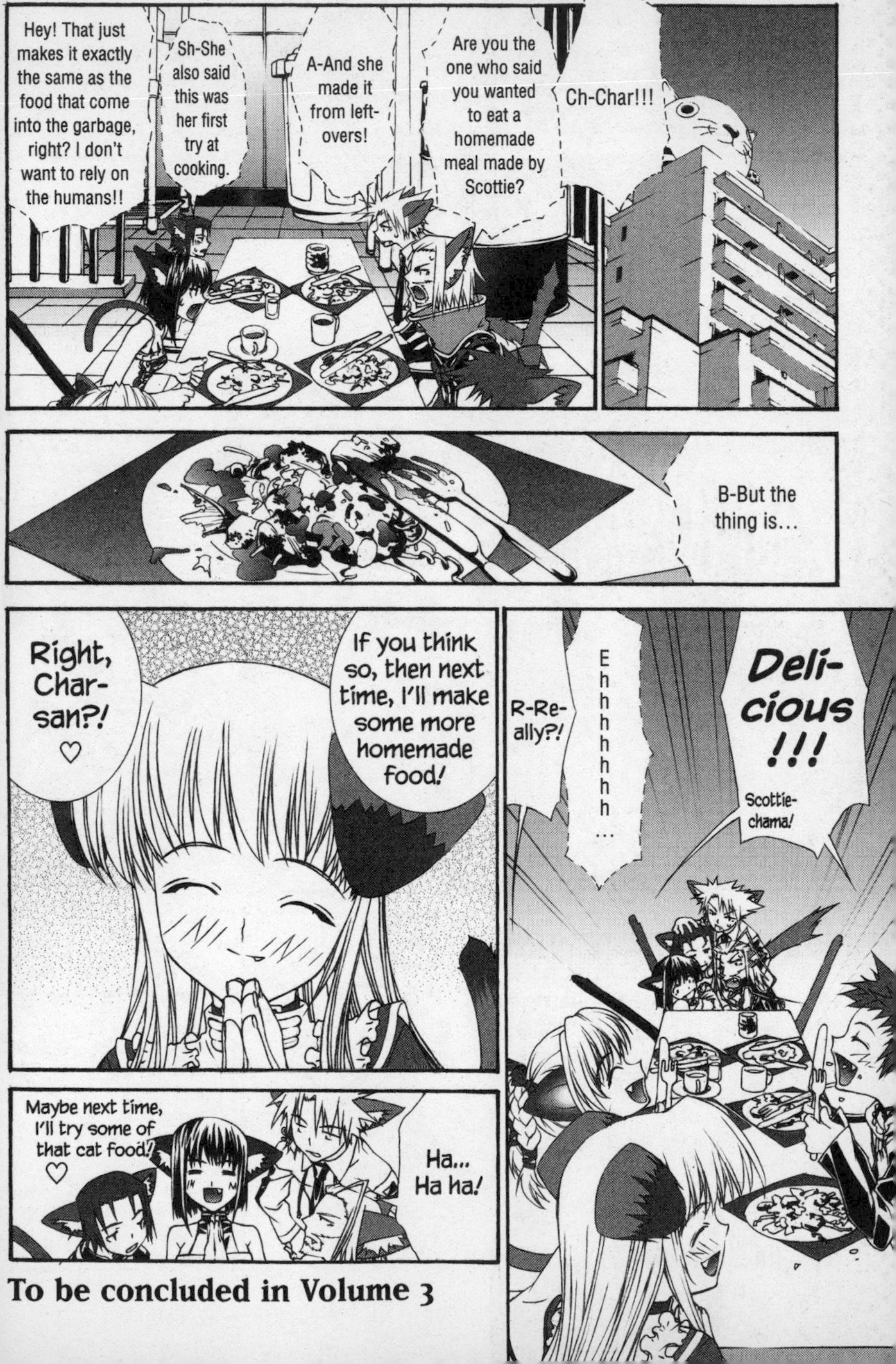
Ch-Char!!!
Are you the one who said you wanted to eat a homemade meal made by Scottie?
A-And she made it from left-overs!
Sh-She also said this was her first try at cooking.
Hey! That just makes it exactly the same as the food that come into the garbage, right? I don't want to rely on the humans!!
B-But the thing is…
Deli-cious!!!
Scottie-chama!
Ehhhhhhhhh…
R-Re-ally?!
If you think so, then next time, I'll make some more homemade food!
Right, Char-san?! ♡
Ha... Ha ha!
Maybe next time, I'll try some of that cat food! ♡

To be concluded in Volume 3

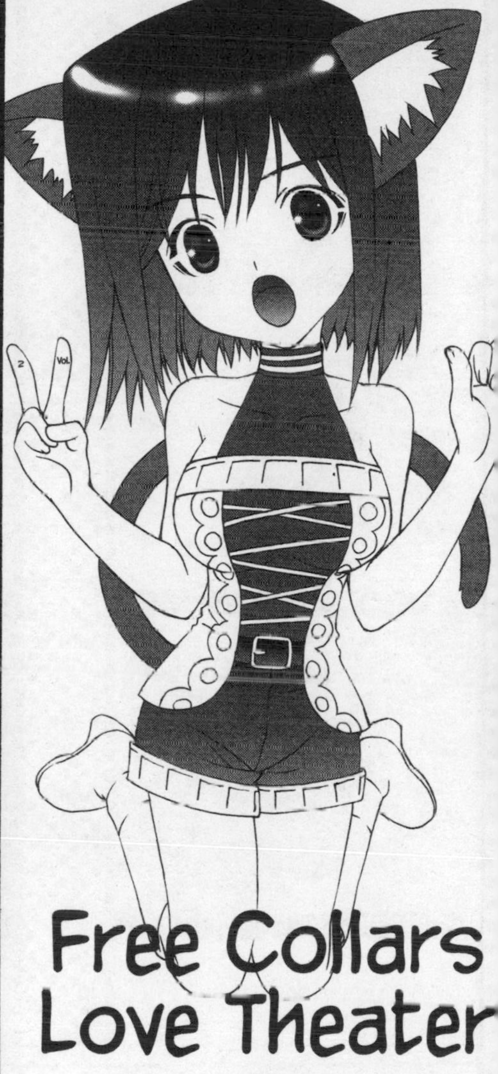

Free Collars Love Theater

②

By Fuji-Taku-chan

I Want to Be Rescued.

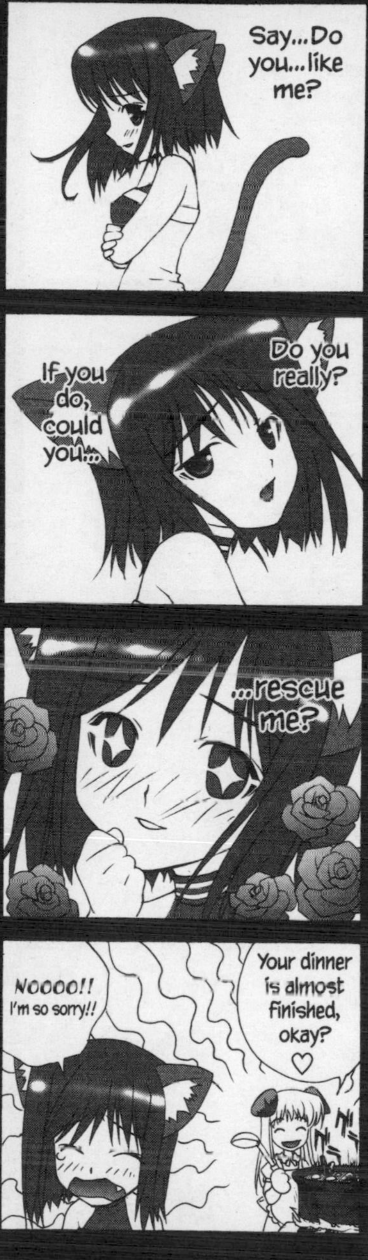
Say...Do you...like me?
Do you really?
If you do, could you...
...rescue me?
Your dinner is almost finished, okay? ♡
NOOOO!! I'm so sorry!!

Churakichi

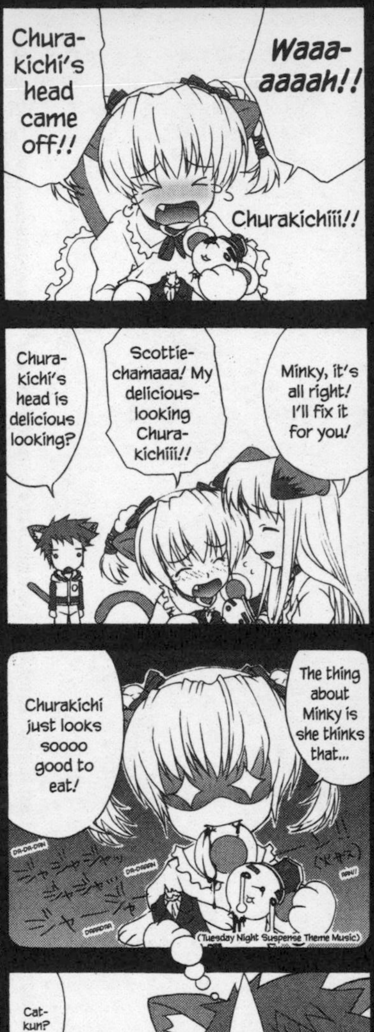
Waaa-aaaah!!
Chura-kichi's head came off!!
Churakichiii!!
Minky, it's all right! I'll fix it for you!
Scottie-chamaaa! My delicious-looking Chura-kichiii!!
Chura-kichi's head is delicious looking?
The thing about Minky is she thinks that...
Churakichi just looks soooo good to eat!
DA-DA-DAN
DA-DAAN
DAAADAN
DAN!
(Tuesday Night Suspense Theme Music)
Cat-kun?

Unwanted Hair

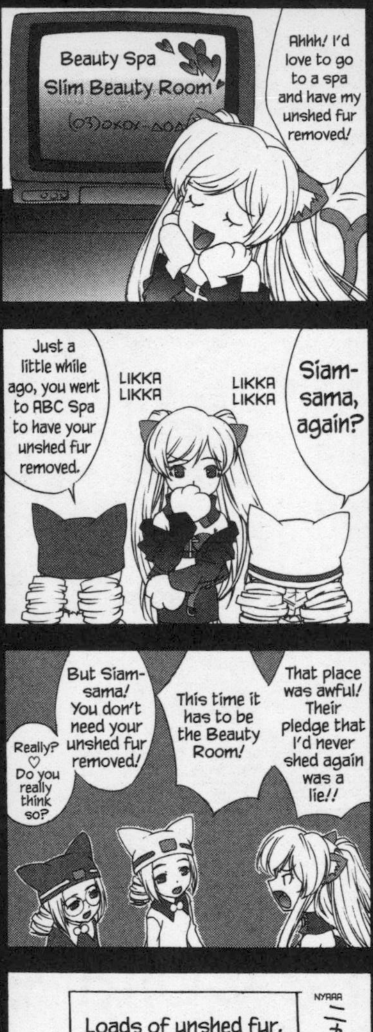
Ahhh! I'd love to go to a spa and have my unshed fur removed!
Beauty Spa
Slim Beauty Room
Siam-sama, again?
LIKKA LIKKA
LIKKA LIKKA
Just a little while ago, you went to ABC Spa to have your unshed fur removed.
That place was awful! Their pledge that I'd never shed again was a lie!!
This time it has to be the Beauty Room!
But Siam-sama! You don't need your unshed fur removed!
Really? ♡ Do you really think so?
NYRRA
NYRRA
NYRRA
Loads of unshed fur.
NYRRA
NYRRA
NYRRA
Oh! Stray cats!

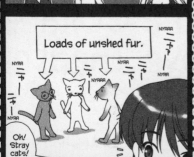

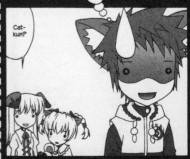

■ Long time, no see. It's been seven months (in the Japanese version)! Since there were more open pages, we used some to describe the characters and had fun on a couple others. With the addition of Minky to the cast, we have more beautiful flowers, so things have gotten lively for the Free Collars. But somewhere around volume 3, the Free Collars' main story, the territorial battle, really starts to get moving. Wait for it, okay? Then let's meet again in volume 3!

Takuya Fujimi

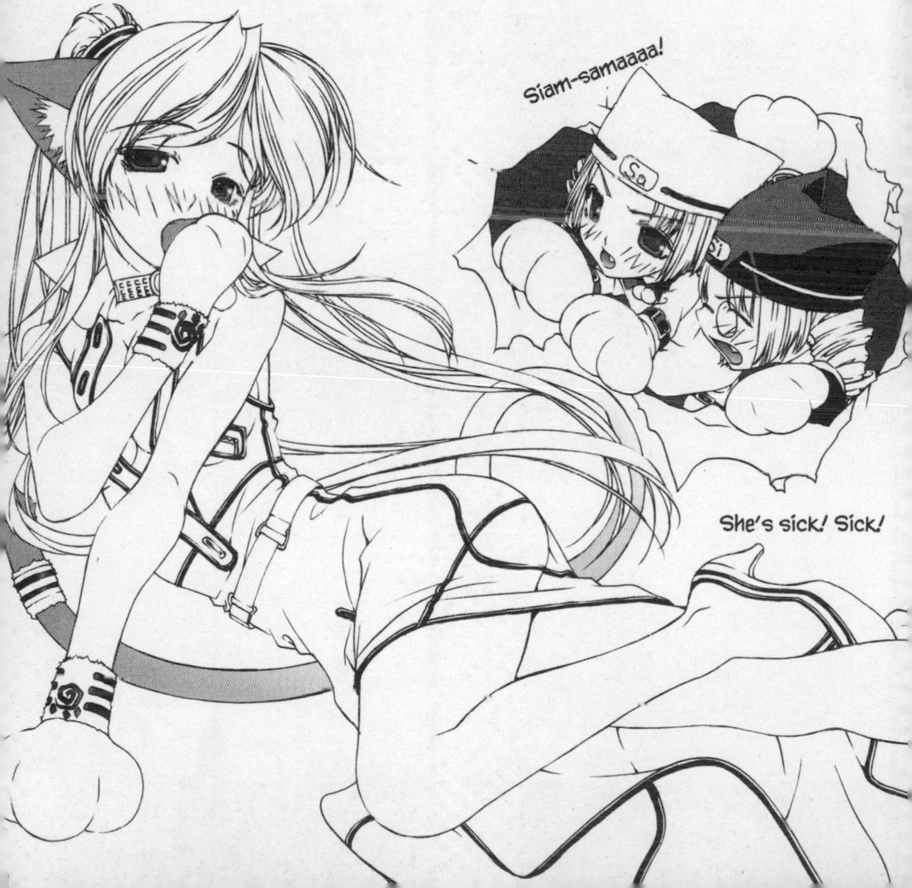
Siam-samaaaa!
She's sick! Sick!

Free Collars Love Theater

In the Bath

It's that time of the day when I can have a great time in the bath!
♥
SPLSH
SPLSH
SHMMP
Is he a voyeur?!
Who are you?!
SPLOOSH
Fan service! ♥
WHOOSH
Again?!

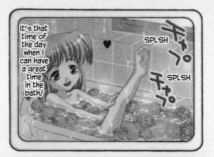

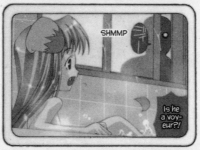

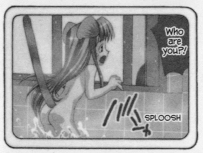

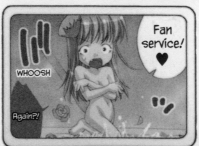

TRANSLATION NOTES

Japanese is a tricky language for most Westerners, and translation is often more an art than a science. For your edification and reading pleasure, here are notes on some of the places where we could have gone in a different direction in our translation, or where a Japanese cultural reference is used.

K Square, page 13

Since Ikebukuro has become almost as large a manga mecca as Akihabara, the manga-publishing giant Kodansha has set up a specialty store called K Square in East Ikebukuro.

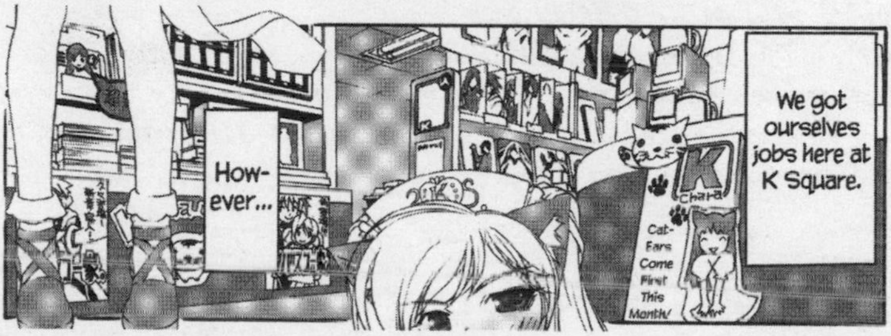

We got ourselves jobs here at K Square.
K
Chara
Cat-Ears Come First This Month!
However...

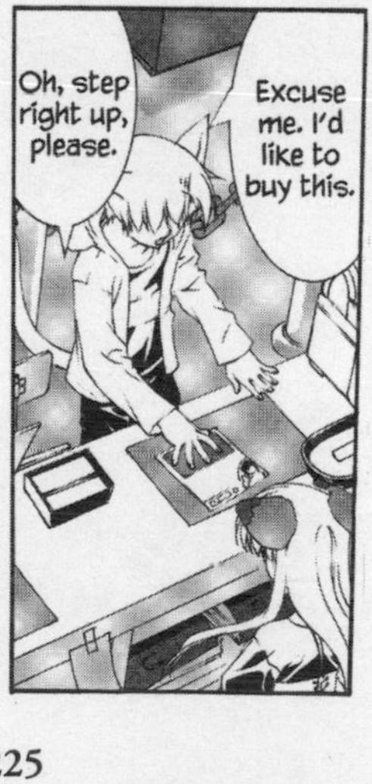

Excuse me. I'd like to buy this.
Oh, step right up, please.

Step right up (Irasshaimase), page 14

Irasshaimase is usually used as a greeting when someone comes into a place of business, but it can also be used when one sees a customer at any time.

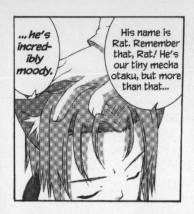

His name is Rat. Remember that, Rat! He's our tiny mecha otaku, but more than that...
...he's incred-ibly moody.

Mecha, page 20

Taken from the Japanese abbreviation for the word "mechanicals," mecha is used to refer to just about anything in anime, manga, games, toys, etc., that is a machine. But usually it refers to giant robots, cool cars, and other futuristic machines.

Rat's Attack, page 38

Usually in this translation we include the Japanese pronunciation of the attack name, but for some attacks, the pronunciation guide next to the kanji in the original edition specifically listed the pronunciation in the English words used in this edition.

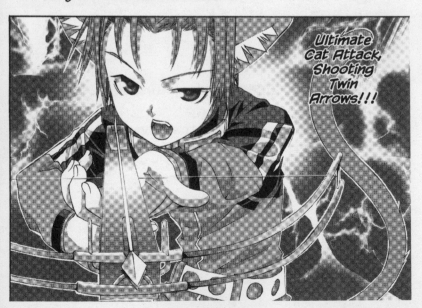

Ultimate Cat Attack, Shooting Twin Arrows!!!

Mon Buran, page 50

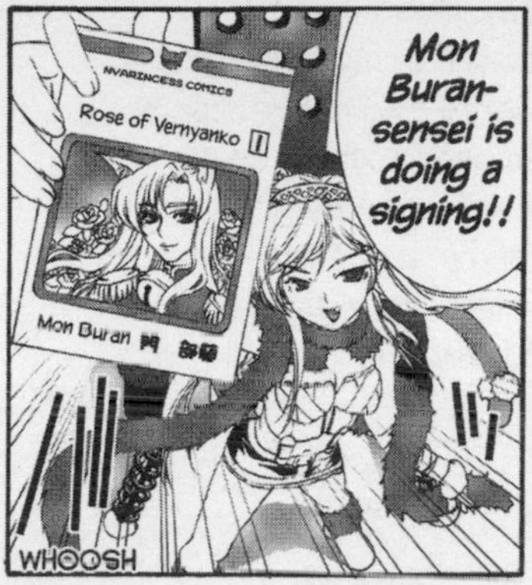
Mon Buran-sensei is doing a signing!!
NYARINCESS COMICS
Rose of Vernyanko I
Mon Buran
WHOOSH

Mon Buran is the Japanese pronunciation of Mont Blanc. Mont Blanc is the name of a French mountain. However, it is also the name of a popular Italian cake, a character in *Tetsuwan Atom* (*Astroboy*), and a character out of *Final Fantasy Tactics Advance.* In this case, Mon Buran was spelled in kanji rather than katakana (the characters for foreign words), so this translation uses the Japanese pronunciation.

Manga no Hayashi, page 53

This is a reference to the famous Manga no Mori chain of manga bookstores in Japan. It's also something of a pun, since the name Manga no Mori can be translated as Manga Forest, and Manga no Hayashi in Cyan's world can be translated as Manga Grove.

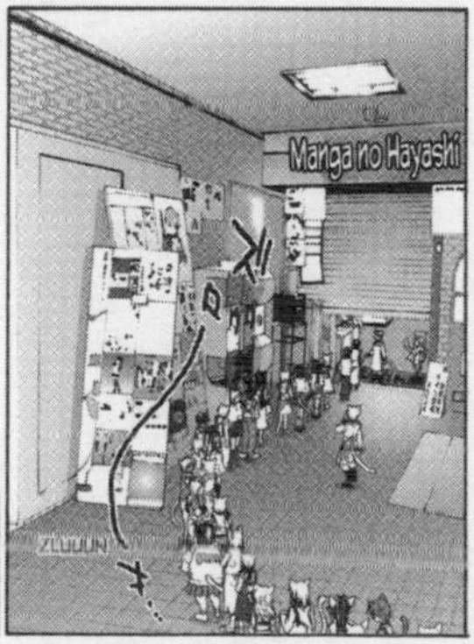
Manga no Hayashi
ZLUUUN

Tokimeki Nantara, page 59

There have been a number of date-sims (computer games that simulate romancing the opposite sex) for men, but Tokimeki Memorial, one of the more popular franchises, put out a female-oriented version that became wildly popular with the fans of *bishônen* (beautiful young men). This is the kind of game that Siam is referring to.

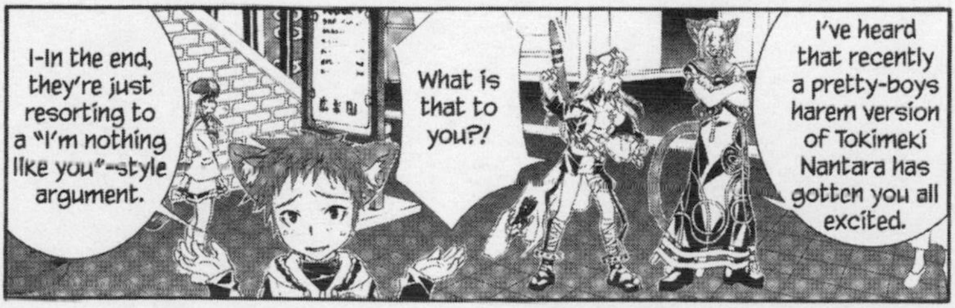
I've heard that recently a pretty-boys harem version of Tokimeki Nantara has gotten you all excited.
What is that to you?!
I-In the end, they're just resorting to a "I'm nothing like you"-style argument.

Revolving Sushi, page 121

In a revolving sushi restaurant, sushi is placed on a revolving belt and sent throughout the restaurant. There are methods for ordering special dishes and other items such as drinks and side dishes, but the sushi moving through the restaurant is the main attraction. This type of sushi shop (and its boat-based cousin) has even been brought to other countries and locations with large Japanese communities, including quite a few in North America.

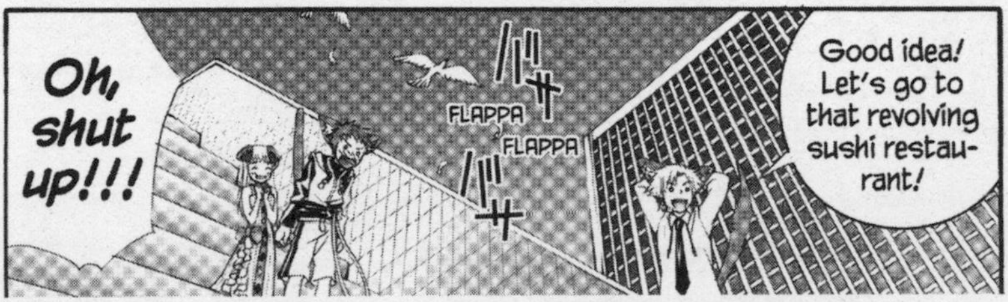
Good idea! Let's go to that revolving sushi restaurant!
FLAPPA
FLAPPA
Oh, shut up!!!

-chama, page 166

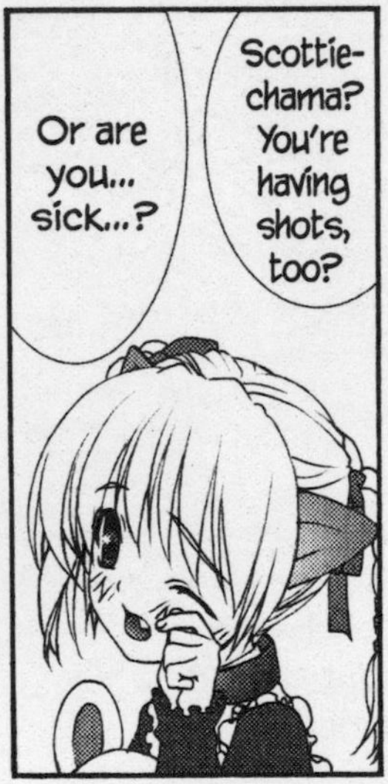
Scottie-chama? You're having shots, too?
Or are you... sick...?

In Japanese, "baby talk" can be simulated by using the "ch" sound rather than the "s" sound. In Minky's case, she says "-chama" rather than "-sama." Adults who want to sound cute and babylike can also use this variation.

We are pleased to present you with a preview of *Free Collars Kingdom*, Volume 3. This volume will be available in English on July 31, 2007, but for now, you'll have to make do with the Japanese!

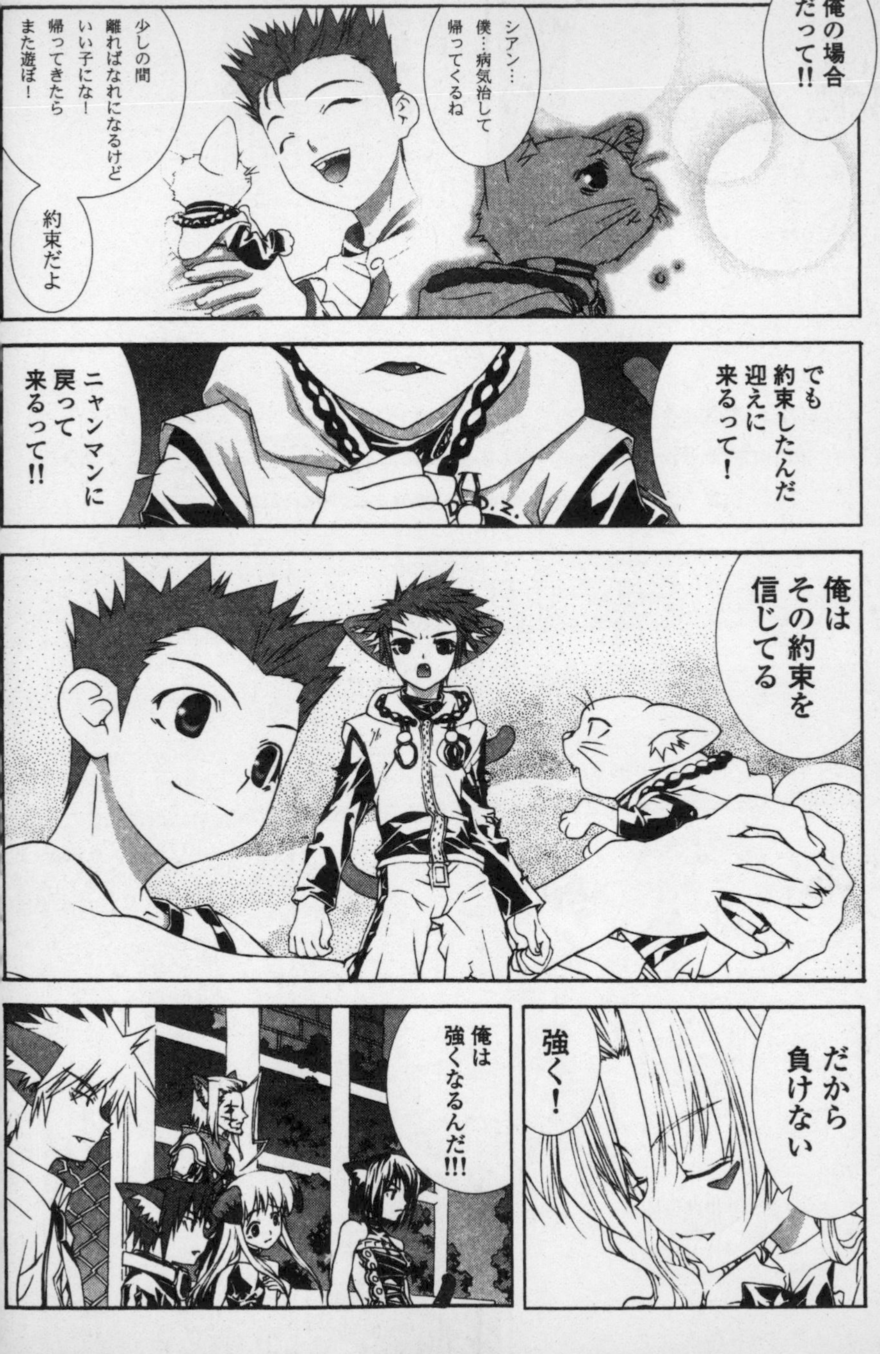
俺の場合だって!!
シアン…僕…病気治して帰ってくるね
少しの間離ればなれになるけどいい子にな!帰ってきたらまた遊ぼ!
約束だよ
でも約束したんだ迎えに来るって!
ニャンマンに戻って来るって!!
俺はその約束を信じてる
だから負けない
強く!
俺は強くなるんだ!!!

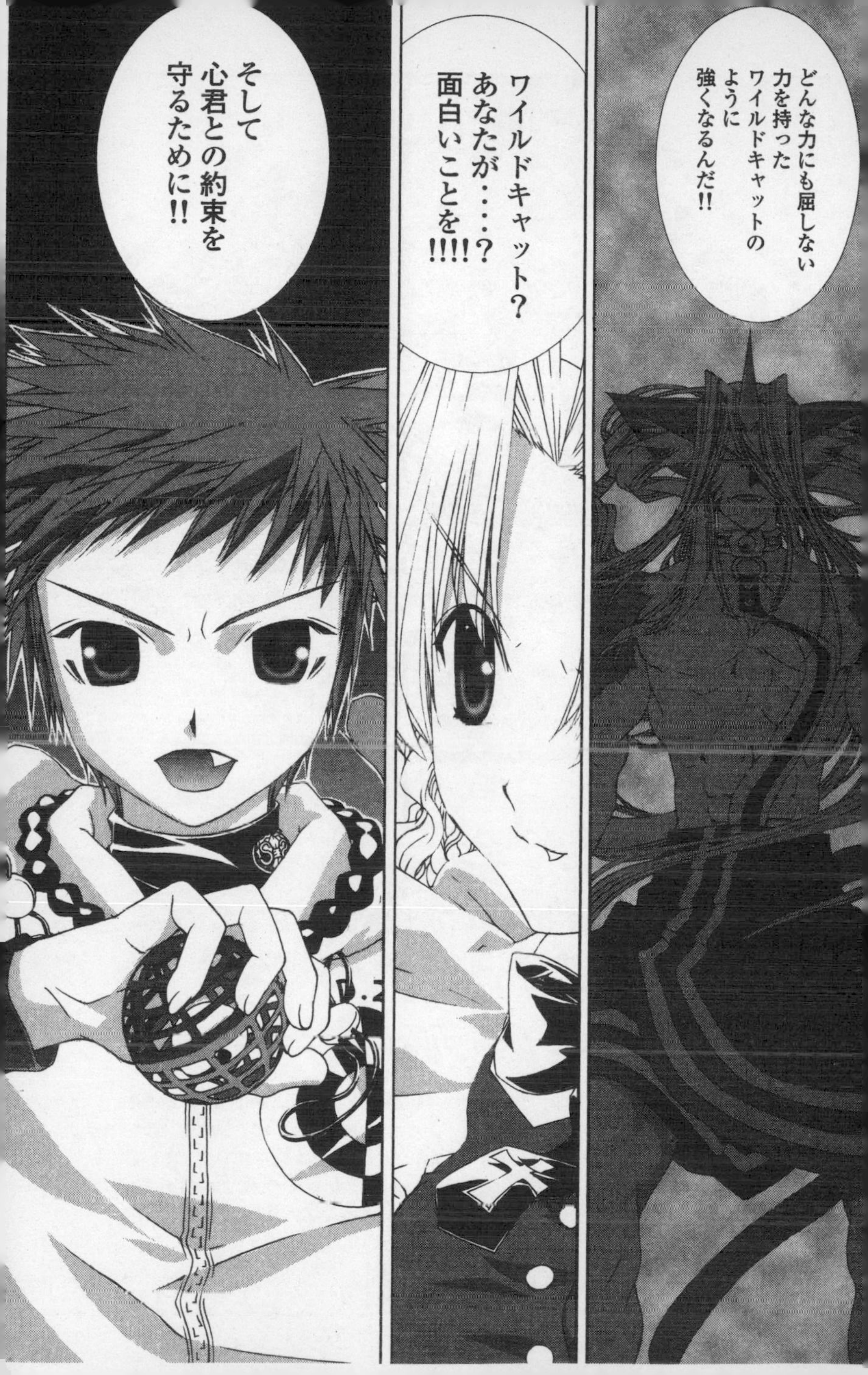
どんな力にも屈しない力を持ったワイルドキャットのように強くなるんだ!!
ワイルドキャット?あなたが・・・?面白いことを!!!!
そして心君との約束を守るために!!

TOMARE! [STOP!]

You are going the wrong way!

Manga is a completely different type of reading experience.

To start at the *beginning*, go to the *end*!

That's right! Authentic manga is read the traditional Japanese way—from right to left. Exactly the *opposite* of how American books are read. It's easy to follow: Just go to the other end of the book, and read each page—and each panel—from right side to left side, starting at the top right. Now you're experiencing manga as it was meant to be.